THE INFORMATION SYSTEMS ENVIRONMENT

IFIP Working Conference on
The Information Systems Environment
Bonn, West Germany, 11-13 June 1979

organized by
IFIP Technical Committee 8, Information Systems
International Federation for Information Processing

NORTH-HOLLAND PUBLISHING COMPANY
AMSTERDAM • NEW YORK • OXFORD

THE INFORMATION SYSTEMS ENVIRONMENT

Proceedings of the IFIP TC 8.2 Working Conference on
The Information Systems Environment
Bonn, West Germany, 11-13 June 1979

edited by

Henry C. LUCAS Jr.
New York University

Frank F. LAND
London School of Economics

Timothy J. LINCOLN
IBM UK, Ltd.

Konrad SUPPER
MBP Germany, GmbH

1980

NORTH-HOLLAND PUBLISHING COMPANY
AMSTERDAM • NEW YORK • OXFORD

ISBN: 0 444 86036 3

Published by:
NORTH-HOLLAND PUBLISHING COMPANY—AMSTERDAM • NEW YORK • OXFORD

Sole distributors for the U.S.A. and Canada:
ELSEVIER NORTH-HOLLAND, INC.
52 Vanderbilt Avenue
New York, N.Y. 10017

Library of Congress Cataloging in Publication Data

IFIP TC 8.2 Working Conference on the Information
    Systems Environment, Bonn, 1979.
    The information systems environment.

    "Organized by IFIP Technical Committee 8, Information
Systems, International Federation for Information Pro-
cessing."
    1. Management information systems--Congresses.
I. Lucas, Henry C. II. International Federation for
Information Processing. Technical Committee for Infor-
mation Systems. III. Title.
T58.6.I14 1979   658.4'0388   80-17839
ISBN 0-444-86036-3

PRINTED IN THE NETHERLANDS

To Jan Joele

PREFACE

This book contains the papers presented at the Working Conference on the Information Systems Environment sponsored by IFIP Working Group 8.2. The Working Group focuses on problems of the interaction between organizations and information systems. The papers in this volume all address different aspects of the information systems environment; we feel they are an important contribution to the field of practice and theory and hope they will stimulate further research in this most important field.

The Conference was held in Bonn, Germany, from June 11-13, 1979. The host for the Conference, Gesellschaft fur Mathematik und Datenverarbeitung (GMD), provided financial and administrative support and a most congenial environment for the Conference. We are particularly indebted to Director Friedrich Winkelhage of GMD for making the Conference possible. Financial support for the Conference was also provided by IBM UK, Ltd.

The efforts of a number of people contributed to the success of the Conference. The Program Committee of Jan Joele, Frank Land, Enid Mumford, Konrad Supper and the Conference Chairman, Tim Lincoln, labored diligently for over a year to prepare for the meeting. Alex Verrijn Stuart, Chairman of Technical Committee 8 of IFIP helped bring WG 8.2 into existence and encouraged the Working Conference project. Finally, we are indebted to the authors and participants in the Conference.

This book is dedicated to our colleague, Jan Joele, whose tragic death came a few short months before the Conference.

Henry C. Lucas, Jr.
Chairman
Working Group 8.2

CONTENTS

The Information Systems Environment
Lucas, Land, Lincoln, Supper (Editors)
North-Holland Publishing Company
© *IFIP, 1980*

THE INFORMATION SYSTEMS ENVIRONMENT

CONFERENCE COMMITTEE REPORT

F. F. Land, T. J. Lincoln, E. Mumford, K. Supper

CONFERENCE BACKGROUND

The past few years have seen rapid improvements in the price/performance
of computer technology and there is every indication that this trend will
continue into the foreseeable future. As computers become cheaper, more
powerful and easier to use, computer systems will become increasingly
integrated in the basic operations, planning and control systems of an
organisation. These developments can potentially bring significant
commercial and administrative advantages if they can be introduced
successfully.

Computer systems are now a well established part of most large
companies. In many cases, data processing departments have a history
going back 15-20 years and DP management and professionals have
considerable experience in developing systems. The current trends in
performance-price of computing technology suggest that many new computing
applications will become cost-effective and should be implemented given,
of course, that human costs, such as lowering of job satisfaction, or
decrease in quality of working life, are fully taken into account. It
appears on the surface therefore that most large organisations should
have an experienced, proven DP department able to take advantage of the
exciting computing opportunities coming available. Senior executives
should be looking forward to the future with anticipation and be willing
to invest substantial money and resources into DP systems to gain the
competitive edges essential for survival. However experience suggests
that only a small minority of senior executives have confidence in the
ability of their organisations to make the best use of computerised information systems. This may be associated with a fear that major technical
change may be accompanied by considerable distruption and stress.

The probability of successful implementation of computerised systems
depends of course on the ability of the design and implementation team to
overcome the constraints inhibiting successful implementation. One of
the major constraints is human acceptance of the system, and to overcome
this problem the DP professional needs to acquire an awareness of the
need to design good social as well as good technical systems. This
awareness needs to be supplemented by the appropriate skills within the
D.P. team. As organisations gain experience, policies, procedures and
standards are established which help avoid the more obvious pitfalls. In
this way management systems must evolve which will assist the planning
and controlling of the systems development effort. The management
processes and systems thereby evolved will reflect the prime constraints
which they are designed to overcome.

In the early days of computing the prime constraints lay, in most cases, within the DP department itself. This was a reflection of three things. Firstly, DP technology was new, limited in capacity and function and often unreliable. Thus there were technological constraints associated with even simple systems. Secondly, systems analysis and programming were virtually 'black arts' without formalised methods or a disciplined approach. Thus there were constraints associated with the internal DP management process which often lead to dramatic cost and schedule overruns. Thirdly, the applications or systems attacked first were usually simple, formalised applications. These were well-understood and established and therefore computerization had little impact on the organisation or on user attitudes.

Perhaps inevitably therefore, the management processes and systems evolved to deal with these DP constraints emphasized those characteristics of the total Information Systems process which were associated with the DP department. Accordingly most organisations control their Information Systems development effort by monitoring characteristics such as DP costs, machine utilization, project costs and schedules and programmer productivity. The non-DP characteristics of the Information Systems process were either ignored or noted in terms of their impact on the DP characteristics. A common example of this was 'user resistance has impacted the project schedules'.

This situation is not too bad as long as the management system remains sensitive to the complex and varied needs of the different interest groups within and outside the organisation and provided it allows effective planning and control. However DP technology, social attitudes, management philosophy and employee expectations are currently subject to a remarkable rate of change. It must be expected therefore that the key constraints which inhibit the development and use of technology will also change. As this occurs the traditional DP management system will come under increasing stress and will become increasingly ineffective. An example of this is the often heard comment 'We implemented the project within budget and schedule, but we implemented the wrong system'.

Studies have shown that the key constraints to the development of computerised information systems are changing and in most cases no longer lie primarily within the DP department. It has been shown that the key constraints increasingly lie in three areas:

- Non-formalised, inappropriate and changing basic business systems

- Lack of effective user/DP department communication, epitomised by failure to involve users effectively.

- External constraints impeding DP development.

An analysis of the major trends impacting DP suggests that these constraints will continue to be critically important compared with technology.
This situation clearly places stress on the traditional DP management system which can only be relieved by the management system evolving to better assist management cope with the non-DP constraints. While the direction of this evolution is clear, the structure of a desired management system or the tools and techniques to be employed are far from clear. Indeed most organisations are still struggling to implement DP department controls and have yet to seriously consider the non-DP measurements and controls which will be required.

The Information Environment conference was established so that
researchers and practitioners could meet to discuss the non-DP
constraints to the development of Information Systems. Participants were
invited who had experience in each of the three areas listed above. It
was clear from the beginning that definitive answers would not be
forthcoming. The best that could be hoped for was to bring together in
both formal and informal sessions those people who could best contribute
to the debate. By this way it was felt that the dimensions of the
problem could be better understood, experience gained with specific tools
and techniques could be evaluated and proposals for future research and
practical work could be discussed.

CONFERENCE PAPERS

Speakers at the Conference came from all over the world and from a wide
variety of backgrounds and disciplines. Academics and practitioners
presented papers but a feature of the Conference was that all speakers
dealt with research or experiences which had to do with the real world
problem of developing effective information systems. Although the themes
covered by the speakers covered a wide range of ideas it was possible to
classify the papers under four major headings:

1.   Organisation and Behaviour

2.   Participative Design Techniques

3.   Methodologies and Tools

4.   Personal Views and Speculations

Organisation and Behaviour

Papers under the first heading set out to analyse the organisational and
behavioural context in which information systems are developed and are
expected to support the goal seeking activities of those who work in the
organisations. Some of the authors go on to suggest solutions to the
many problems thrown up by their analysis. The papers by Earl and
Hopwood and Argyris provided evidence from research about organisational
realities which run counter to widespread beliefs held too tenaciously by
professional systems analysts. Earl and Hopwood pointed to the need
within organisations for informality and informal systems, and that a
formal MIS is neither a necessary or sufficient condition for effective
management. Many managers prefer to look to informal sources for help in
planning and decision-making. Indeed, successful organisations are the
ones with an appropriate mix of formal and informal systems. Argyris, in
his paper, succeeds in questioning some of the basic tenets of
conventional systems analysis - that in order to capture the real needs
of managers and to discover how an organisation works, the systems
analyst has to interview the executives and the clerks and others who
make the system work. He provides evidence that such interviews only
lead to a distorted model of the real world. What the respondent
'espouses' is very far from what the respondent actually does when faced,
for example, with the task of making a decision.

Szyperski analyses the present status and trends in the development of
information and communication technology, and present-day attitudes
within organisations to the use of such technology. He points out that
the changes in the technology represent a discontinuity in the evolution
of opportunities, and that management is by and large not prepared to

take hold of the opportunities provided. He discusses some of the myths
and illusions which are pervasive amongst systems designers and
management, and which can constrain the advances, in social and technical
terms, which the technology makes possible. The paper sets out a series
of issues which Szyperski regards as vital to any discussion on the
effective use of the technological opportunities and attempts to provide
at least some of the answers. Like many other speakers at the Conference
he selects user participation as one important element in any design
process.

Ciborra and his colleagues (G. Bracchi and P. Maggolini) review the
developments of systems analysis methodology over the past decade and
point to the range of practices which have evolved in this period. They
conclude that four contingent factors influence that success of a given
systems analysis method - the nature of the processes to be automated,
the data processing technology available, the extent of user awareness,
and the type of project management system deployed. The authors
considered the ability of a variety of formalised systems analysis
methods for establishing systems requirements, of coping with wide
variations in the contingent factors and conclude that of the methods
under investigation, those developed by Lundeberg in Sweden, the PORGI
project in Germany and the socio-technical methods of Mumford and her
collaborators in England and De Maio and his collaborators in Italy,
offer the best chance of success.

The paper of J.P. Campagne, J. Favrel and J.F. Petit is complementary to
the papers of Earl and Hopwood and to the Ciborra paper. The authors
review models of the change process and have developed the ideas of Alter
and Ginzberg (Managing Uncertainty) in MIS implementation. They draw
attention to the fact that a change in DP systems has to be considered as
a type of risk analysis in deciding upon a strategy for change.
Motivation for changes seem to be a vital factor, and a question of
importance for the designer is the stability of motivation through the
various stages of the project.

Dumas reminds us that every organisation has an information processing
capacity and that this is made up of human as well as machine information
processors. The information processing capacity of an organisation can
be enhanced by a variety of strategies of which making more use of
computers is only one strategy. The choice of best strategy is dependent
on many factors. In any case, the systems designer has to consider the
total capacity of the organisation to process information and not only to
concentrate on computer possiblities.

Olerup presents a conceptual framework for analysing information
systems. She, as does Dumas, conjectures that significant
characteristics of information systems are dependent on the
organisational context in which they are developed and selects as the two
most important contextual factors the complexity and stability of the
organisation's environment. Her research findings confirm, for example,
that reporting frequencies in similar size, but otherwise different
concerns are related to these factors.

The message that comes across most strongly from papers in this section
is that what actually happens in organisations is dominated by people's
perceptions, preferences, prejudices and judgements and that without a
better understanding of human behaviour within organisations, systems
designers will continue to design computer systems which are perceived
not to meet the real needs of the organisation.

The papers collected together in Section 1 provide a first class review
of the new views of the place of information systems in organisations.
As such the section should be compulsory reading for all practicing and
student systems analysts.

Participative Design Techniques

A constant theme at the Conference was that of participation by users in
the design and implementation of computer based systems. Many of the
speakers and most of the delegates at the conference seem to see in user
participation a way of overcoming the problem identified by the speakers
in the first section.

Speakers attacked the topic from a number of different directions. A
number attempted to provide a rationale for participation. Others
described particular techniques for involving users in the design process
and others again reported particular experiences with the use of
participative techniques or provided a survey of participative methods.

Winkelhage and Marock considered the Mumford "consensus" approach to
participation (discussed in the Land, Mumford, Hawgood paper in
conference) in the context of cooperation by a number of small
organisations attempting joint systems design. The authors considered
the problems that could occur and stress a need for further research techniques.

De Maio contrasts the traditional methods of design with the methods
based on socio-technical approach. He subjects the traditional methods
to a rigorous critique, before going on to examine and classify
alternative socio-technical methods. He identifies two main schools of
thought - one which stresses the need for participation, and the other
which attempts to define more or less formal methods for the
identification of information requirements. This school differs from the
traditional school in insisting on the need to look for social goals, and
in its tendency to enlist user participation in the design process. De
Maio provides a detailed analysis and comparison of some of the principal
socio-technical methods described in the literature, including in this
the methods he himself has developed and used.

Rajkovic describes the self-management philosophy in use in Yugoslavia
but points out that despite State support for the principles embodied in
self-management, many information systems projects have been developed on
conventional lines. However, it is becoming recognised that the
development of information systems should follow the self-management
philosophy and this had lead to experiments in a variety of participative
techniques. Rajkovic picks out in particular the ISAC methods developed
by Lundeberg in Sweden.

Hoyer examines participation in the context of Scandinavian practice and
Scandinavian Law. He distinguishes between participation and
co-determination. The latter implies the right of employees to be
consulted and to decide upon the properties of the system. Participation
only implies a user involvement in the design process where the main
properties of the system are determined before the user is involved.
Despite legislation in both Norway and Sweden, the actual practice has
only made slow progress towards genuine implementation of
co-determination. Hayer analyses the cause for this and suggests a model
of organisional attitudes based on the dominant ideology of systems

designers and the dominant ideology prevalent within the organisation to explain the way changing methods might be implemented.

Courbon and Bourgeous distinguish between the technical process of information systems design where analysis leads to the implementation of a new system and the social process of systems design in which consciousness of the change taking place leads gradually to the adoption of new norms of behaviour. They suggest that many of the disappointments in implemented systems stem from the failure of conventional methods of design to take account of this social process. The authors go on to stress a need for a single approach which couples the technical and social processes. They argue that participation of users is an important element in such an approach. At the same time the role of the professional DP designer becomes more that of a nurturing agent to help the process along. The more systems become management or management support oriented the more important it becomes to adopt an evolutionary, incremental, highly participative strategy of systems development.

Saaksjarvi sets out a methodology for involving different levels of management and end users in the planning and evaluation of information systems projects. The principal aim of the process is to reconcile the systems objectives with the objectives of the organisation and at the same time to set priorities in the context of conflicting user needs and demands. The author points out that if only one group of managers, say top managers, are involved in the planning procedure, the plan is likely to be unbalanced. Saaksjarvi suggests that experience in the use of participative planning techniques have shown that they can be successfully used in practice.

Paul Blokdjik from IBM in the Netherlands describes how, for a major DP project, an attempt was made to overcome frequently observed user versus DP professional communication problems by setting up separate design teams based on representatives of user managers and end users. The two teams met on a part-time basis and were instructed first in the uses of the formal design methods chosen for the project. These included top-down design techniques and some associated graphical representation methods such as Nassi-Schneiderman charts. A survey of the participants carried out at the end of the logical design phase suggested considerable satisfaction with the process and it was deemed to be of value to the project.

It was clear that despite problems and setbacks all the speakers had confidence in the principle of participation and felt that experiments with participation had yielded positive results. More work was needed in educating users to play a bigger role in the design evaluation and implementation of systems. At the same time, professional DP people had to learn to recognise that their role was changing and that they would no longer carry the prime or sole responsibility of the design of new systems.

Methodologies and Tools

In this section speakers presented a variety of different methodologies and tools. These fell into a number of broad schools - socio-technical approaches were espoused in the papers by Land, Mumford and Hawgood, in the paper by Efstathiou and by Oplland and Kolf. Kerola in his paper, and Espejo, provided methodologies based on cybernetic thinking whilst the papers of Methlie and the paper of Bosman and Sol could be classified as of the Scandinavian school, developing methods which stress the difference between the infological and datalogical approach. They, as do

Ben-Nathan and Cook and Stamper and Mason and Jones define rather formal techniques of analysis and design using special languages (Cook and Stamper) or graphical notation (Methlie) or documentation methods (Ben-Nathan).

Methlie presents a conceptual framework for the development of information systems in which particular stress is placed on defining requirements on the basis of organisational needs. A key feature in defining needs is what he calls 'task uncertainty'. The more uncertainty, the greater the need for information. He goes on to describe a method for modelling the organisation based on diagramatic techniques - a graphic language for analysis.

Efstathiou in her paper points out the difficulty of arriving at objective quantified measures of the value of specific systems features. This is particulary so where users are involved in the evaluation of systems objectives. She describes a technique developed with a number of collaborators, which permits evaluation to be carried out in terms of preferences described in natural language rather than numerically. Experience suggests that the use of the technique is welcomed by participants in evaluation.

Kerola models the life cycle of an information systems project, basing his model on a conceptual framkework derived from general systems theory and cybernetics, and couched in the language of semiotics. He conceives the systems design and implementation process to be more closely related to that of the social and behavioural sciences than to that of the exact sciences. Kerola's model identifies the complex factors relevant to the 'infological' design of an information system, and which represent a starting point both for further research and for solving practical problems.

Two sets of authors - Oppeland and Kolf, and Land, Mumford and Hawgood, discuss tools they have developed to support user participation in the process of analysis, design, evaluation and implementation of information systems project. Both sets of authors base their tools on a socio-technical approach to systems change.

Opperland and Kolf are responsible for the PORGI project of BIFOA at the University of Cologne. The project provides support tools in the form of checklists, questionnaires and tables. The tools cover many aspects of the processes in the life cycle of and information systems project. A feature of the methods proposed by Oppeland and Kolf is that the diagnostic tools provided enable other tools to be modified to provide a better fit with the capabilities and situations existing in the organisation using the PORGI approach. The paper cites two cases where the approach was used and indicates the results achieved and the lessons learned.

Land, Mumford and Hawgood describe a general method, and some tools which enable users to play a crucial part in the design of their own systems. Although the tools are intended to assist participants drawn from the user population, the tools can be applied in more conventional design situations. The method proposed differs from other methods frequently advocated, in that it suggests that the analysis of systems be carried out not in terms of an analysis of an existing system, but in terms of an 'essential' system, i.e. the set of operations which are necessary to carry out the objectives of the organisation in question. This 'essential' system can then be scanned for inherent weaknesses (variances) and compared with the existing systems to define

discrepencies and the reason for the discrepencies. The analysis can be
used to derive some of the operational objectives of the new system.

Bosman & Sol observe that most existing information processing systems
deal with well-structured problems. However, organisational problems
often fall into the category of ill-structured problems, for these there
are no consistent solution methods. They suggest the need to use
computer systems as an extension of human cognitive capabilities. The
paper develops a formal approach to coping with the ill-structured
problems by means of a process of modelling and simulation, using SIMULA
as a tool. The process commences with the conceptualisation of the
'real' system. This is developed into a conceptual model, from which a
simulation model is derived. The process is iterative and leads
ultimately to the implementation of the information system.

Ben-Nathan in his paper postulates the need for the function of an
Information Systems Architect within Systems Development. The architect
is concerned with ensuring coordination as between individual application
projects within the context of an integrated data base for the organisation. The job of the architect is to develop in association with the
prime clients models of the enterprise's processes, and to document
these in a standard and consistent manner. The Information System
Architect clarifies the objectives of systems and sets out the organisational plan for the implementation. He has the authority to reject
individual projects if they are not consistent with the overall
architecture.

Espejo uses a cybernetic approach to analyse the effectiveness of an
organisation and to identify areas of weakness in the organisation or in
its systems. He bases his analysis on the Stafford Beer model of the
organisational structure of any viable system. Espejo presents a case
study of a small engineering company in England which is analysed on the
basis of the Beer model. He is able to show a number of weaknesses in
the organistation of the company and the analysis could form the basis
for the redesign of the information system.

The papers of Cook and Stamper and Mason and Jones should be read
together. Cook and Stamper propose that the LEGOL language developed by
them for representing and simulating complex organisational systems -
such as the systems defined by administrative law - forms a useful tool
for solving problems of information systems analysis and design. The
Mason and Jones paper provides an example of the use of LEGOL which makes
it possible for reader to get a better appreciation of the capabilities
of the LEGOL language. LEGOL provides a means of modelling organisational rules and norms, and it provides a tool aimed to improve the
understanding of organisational concepts such as power, responsibility
and authority.
Some of the papers in this section give case studies of the application
of the methods, other authors simply present their tools. It is up to
the reader to judge which tools are most suitable for his own environment.

Personal Views and Speculation
_____

The final section of the book presents two papers which, though based on
a great deal of practical experience in industry and administration, and
sensible analysis of current trends, are rather more speculative than the
other papers in the volume.

Stanley Day with many years experience in designing and implementing systems in one of the major oil companies, presents a rather pessimistic view. Basing his argument on a broad historical view, and discerning the basically conservative attitude of management, and the frequent failures of the more adventurous spirits, he is concerned that the more turbulent situation brought about by many factors, including changing in technology, whilst providing many opportunities for simplification and reversing the trends towards more complex organistaions, cannot be coped with by our democratic processes. He suggests that the demand of the technology will create a new class driven society with an aristocracy of the intellect.

Charles Read who professionally examines trends in one of our large industries – banking, finds that our ability to predict behaviour in relation to technology is poor, and that many designers operate on the basis of illusions about the real world their systems have to operate in. His paper reports research results and examples which explode the myths which many EDP people believe in. It is a salutory reminder to professional EDP people to retain at least some degree of humility.

CONCLUSION

The Information Systems Environment conference was established so that researchers and practitioners could meet to discuss the key constraints to the development of Information Systems. The papers read at the conference and the accompanying discussion indicate strongly that technology is no longer (if indeed it ever was) the prime constraint. Indeed the conference provided clear evidence that informations systems interact closely with the organisational structure and the way people work within the organisation. Accordingly information systems cannot be realistically designed without knowledge and experience of the ways in which these systems impact people and organisation. The Information Systems Environment conference gave many examples of this interaction.

The conference also indicated the gap which exists between the opposing design philosophies apparent today. At one end of the spectrum are the technologists who place the hardware and software design requirements first. At the other end of the spectrum are those who feel that human and organisational factors are the most important. Whilst this distinction has been apparent for many years, the conference illustrated again how difficult it is for designers who follow one extreme to come to terms with the necessity of taking other design criteria into account.

The conference provided indications of how this gap may be overcome but much research work is still required. In particular research is needed to understand the interaction between information systems and human and organisational factors. Case studies must be documented to lend weight to the research findings and education is required to communicate these findings to young system designers. It is most important that convincing evidence supporting the human and organisational view of information systems design becomes more widely known to counterbalance the apparently hard data employed by technologists. Until a situation exists in which senior executives, users and technologists are able to take a balanced view of conflicting design criteria we must not expect information systems to play a fully effective role within the organisation.

ORGANIZATION AND BEHAVIOR

The Information Systems Environment
Lucas, Land, Lincoln, Supper (Editors)
North-Holland Publishing Company
© *IFIP, 1980*

FROM MANAGEMENT INFORMATION TO
INFORMATION MANAGEMENT

Michael J. Earl
Oxford Centre for Management Studies

and

Anthony G. Hopwood
London Graduate School of Business Studies

Michael J. Earl
Oxford Centre for Management Studies

and

Anthony G. Hopwood
London Graduate School of Business Studies

Systems designers, managers and researchers increasingly
recognize that there are problems in the development and
operation of MIS.   Frequently lack of management support
and involvement are cited as causes of inadequate MIS and
calls are made for managing information as a resource.

In this paper the authors argue that a new perspective is
required, from a concern with management information as a
technical phenomenon to a concern with information
management as a substantive organizational phenomenon.
Such a re-direction may depend on new metaphors, language
and frameworks being derived first.

Among both researchers and managers there is an increasing realization of problems
in the management information area.   A recurring theme in the literature is that
MIS have been disappointing in so far as they commonly have failed to meet
expectations (Argyris 1977).   In management courses,sessions on MIS rarely want for
lively discussion, heated debate and general concern.   Managers frequently complain
of information overload on the one hand and an information gap on the other.   The
professional information providers - systems analysts, accountants and management
scientists - proudly describe their achievements and earnestly explain their current
plans.   The information users listen with mixed feelings ranging from hope to
scepticism, from commitment to antagonism and from understanding to incomprehension.
There are problems in the current state of MIS.

Meanwhile substantial sums of money continue to be spent on information processing.
Companies commonly claim that their data processing budgets consume 2% of sales
turnover.   One major multinational company has estimated that 10% of its world-wide
corporate turnover is spent on information processing.   Ten percent of net assets
on world-wide balance sheets are thought to be explained by hardware investment and
a UK multinational's data processing budget is currently growing by 30% per annum
compound.   Top management understandably is becoming concerned with "value for
money".

Gibson and Nolan (1974) have suggested that DP budgets follow an S-shaped curve
characterized by increasing management attention to planning and control of the
computer resource.   Concern with efficiency of information processing is expressed
by productivity audits, performance monitoring and proliferation of controls.
Effectiveness is emphasized by the introduction of steering committees, attempts at
cost benefit analyses and charging for computer services.   Maturity, they suggest,
is reached only when the computer resource is fully integrated into everyday
management practice and thinking.   Our evidence would suggest that such a maturity
has yet to be achieved however.   While continual thinking and concern may be
evident, it would appear that we are a long way from gaining the full integration
of the computer resource into management practice.

4   M.J. EARL, A.G. HOPWOOD

Meanwhile information processing technology continues to advance. Mainframes and
mass storage continue to approximate to Grosch's Law providing more power for less
money. Minicomputers, and now microcomputers, threaten to change the shape of
data-processing and perhaps of MIS. "Convergence" of computing, data communication and word processing will extend the scope of formal information processing.
Managers and specialists are both excited and alarmed. The specialist contemplat-
es new techniques and new applications. The DP manager sees new options and new
anxieties. Managers wonder whether an opportunity has arrived to regain control
or, more frequently perhaps, whether the technology will finally leave them
stranded.

Yet despite some of the fundamental questions posed by these trends, investment in
formal MIS continues. With the persuasiveness of so many interested parties,
particularly the information providers, the appeal of sophisticated technology
and the felt need to keep up with others, it is easy to justify ever more information systems. There is always an information need, the system always needs
improving and incremental growth is generally invisible. Indeed MIS perpetuate
themselves: they are necessary because they are there. Professions and disciplines such as accounting, computer science and cybernetics are built around them.
Other seemingly successful organizations have MIS and publicize them. Yet in
transferring systems from other organizations we fail to examine the context in
which they originally operated, often implementing misfits as a result. Finally,
we seek spin-offs, trying to satisfy management information needs on the basis of
existing data-orientated systems (Zani 1970). In short, MIS are assumed to be
good for us. After all, or so it is frequently claimed, is not information the
raw material of decision making, the sine qua non of planning and control and
the life blood of organizations?

Increasingly however the existence of any a priori relationship between formal MIS
as commonly conceived and effective organizational performance is being questioned.
In a planning context, for instance, Grinyer and Norburn (1975) found no significant relationship between formal information systems and financial performance.
Instead they found use of both informal channels of communication and informal
decision-making processes was associated with success. Lorsch and Allen (1973)
found that complexity of management control information systems facilitated upward
information flows, but not downward flows. However both downward and upward flows
were found to be associated with favorable financial performance with alternatives
to formal MIS appearing to be essential.

Indeed it is the "newly poor" (Olofsson and Svalander, 1975) that invest heavily
in additional mechanisms for internal visibility and control, although often in so
doing they may further dislocate themselves from their problematic external
environments as they consciously or unconsciously succumb to the demands of their
ever more visible internal environments. Financially efficient, they may still
walk to their economic grave (Hopwood, 1979). And the financially successful, on
the other hand, tend to avoid many of the rigors of ever more sophisticated
information and control systems (Child, 1973, 1974, 1975; Rosner, 1968; Turcotte,
1974). Seemingly they revel and flourish within the context of informal planning
and assessment practices (Child, 1974), multiple and overlapping flows of information (Grinyer and Norburn, 1975) and continually renegotiated exchanges between
organizational participants (Georgiou, 1973). Indeed the hearsay evidence of many
managers suggests that the information they use in critical decisions does not
emanate from the formal MIS. As Mintzberg (1972) discovered, top managers select
and prefer informal information processing in most of their work.

Thus with the past disappointments with information systems which explicitly have
claimed to facilitate the process of management, the growth of expenditure on
information processing and the newly emergent technological developments, pressures on both MIS designers and users are undoubtedly increasing. Concerns and
dissatisfactions are being expressed and at least some are starting to probe for
alternatives.

The theme of our paper is that a major constraint on both current practice and the delineation of alternatives is that information processing is viewed in too narrow and technical a manner.   Information is still seen as a technical phenomenon, a "thing" that has a seemingly problematic relationship to the intricacies of organizational processes and practices.   And, as a consequence, our underlying information concepts and language tend to encourage the formalization, bureaucratization, standardization and mechanization of information processes - the very things which the recent studies quoted above suggest neither fit nor suit the realities of organizational activity.   If this is the case, and we think that it is, then the alternatives to present practice may not be recognized because our existing MIS perspectives are outdated and not descriptive of even present organizational practice.

In this paper we argue for a new perspective, from a concern with management information as a technical phenomenon to a concern with information management as a substantive organizational phenomenon.   Our theme is not just a play on words or a mere evangelical call to put management back into information systems.   The perspective which we seek is one that is concerned with a broader appreciation of information processing in organizations.   We are urgently in need of some new and very different metaphors for considering the roles which information does, can and might play in organizational functioning.   To illustrate this we start by examining the variety of ways in which organizations process information.

THE INFORMATION PROCESSING MIX IN ORGANIZATIONS

Despite the emphasis which has been placed on MIS, organizations have invested and continually do invest in a multitude of ways of processing information.   One way of looking at the variety of approaches used in practice is to distinguish between routine and non-routine and official and unofficial modes of information processing. The resulting array of information possibilities is depicted in Figure 1.

	Routine	Non-Routine

Official	MIS
	Management Accounting
	   Systems;
	Production Control
	   Systems
		Access Facilities;
		Task Forces;
		Liaison Roles

Unofficial	Black-books; Just in Case Files	The Grape Vine; Lunch Table Chats

Figure 1.   The Information Processing Mix

The official, routine information processing box contains the MIS which have been emphasized so much.   They are often the operational systems upon which our organizations depend from day to day.   In some businesses they have even become a substantial part of the business itself; for example air-line reservation systems, production control systems in the engineering sector and transactions systems in banking.

The unofficial, routine category of information processing contains systems which serve local needs.   In some cases these strive to compensate for the inadequacies of the routine systems; in other cases they are maintained as defensive information against attack from superiors and peers.   It is evident from research (Hopwood

1973; Simon et al., 1954) and from discussions with managers that such informal, but nonetheless routine, approaches to information processing are ubiquitous. Hedberg and Johnson (1978) saw them as having value in creating and maintaining subcultures to question and challenge the status quo and stability.   Also they suggested that they often provide more flexibility and discretion to managers than the official counterparts.   Argyris (1977) suggests that unofficial, routine systems often represent actuality, provide concrete descriptions of unique situations, indicate true causality and provide private and tacit views.   Earl (1978a) suggests that they may be attractive because they are simple and may serve as unofficial prototypes for subsequent official routinization.

The non-routine, official category includes purposive approaches to facilitating the processing of information such as investments in the capability to provide ad hoc information and mechanisms for furthering access to information.   Also included in this category are those structural approaches to information processing which are effective because they are based on managerial actions and interpersonal activities through which "things get done" and by which we can learn from experience.   Such structural mechanisms provide means for crossing intra-organizational boundaries, for transcending levels of authority and influencing others by discourse and persuasion.   Meetings, conferences and task forces provide channels of lateral and downward communication when often the routine MIS are predominantly upward. By being less formal and structured, non-routine and official "information systems" may also help achieve "control with" rather than "control over".   They may perhaps offer top management a means of keeping "in touch", when the formal and official MIS no longer represent the reality they once measured.   Finally they can often be created quickly and then killed when their purpose has been satisfied. Conversely the routine, official forms of information processing take a long time to create and may never die.

The unofficial, non-routine category comprises many of the informal information systems upon which managers depend.   These devices carry news quickly, convey nuances, and can process qualitative information.   To discover what is important, one joins the grape-vine.   To influence some-one or break down the system one sits at the right lunch-table.   To try and make sense of complexity we share the problem and construct our organization and world through and with each other.   These forms of information processing are personal and private and accordingly fulfill purposes which the official or routine system could never attempt.

The reality of information processing in organizations is the vibrant and varied mix depicted by this framework.   Organizations both have and require a balance of complementary information processing forms, including the more personal and structural varieties.   However it seems to us that so much of this reality does not influence or enter into legitimate professional discourse in the MIS area, and this may well be a major constraint on organizational adaptation or change. Investing heavily in routine, official MIS we often forget and exclude investment in, and development of, competing, counter-balancing, overlapping and reinforcing information flows and processes.   Just why does the emphasis on the formal and routine continue?   What is at stake with the development of MIS as we now know them? What organizational roles do they really serve?   To address such questions, let us consider further a key aspect of the interface between information and organization, namely the roles which information plays in decision-making.   How is the development of MIS implicated in the very different types of decision-making processes which constitute organizational life?

INFORMATION AND DECISION

Many writers have seen MIS as servants of decision making and several authorities have devised decision-orientated strategies for MIS design (Ackoff 1967; Zani 1970; Mason 1969).   The relationship between information and decision making has been an influential basis for the analysis, development and articulation of normative MIS "solutions".   Indeed some have even described MIS as Decision Support

Systems (Gorry and Scott-Morton 1971).

However, one problem with the use of the decision-making perspective for the analysis of both information needs and information systems is that the relationship between information and decision has rarely been critically examined. The link has, in other words, been presumed rather than described and analyzed. A particular view of human rationality and the attendant relationship between information and decision-making has been uncritically adopted. We have tended to presume, for instance, that the specification and analysis of information preceeds decision-making, that the roles played by information in decision-making are invariate across a multitude of different decision situations. Information is there to facilitate and ease rather than more actively influence, if indeed not frustrate, the decision-making process. Such presumptions are however little more than abstractions from the complex reality of information processing in organizations. While they might simplify the information system design process, their relationship to the realities of organizational life is questionable.

One way of looking at the relationship between information and decision-making in more detail can be based on the analysis of Thompson and Tuden (1959) which adds to the traditional view of the link between decision-making and uncertainty by classifying various states of uncertainty and different types of decision-making processes. As can be seen in Figure 2, they distinguish between uncertainty (or disagreement, for that is the same at the organizational level) over organizational objectives and the uncertainty over the cause and effect relationships which are embodied in particular organizational actions. When objectives are clear and undisputed, and cause and effect certain, Thompson and Tuden highlighted the potential for decision-making by computation. As cause and effect relationships become uncertain, however, that potential diminishes and decisions start to be made in a judgemental manner. If the focus of uncertainty resides in the specification of objectives, however, decisions tend to be the result of compromise when cause and effect relationships are certain, and of a more "inspirational" nature when even that clarity disappears.

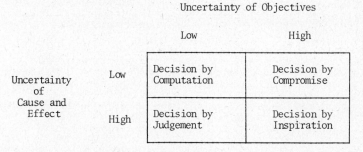

Uncertainty of Objectives

		Low	High
Uncertainty of Cause and Effect	Low	Decision by Computation	Decision by Compromise
	High	Decision by Judgement	Decision by Inspiration

Figure 2.   Decision-Making and Uncertainty

By being based on a more detailed characterization of the ways in which uncertainties are perceived and located in organizations, we believe that such an array of decision possibilities is of real significance in trying to understand the emergence and functioning of information systems in organizations. Moreover the framework relates to the views of those who have seen information processing as a means of uncertainty reduction (Galbraith, 1973) and information value as the degree to which uncertainty is reduced. However rather than presuming the link between information and uncertainty, let us consider the roles which information processing and information systems might and do play in the different decision situations described by Thompson and Tuden.

First we strive to articulate a normative view. Using an all too unsatisfactory "machine" analogy, Figure 3 outlines the orientations which information systems perhaps might adopt in the best of all possible worlds. Given low uncertainty on each dimension, we approach the management scientists' definition of certainty, where algorithms, formulae and rules can be derived to solve the problem by computation. Alternatively it may represent Simon's structured decisions (1960) where the intelligence, design and choice phases are all programmable. In either case stock control systems, credit control routines and linear programming models are all examples of what we call "answer machines".

Uncertainty about Objectives

		Low	High
Uncertainty of Cause and Effect	Low	Answer Machines	Dialogue Machines
	High	Learning Machines	Idea Machines

Figure 3. A Normative View of the Relationship

Between Information Systems and Uncertainty

Given clear objectives but uncertain causation, we need to explore problems, ask questions, analyze the analyzable and finally resort to judgement. Here MIS cannot provide the answer but they can go part of the way, providing assistance through what Gorry and Scott-Morton (1971) would call decision support systems, Mason and Mitroff (1973) might call dialectical systems and Churchman (1971) calls inquiring systems. Examples of what we refer to as "learning machines" are enquiry facilities, sensitivity analysis and what-if models.

Given uncertainty or disagreement over objectives but relative certainty on causation, then values, principles, perspectives and interests conflict. In a rapidly changing economic, social and political environment, such bargaining situations may be increasing. Here political processes are important where often the vital tasks include discussion, intelligence and problem-sharing to gather different points of view, seek conflict resolution or just keep talking. Examples of relevant information processing here might include 'think-tanks', information centers, consultative and participative processes, retreats and the like - all examples of what we refer to as "dialogue machines". The orientation is towards freeing channels of opinion and communication and toward polemics and debate, with the value of information being measured by the number of consistent points of view that can be persuasively argued with the data and within the context provided by the information system (Boland 1979).

Finally given uncertainty in both dimensions, or decision by inspiration, we seek "idea machines". Here the formal MIS may provide multiple streams of thought which Koestler (1964) suggests triggers creativity. Other information processing forms may include the semi-confusing information systems suggested by Hedberg and Jonsson (1978) and the use of creativity techniques, such as Delphi processes or brainstorming. They will also include experience sharing and contact with other organizations or related thinkers. Certainly fluid or organismic organization design will be advantageous, encouraging boundaries to be crossed and the fertilization of ideas (Burns and Stalker, 1961).

Most people will not argue with this exposition. When presented in such terms they are prepared to acknowledge the variety of roles which information systems might serve and even the consequent variety of approaches to information system design and operation. However although the analysis may be acceptable, it describes, we would venture to suggest, a set of circumstances which is very different than the reality of the relationship between information and decision-making which exists in many organizations. That reality which is so fundamental to our argument is illustrated in Figure 4.

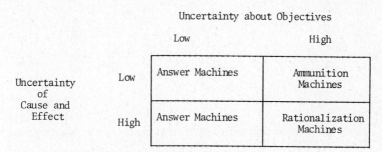

Figure 4.   Uncertainty Decision-Making and the

Roles of Information Systems

On the whole we have learned how to develop MIS for decision by computation. While some problems may remain, quite successful "answer machines" are in wide-spread use. Thereafter, however, organizational reality starts to diverge from the normative and all too appealing set of circumstances outlined in Figure 3. Rather than using "learning machines" to confront the uncertainties inherent in cause and effect relationships, information system designers have sought to reduce or even camouflage them. Uncertainty, it would appear, is seen as a threatening rather than inevitable state of the world, which rather than being exploited for what it is, needs to be masked by an enormous investment in tidy minded systems and in pushing down the boundaries of computational practice. So in circumstances which cry out for information which can stimulate learning and the exercise of judgement, we find routine MIS which often assume the very certainties which cannot be found.

The management scientist seeks to develop optimizing models where descriptive models can only be appropriate. The same specialist promotes the use of probability models and modes of risk analysis where a sensitive use of deterministic models may better facilitate the exercise of judgement. The systems analyst prescribes enquiry systems which have specified answers rather than interrogation facilities for the user to select and develop, and the modeller seeks solutions as answers rather than frameworks for decision-making. All the above assume a certainty which the user has never readily experienced. Designers simply forget how much prior knowledge and insight their procedures require, or impute, and by so doing they are rarely, if ever, able to come to terms with the "wicked" (Mason and Mitroff 1973) problems which constitute an important part of management practice.

In emphasising the more technical mechanisms for the improvement of information, designers so often ignore the complementary but equally essential investments which need to be made in interpretative and decision skills. In other words our parent disciplines of computing, accounting and management science have sought for answers where they cannot always be specified, aiming for technocratic solutions regardless of the context of either the user or the organizational environment.

Such approaches result in the presumption of states of quasi-certainty which do not exist and the use of particular forms of economic and scientific rationality which bear little or no relationship to those which are implicit in the processes of management decision-making.

Then as we also suggest in Figure 4, far from creating a basis for dialogue and interchange, MIS tend to be used as "ammunition machines" in decisions by compromise. By the use of this perhaps emotive term, we wish to point to the ways in which information systems serve to promote and articulate particular interested positions and values. Political processes in organizations give rise to the emergence and elaboration of information systems as one party or interested group seeks to influence others. For as Bariff and Galbraith (1978) point out, information systems may be used to perpetuate or modify decision-making processes and social structures. By influencing the accepted language of negotiation, such systems can help to shape what is regarded as problematic, what can be deemed to be a credible solution and, most important of all, the criteria which are used in their selection. In ways such as these, traditional management accounting systems and mechanisms for financial appraisal can be used to reduce the complexity of a decision environment into a simple uni-goal economic system that has a life of its own divorced from the broader realities of organizational functioning. As one manager put it: "given a sensitive strategic decision (for example divestment) the information on the table is generally financial. Once the decision is made and we discuss its implementation other information is used, such as engineering, marketing or personnel considerations".

The "idea machine" we suggested for decision by inspiration may appear to be the only contribution that MIS can make in the context of such extreme uncertainty. However we suspect that that very uncertainty creates the need for other roles which they can and do serve. Rather than seeking to promote the creativity, inspiration and entrepreneurship which is so vital in such strategic contexts, MIS may more often than not operate as "rationalization machines" seeking to legitimize and justify actions that have been decided upon. As Bower (1970) discovered, and as many managers have described to us, the widespread adoption of capital budgeting procedures has resulted in the availability of justification devices rather than the simple and unproblematic provision of information for, and prior to, decision-making.

We do not seek the question the necessity for rationalization machines, for organizations require mechanisms through which they can legitimize what is to be done and retrospectively create a rationale for action. What we do suggest is that the information processing which is typical of such procedures be recognized for what it is, and that more active acknowledgement be given to the fact that the creativity and inspiration, which are so necessary in such contexts, are more likely to spring out of socially interactive forms of information processing.

By introducing our rather strong metaphors for information and decision, we are calling for a re-orientation away from the exclusive emphasis on technocratic and bureaucratic forms of information processing which is so characteristic of today's information system practice. There is, we think, an urgent need to acknowledge the reality of information practice in its full diversity; to see, in other words, the processes which create the roles for information processing and give rise to information systems in their wider organizational context. Such metaphors point to both the present existence of, and extended future possibilities for, MIS designs which acknowledge the uncertainties of organizational life. Hedberg and Jonsson (1978) in prescribing semi-confusing information systems called for a similar re-orientation. Like them, we advocate a move to a process view of MIS rather than the structured view which has been prevalent hitherto. Such a view would be dynamic rather than static, emphasizing the roles which information processing plays on the actions and interactions through which and by which managers make sense of their environments and cope with uncertainty.

TOWARDS INFORMATION MANAGEMENT

In summary, we can state that many MIS specialists adopt a partial and rather idiosyncratic view of the role which information processing does and can serve in organizations. Emphasizing the importance of formal and systemic approaches, they invest heavily in a perspective and approach which can be, and often is, radically at variance with the way in which managers in their own organizations engage in the active and influential processing of information. Indeed we frequently get the impression that the MIS function is increasingly operating in a rather isolated, albeit comfortable, organizational niche. That is not to say that it lacks influence. Isolated though it may sometimes be from the more active processing of information in organizations, it can nonetheless have an important influence on the delineation of the desirable and the possible. However that influence stems not from the appropriateness of the MIS designs, but from the way in which the resultant information is taken up and used by those managers who strive to personally influence ongoing processes of organizational control. So, in the last resort, it may well be that it is the managers, or at least some of them, who put the management into MIS!

If these claims are valid, it becomes apparent that information management which emphasizes the development of conventional MIS in isolation from their organizational context will only at best yield marginal gain. At worst it might be dysfunctional for it can perpetuate and strengthen information processing forms which neither represent the social reality of organizations nor the real complexity and uncertainty of the organization and its environment. Indeed it is by no menas unlikely that such a limited view of information processing may be impairing organizational performance and threatening organizational survival.

However, we should not overlook the fact that today's organizations do contain a mix of vibrant and varied information flows and processes. The routine co-exists with the non-routine, the official with the unofficial and despite the massive investment in formal MIS and the application of limited information-decision concepts, the undercurrents of the non-routine and unofficial have survived. Indeed we would like at least to acknowledge the possibility that their survival is the result of under-emphasis and inattention. It could well be that if we attempt to plan, organize and control them too much, we may kill the very spontaneity, flexibility and informality on which their effectiveness depends. This is indeed a real possibility. Nevertheless we are still convinced that if information management is to offer something of real benefit to organizations, it has to have a framework that can at least place the formal within its wider context. Otherwise a continued focus on the narrow, technical aspects of information processing may not only ultimately drive out these very necessary complements and counterparts, but also we may fail to fully exploit the real possibilities for the organizational processing of information which emerging technologies may offer (Earl, 1978b).

The wider, alternative and complementary forms of information processing which currently co-exist in organizations must therefore start to enter into the discourse of MIS designers, managers and even users. Indeed a vital task of information management needs to be the explication of a broader framework for the consideration of information processing in organizations and an understanding of its implications for MIS analysis and design.

We can summarize our own, albeit tentative, suggestions for the outline of such a framework in the following way:

*   New frameworks and metaphors are required to re-orient our information thinking.

*   A major goal of such frameworks and metaphors is to explicate social reality and challenge technocratic wisdoms.

* Information problems do not necessarily require information systems; alternative forms of information processing can, do and should exist in organizations.

* Investment in organizational processes and structural forms of information
  processing are required to complement the MIS.

* We need to improve our understanding of how organizational decision-making and
  control is achieved, before major advances in MIS will be possible.

* Many MIS will need to generate frameworks rather than providing mere solutions.

With such a broader organizational perspective, tasks and responsibilities of
information management will take on a very different form.

With the technical so explicitly linked to the organizational, no one management
function can be, or should be, responsible for the whole of information processing.
The role of the information specialist therefore will need to become that of a
catalyst for change. The user in contrast will need to have the confidence to
explicate and describe his own information environment, processing and problems.
In such a context progress in information management therefore will depend on us,
as managers and users as much as, if not more than, on them as specialists.

REFERENCES

(1) Ackoff, R.L., Management Misinformation Systems, Management Science, Dec.
     (1967), 147-156.

(2) Argyris, C., Organisational Learning and Management Information Systems.
     Accounting, Organisations and Society, Vol.2. No.2. (1977), 113-123.

(3) Bariff, M.L., and Galbraith, J.R., Intraorganisational Power Considerations
     for Designing Information Systems. Accounting, Organisations and Society,
     Vol.3. No.1. (1978), 15-28.

(4) Boland, R.J., Control, Causality and Information System Requirements,
     Accounting, Organisations and Society, Vol. 4. No.4. (1979), forthcoming.

(5) Bower, J., Managing the Resource Allocation Process (Division of Research,
     Graduate School of Business Administration, Harvard University, 1970).

(6) Burns, T., and Stalker, G.M., The Management of Innovation. (London,
     Tavistock, 1961).

(7) Child, J., Strategies of Control and Organisation Behaviour. Administrative
     Science Quarterly, (1973), 1-17.

(8) Child, J., Management and Organisational Factors Associated with Company
     Performance, Part 1. Journal of Management Studies (1974), 175-189.

(9) Child, J., Managerial and Organisational Factors Associated with Company
     Performance - Part 2. Journal of Management Studies, (1975), 12-27.

(10) Churchman, W., The Design of Inquiring Systems. (Basic Books, New York, 1971).

(11) Earl, M.J., Prototype Systems for Accounting, Information and Control,
     Accounting, Orgnisations and Society, Vol.3. No.2. (1978a), 168-172.

(12) Earl, M.J., What Microprocessors Mean. Management Today, December (1978b),
     67-74.

(13) Galbraith, J., Designing Complex Organisations (Addison-Wesley, 1973).

(14) Gibson, C.F., and Nolan, R.L., Managing the Four Stages of EDP Growth.
      Harvard Business Review, (Jan.-Feb. 1974), 76-88.

(15) Gorry, G.A., and Scott-Morton, M.S., A Framework for Management Information
      Systems, Sloan Management Review, (Fall, 1971), 56-70.

(16) Georgiou, P., The Goal Paradigm and Notes Towards a Counter Paradigm.
      Administrative Science Quarterly. (1973), 291-310.

(17) Grinyer, P., and Norburn, D., Planning for Existing Markets: Perceptions of
      Executives and Financial Performance. Journal of the Royal Statistical
      Society, Series A, (1975), 70-97.

(18) Hedberg, B., and Jonsson, S., Designing Semi-Confusing Information Systems
      for Organisations in Changing Environments, Accounting, Organisations and
      Society, Vol. 3., No.1 (1978), 47-64.

(19) Hopwood, A.G., Criteria of Corporate Effectiveness, in Brodie, M., and
      Bennet, R., (Eds.) Managerial Effectiveness, (Thames Valley Regional
      Management Centre, 1979).

(20) Hopwood, A.G., An Accounting System and Managerial Behaviour, (Saxon House,
      1973).

(21) Koestler, A., The Act of Creation, (Hutchinson,London, 1964).

(22) Lorsch, J., and Allen, S., III, Managing Diversity and Independence,
      (Division of Research, Graduate School of Business, Harvard University, 1973).

(23) Mason, R.O., Basic Concepts for Designing Management Information Systems,
      (AIS Research Paper No. 8. Graduate School of Business Administration,
      University of California, Los Angeles, October, 1969).

(24) Mason, R.O., and Mitroff, I.M., A Program for Research on MIS. Management
      Science, (Jan. 1973), 475-487.

(25) Mintzberg, H., The Myths of MIS. California Management Review. (Fall, 1972)
      92-97.

(26) Oloffson, C. and Svalander, P.A., The Medical Services Change Over to a Poor
      Environment - "New Poor" Behaviour. Unpublished Working Paper, University
      of Linkoping. (1975).

(27) Simon, H.A., Guetzkow, G., Kozmetsky, G., and Tyndall, G., Centralisation
      v. Decentralisation in Organising the Controller's Department. (New York,
      Controllership Foundation Inc. 1954).

(28) Thompson, J.D., and Tuden, A., Strategies, Structures and Processes of
      Organisational Decision, in Thompson, J.D., et.al. (Eds.), Comparative
      Studies in Administration, (University of Pittsburgh Press, 1959).

(29) Turcotte, W.E., Control Systems, Performance and Satisfaction in Two State
      Agencies. Administrative Science Quarterly, (1974), 60-73.

(30) Zani, W.M., Blueprint for MIS. Harvard Business Review, (Nov.-Dec.1970),
      95-100.

The Information Systems Environment
Lucas, Land, Lincoln, Supper (Editors)
North-Holland Publishing Company
© *IFIP, 1980*

SOME INNER CONTRADICTIONS IN MANAGEMENT INFORMATION SYSTEMS[1]

Chris Argyris

Harvard University

Most management information systems are designed to use information that is objective, precise, generalizable, trendable, and comparable. These very features generate conditions of distancing and injustice which, in turn, may lead individuals to distort the information in order to protect themselves. Hence, a contradiction: the conditions required for useful valid information lead to conditions that may distort the information.

Administrators require management information systems to fulfill their responsibility for managing the system. In order to fulfill responsibility, it is necessary for the organization to be able to detect and correct error which, in turn, also implies detecting when the unit cannot detect and correct error. If we define learning as the detection and correction of error, then learning is a core activity of any organization and any MIS.

Inner contradiction: Learning about other's performance in order to control their performance may inhibit learning

It may appear trivial and obvious, but it is important to point out that the purpose of the learning that we just identified is to control the performance of others. Herein, we shall see, lies the basis for a contradiction. Control, in order to be effective, is designed in many organizations to be unilateral. Along with the unilateral feature, there tend to exist sanctions in order to make certain it has "teeth." The theory of how to monitor the performance of others is basically, therefore, a theory of unilateral control, or rewards and punishments designed on the assumption that "people respect what you inspect."

The designers of such control activities are aware that they may see unintended consequences on learning. Unfortunately, as we shall see, instead of dealing with the dilemma in a straightforward manner, all sorts of caveats are included that are so general that they act as a camouflage of the unilateral control features. Since the camouflage is understandably seen as a message that the system of unilateral control is undiscussable, rules soon develop about keeping the undiscussable, undiscussable.

If the theory of unilateral control combined with rules for camouflage is to be used, it must first be learned. Hence, the participants must learn a theory of control that is counterproductive to the detection and correction of important errors. This marks the beginnings of the contradiction. The MIS "sold" as a learning device requires that the users learn a theory of unilateral control that is counterproductive to learning about important errors. If, as we shall see, it is not easy for subordinates to discuss this contradiction (because

it may appear as disloyal and troublemaking), then they will camouflage their
doubts. They will then be learning that for the sake of survival, they must
deceive and camouflage: the very type of activities that they wished the others
did not do.

We now have the proponents of MIS requiring contradictory actions; the
users learning to adhere to the contradictory actions and hiding the contradic-
toriness. These users have difficulty in dealing with some real issues of implementing MIS but act as if this is not so; hence, they contribute to the contradiction while simultaneously acting as if there is no contradiction.

Thus, the theory used to monitor and control the performance of others can
lead to inhibiting the learning required to accomplish the monitoring and control.
This is a contradiction because the activities that lead to successful monitoring
and control may also lead to ineffective learning. Ineffective learning, in
turn, may lead to less effective monitoring and control. The contradiction is
"inner" in the sense that it is inherent in the way MIS are presently designed.

There are several other inner contradictions that flow from the one just
described. Some are related to the way administrators tend to use MIS while
others are related to the very fact that MIS must use information if they are to
be effective. Let us examine the latter first.

A map for understanding may not be adequate as a map for taking action

In order for administrators to coordinate actions, they must have pictures
or maps of what is happening. But in order to have a map of what is happening,
it must have happened. In order to know what has happened, one must reflect
backward (in time) and piece events into some recognizable pattern.

But it takes time and skill to recreate events so that history can be used
to manage the present and the future. It is the task of management information
specialists to design maps for understanding the past and present realities in
order to help line management enact future realities. But there may be a
dilemma embedded in these objectives because valid maps for understanding reality
may have different properties than the maps people utilize to take action.

Maps based upon reflections of experience may be more complete than the
maps used to create the experience in the first place. The first reason is that
all human beings know more than they can say. In other words, the personal
information systems humans use to design and execute their actions are so complex
that they must be kept tacit in order to be effective. But in order for maps to
be tacit so that they can be used, people must be so skillful at what they are
doing that they need not pay conscious attention to their actions. A person
riding a bicycle uses a map that is over 400 pages in length, yet he cannot
articulate the map. Indeed, one way to immobilize the rider is to require that
he read the map while trying to ride the bicycle.

Second, if people rarely have complete pictures of what is going on in
their heads, they also have difficulty in knowing what is going on in the heads
of others. Hence, people will always have scattered, incomplete information
about any complex episode. Third, people rarely have the time to reflect on
practice adequately and, at the same time, continue to take action to get their
jobs done.

These possibilities may inhibit the use of MIS as proposed by the designers
and the line managers who support the system. This could lead to the ineffective
use of MIS which, in turn, could get the MIS designers in trouble. One consequence of misuse may be that designers strive to make their system as "tamper

proof" as possible, for example, by making it as precise as possible.

Note what has happened. We have an MIS that may contain inner contradictions. These inner contradictions may lead to the ineffective use of MIS. The reaction of the MIS designers is to build into the system features to minimize the MIS being blamed unjustly. These features act as controls to minimize the unfair or incompetent use of the MIS. But such controls may reinforce the unilateral theory of control, the "respect what we inspect" policy that we described previously.

The use of information to manage a system may create conditions of injustice

Another feature of maps for understanding that may inhibit their use as maps for action is that, in order to produce useable maps, people must abstract from reality that portion which their theory of management tells them is important. In order to do this, they must uncouple some variables that are coupled in the action context and couple other variables that are not. This artificial coupling and uncoupling leads to abstract information that is distanced from the action context. But the distancing is necessary in order to chunk the information.

To use reconstructed information to manage many parts requires categories that are trendable and comparable which implies a stable variance. Moreover, the logic that underlies the categories used should be explicit. The logic and the categories should also be disconfirmable. The more all this can be done with minimal ambiguity and maximum reproducibility, the more precise the information. Hence, top management maps for understanding tend to be characterized by information that is distant and strives for increasing precision.

Now, picture first-line supervisors dealing with their employees. They, too, have the same information-processing limits as the top. They, too, will create maps of understanding that reflect backwards in order to work forward (in time). They, too, must chunk their information.

But the kind of information first-line supervisors use to accomplish these requirements is quite different. MIS, at the point of action in a given situation, requires (1) concrete descriptions of unique situations; (2) representations of actual processes, whether they are rare or repeatable; (3) connection of performance to the process of the situation; (4) implicitly rational logic in that the rules for defining categories, for making inferences, for confirming or disconfirming evaluations are private, subjective, and based upon (5) tacit knowledge and tacit processes.

Such information may be effective for the action context but it is not trendable or comparable, and it is also difficult for others to replicate or publicly disconfirm. In other words, it cannot be used much beyond the concrete situation and usually not by others except that particular first-line supervisor.

The characteristics of distant and local MIS emphasize different ways of thinking, different ways of dealing with people, different concepts of dealing with causality, and above all, different conceptions of how order is defined and managed.

For example:

Distant MIS induces individuals	Local MIS induces individuals
To think abstractly and rationally	To think concretely and intuitively
To conceptualize stable variance and general overall conditions and trends	To conceptualize variable processes and specific conditions
To distance self from processes that produce results, and focus primarily upon the results or the performance	To become close to the processes that produce results, and focus on them as much as on the results
To identify errors that are exceptional	To identify errors and correct them before they become exceptional
To infer causality from information lacking specificity of causal processes or mechanics	To infer causality from information rich with situational causality related to specific mechanisms

The distant MIS will tend to reward abstract conceptualization, impartiality, publicly verifiable rationality, distancing from individual cases, and inferring personal responsibility from abstract data and overall trends. The local MIS will tend to reward concrete thinking, intuition, privately verifiable rationality, closeness to the individual case, and inferring personal responsibility from concrete specific processes.

People who live over periods of time in either of these worlds may come to hold different conceptions of the meanings of responsibility, competence, causality, and the requirements for effective order. Human beings' sense of justice may be a function of their concepts of responsibility, competence, and the requirements for effective order.

For example, we may learn by observing the operations of our courts that justice requires that all parties have equal access to the same information and an equal opportunity to confirm or disconfirm it. Yet top managers have access to different information than the locals; the locals rarely have the opportunity to confront the information used by the top. If the locals were to have such an opportunity, it is questionable whether they would have the information-processing competences required to deal with it effectively. Justice also requires that errors be directly and unambiguously coupled to individuals' actions (the smoking gun). Yet MIS for top management does not attend to such rules of evidence.

The paradox therefore is that in order to manage through the use of information, we have had to design a world that produces competence and justice along with incompetence and injustice, the latter mostly around the difficult problems of the organization.

The sheer information-processing requirements and the costs that would be necessary to assure minimal misunderstanding and minimal injustice may be so high that such assurances would not be possible. Employees who are responsible and loyal understand these constraints, but in doing so, place themselves in a dilemma. If they accept the high probability of injustice as necessary, then they have acted to legitimize injustice. If they do not accept the necessity of injustice, they would be seen as disloyal. Those at the upper levels may find it necessary to defend themselves from the dilemma of having to be unjust in order to make the organization effective.

We may ask, how do people deal with the dilemma of being exposed to necessary and self-legitimated injustice? Some possible adaptive activities at the lower levels may be:

(1) They may consider the basis for, and the meaning of, justice to be embedded in the nature of their type of MIS. But such an action leaves them open to potential conflict with the top because, as we have suggested above, each MIS implies a different conception of order.

(2) They may reduce their risks by withholding information or sending doctored information upward.

(3) They may reduce the tension of living in a world of unpredictable and uncontrollable injustice by withdrawing their energies and commitments, and hence feeling less of a sense of personal responsibility.

Reactions such as these reduce the probability that the top will get the information it needs and the commitment it desires on the part of the lower levels in order to manage effectively.

Compounding the top's problem is the previously stated possibility that it may be forced to be unjust even when it does not wish to be. Top managers may react to this possibility by developing attitudes and values such as that they must be tough because, as one president said to the writer, "Five percent of the people work; ten percent think they work; and eighty-five percent would rather die than work." Another set of attitudes usually developed is that lower-level managers and employees can be trusted only to the extent that they can be monitored.

These attitudes and values, combined with the top management's reactions described above, may lead to at least three counterproductive tendencies:

(1) Lower-level managers may become more fearful, take fewer risks, and increase their defensive and protective activities.

(2) These actions may deepen the degree of penetration that management must take into the local MIS. This can lead to confusion because the properties of top management MIS are incongruent with the properties of the local MIS.

(3) These actions may increase the probability that the subordinates will attempt to turn the top MIS into a way of getting even with, or generating some control over, the top. For example, air traffic controllers can "strike" simply by following the defined procedures rigorously.

"Tightening up" MIS in order to "get performance under control" may inhibit the achievement of performance

Recall at the outset I suggested that people tend to control any activity that could be counterproductive by the use of unilateral control. The conditions above could understandably be seen by line management as a threat to their ability to control and manage. Hence, they may request that the MIS designers tighten up their systems and make them more tamper proof. The result usually is for the MIS designers to seek to produce an MIS that is more unilaterally controlling than the previous one (Zamanek, 1975).

There are two important consequences of tightening up. The more comprehensive and the more precise the control, the more the actions of the performers are guided by the monitoring system. More specifically, this means that the MIS produces greater influence by the monitoring managers over (1) the goals to be achieved by the individuals, (2) the processes or steps by which they will achieve them, (3) the level of challenge to be overcome, and (4) the importance all of these factors should have for the performers. The more these features are approximated, the greater the probability that the performers will experience psychological failure (Lewin, Dembo, Festinger, Sears, 1944). Psychological failure occurs to the extent that the performers are told what their goals are, the paths to the goals, their level of aspiration, and the meaning the goals should have for them.

Under conditions of psychological failure, people may produce the required performance targets but feel little personal involvement in doing so. With the lowered sense of involvement usually goes a lowered sense of responsibility for detecting and correcting error. The performers are content to let the definers of the MIS discover and correct errors, including those that may exist in the design and execution of the MIS.

Psychological failure, therefore, tends to lead to conditions where performers feel a lower sense of responsibility and vigilance to detect and correct error. There is a compounding of the contradiction described above, namely that MIS appear to be designed in ways that inhibit the learning they are supposed to carry out.

There is still another compounding of the contradiction. As the MIS becomes tighter, the result may be not only to reduce the discretion and choice the performers have in defining the criteria for acceptable performance, but also the way they go about producing the performance. These conditions are akin to what Lewin (1951) called the reduction of space of free movement. The smaller the space of free movement, the greater the probability that the actors will feel tension, anxiety, and frustration. If they are not able to reverse the process, the other way to reduce the tension is to become less involved in the work. If the space of free movement is to be small, at least the performers can feel that they do not give a darn about the job in the first place. The resulting withdrawal leads to less concern for the detecting and correcting of error.

MIS, management by exception, and management by crisis

It makes little sense to detect and correct all errors because that would require an army of monitors almost as large as the performers. Even if the organization could afford such monitoring, it is likely that it would be experienced as meddling pressure by those being monitored.

The challenge, therefore, is to define criteria that make it unnecessary to examine every error that is made. This is usually accomplished by defining a level of acceptable performance. Errors within a range of acceptable performance are ignored, a strategy called management by exception.

Management by exception makes organizational learning feasible because it permits us to ignore all "small" errors. One unintended consequence, however, is that in some cases the small errors are indicators of an impending major problem. Under these conditions, the organization remains blind to major error until the small error becomes large.

Once the error becomes large and surfaces, it also attracts the attention of top management. People at the lower levels begin to feel vulnerable and prepare their case as to why the error occurred, and more importantly, what they are doing to correct the error. One frequent consequence is that an atmosphere of crisis is created. The crisis becomes necessary in order to overcome any barriers to action and to sidetrack, temporarily, bureaucratic attention to less important issues. In terms of our model, the crisis is an attempt to overcome

the barriers to learning. Paradoxically, the use of crisis is itself a game.
Hence, the very activities that may lead to success also reinforce the factors
that may lead to failure.

The case for escalating error

So far, I have suggested that present concepts for the effective design and
use of MIS may have embedded within them features that make the detection and
correction of error difficult.

The natural question to ask is, what can be done to correct the situation?
We have found that this question cannot be answered adequately without describing
one additional feature of reality in most organizations. The feature to which I
refer is the predisposition to create constraints for learning that lead to
escalating error.

Figure 0-I represents a model of the learning system that, to date, mirrors
the conditions in all the organizations that we have studied (Argyris and Schön,
1978). The model begins with the cognitive features of information. The sub-
stance of the information is irrelevant. Information may vary from inaccessible
to accessible, ambiguous to unambiguous, vague to clear, inconsistent to consistent, and incongruent to congruent.

When such information interacts with individuals, a primary inhibiting loop
for learning is created due to the tendency of these individuals to reinforce
whatever degree of inaccessibility, ambiguity, vagueness, inconsistency exists
in the information. By inhibiting loop, I mean simply that the consequences of
the interaction between Columns (1) and (3) are loops that tend to maintain and
reinforce the original conditions that produce error. Feedback is positive in
that it reinforces the original qualities of the information; it is not corrective. (Feedback is represented by arrows that return to a previous condition.)

Why should an inhibiting loop always occur? In order to answer that question, I must introduce the concepts of theories of action, espoused theories,
and Model I theories-in-use.

What is Model I theory-in use? People design and guide their behavior by
the use of theories of action that they hold in their heads. Espoused theories
of action are the theories that people report are governing their actions. Most
people studied so far manifest theories-in-use that are remarkably similar and
fall into a pattern we have called Model I.

Model I theories-in-use are theories of top-down, unilateral control of
others in order for the actors to win, not to lose, and to control the environment in which they exist in order to be effective. But it can be shown that
Model I theories-in-use lead to effective problem-solving, primarily for issues
that do not require that the underlying assumptions of Model I theories-in-use
be questionable; that is, single-loop learning. Model I theories-in-use do not
make it possible for people to have problem-solving skills that question the
governing values of their theory-in-use; that is, double-loop learning (Argyris
and Schön, 1974).

Back to our model of organizational learning. I am asserting that people
studied so far manifest similar theories-in-use which are oriented toward unilateral control and lead to single-loop learning. There are four consequences
of the above (Column 5). People tend to be unaware of their impact upon error,
discovery and correction. If A makes an error and others tend to hide the impact
it has on them, then A will not be aware of the impact. A second result of
primary inhibiting loops is that people tend to be unaware that they are unable

to discover-invent-produce genuinely corrective solutions to problems. A third
result is defensive group dynamics (e.g., little additivity in problem-solving,
low openness and trust, and high conformity and covering up of threatening
issues). A fourth result is intergroup dynamics that are also counterproductive.

These four results create secondary inhibiting loops. They are called
secondary inhibiting loops because they arise out of interaction with the
primary inhibiting loops. Secondary inhibiting loops also feed back to reinforce
the primary inhibiting loops and the previous conditions that predispose error
(Columns 2, 3, 4, and 5).

What kinds of errors tend to be correctable and uncorrectable under these
conditions? Errors that tend to be correctable (see top of Column 7) include:
(a) errors whose discovery is a threat to the individual's system of hiding
error, and his or her inability to correct error; (b) errors that predispose
primary inhibiting loops because they are threatening Model I values (e.g., win-
don't lose, suppress feelings, etc.); and (c) errors whose correction violates
organizational norms.

The errors that tend to be uncorrectable (a) are camouflaged, (b) the
primary and secondary inhibiting loops associated with them are camouflaged, and
(c) the camouflage is camouflaged with (d) the development of protective activities such as "j.i.c. files" ("just in case" the superiors ask) (Column 8).
Again, the conditions described in Columns 7 and 8 feed back to reinforce the
previous conditions.

The conditions described in Column 8 also tend to increase the predisposition of competitive win-lose games, deception, not taking risks, the potency of
the attribution that the participants will make to the effect that their organizations are brittle and unchangeable, and the potency of their expectation that
organizations are not for double-loop learning (Column 9). These conditions
feed back to reinforce the previous error-producing conditions and simultaneously
tend to reduce the probability that the organization will examine effectively
the processes of how it examines and evaluates its performance. And again, this
feeds back to reinforce the previous conditions. Every time the previous conditions are reinforced, the consequences that follow are also reinforced. Hence,
we have a system that is not very likely to learn except when dealing with those
problems that are correctable (top of Column 7). The participants will tend to
experience double binds. If they follow the requirements of the system, little
learning will occur about issues that question the underlying objectives and
policies. If they consider changing the system, they will tend to take on a
task that they consider foolhardy and dangerous to their survival.

A summary of the diagnosis

The design of MIS, according to present conceptions of sound practice,
leads to systems that have embedded in them inner contradictions. Inner contradictions are features of systems that lead to success and failure, effectiveness
and ineffectiveness. Unfortunately, most organizations contain people who are
programmed with Model I and who therefore create O-I learning systems in their
organizations. These learning systems are ill-suited to dealing with such
double-loop problems as contradictions, paradoxes, and dilemmas that are
embedded in the underlying theory of design of MIS.

Implications for practice

The first implication is that we must teach people how to deal with inner
contradictions. If this analysis is correct, it is highly unlikely that the

solution is for people to grab one horn of the dilemma. For example, the reaction of "tightening up" will lead to increased effectivness and increased rigidity of the MIS because the predispositions to compete, play political games, and to camouflage will go even further underground.

In a large newspaper, the top management decided not to deal with their O-I learning system. They chose to develop a new financial MIS which they felt would bring order and make sense out of the confusion. One year later, the proponents of the financial system reported that it had enhanced organizational learning primarily at the single-loop level. Double-loop learning was now even more difficult because those who resisted it did so by creative manipulation of the financial system (Argyris, 1974).

What is needed is an organizational learning system that encourages double-loop learning. We have been experimenting with implanting such systems into organizations and have found that it is not possible to make the transplant successfully without teaching the participants a new theory-in-use. The reason that a new theory-in-use is required is, as pointed out above, that people can implement actions and systems only if these are congruent with their theories-in-use.

A Model II theory-in-use is needed that includes behavioral strategies such as advocacy combined with inquiry; the minimal use of face-saving and unilateral censorship actions, the advocating of positions in ways that are publicly disconfirmable, and making discussable any information (cognitive or emotional) that is relevant to the problem. Teaching Model II and helping people to create an O-II learning system is not easy but it appears doable. Ginzberg (1975) and Keen (1975) have made some interesting and useful suggestions. Don Schön and I would agree with their emphases on changing attitudes and behavior but would add that these are not adequate. The change must reach the individual participant's respective theories-in-use and the O-I learning system.

A more immediate recommendation is to re-examine the present advice being given management in order to help them understand the enormous gaps embedded within it, if the advice is to go from ideas to actions.

For example, in a thoughtful article, Hammond (1974) notes that effective MIS (1) provide a structure to a situation which is initially relatively unstructured, (2) extend the decision maker's information-processing ability, (3) facilitate concept formation, (4) stimulate the collection of data that otherwise might not be collected, and (5) free the manager from existing mental sets. All these are potential benefits. But it may be that they are obtained at a a potential cost of some degree of psychological failure, injustice, and escalating error.

Similarly, Neuschel (1976) advises administrators to believe "...in the idea that continuous adaptation, simplification, and strengthening of systems is important" (page 58). In order to do so, the administrator's basic task is "...to stimulate among the entire executive and supervisory force an understanding of the problem and opportunities it holds, and a will for united action." (This is the author's underlining.)

What this advice fails to alert the administrators to are the consequences that will occur as they strive to succeed in the above. A united drive for continual adaptation, simplification, and strengthening of systems may also lead to a reinforcement of psychological failure, injustice, and escalating error. Thus, making the above a part of the sinews of the organization through management determination to systems improvement (another recommendation by Neuschel) may also lead to the probability of psychological failure, injustice, and escalating error becoming part of the sinews of the organization.

Zannetos (1978) has made an analysis as to why managers appear adverse to intelligent information systems that are designed to use proabilistic thinking and to experiment and test various solutions. Among the several interesting hypotheses are that managers dislike probabilistic thinking and have an aversion to making decisions on the basis of incomplete information.

There is a puzzle embedded in these hypotheses because managers make decisions on incomplete information; indeed, many even define "managerial toughness" as precisely that ability (Argyris, 1976). One solution to the puzzle is that intelligent information systems make probabilistic thinking explicit, and in doing so, expose it to more rigorous and systematic analysis. This leads, as Zannetos points out, to making error more visible.

Under these conditions, the managers will behave, if our analysis is correct, in contradictory ways. If asked whether they wish more information, they will respond affirmatively to the point of asking for too much, as Ackoff (1967) suggests. The reason is that they are playing the Model O-I games of "just-in-case" and "cover-your-ass." Similarly, they make decisions under uncertainty but do not wish to make the uncertainty explicit in order to cover themselves. In our terms, the properties of intelligent information systems that Zannetos recommends, in addition to making the managers vulnerable, also reduce their space of free movement and increase the probability of their experiencing psychological failure when the information is operating effectively.

The "sales job" that may have to be done will include, as Zannetos suggests, developing healthy attitudes toward accounting data, toward probabilistic thinking, toward the effective use of computers. It also must include, if our analysis is correct, an unfreezing of the Model I theories-in-use and the O-I learning system.

---

[1] This paper was written jointly for the Bonn Working Group 8.2 Working Conference on the Information Systems Environment (June 1979) and the Conference on Managerial Accounting, University of Illinois, Department of Accounting (November 1979).

REFERENCES

1. Ackoff, Russell L., Management Misinformation Systems, Management Science, 14, 4 (1967) B147-B156.

2. Argyris, Chris, Behind the Front Page (Jossey-Bass, San Francisco, 1974).

3. Argyris, Chris, Increasing Leadership Effectiveness (Wiley-Interscience, N.Y., 1976).

4. Argyris, Chris and Donald Schön, Theory in Practice (Jossey-Bass, San Francisco, 1974).

5. Argyris, Chris and Donald Schön, Organizational Learning (Addison-Wesley, Reading, MA, 1978).

6. Ginzberg, Michael Jay, Implementation as a process of change: A framework and empirical study, Center for Information Systems Research, M.I.T. Report No. 13 (1975).

7. Hammond, John S., The Roles of the Manager and Management Scientist in Successful Implementation, Sloan Management Review (1974) 1-24.

8. Keen, Peter G.W., A Clinical Approach to the Implementation of OR/MS/MIS Projects, Working Paper 780-75, Sloan School of Management, M.I.T. (1975).

9. Lewin, Kurt, Field Theory in Social Science, Dorwin Cartwright (ed.) (Harper & Row, N.Y., 1951).

10. Lewin, Kurt, Tamara Dembo, Leon Festinger, and Paul Sears, Levels of Aspiration, in: J. McV. Hunt (ed.) Handbook of Personality and the Behavioral Disorders (Ronald Press, N.Y., 1944).

11. Mintzberg, Henry, Impediments to the Use of Management Information, National Association of Accountants, 1975.

12. Neuschel, Richard F., Management Systems for Profit and Growth (McGraw-Hill, N.Y., 1976).

13. Zannetos, Zenon S., Intelligent information systems: a decade later, Working paper 1028-78, Sloan School of Management, M.I.T. (1978).

15. Zemanek, H., The Human Being and the Automaton, in Enid Mumford and Harold Sackman (eds.) Human Choice and Computers (American Elsevier Publishing, 1975).

The Information Systems Environment
Lucas, Land, Lincoln, Supper (Editors)
North-Holland Publishing Company
© *IFIP, 1980*

Planning and Implementation of Information Systems

N. Szyperski

Betriebswirtschaftliches Institut für Organisation und Automation
an der Universität zu Köln (BIFOA)
Cologne
Federal Republic of Germany

This paper concentrates on issues and aspects of systems development of strategic importance. The future of information systems
raises a number of questions for both operational and strategic
information management. In order to deal more closely with these
questions, the paper states ten propositions which cast some light
on the present situation. These more or less well known facts form
the basis for information-system planning in the broadest sense.
They represent the starting-position for further developments in
this field. The next step will be to highlight certain points in
the development of information systems through a series of ten
questions. This latter section will represent not so much a cool
scientific analysis as a formulation of certain provocative
theses.

THE PRESENT STATUS OF SYSTEMS

(1) The computer world picture has undergone a fundamental change

The era of centralized information systems, of the isolated central
master-computer with a greater or lesser number of dependent sa-
tellites is coming to an end. In the course of these changes communication networks have come into existence with network processors as their central hardware[1]. The periphery can then consist
of similar large computers connected through the network. The
networks serve computer-supported communication-systems designed,
realized and operated not for their own sakes, but in order to
ease communications between people. Although these changes have
already taken place in principle, not all institutes and levels of
management are yet aware of them. Whether they constitute a re-

volution of Copernican proportions is a question we can not yet
answer, but there can be no doubt that a fundamental transformation in our view of information systems has taken place.

(2) Different technologies are coalescing

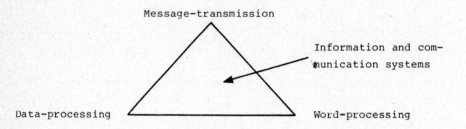

The shifting of technical barriers has caused boundaries to become
blurred, with the result that there is more freedom for the development of information systems. This is reinforced by the drastic
improvement in the price/performance ratio which has accompanied
the technical development of information systems: more comprehensive technical alternatives in the field of information and communication are now available at economic rates.

(3) Information and communication are two sides of the same
      coin

The fusion of technologies opens the possibility of considering
both information and communication aspects at the same time, and
of taking account of interdependence relations while developing
the systems.

The interdependence relations are clearly seen in the fact that
there can be no communication without information and vice versa.
It is advisable to conceive of them as a pair of inseparable
Siamese twins.

(4) The peripheral equipment of the information systems can be

reintegrated into the organization of the place of work

This integration is particularly true of intellectual work, as in
management, professional departments and in research. Computer-
supported information systems need no longer be separated functionally and spatially from the human being at work. The dichotomy
between the computer center where the processing is carried out,
and the places of work where the data are prepared and the output
evaluated can be abolished. In the future, the task will be to
design 'workshops' for 'knowledge workers', so that modern information and communication technologies can be used in the context
of work in a meaningful fashion. We must address ourselves to the
computer-supported integration of all intellectual activity,
including all human, social and political problems.

This brings us back to the change mentioned under proposition (1).
The human being in his working and thinking capacity is no longer
tied to a 'peripheral unit' attached to a central computer. The
participating human being can once more play his role of master in
his own sphere of activity, if he uses the information technology
and knows how to maintain his primary and central role in the
design and implementation process.

(5) The functional spectrum of information systems has greatly
    expanded.

The most obvious indicator is the development and application of
new areas of information technology that are appearing beside the
traditional areas of data-processing and message-transmission, for
example:

- telecommunication,
- word-processing,
- Telefax, television,
- electronic mail,
- library facilities,
- printing and mailing.

As a result the sphere of activity and responsibility of information management is expanding. The organizational structures have

not, however, changed to the same degree.

Have the developments in information technology been given enough
attention by business, as on actual or potential user? There is
considerable evidence that this is not in fact the case. The
application potential of new developments has not yet all been
explored.

(6) The human being in his capacity as a naturally intelligent
    information processor and communicator has been rediscovered.

For the use of information systems, it is of critical importance
to realize that people have different attitudes toward information
and that they differ in their qualitative and quantitative abilities in respect of information processing. The human being still
often represents for science the Unknown User whose behavior in
the face of information systems is difficult to explain, can hardly
be predicted and can only be influenced to a limited extent.
Because of these facts it is very difficult to say what can be
planned at all in the framework of a user-oriented systems development. In spite of this, the transition from their role as routine
operators to their role as experts and managers, people's natural
intelligence and their knowledge gained from experience will come
to occupy the center of the stage once again.

(7) Most large organizations are still at Stage 3 of Nolan's
    4-Phase scheme.

Organizations aim for low slack and high control standard. They
are concerned to perfect the 'industrial' application of data-
processing and thereby partly lose sight of the necessary experimental and developmental aspects.

It is at least questionable whether organizations can maintain
this control standard on the introduction of decentralized sytems.
A precondition for this is that organizations have sufficient
capacity to learn. However, corporate learning is a difficult and
strenuous business; moreover, it presupposes a certain degree of
organizational flexibility.

(8) Management is not prepared for the current developments in
    information technology

DP-management is seeking in many cases to halt the "evolutionary
process." Data processing chiefs are often - and usually not
without reason - conservatively inclined. They are out to maintain
the control standard and the efficiency level. General management
on the other hand is not sufficiently sensitive to the problems
looming on the horizon. Nor are the information systems of the
companies themselves able to reflect the symptoms of development.
They should actually be reminding those responsible that it is
time to react, and that the development of information and communication systems is of direct and central importance for the
latter themselves.

(9) The rational use of information and communication technologies
    is a vital factor in competition.

These technologies and their application and future potential are
more than just a means of increasing productivity. Without a
modern communication system the very survival of a company is at
risk. The character of the informational infrastructure of an
organization can easily determine the viability of the company, if
competition on the national and above all on the international
level goes beyond price and product competition in the areas of
adaptability and speed of response. Response competition of this
kind can be superimposed on price and product competition, and
have a decisive effect. This effect is especially when strong in
the other competitive dimensions a tendency towards diminishing
differentiation possibilities can be observed. In companies whose
primary function is to offer information, for example news
agencies, this tendency is of especial importance, but it is true
of whole service-industries, and is gaining in importance in the
manufacturing industry.

Increasing responsive-competition is also the way in which the
conditions in an information-based or 'communicative' society
express themselves. Technological development creates the conditions for this change. Anyone who does not conform, and can not
make up for this self-imposed disadvantage in some other way, is

bound to suffer considerable economic loss.

(10) The practical problems of any company with an explosive de-
     velopment of information technology extend beyond the con-
     fines of systems development.

The general context of implementation can not remain untouched by
technological development. Organizational structures, assessment
scheme, reward and punishment procedures and the states of specialist and systems development must be open to reappraisal no
matter which member of the organization is concerned. This fact is
of particular importance for corporate philosophy and practical
management.[2]

Within companies the style of management must be examined critically to the extent that it is a source of streams of information
and necessary documentation. For example, it is no longer enough
to optimize the information system set up by a given style of
management; rather, the informational consequence of alternative
styles must be analyzed. The 'Parkinson Ratio' demonstrated by
Paul Strassman may serve as an illustration: an incoming letter
may generate a multiplicity of consequential documentation within
an organization - in industrial organizational ratios of 1:15, and
1:25, in medical institutions even of 1:125 have been attested. In
such cases it is certainly not enough to accept these processes
and optimize them on the basis of new procedures. Informational
relationships and documentation habits must, rather, be examined
in respect of their usefulness. Initiatives of this kind have far-
reaching effects on the informational consciousness of an organization.

PLANNING AND IMPLEMENTATION PROBLEMS

(1) How can present illusions and fictions be overcome?

Examples of such are legion:
     - the 'normal' manager, rational and fact-oriented,
     - allegedly stable informational needs,
     - the planned-for division of tasks into sequential phases

and stages,
- priority given to optimization of storage facilities,
- the negative illusions that the development of information
  systems is bound always to be a failure.

In order to overcome these and other notions, it seems necessary
to change one's view of the world, including the way one looks at
problems, and including also one's necessary prior understanding
of information systems. For example an information system is an
open system in which human beings made of flesh an blood, with
changed opinions, attitudes and experiences, have varying needs
for personal contact. Their informational needs are dependent on
learning-processes. Thus static and stable informational need
structures are only conceivable in a world where cognitive and
real development are unknown. Any attempt to develop a complete
computer-supported information system for a rational management
and its stable information requirements, a system whose life
expectancy is seen from the first as unlimited, is very likely to
be a failure as a result of these preconceptions.

Experience with actually developed, operated and used subsystems
shows that they have different useful lifetimes in different functional spheres, for example in R&D and administration of between 2
and 3 and between 5 and 7 years respectively. Yet the 'replacement
period' is fairly stable. Why is it that no one in systems planning begins from the assumption, that the lifetimes of systems
will be different, as is the case in other spheres of investment.

Widespread scepticism is understandable in view of the many
failures we have experienced; the expectations that were awakened
were too great and sometimes simply wrong. In addition, however,
as has been demonstrated by Lübbe there is a still more general
orientation crisis resulting from a too rapid pace of development
and change, which has not left people with enough time to gather
relevant experience with the new technology. For this reason
people like to turn to myths that relieve them of the worry of
having to deal with real problems of development more closely.
Both the path to the illusory resurrection of past situations and
solutions i.e. the trend to nostalgia, and the push to get into
the futuristic Utopian palace, are motivated by the desire to
relieve oneself of the responsibility for taking the next step. To

overcome these inhibiting myths and illusions means constructive
discussion of the practically feasible and practically necessary
data-processing and word-processing systems and corresponding communication systems. In this process economic, social and human
aspects must be related and evaluated in the international context
of development.

(2) How can we take account of and come to terms with the emerging
    discontinuities in our environment?

For a start it is indispensable for information-system managers to
recognize discontinuities as such. Otherwise it can easily happen
that they will attempt - in the figurative sense - to aim for pro-
fits in the wrong market by means of rationalization of production.
Strategic insights can only be obtained with difficulty, and all
the more so the weaker the signals and indicators are.

Possibilities of dealing with discontinuities are offered by strategic management together with technological forecasting and
research into opportunities and risks.

What is technically feasible in the next five to eight years can
be fairly reliably predicted on the basis of laboratory work
completed or still in progress, but the question of who is to use
the new technologies and what economic opportunities they will
create, is still open. In other words, the largest uncertainty
factor is represented by the product and marketing strategies of
the manufacturing industries.

An important requirement, however, for all successfull measures to
be taken by information and communication management is the attitude of the systems-managers and general managers themselves. They
need to develop an intuition for which developments in information
technology are of strategic importance for their own organizational infrastructure. Just as Portfolio Analysis has given rise
to Strategic Business Units, so corresponding methodological
approaches must be found and acted upon in order to assess information-systems complexés for their strategic importance.

(3) How can we react in the face of incipient problems and predic-

table crisis?

From among the many possibilities which have been put forward, I
shall present a few selective examples:

- The integration of strategic information-systems management and
  strategic corporate management
  Here we have to bear in mind the fact that information systems
  are aids to operating in spheres of action which have been stipulated by strategic planning. Conversely, new information
  systems and different information resources can open up new
  spheres of action for a company. How this strategic interrelationship is characterized can vary. The more one's own business
  is characterized wholly or partly by information and communication services, the greater the influence of developments in
  information technology on business strategy. Information
  Resource Management and strategic information-systems planning
  are coming to be matters of urgent necessity.

This strategic information-systems planning must be based on a
corresponding analysis of the possible spheres of action of
information systems and an appropriate strategic evaluation of
these spheres of action.

- A Momentum-Strategy starts out from the assumption that developed and developing information and communication systems
  will stand up to future strategic demands. Logically consistent measure: a research group into information technology
  is set up.

- An aggressive development strategy is based on the manifest
  strategic relevance of developments in information technology
  for securing the success potential of one's own business. The
  result is a deliberate attempt to operate on the technological
  frontline and to push this front forward at one's own cost.
  Logically consistent behavior: developments in information
  technology determine the whole strategic approach of the
  organization, R & D projects in the field of information and
  communication technology are given own budgets; manufacturers
  of hard and software are presented with tasks which stimulate
  development - at least, if not research.

- A <u>moderate development strategy</u> is, in intention, somewhere
  between the two preceding ones. It is the expression of the
  strategic concern of the whole organization. Logically consistent measures: design and execution of pilot projects on
  information and communication technology, on the basis of and
  together with strategic analyses and studies of effects and
  implementation procedures.

- A <u>more defensive or even destructive strategy</u> would attempt to
  force back the influence of information and communication
  technologies.

All those concerned with information systems planning should
reveal their preferred basic strategy in terms of the categories
set out above, so that a consensus can be achieved on the basic
strategy of the organization, before individual measures and
developments are discussed.

· <u>Improved consideration for the demands of information-systems</u>
  <u>and for informational requirements</u>
When these demands or requirements are being determined, different principles or combinations of principles can be applied.
The methods of information Requirement Engineering are concerned
with such questions.

It must be remembered that these requirements and demands are
dependent on the decision-task and decision-situation which the
system is to support. They may therefore be stable, but as a
rule are dynamically dependent on learning processes and changed
decision-conditions. Actual communication and the utilization of
information should be accompanied by intensive studies of
demands and requirements.

· <u>Participation by experienced users</u>
The first people to be supported as 'users' should be the most
able managers, specialists and administrators. In this way,
experience can be gained which will be helpful in facilitating
the use of information systems by others. Information-systems
developments should not be regarded as ways of making up for the
deficiencies of the tail-enders, but as aids to the work of

experienced, committed and able members of an organization. The
idle periods, burden of routine and informational and communicative bottlenecks which they experience are the ones which
must be eliminated. Seen in this light, it is the human worker
with his tasks and responsibilities who occupies the center of
the stage, not the installations or the technical systems.

If the central requirement is that the data-processing installation should be used to its full capacity, and the work of human
employees organized around it, then problems and crises are
inevitable. Information and communication are the vital nerve of
those engaged in intellectual activity, and are bound to end up
as also rans if one looks at the problem from the narrow standpoint of data-processing technology. The employee, whether as
manager, professional or clerical worker, must be the starting-
point for systems planning, both for organizational, and, given
the expected level of wages and salaries, economic reasons. Thus
his participation in systems planning is an expression of organizational wisdom and not a piece of humanitarian charity.

Limitation of risk by means of improved assessment of future developments and consequences

Many mistakes and risks arise as a result of careless planning:
available knowledge concerning foreseeable developments and consequences is not called upon. Not infrequently, information-
systems specialists are simply bad at seeking out and using
information. There are many barriers to be overcome here. Development studies however cost money. They require a budgetary
framework which will allow field studies, simulation techniques
and pilot developments. The basis of such analyzes is information-systems research. Research into information technology by
the user in his own organization appears at the moment however
to be an utopian dream. In the right circumstances user research
is a logical consequence of the strategic importance of the
informational infrastructure in response-competition.

(4) How can the limits of information-systems planning be de-
    monstrated?

In principle, not everything can be planned without serious disad-
vantages resulting. The limits of planning can be demonstrated

under the following aspects:

. Planning is only possible on the basis of a compromise on
  objectives, without a general acceptance of the results being
  assured in every case (especially when those involved have
  incompatible objectives).

· Planning is based on the given priority-structure at the time,
  although its results will be judged in the light of future
  priorities.

. New knowledge and learning processes change prognoses and
  premisses, with the result that planning cannot remain static,
  and planning adjustments often follow in the wake of changes
  arising from relevant studies.

The fulfilment of particular needs conceals the needs
themselves; these come to light only when, later, they are not
fulfilled. An analysis of the situation as it is cannot uncover
them, since they only come to light when they are seen as short-
comings in the new context.

In view of the fact that planning, or the validity of its results,
is thus restricted, we are left with the following possible
procedures. Either we plan only on a very limited scale and for
the very short term, leaving the requirements to develop on their
own and accepting the changing planning conditions; or else we
plan on a comprehensive scale, regulating the requirements and the
discussion of objectives by the formation of an ideology on more
or less totalitarian lines. Which path is more appropriate for the
planning of information systems in organizations must remain an
open question for the time being. It must be remembered, however,
that those concerned can avail themselves, in the event of their
objectives being thwarted, of numerous means of reacting to such
an event and of influencing the success of the information
systems.

(5) How can we establish what is a good – or the best – combina-
    tion of competing information systems within the info-infra-
    structure of a company?

Within organizations there will and cannot be unitary, comprehensive and total information systems, because different systems are
suited best to different tasks. Analogously to passenger and
freight traffic, which can be transported by road, rail, sea or
air, communication within companies has various channels at its
disposal, such as conversation, mail, data-communication and fac-
simile transmission, computer-networks in conjunction with mail,
etc..

The planning of the actual info-infrastructure takes place in
various stages, according to:

• the particular utilization of the systems (Information Management),
• the design of the systems (Information System Management),
• the basic information and communication potentialities (Information Resource Management).

Anything which cannot be planned on the basis of the resources and
is not organizationally permissible, cannot be executed on the
systems-technical plan. Only those information systems which have
actually been set up can actually be used for practical work. From
the point of view of individual information and communication
requirements, a diverse and competing supply of information and
communication services is to be welcomed. Competition enhances the
performance of systems and freedom of choice improves optimization
opportunities for the user. The interests of global systems-design
may conflict with this. On no account must a design be approved
from the outset without discussion if it excludes all competition.
The best communications results are manifestly achieved by using
different media in conjunction, such as telephone conversation,
correspondence by letter, computer-conferencing, and perhaps the
use of individual television receivers. Monocultures might well be
inappropriate at the info-infrastructure level too.

(6) How can technical and economic changes in information systems
    be exploited to the best advantage?

Technological development opens up on the one hand the opportunity
for new applications at an advantageous level of cost, but on the
other hand the costs of one's own systems development will also

rise at an increasing rate. It almost looks as if individual development costs will become too great in the future to permit individual development projects. In any case, development costs must
be reduced, and development periods shortened, in order that the
increasingly cheaper hardware and system software can be used
appropriately. This can be achieved through higher productivity on
the part of the development departments, and/or by using prefabri-
cated systems or components, capable of being used in various
ways. The consequence for the organization is that info-infrastruc-
tures, and functions and their execution, can have a less exotic
appearance and must be much more highly standardized in their
basic patterns.

At the present time we can observe two trends, which both serve to
exhaust new possibilities of economic and technical utilization:

. Increasingly, standardized and inexpensive application systems
  are being installed as information systems for the basic and
  central information problems of an organization. This is true
  both in relation to individual sectors of large concerns, and on
  a supra-company basis, to small and middle-sized firms.

  At the same time, however, we are seeing more and more frequently simple, ad hoc programmed systems, produced at low cost,
  directly supporting their users. Such adapted, usually unstable
  information systems can then be trimmed to the user's implicit
  decision-making model ('actual used theory'); they build on the
  info-infrastructure of the company.

(7) How is the comprehensive information function to be
    organized?[3]

The organizational structure influences the course of events, and
the type of organization has an important bearing on the ability
of the company to perceive, understand and cope with outside
influences. This is also true - perhaps especially so - of such
cross-section functions as the information function. However there
are no analytic rules and methods with whose help the organization
can be optimized with respect to the operations, development and
management of its information systems.

Organizational arrangements and alterations usually proceed on the basis of a compromise between different structural conditions. This compromise must be borne by the influential members of the management and the organization as a whole. Structural solutions such as centralization and decentralization look different on different levels. In the case of the operations, systems development and management of information and communication systems, this could lead to a central information resource management in conjunction with a decentralized systems development and shared operations.

* First, the following must be decided:
  - the underlying philosophy of the organization, including the desired style of management and the general organizational structural guidelines (such as the extent of divisionalization, or the degree of management decentralization, for example),

  - the strategic and operational demands on the information and communication system deriving from this philosophy, and the resulting objectives of the information function.

* Second, the necessary subtasks and activity-packages within the very broadly defined information function are to be stipulated as globally as possible and in as much detail as necessary.

* Third and finally, a structure matrix of persons responsible must be developed. In this matrix, those responsible for the various tasks are to be arranged along three dimensions:

First dimension
  - Corporate leadership and central corporate functions (in respect of standards, decision-making rules, corporate philosophy)
  - corporate sectors and coporate leadership as systems users
  - cross-sectional domain 'systems'
  - external aids (consultancy firms, producers of hard and/or software)

Second dimension
  - general understanding (in respect of matters concerning the business)

- understanding of systems (in respect of information and communication systems)

3rd dimension
- management
- professional and clerical worker
• Fourth, the delimited subtasks are to be assigned to those
responsible according to the above mentioned structure matrix,
without residue, so that every subtask is assigned at least one
responsible person. This guarantees that no subtask is forgotten
when the information function is being organized.

In this 'organization game' organizational principles, precepts
and experiences must be taken into account to the extent that they
limit individual organizational space and prevent inapporiate
design. The form of organization advocated here has the advantage
of greater transparency. The interim results of the process of
opinion formation and compromise can be optically captured. In
this way redundancy and gambling can be avoided, and agreements
reached more easily. The outcome remains open for the solution
most appropriate to each individual situation.

8) How can corporate philosophy be changed?

For the future it seems inevitable that the problem of centralized
vs. decentralized organization of the information-systems function
within companies must be raised to the level of consciousness.
Moreover, a fundamentally positive attitude towards planning
appears necessary, since planning-oriented managers are more sensitive to the exigencies of systems development.

Centralists, decentralists, not to mention federalists, vary
widely in their attitudes and basic philosophies - but these are
extremely stable. It is just as difficult to change these attitudes as it is to change a given und usually deeprooted corporate
philosophy. Everything connected with human behavior is extremely
stable in an organizational context.

However, in particular vis-à-vis the information and communication
function, these attitudes, and business and corporate philosophies
must in most cases be modified. Otherwise the awareness necessary

for a comprehensive operational and strategic information and communication management cannot be developed. In many cases the
discussion and revision of the corporate philosophy must begin all
strategic considerations in respect of information.

(9) How can we achieve a better understanding between those
    involved?

Managers and professionals at various levels, and systems-specia-
lists, all regard information systems from their own individual
perspectives. The consequence is that rolespecific barriers appear
which inhibit all communication and in extreme cases prevent it
altogether. Those involved must therefore help each other to start
a process of communication. This needs effort on all sides.
Without adequate communication requirements in respect of the
development of one's own info-infrastructure, this is impossible.
Anyone who doesn't know why he should talk to anyone else, and
what about, is hardly likely to have much unterstanding for the
views of the 'other side'. Agreement presupposes a common interest
in the development of systems and in information resources.

Technological developments, and the opportunities and risks which
they present, and the consequences of different individual strategies in respect of these, must be made known within the organization in good time. For the same reason, longer-term development
objectives in this field must also be made known and discussed.
Anyone who expects others to understand his or her point of view
must also be prepared to provide sufficient informations as input.
By these means, those concerned are involved in good time in the
process of defining problem areas and establishing and evaluating
alternatives on a strategic level with respect to information.

(10) How far can information-systems research be extended and
     improved?

Information and communication research, including research in the
field of word-processing, are in technological terms, young
sciences. The development of info-infrastructure at the level of
individual companies, and at supra-company level, is fundamentally
dependent on the further development of this research. Individual

companies will have increasingly to ask themselves what R&D conclusions they wish to - or must - draw from their strategic attitude towards response-competition. When more than 50% of the staff
are occupied with 'information', one is justified in asking why
actually there are no, or such small, R&D groups for information
systems in user companies. Strategic information management must
answer this question in one way or another. More information and
communication research within companies is thus one answer to the
question posed above.

The intensification of company-external and university research,
preferably in co-operation with practical users, is another
answer. This research must be drawn closer to the object of its
experience, that is the actually existing information and communication systems. Research through development must not remain
only a slogan. Co-operation with outside scientists on systems
development within organizations is an important, prerequisite for
scientific progress in this field. In this context, the degree of
co-operative-mindedness among those involved in everyday practice
is once more the bottleneck. Here the cirles begin to close:
science must realize the central importance of the corporate philosophy as the determining factor in development, when it designs
its own future research projects relating to the development of
information and communication systems in organizations.[4]

Besides this, it seems inevitable that results and ideas will be
exchanged on a much greater scale at the national and international levels. A technocratic attitude is to be opposed. The
human being, in his or her constitutive role in the organization,
must remain at the center of information and communication
activity. She or he cannot be degraded to being the peripheral
unit of the installation, or simply the operator for user. The
user is and will remain the bearer of responsibility. The development of information technology will also offer the world of
research new opportunities to help to design an organizational
environment in harmony with human dignity.

4. References

(1) To the same subject see: Gosden, J.A.: Some Cautions in Large-
Scale System Design and Implementation, in: Information & Ma-
nagement, Volume 2, 1979; Rockart, T.F.; Bullen, C. V.; Kogan,
J.N.: The Management of distributed Processing, Massachusetts
Institute of Technology (MIT), Dec. 1978; Szyperski, N.; Kolf,
F.: Integration der strategischen Informati̅ons-System-Planung
(SISP in die Unternehmungsentwicklungsplanung, in: Hansen,
H.R.   (ed.): Entwicklungstendenzen der Systemanalyse, München
1979, S. 59-81.

(2) Information systems have reached critical importance not only
with respect to corporate level, but the development of the
whole society depends on the resource 'Information'. Government and business have to pay more attention to the international information markets.
See Szyperski, N.; Nathusius, K.: Information und Wirtschaft,
Frankfurt, New York 1975; Auerbach, L.L.; Slameka, V.: Needed:
Executive Awareness of Information Resources, in: Information
& Management, Vol. 2, 1979, S. 3-6

(3) See: Schmitz, P.; Szyperski, N. Organisatorisches Instrument
zur Gestaltung von Informations- u. Kommunikationssystemen in
Unternehmungen, in: Angewandte Informatik, 20 Jg., 1978, 2.
281-292.

(4) See: Resnikoff, H.L.: The Need for Research in Information
Science, in: Information & Management, Vol 2, 1979, S. 1 f.;
Szyperski, N.; Grochla, E. (ed.): Design and Implementation of
Computer-based Information Systems, Alphen aan den Rijn, 1979.

The Information Systems Environment
Lucas, Land, Lincoln, Supper (Editors)
North-Holland Publishing Company
© IFIP, 1980

A MULTIPLE-CONTINGENCY REVIEW OF SYSTEMS
ANALYSIS METHODS AND MODELS

C. Ciborra, G. Bracchi, P. Maggiolini
Istituto di Elettrotecnica ed Elettronica
Politecnico di Milano
Piazza L. da Vinci 32
20133 Milano
Italy[1]

A general framework for the review, comparison and evaluation of the present methodologies for analyzing and design
ing information systems is illustrated.
Four major contingent factors are shown to affect the analyst's task environment: the nature of the organization and
information processes that have to be investigated, the
available data processing technology, the relationships
between users and designers in the development cycle, and
project management strategies.
On the basis of these factors the deficiencies of the vari
ous existing system analysis methodologies are discussed
and the need to explicitly consider the problems of social
change in the implementation of systems in the organization
is shown.

INTRODUCTION

Study on information systems development suggests a casual link exists
between the failures of many applications in management (or at least
the post-implementation disillusions) and the lack of a sound methodology to capture user information needs and to design a new system
accordingly. A number of researchers have felt the need to consider
retrospectively the whole development of systems analysis methodologies and to identify their intrisic rationale to point at possible
improvements, to find out new research paths, and to provide a guide
to use different methods (Miller (1964), Bostrom and Heinen (1977),
Taggart and Tharp (1977), Couger (1973), Munro and Davies (1977),
Teichroew (1972)).

The basic aim of this paper is to present a general framework for the
review, comparison, and evaluation of systems analysis (SA) techniques. This framework is based on hypotheses that have been widely
tested in the Artificial Intelligence environment (Newell and Simon
(1972) and Polya (1957)) and it identifies four contingent factors that influence the adequacy of a given SA technique: the nature of the decision
process to be automated, the data processing technology available,
user awareness, and the management of the information systems project.

A general assumption of the paper is that an organizational perspective is relevant for the evaluation of current efforts in SA techniques development, and a general conclusion is that there cannot be
one optimal method to be applied in every information system design
effort.

---

[1]This work was partially supported by the Italian National Research
Council, Project 'Informatica', and by Fondo Fiorentini Mauro -
Politecnico di Milano.

In the paper the evolution of the state-of-the-art SA techniques is
briefly reviewed, and the emergence of a contingent approach to system analysis is to be discussed. The basic assumptions and the gene
ral framework of the contingency approach are then be illustrated,
and the different types of the analyst's task environments are discus
sed in detail. On the basis of this discussion, a qualitative evaluation of existing SA methods is presented, and guidelines for selecting and/or tailoring SA techniques adequate to the particular environ
ments are introduced.

SA METHODS: DISSATISFACTION AND EMERGENCE OF A CONTINGENT APPROACH

Miller (1964)   comments that progress in developing a methodology for designing management information systems (MIS) has been
slow. The problem of developing and defining the proper content of an
information systems has been slighted in the general work of systems
analysis and design. Around 1970 the solution seemed to be envisaged
in the automation of the system development process: the automated
system comes then of age with the far-reaching example of the ISDOS
approach (Teichroew (1972), Teichroew and Hershey (1977)).

However, the past few years seem to have shown that disillusionment
is here to stay. Bostrom and Heinen (1977) suggest reasons for many
failures and problems lie in the way systems designers view organizations and the function of an MIS. These views are embedded in the design methods which lack a sound understanding of information needs
and of social change exigencies and a truly systematic approach. What
is needed is a more realistic view of organizations embedded in a solid design methodology through which various interventions can be integrated into effective change programs.

One of the first comparative studies of SA methods is based on a hi-
storic perspective: Couger (1973) recognizes an evolution of SA techniques almost concomitant with the degree of sophistication of dp-
technology.

A more comprehensive attempt in the direction of a critical evaluation of SA techniques is the one by Taggart and Tharp (1965 and 1977).
Starting from the empirical fact that the identification of information needs of management is a most critical factor in successful MIS
implementation, the authors review analytically more than twenty SA
methods. Four main parameters are selected for comparison:

- information (intrinsic characteristics, current scope of need
  satisfaction, degree of sophistication),

- decision making (decision process, decision-making hierarchy, the
  characteristics of the decision maker),

- organization (external and internal environment, management functions and level),

- development process (evaluation criteria used).

Such parameters although discussed in detail seem to have been select
ed primarily on the basis of sound intuition.

Finally, to asses the SA methods effectiveness a systematic investiga
tion on the performance of two specific approaches has been carried
out by Munro and Davis (1977). They compare for a variety of situations top-down and bottom-up information requirement analysis. The
former approach is characterized by its focus on the data at the operational level of the organization while the latter focuses on deci-

sions at the managerial level. The results are not discriminating, nevertheless, the hypotheses put forward are interesting:

- a method may perform better in some functional areas than in others,
- the type of decision (programmed or non-programmed) affects the values of information obtained using a method,
- SA techniques cannot be considered apart from the organizational context in which they have to be applied.

Following similar ideas, in this paper we will try to justify the need for a contingent comparison and selection of SA techniques in a more systematic way. We identify a number of relevant contingent factors, and evaluate the techniques according to parameters derived from the factors. However, some basic assumptions need to be made explicit before the comparison.

BASIC ASSUMPTIONS AND A FRAMEWORK FOR THE CONTINGENT APPROACH

Systems analysis methodologies embody a number of conceptual models, beside the explicit rules or documentation tools provided to the analyst. The models usually refer to some issues which build up the frame of reference of the system designer. Critical issues are for example:

- the definition of an information system,
- its relationship with the organizational structure,
- the roles of analyst and user during the design, etc.

The core assumption regards the relationship between the information system (technology, procedures, information flows) and the organization (the structures and the people somehow exposed to the IS design and operation, including both users and designers). Such an assumption has far-reaching consequences on:

- how the analyst understands his own role in designing a new "object" to be inserted into organization,
- how the user's role is understood by the analyst,
- what aspects will be selected during the analysis (information flows only, or also decision-making and control processes, and the quality of working life standards, etc.).

"A highly desirable aim is to define systems to be as independent of a specific organization as possible. This principle does not imply that specific reports from a system should not be designed for a specific organization's use; it does mean that system support boundaries should be relatively free of organization constraints and that multiple organizations should share in the use of consistently defined data in the solution of business-oriented problems"(IBM (1975), page 9). Other methods assume that one cannot specify what information is required for decision making until an explanatory model of the decision process and the system involved has been constructed and tested: information systems are seen as subsystems of control systems (Ackoff (1967)).

These two opposite approaches can be understood if we consider different modelling view-points (Argyris (1977)). The former perspective tends to focus on "distant" information systems (i.e., on formal information and control systems which are at a distance from the operative processes, which rely on norms, on the formalization and standar-

dization of behaviors and information exchanges) that are consequently assumed to be easily representable by means of rational and abstract
categories.

The latter perspective on the other hand focuses on "local" information systems that are characterized by a strict adherence to the control and the coordination of local processes. Such different approaches suggest divergent design strategies. Quite often the dynamics of
the events (failures, inefficiencies, user's protests, etc.) are the
factors that compel the designer to switch from the "rational" approach
to the idiosyncratic one.

A Framework for Comparison

To find criteria for comparison, selection and development of design
strategies, only the "object" to which the analysis effort is applied
has been considered. We suggest that instead of considering only the
nature of the information system to be computerized, we examine the
whole analyst's job, looking at its aims, structure and constraints,
because of the systemic links which bind all these aspects. Only the
requirements-analysis phase will be examined, since it constitutes
one of the most serious parts of the analyst's job, and surely the
least structured one. The study of the analyst's work leads us   to
describe a new contingency approach to the choice and development of
SA methods.

Systems analysis may be considered as a process of perception and selection of organization processes, followed by their description in
terms of a formal model, and by the building of a "data-logical" model, which is the input to the implementation of the new system
(Langefors (1978)). The work of the analyst may be thus regarded as a
problem-solving activity of a symbolic nature, consisting of observations, abstractions, and adaptations of abstractions to a limited set
of rules. The rules are derived from a variety of different sources:
methods, prescriptions, "computer-logic", education; their nature will
be discussed later. Problem solving means achieving an outcome which
initially does not exist starting from a set of givens. In our case the
outcome is the final design of the new system and the givens are basic
know-how, methods, and knowledge obtained from the study of reality

Newell and Simon (1972) suggest that humans, when engaged in problem
solving, are representable as information processing systems (IPS) com
posed of:

- a memory containing symbol structures,

- an information processor which transforms the symbol structures,

- receptors and effectors to capture and communicate information.

The designer (our IPS) when creating a new system operates with symbol
structures which summarize the knowledge he has regarding organizational structures, decision processes, information flows, etc. He
transforms such symbols according to rules and models he has at dispo
sal in his own memory, using available and known tools in order to
solve his problem (that is to reach the objective of analyzing and designing the system).

Extending the results tested by Newell and Simon (1972), we suggest
that the designer while carrying out his job uses a conceptual problem
space. The analyst's problem space contains a number of elements:

- symbol structures representing the state of knowledge about the task
  and the "object" system,

- sequence of operations on symbols,
- problems, i.e. sets of final, desired states,
- general knowledge available (memory).

Problem solving takes place by <u>search</u> in the problem space. The problem space also determines the possible programs (i.e. methods) used in problem solving.

Let us now discuss what factors affect the structure of the problem space available to the analyst. Newell and Simon (1972) point out that it is the <u>task environment</u> which determines the possible structures of the problem space: the task environment may be described as the environment in which the analyst operates coupled with a goal, problem or task. The main features of the information system task environment (its so-called "texture") can be summarized following the guidelines set by Leavitt (1964):

- the <u>task</u>: i.e., the nature of the organizational, technological and information processes that have to be investigated and redesigned by the analyst.

- the <u>technology</u>: i.e., the data processing technology for implementing the new systems, as well as methods and procedures available. The latter are the SA methods, defined as disciplined approaches which govern the design activity, by providing symbol structures (e.g. diagrams and other documentation aids), operators (e.g. the functional decomposition), problems and search-process structures (goals setting and design phases), knowledge of the organization, and rules to increase the amount of knowledge (about the organization, the structure of its information system, the user, etc.).

- <u>people</u>: the social system which comprises the analyst and the "object system" (users, other specialists, vendors, etc.).

- the <u>structure</u>: the management of the project and the relevant authority structure.

Figure 1 is a simplified view of the interrelationships of the factors.

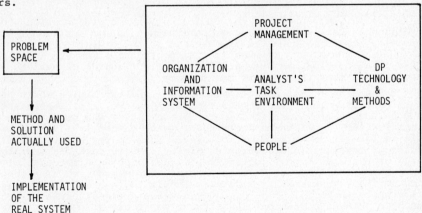

Figure 1 - Systems Analysis as a Problem Solving Activity

Applying the above considerations we can reformulate the contingent approach by stating that <u>different task environments imply different problem spaces</u> and, <u>above all, different methods or approaches</u> that are actually implemented to design the information system.

This assumption seems to justify a number of observable facts:

- the existence of a large number of <u>ad hoc</u> system design methods, each adapted to the idiosyncracies of the designer and of the situation;

- the low degree of utilization of those methods that we might call "universal SA methods", especially in small-and middle-sized companies;

- the soundness of the prototype approach, according to which the computer-based information system should be designed on an experimental basis, thus building <u>ad hoc</u> problem spaces and methods (Earl (1978)).

In the next section, we try to classify different task environments whose features require specific characteristics of SA methods.

TYPES OF TASK ENVIRONMENTS

In presenting the task environments which may be faced by the designer, we consider the following aspects:

- the nature of organization and information technology in the area exposed to analysis and design activities,

- the available data processing technology,

- the relationship between users and designers in the development cycle,

- project management strategies.

Organization and Information System

As far as the nature of the relationships between organization and in formation system is concerned, we recall that in our approach the information system is regarded as embedded in the organization and its control mechanisms and relevant decision processes (Ackoff (1967)). These relationships can vary providing a first source of variety (and uncertainty) that the analyst has to face.

Many authors have proposed classifications and typologies which help us in understanding how such relationships change. A first synthetic proposal comes from Gorry and Scott Morton (1971) who combine the Simon's (1960) decision-making typology with Anthony's (1965) framework to identify nine information system ideal types related to nine different organizational contexts. Highly structured decisions are lo cated at the operational control level (e.g. accounts receivable), where the problem is to implement already formalized decision models with software programs. At strategic levels there are unstructured areas where there is a need of model development and formalization before any computerization. The authors point out also the relevance of the typology when considering implementation problems, the skills required by managers and analysts, and the characteristics of the design process. In fact, information requirements differ sharply in the nine areas, and systems analysts who deal with groups of top managers may require different backgrounds and skills from those who have to communicate mainly with production personnel, etc.

A similar argument is proposed by MacIntosh and Daft (1978). On the basis of research carried out in twenty-four work-units, they have been able to establish an empirical relationship between four types of work-unit "technologies" and four types of information systems, crossing two criteria: task knowledge and work variety (see Figure 2).

Not understood	Craft technology Cursory IS	Research technology Diffuse IS
Well understood	Programmable technology Concise IS	Technical-professional technology Elaborate IS

Task knowledge (left side)

Low   High

Variety (uncertainty)

Figure 2 - Typology of Work Technology and Information Systems (adapted from MacIntosh and Daft (1978))

The main information design problems consists then in matching the underlying technology of a unit with the appropriate information system, trying to avoid errors such as implementing a large data base from a craft-technology situation, etc.

Another typology of organizations (and related IS) which may be of interest refers to the degree of integration. Where low integration exists, the joint effects of a lack of structure, coordination and purposefullness of the various parts of the organization and the inability of the decision maker to know and govern these loosely connected subsystems pose severe design problems. For example the definition of an MIS or a data base for an insufficiently integrated system creates a need to:

- identify and co-ordinate users who have different goals, knowledge, interests and no specific organizational constraints which guide their behavior;
- create and design decision and control models, where nothing similar exists;
- define the boundaries of the system, etc.

In this context the design of user participation seems to play a relevant role in the whole design process (Nygaard (1978)).

Summarizing, different types of organization structures and technologies not only create different types of information system but also require different problem solving capabilities on the part of the analyst.

Technology

Not only the technology of the work system influences the analyst's approach, but also the available data processing technology.

The availability of new hardware and software tools continuously poses to the analyst new design problems, and quickly make obsolete the pre-existent development techniques.

A vaste literature is already developed on how to design information systems that take into account the most recent technologies, such as distributed computer systems, data bases, user-oriented languages, etc. However, we can easily notice a gap between the availability of the technology and the capability of the specialists to master it through systematic design methods.

It is not in the scope of this paper to discuss the specific analysis and design techniques that have been proposed or are presently investigated for emerging hardware and software technologies. We would like here to describe,as an example, the difference in design strategies between a data-base approach and a more conventional processing-oriented approach. In the logical data base design activities we may distinguish five general steps (Yao et al. (1978)):

- requirements analysis,

- modelling of users' view,

- integration of views of different users into one logical schema,

- restructuring and optimization of the logical schema,

- mapping the logical schema into the specific data model that is utilized by the data base management system on which the system implementation is based.

While the first step involves similar techniques both for conventional IS design and data base design, the subsequent steps are dependent on the specific software environment. Without going into further details it appears that when designing a data base, the data and their definition and relationships enter into the design at a much earlier stage than in the traditional approach.

Further problems are posed by the view integration phase when several view representations produced in view modeling have to be merged into one logical schema. The analysis problems regarded here include:

- what are the significant representations among the existing ones,

- how to find technical and organizational arrangements in order to build a unique model where different views are taken into account.

Such problems may become critical when the analyst has to deal with different interest groups (see next section).

People: The Users

The social interaction level between the user and the designer may influence the design approach. We have seen that the type of work-unit technology and its information system (as well as the dimensions of the project management in the next section) require different degrees and modes of user participation. Here we consider the opposite pole of the relationship between the user and specialist: it is the user and the social situation of design that actively put requests and constraints to which the analyst has to adapt tools and their application. We may categorize users according to their degree of activity or consciousness into three classes:

a) users with no or low degree of consciousness about what data processing means for them,

b) users who have (or are willing to get) a professional understanding of their roles and power bases with respect to the system,

c) users who have a widespread consciousness of the opportunities and constraints offered by automation, and are willing to influence the design of their work environment according to some socially shared criteria.

Two reasons seem to be most important in determining to what class a user belongs:

- the degree of confidence with the technology within the organization (and society) where the user operates. The introduction of new and sophisticated technologies requires a certain delay before learning phenomena can take place, self-consciousness is gained, and actions are taken to influence systems.

- the "status" of the user in the organization: when "efficient" systems are implemented, it is probable that middle managers will tend to behave according to class b). Workers and unions, once they have developed a consciousness of the social and work effects of dp technology, tend to behave according to class c).

In each of three cases the analyst needs specific tools and education:

- in the first situation, "edp imperialism" has been the common experience: it is the analyst who designs and creates the system and sells it to the "stupid user". In some SA methods the role of the user is completely neglected and the "computer logic" prevails upon the organization-oriented approach.

- in the second situation, users are considered functionally important to the successful design of an MIS. A number of user-oriented methods have been developed, where the role of the user is emphasized, he provides his knowledge to rightly specify his information needs and decision models, and he participates in project management. Also the analyst's education is improved and more concepts deriving from management sciences and organization theories are included in the training menu.

- as an example of the third situation, where social influence of the analyst's task environment is present, one can refer to the Scandinavian data agreements (see Nygaard (1978), Docherty (1978). Those state that it is important for computer-based systems to be evaluated not only from technical and economical, but also from a social perspective. Management must provide information concerning systems clearly and in a language easily understood by persons lacking special knowledge of the area concerned.

These and other requests pose a series of problems regarding methods and eduction. Methods have to be developed which can easily show social and organizational consequences of systems. Documentation aids should not be sophisticated and clumsy, but easily interpretable by various interest groups which may lack technical knowledge.

These requirements attack the traditional power bases of the expertise, and eliminate any possibility for "independent" and "neutral" behavior of the analyst. Education models have to be changed accordingly.

A number of issues (both technological and social) which are going to change the analyst's skills can be determined, e.g.:

- participation in system design teams where representatives from various interest groups are present; consequently, the necessity of communicating and negotiating systems properties with users;
- development of user-oriented computer languages;
- implementing more sophisticated operating systems for a larger and varied group of information processing and communication equipment (characteristics dependent upon technological development).

Project Management

The contingency view of SA method is supported and specified also when project management (i.e. the structure of the design activity) is considered. Nolan and McFarlan (1974) have monitored companies efforts at computerization and they have found out that each project of a new system has three major dimensions which influence its management and probability of success:

- the degree of inherent structure of the project, i.e., the degree to which inputs, outputs and programs can be defined by the users and the analysts,
- the confidence level with dp technology in the company,
- the size of the project.

For each combination of the three criteria, a qualitative risk measure of the project can be found, and a corresponding project-management strategy can be developed.

Thus, for example, in a large-sized project, with low inherent structure and highly sophisticated (new) technology involved, the risks of failure are high. One has to select strategies such as splitting the project into a number of independent subsystems, increasing user involvment through institutionalized mechanisms (committees, user's responsibility for the project, etc.), and finally increasing the competence and integration among the specialists staff to face the complexity and uncertainty brought in by the new technology.

EVALUATION OF EXISTING SA METHODS

In the previous section various facets of the analyst's task environment have been identified together with modifications of the analyst's "problem space" for different contingencies.

It is now possible to evaluate the flexibility of current methods on the four contingent factors:

- type of relationship between organization and its information systems,
- type of edp technology available (e.g. data base vs. conventional processing),
- role of the analyst (abstract and rational vs. strongly dependent upon the study of the actual organization) and role of the user (degree of consciousness),
- project-management strategies (how the method takes into account the "risk factor"?).

Each of these factors allows to define a number of situations. The extreme ones are shown in Table 1.

FACTOR	SITUATION'S SPECTRUM	
Organization and information system	known program-med ————	unknown, complex relationship
dp technology	new technology ————	conventional processing
role of analyst	"stand alone" ————	involved with users
and user	passive user ————	active user
project management	low risk ————	high risk

Table 1 - Types of Task Environments

In Table 2, eleven well-known SA methods developed in the last fifteen years by hardware suppliers, user companies and universities are listed and evaluated on the basis of their effectiveness in matching the multiple situations posed by each contingent factor describing the analyst's task environment. In other words, the table shows a qualitative evaluation of the flexibility of SA methods, flexibility being defined as the capability of each method to suggest to the analyst appropriate problem-solving tools in each specific situation along the four main axes of his task environment.

In the table the main assumption regarding the relationship between information system and organization for each method has been added and for reasons of clarity the user's role has been separated from the analyst's.

Each entry of Table 2 represents our qualitative judgment regarding the flexibility of the method in the whole range of situations depicted in Table 1; for example, "low" under "task" means that a specific method prescribes the investigation of "regular processes" only, while it fails if processes are uncertain and rich in variance; "low" under "analyst's role" means that the method gives instructions to the analyst to behave as a "stand alone" specialist, etc.

It can be noticed that very few methods show a high degree of flexibility to adapt to multiple social and technical contingencies (Lundberg et al. (1978)). In particular the Socio-Technical Systems (STS) (Hagwood et al. (1978), Bostrom and Heinen (1977)) methodologies seem to be well suited for understanding organization and information problems. ISAC (Lundberg et al. (1978)) seems to be a very sophisticated tool for connecting the organizational analysis to the logical design of information systems.PORGI (Kolf et al. (1978)) seems to be a well suited method for a contingent project management.

METHOD	INTERACTION BETWEEN IS AND OS	TASK (nature of OS and IS)	TECHNOLOGY	PEOPLE		PROJECT MANAGEMENT
				USER'S ROLE	ANALYST'S ROLE	
ARDI (Hartman et al. (1978))	existent(low)	low	low	low	medium	low
BISAD (Honeywell (1973))	non existent	low	low	low	medium	low
BSP (IBM (1975))	non existent	low	medium	medium	medium	low
HIPO (Stay (1976))	non existent	low	low	low	low	low
ISAC (Lundeberg et al. (1978))	existent	medium	high	high	medium	medium
ISDOS (Teichroew and Hershey (1977))	non existent	low	medium	low	low	low
ORGWARE (D.V. Orga (1976))	existent	low	medium	low	medium	medium
PORGI (Kolf et al. (1978))	existent	medium	low	medium	medium	high
SADT (Softech (1978))	existent(low)	low	medium	medium	medium	medium
SOP (IBM (1961))	existent(low)	low	low	low	low	low
STS (Hagwood et al. (1978))	existent	high	to be developed	medium	medium	low

Table 2 - Comparison of Some Existing SA Methods

CONCLUDING REMARKS

A review of system analysis methods has been conducted on the basis of the main tasks which face the system analyst. The need for multiple approaches to match multiple contingencies has been shown to be an answer stemming from critical perspectives on existing methods.

Most probably, there is no method able to match the whole range of specific contingencies which characterize a given project. We have proposed a framework and a qualitative classification as an intermediate tool able to guide the project team in choosing a method appropriate to the main idiosyncracies of the project situation. Consequently, the classification shows possible "mixes" of methods to be applied and eventualy points out the need of further research and development activities aimed at creating new methods to integrate and extend the existing ones. Finally, if the "social" dimensions of the analyst's task environment are considered,from the review and classification it appears that existing methods are not always adequate, the few exceptions being those methods which explicitly consider the problems of social change taking place with the implementation of data processing technology in the organization.

REFERENCES

/1/ Miller, J.C., Conceptual models for determining information requirements, Proc. AFIPS 1964 Spring Jt.Computer Conf. (1964), 609-620.

/2/ Bostrom, R.P. and Heinen, J.S., MIS problems and failures: A socio-technical perspective. Part I, The Causes, MIS Quarterly (sept. 1977) 17-32.

/3/ Bostrom, R.P. and Heinen, J.S., MIS problems and failures: A socio-technical perspective. Part II, MIS Quarterly (dec. 1977) 11-28.

/4/ Taggart, W.M. Jr. and Tharp, M.O., A survey of information requirements analysis techniques, ACM Computing Surveys, 9, n. 4 (dec. 1977) 273-290.

/5/ Couger, J.D., Evolution of business system analysis techniques, ACM Computer Surveys, 5 (sept. 1973) 167-198.

/6/ Munro, M.C. and Davis, G.B., Determining management information needs: a comparison of methods, MIS Quarterly (june 1977) 55-68.

/7/ Davis, G.B., Management information systems: conceptual foundations, structure and development, (Mc Graw-Hill, 1974).

/8/ Teichroew, D., A survey of languages for stating requirements for computer-based information systems, AFIPS Proc. Fall 1972, 1203-1224.

/9/ Newell, A. and Simon, H.A., Human problem solving, (Prentice Hall, 1972).

/10/ Polya, G., How to solve is, (Doubleday - Anchar, 1957).

/11/ Teichroew, D. and Hershey, E.A., PSL/PSA: A computer aided technique for structured documentation and analysis of information processing systems, IEEE Trans. on Software Engineering (Jan.1977).

/12/ Taggart, W.M. and Tharp, M.O., Dimensions of information requirements analysis, Data Base, 7 (1975) 5-13.

/13/ IBM, Business Systems Planning, Report, New York (1975), GE-20-05027-1.

/14/ Ackoff, R.O., Management MIS information systems, Management
     Science, 14, n. 4 (dec. 1967).

/15/ Argyris, C., Organizational learning and management information
     systems, Accounting, Management and Society, n. 3 (dec. 1977).

/16/ Langefors, B., Analysis of user needs, in:Bracchi, G. and Locke-
     mann, P.C. (Eds.), Information Systems Methodology (Springer
     Verlag, Berlin, 1978).

/17/ Leavitt, H.J., Applied organization change in industry: structu-
     ral, technical and human approaches, in:Cooper, W.W. et al (Eds.),
     New Perspectives in Organization Research (New York, 1964).

/18/ Earl, M., Prototype systems for management information and con-
     trol, Accounting, Management and Society (1978).

/19/ Gorry, G.A. and Scott Morton, M.S., A framework for management
     information systems, Sloan Management Review, 13, n. 1, (1971)
     55-70.

/20/ Simon, H.A., The new science of management decision, (Harper and
     Row, New York, 1960).

/21/ Anthony, R.N., Planning and Control Systems, Boston, Harvard
     University Graduate School of Business Administration (1965).

/22/ MacIntosh, N.B. and Daft, R.L., User department technology and
     information design, Information & Management (1978) 123-131.

/23/ Nygaard, K., Trade union participation, in:Sandberg A. (Ed.),
     Trade Unions, Planning and Computers (Stockolm, sept. 1978).

/24/ Yao, S.B., Navathe, S.B. and Weldon, J.L., An integrated approach
     to logical database design, Proc. NYU Database Symposium (New
     York, may 1978).

/25/ Docherty, P., Some consequences of acts and joint agreements in
     Norway and Sweden affecting user participation, Proc. Computer
     Impact Conf. (Copenhagen, oct. 1978).

/26/ Nolan, R.L. and Mac Farlan, Effective edp project management,
     in: Nolan, R. (Ed.), Managing the Data Resource Function,(West
     Publishing, 1974).

/27/ Hartman, W., Matthes, H. and Proeme, A., Management information
     systems handbook (MacGraw-Hill, New York, 1968).

/28/ Honeywell Information Systems, Bisad Manual (1973).

/29/ Stay, J.F., HIPO and integrated program design, IBM Systems
     Journal, 15, n. 2 (1976) 145-154.

/30/ Lundeberg,M., Goldkuhl, G. and Nilsson, A., A systematic approach
     to information systems development, General Report, University
     of Stockolm (1978).

/31/ D.V. Orga, Orgware Handbook (1976).

/32/ Kolf, F., Opelland, H.J., Seibt, D. and Szyperski, N., Tools for
     handling human and organizational problems of CBIS, in Bracchi, G.
     and Lockemann, P.C. (Eds.), op.cit. (1978).

/33/ Softech inc., An introduction to SADT, Report, Waltham, Mass.
     (1978).

/34/ IBM, SOP Manual, New York (1961).

/35/ Hagwood, J., Land, F. and Mumford, E., A participative approach
     to forward planning and system change, in:Bracchi, G. and Locke-
     mann, P.C. (Eds.), op.cit. (1978).

The Information Systems Environment
Lucas, Land, Lincoln, Supper (Editors)
North-Holland Publishing Company
© *IFIP, 1980*

INTRODUCTION OF CHANGE IN ORGANIZATIONAL DATA SYSTEMS

J. P. CAMPAGNE, J. FAVREL, J. F. PETIT

INSA and GRECO Rhone-alpin d'Analyse de Systèmes
Département Informatique, Bât. 502
69621 - VILLEURBANNE CEDEX
FRANCE

A general framework for considering the problems arising out of change in data systems within an organization is needed. The present ways of developing these data systems fall into two categories depending on whether they aim at data production or at decision support. The article by Ginzberg and Alter (1978) is an important step for defining the ways to implement decision support systems within an organization and for defining a general framework for implementing all data systems within an organization. These authors rely on Kolb and Frohman's model for introducing organizational change. They refer to the importance of risk factors which make the change process more complex or which can lead to its failure, as well as to the bringing together of strategies which are liable to inhibit these risk factors or reduce their impacts.

The purpose of this paper is to put forward four proposals which we feel should guide the process of introduction of change in data systems within organizations and which should allow us to develop a methodology for implementing such changes. Four proposals are presented :

- we must consider all changes in a data system within an organization as organizational change,

- we must consider the motivation for change and make sure of its stability,

- we must carry out a clinical analysis in order to define the change and to decide which strategies are best adapted to the implementation of this change,

- we must always consider such a change in a contingent manner.

BASIS FOR CONSIDERING CHANGE IN DATA SYSTEMS WITHIN AN ORGANIZATION

An overall framework for change should include :

- how an organization grows up and works,

- the part played by data systems within the organization and how they develop,

- the motivations for change in these data systems.

The organization

The organization should be considered from two points of view :

- from the formal point of view as a structure which coordinates the activities and operations,

- from the informal point of view consisting of actors with bounded rationality concerned in power games.

The formal structure of the organization.

According to Lorsch and Lawrence (1969), the structuring of the organization is first defined by the needs for differentiation linked to the environment. Needs for integration appear according to the degree of differentiation reached ; integration and differentiation reinforce each other. The needs for integration grow as differentiation grows and every time there is an organizational change, it is necessary to maintain the balance between the level of differentiation reached and the level of integration required.

In order to describe the structuring of an organization and its dynamics, J. Melese (1979) distinguishes transverse systems in the Organization-Environment system. Transverse systems, such as the economic system, the financial system or the legal system, have their own logic and condition and control specific flows into the company and its environment. The organization can then be seen as the place were this logic is superimposed upon different components. Structuring is the result of the search for a counterbalancing and for the resolving of conflicts which are inherent to the contradictory logic of these transverse systems. Dynamics are at intermediate levels of stabilization, and the corresponding units in the company function like variety generators. They receive and transmit meanings and projects. If there were no absorbing of uncertainty at these intermediate levels, the organization would become far too complex at a higher level.

If we consider the organization from the formal point of view, for each unit we must consider the contradictory logic depending on the various transverse systems in which the unit is concerned. This means looking for the way the actors make a synthesis of this contradictory logic at a given level of stabilization. This also means determining how various units are coordinated within the framework of each transverse system.

The informal structure of the organization.
The way an organization is structured and works is only partly determined by the specific character of its environment, the needs of coordination and the necessities of absorption of uncertainty at a local level. Power games around zones of uncertainty which actors master according to their position and/or their knowledge grow out of these specific characters. Crozier and Friedberg (1977) suggest that real systems of action built by actors belonging to the organization or to its environment develop around the tasks, around the decisional processes, or from the sharing by a set of individuals of the same job, the same language or more generally the same culture.

The functionning of an organization cannot be described in a purely rational manner with reference to the hypothetical objectives of the company. It must be described in a contingent way with reference to the bounded rationality of each actor or group of actors. This bounded rationality results from the cognitive limits of each actors which tally with his capacities and his way of considering his environment, as well as with his own objectives which are conditionned by the organization's power and control system and by his own criteria for judgment.

The functions of data systems and principles for development.
The fact that there are real systems of action means that there are communications systems between the actors who take part in them. These communications systems can be formal or informal or partially formal and partially informal. They are based on a language, on codes and syntax and presuppose semantics which are specific to these real systems of action.

Communication between these real systems of action is principally ensured by individuals because they belong to several real systems of action simultaneously. This communication is essential for the evolution, the stability and the survival of an organization.

However, because of the legal constraints placed upon the organization, because

of the need to ensure the perpetuity and the stability of operational processes
and because of the necessity for structuring and formalizing their knowledge of
these processes and of the Organization-Environment system, the actors develop
data systems. The function of data system is to acquire, treat and transmit data
within the Organization-Environment system. Data systems can be clerical replacement systems, or they can be systems for management support to guide or control
the activities of the actors, or they can be decision support systems.

The distinction between data and information (a datum or a set of data meaningful)
for an individual) just as the consideration of the roles of data systems within
organizations lead us to distinguish :

- The information system which each individual or group of actors builds for
himself taking his specific informational system into account. J. Melese (1978)
defines the informational system of a unit in a given organization as being all
the information transmitted and received by the unit.

- Informal data systems which exist within real groups of action or between real
groups of action.

- Data systems built for documentation or for data processing which have no part
to play in the communication between actors or groups or in decision processes.

- Formal communications systems which exist within real groups of actions or between real groups of action.

- Data systems built to support one or more actors in a particular decision
process.

These data systems are artefacts of the organization at any given moment. They
correspond to a structure and to organizational models which are imposed by actors or by groups of actors as a result of the power they wield.

Data systems correspond to a continuously changing balance between a degree of
differentiations, a degree of absorption of complexity at local level, and a degree
of integration. Peter G. W. Keen and Michaël S. Scott-Morton (1979) distinguish :

- Management Information Systems (M.I.S.) whose main impact has been on structured tasks where standard operating procedures, decision rules and information
flows can be reliably defined. They constitute what J. L. Le Moigne (1978) calls
the Organizational Information System (O.I.S.). The O.I.S. is task oriented and
ensures the production of legal, operational or administrative data, as well as
the production of signals for the purpose of automatic task control. It equally
ensures all the elaboration of knowledge founded on mechanistic models of the
organization. The computer based information systems within the O.I.S. ensures
clerical replacement systems and data production for managerial decision making.

- The Decision Support System (D.S.S.) whose main impact is on decision in which
there is sufficient structure for computer and analytic aids to be of value but
where manager judgment is essential. They are oriented toward individuals and decision processes.

The distinction above is important because of the wide consensus on the methodologies to be used for the introduction of change in each of these types of information system. J. L. Le Moigne continues "the process of formalizing operational
system models by organizational information is controlled by a now well explici-
ted formalism : The ANSI-SPARC paradigm. It enables the notion of the conceptual
formalism of "reality perception" on which the following models are defined to
be brought out : "external" models of data which are activited by various processes within the O.I.S. and "logical" and "internal" models strictly formalized
and "addressed" data which the memorization system generates". This means that
today we have some methods which allow us to describe an organizational Information Subsystem, to integrate independently developed external models into a common conceptual model, and which allow us to preserve the semantics of these external models.

Likewise as far as decision support systems are concerned, we now agree Ginzberg (1978) on the necessity for :

- user participation in implementation to incorporate user knowledge and to bolster user commitment to change,

- normative system modeling to underscore the necessity for change and to give some direction to it.

- evolutionary or iterative design to ensure learning processes at the actor level and correct definition of goals, and to assure proper adjustment of other organizational components.

What these methodologies of approach do not control, beyond technical and individual change, is the importance of organizational change. This distinction explains the differences in conclusions related to D.S.S. when we examine actual cases of implementation or when we carry out laboratory experiments. It also explains the failure of integrated information systems : the integration solves syntactical problems, but does not take the reality of the organization into account. Integration raises problems at semantic or pragmatic level. The political level and the artificial nature of these data systems has been considerably underestimated.

   Motivations for change in data systems.

The motivations for change in data system are multiple.
They result from the distinction existing between data and information, from the part played by data systems and their possibilities for carrying out tasks, in the running and the coordination of activity, in the running of decision processes, and from the power attached to the control of the zones of uncertainty and the imposition of organizational models.

We may either be dealing with :

- economic motivations, viz. the search for greater data system efficiency through clerical replacement systems. Basically these changes have technological origins and come from new capacities for acquisition, treatment, memorization and communication of data.

- organizational motivations, viz. the organization's search for greater efficiency by modifying its structures, its procedures, its rules for command and control. These changes can either be the result of the organization's need to adapt to the evolution of one or more of its environments or to new capacities for integration which allow it to increase differentiation and to reconsider the organization as a whole.

- political motivations, viz. the desire to modify the rules of the game by modifying the control of the zones of uncertainty or the organizational models and thus the criteria for evaluation and control.

- individual motivations, viz. the desire to develop decision support systems to guide an actor or a group of actors in the running of a decision process.

These motivations generally appear simultaneously. Consequently, the change introduced can either be inside data systems or at the interface between data systems and the information system which each individual builds, or concern the organization as a whole.

MANAGING UNCERTAINTY IN M.I.S. IMPLEMENTATION

Ginzberg's study of the M.I.S. implementation process begins by recognizing that M.I.S. implementation is actually a special case of organizational change. He then adopts the Kolb-Frohman's model as a basic normative description of the change process.

This model consists of seven stages :

Scouting : Scouting involves matching the capabilities of the consultant with the needs of the client-organization. It leads to the selection of an appropriate organizational starting point for the project.

Entry : Entry involves ensuring legitimacy   for action : defining the problem situation, the nature of a solution, the criteria for evaluation and the allocations of responsabilities and resources. It leads to the development of a "contract" for conducting the project.

Diagnosis : diagnosis involves the definition of the problem and its solutions and assessing available resources.

Planning : planning involves defining specific operational objectives and examining alternative ways of reach these objectives. It leads to the developement of an action plan taking the impacts on all parts of the organization into account.

Action : action involves implementing the alternative chosen at the planning stage.

Evaluation : evaluation involves assessing the degree to which goals were met. Evaluation requires specifying "key indicators" to the entry stage which are used as surrogate measures here.

Termination : termination involves assuring that effective control over the new systems rests with those who must use and maintain it and that necessary new patterns of behavior have become effective.

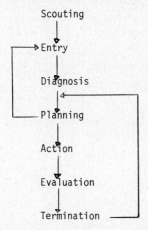

The major hypothesis in Ginzberg's study was that success in implementation is positively correlated with the quality of the implementation process. He verified this hypothesis upon a set from twenty nine computer-based systems.

Alter's study begins by observing that the likelihood of sucessful implementation is positively related to the degree of certainty with which the implementation can be planned. He then documents a series of implementation risk factors in studying fifty-six systems and juxtaposes risk factors against the stages of the Kolb-Frohman model. All eight of the risk factors identified arise for the first time at the early stages of the process.

Alter presents the following table :

Stage	Risk Factor
Scouting	Designer lacking prior experience with similar systems
Entry	Non existent or unwilling user
	Multiple users or designers
Diagnosis	Turnover among users, designers and maintainers
	Lack of support for system
Planning	Inability to specify purpose or usage patterns in advance
	Inability to predict and cushion impact on all parties
	Technical problems, cost effectiveness issues

Alter considers strategies adopted to eliminate or reduce the impact of these risk factors. He catalogues sixteen strategies such as the use of prototypes, the use of evolutionary approach or user participation or commitment. He links risk factors and strategies and observes, for example, that using an evolutionary approach compensates in advance for such risk factors as the designer's lack of prior experience, inability to specify purpose or usage pattern, an evolutionary approach also inhibits risk factors such as unpredictable impacts or technical and cost-effectiveness problems.

We do not think that the enumeration of these sixteen strategies and the links between risk factors and risk reducing strategies is important here. Alter does not try to draw an exhaustive list of the risk factors and of implementation strategies. Ginzberg (1978) has already pointed out the limits of such an approach ; considering 14 factors studies, he identifies 140 distinct factors reported as having a significant correlation with success, of which only 15 appear in 3 or more of the 14 studies .

Alter and Ginzberg's paper offers an important framework which :

- places M.I.S. implementation within the more general framework of the introduction of organizational change.

- emphasizes the importance of pre-design stages in the organizational change process.

- dwells on the importance of the "contract" developed by the user and designer at entry stage.

- places strategies within the context of an organizational change process. They are not methods which are liable to take in the change process as a whole, they are strategies adopted in answer to one or more particular risk factors which appear at a given step in the organizational change process.

- emphasizes the importance of assessing the risk factors present in any system development situation and the importance of trying to develop implementation strategies which will minimize the danger due to these risks. It is an attempt to prevent risk factors by the choice of inhibiting strategies.

Alter and Ginzberg's paper provides guidelines for our research into the way of introducing change in data systems within organizations. The method of introducing such a change is founded on the definition of this change and on the search for the risk factors linked to it.

This leads to the following four propositions :

PROPOSITIONS TO GUIDE IMPLEMENTATION

Proposition 1 : The introduction of any change in data sytems in an organization must be set within the more general framework of organizational change.

We suggest applying the method set out by Ginzberg and Alter for any introduction of change in a data system. We assume that there is no basic difference between the design of a D.S.S. and the introduction of change in an organizational information system (O.I.S.). Therefore, the methodology for implementing this change must be equal for both. Furthermore, because of the impact of a change in the O.I.S. on operational processes and on management methods, any change carried out at this level is more closely linked to organizational change than to certain changes brought about in D.S.S.

It is only the risk factors brought up by these two types of change which differentiate them and justify the use of different strategies. Many failures are caused by the fact that the change carried out has not been considered as a whole. Our first proposition implies that any change can only be defined, measured and introduced with reference to the organization.

We believe that, in order to define the change, the motivation for change is more important than the nature of the data system concerned. We agree with almost all of what Ginzberg (1978) has said about the differences in organizational impacts of change in D.S.S. and in the O.I.S. We equally agree on the need for the actors to be fully concerned with the development of D.S.S. However, we think that if the methodologies are to be different and that if the impacts upon the organization are different, this concern comes rather from the motivation for change than from the nature of the data system involved.

Proposition 2 : The motivation for change must be ranked by priority, and its stability must be ensured.

Change at data system level can either be more important than organizational change, or, on the other hand, can be overridden by it. The motivation for change can result from the desire to carry out a simple change inside data systems, or to help an individual or a set of individuals in a given decision process, or again to modify procedures, management rules or a control system. Because of the possible impacts on the organization of change in the data systems, these changes can only be carried out with reference to a motivation for change at the organization level. This observation confirms the importance of the contract established between the designer(s), the user(s), and the manager(s) during the project entry stage.

Moreover, we believe that it is very important to check the stability of the motivation for change at the end of each stage of the project. The origin of change in data systems is very often technical and comes from new possibilities of treatment and communication. However, the motivation may change. During the running of the project, a process of apprenticeship and a power game exist simultaneously and they are both liable to lead to project evolution. These two processes can change the motivations or superimpose on them the motivations of new actors who become concerned because of the project. We believe that the motivation for change is very important because it essentially justifies the continuation or termination of the project and the implementation strategies to be used.

Proposition 3 : We must carry out a clinical analysis in order to define the change and to decide which strategies are best adapted to the implementation of this change.

If during the predesign stages we are going to find possible risk-factors, and are going to make sure that the contract entered into by designers and users is really meaningful, we must consider the importance of change as a whole. If we are to choose between different strategies which have almost identical effects as far as risk-factors are concerned but which are not equivalent from the cost/ efficiency point of view, we must also consider the overall change.

In order to find these risk factors and to adopt strategies, we must make a clinical analysis of the organization to define the projected change. So that we may define this change, we have decided to consider motivation first and foremost. A change can also be defined with reference to data systems :

- technological change : a hardware change which affects neither individuals nor procedures.

- program change : a change which has been brought about by a modification in legislation, in operating rules or in management rules, but which does not affect the procedures, i. e. the distribution of tasks between men and machines.

- procedure change : the purposes of the data systems remain unchanged, but the methods of data acquisition, treatment, memorization and/or communication are modified, and above all the distribution of tasks between men and machines is modified.

- structure change : change in the data flows, the places and modes of treatment and/or memorization as a result of managerial integration or data systems centralization or, as a result of managerial differentiation or data systems distribution.

- model change : change in data structures or treatment models which is a result of new ways of considering the organization and new management or control rules.

Change occurs also with reference to the environment/organization system :

- definition of the environment :
. stable or shifting environments
. transverse systems in which the system exists.

- definition of the technology :
. well understood or not well understood conversion process
. low or high task variety
. flexibility or rigidness of technologies

- definition of the structure :
. the breakdown into sub-systems and the defining of their roles within the organization.
. the definition of the rules for coordinating the sub-systems.

- definition of the level of impact of the change brought into the organization : this is limited to one actor or to a set of actors, or to the modes of communication and the coordination rules among several actors.

- definition of the nature of the impact on the organization :
. change strictly limited to the data systems
. change in operating rules
. change in managerial rules or in the modes of coordination
. change in the managerial goals
. change in the structures.

INTRODUCTION OF CHANGE IN ORGANIZATIONAL DATA SYSTEMS   69

Change also can be thought of with reference to the individuals or sets individuals concerned by the change
     - change in their tasks.
     - change in their job or in the way they consider it.
     - change in power games, in the control of zones or uncertainty and the
       structuring in real groups of action.

Change can refer to its own dynamics :

     - actors who instigate the change : - the designer(s)
                                         - the user(s)
                                         - the manager(s)

     - projected mode of implementation :
       . system built for the user
       . system sold to the user
       . system forced upon the user

Motivation can justify continuing or abandoning the project. Motivation can also justify strategies like insisting upon mandatory use. The origin of the project underlines risk-factors such as the lack of motivation of users or managers.
Technological aspects guide our choice of the construction of prototypes or the
adoption of an evolutionary design approach. The impacts at individual levels
reveal the risks of rejection by potential users and the individuals'need to
take part, be comitted or to receive training programs.

We believe that a clinical analysis of change, is the only way to guide the implementation of a project efficiently, and to anticipate risk factors before
they can block the project.

Proposition 4 : We must always consider a change in a contingent manner.

We believe that this approach is the only possible one, for the reasons of economy and organization.

Galbraith (1973) has pointed out that investing in a vertical or horizontal information system is one of the means at a company's disposal for resolving problems of coordination. If one wants to introduce a change in the data system in
order to increase coordination possibilities one must first make sure this is
the satisfying solution.

Thompson (1967) has developed rules for structuring organization and for coordination between sub-systems according to the types or interdependency which exist
among sub-systems. The organization's data system can be structured in the same
way as the organization. This means that we must try to integrate data systems
which have reciprocal interdependence. We also should try to coordinate by plan
sequentially interdependent data systems and then try to create an interface
for the transmission of data between them. Finally, we should try to define the
routines or rules which enable data transfers between pooled interdependent
systems to be eliminated.

Lorsch and Lawrence (1969) have argued that the specific nature of the environment of an organization defines its needs for differentiation and integration. A
change in the data system is liable to modify the balance between the degree
of differentiation and the degree of integration and it must be analyzed in a
contingent manner at this level.

The organized social structure which makes up the organization is based on
communications systems which exist among the actors within real groups of action.
Since a change in the data system is liable to put these communications systems
in doubt, any change at this level must be analyzed with reference to the organized social structure.

If we make a contingent approach we assume that there is no perfect way of organizing. This refusal to accept "one best way" leads one to consider the specific nature of an organization, its needs for differentiation and integration linked to its environment, and the means to fulfill these needs. Once the motivations for change have been defined, we must look for the means of carrying out such a change. Intervention in the data system is one of the means to do so, or may indeed be one of the results of such a change.

CONCLUSION

Whatever the nature of the change in the data systems in an organization, this change must be considered as an organizational one. The basic motivation for this change must be considered first and foremost as well as its stability. In order to foresee risk-factors and to avoid those which are linked to the change by adopting appropriate strategies, we must make a clinical analysis of the change. We must also define change from the point of view of its impacts on the individuals and on the organization. Finally, since the change can only be defined within a given organizational context and with reference to its own dynamics, the manner of approaching this change will have to be contingent.

We have made these four propositions to refine Kolb and Frohman model for implementing organizational change, and in order to give guidelines for determining risk-factors and for adapting the strategies used to implement the change. These propositions originate from the way we consider the organization, the way the data systems act within the organization and the organization's motivations for change. They reinforce Ginzberg and Alter's conclusions for the need to adhere to the Kolb and Frohman model and for the need to anticipate risk factors linked to any change.

In future research, we must try to develop this definition of change in order to specify the risk factors associated with change and the strategies which are best adapted to implementation.

BIBLIOGRAPHY

(1) Alter, S., Development patterns for decision support systems, MIS quaterly,
     Sept. 78
     A taxonomy of decision support systems, Sloan management review, Fall 1977.

(2) Alter, S. and Ginzberg, M. J., Managing uncertainty in MIS implementation,
     Sloan management review, Fall 1978.

(3) Couger, J.D., D.S.S., the new thurst in the MIS course, Computing newsletter
     oct. 1978
     Ad hoc versus institution D.S.S., Computing newsletter nov. 1978
     Evolving from MIS to D.S.S., Computing newsletter dec. 1978.

(4) Courbon, J. C., Grajew, J., Tolovi, J., Conception et mise en oeuvre des
     systèmes interactifs d'aide à la décision : l'approche évolutive,
     Informatique et gestion n° 103 février 1979.

(5) Crozier, M., and Friedberg, E., L'acteur et le système (Ed. du Seuil) 1977.

(6) Daft, R. L., and Macintosh, M. B., A new approach to design and use of
     management information, California management review, Fall 1978.

(7) Dickson, Seen, Chervany, Research on management information systems : the
     Minnesota experiments, Management science, vol. 23 n° 9, May 1977.

(8) Galbraight, J., Designing complex organizations, (Addison Weshley Publishing
     company) 1973.

(9) Ginzberg, M. J., Redesign of managerial tasks : a requisite for successfull
     decision support systems, MIS quaterly, March 1978.

(10) Ginzberg, M. J., A process approach to management science implementation
     PHD dissertation, MIT 1975.

(11) Hedberg, B., On man computer interaction in organizational decision,
     Making business administration studies in Gothenberg 1970.

(12) Keen, Peter G. W., and Scott-Morton, M., Decision support systems : an
     organizational perspective, (Addison Whesley Publishing company) 1979.

(13) Keen, Peter G. W., Interactive computer systems for managing : a modest
     proposal, Sloan management review, Fall 1976.

(14) Kolb, D. A., and Frohman, A. L., An organization development approach to
     consulting, Sloan management review, Fall 1970.

(15) Lawrence, P. R., and Lorsch, F. W., Developping organizations : diagnosis
     and actions, (Addison Whesley Publishing company) 1969.

(16) Likert, R., and Likert, J. G., New ways of managing conflict, Mc Graw hill,
     1976.

(17) Le Moigne, J. L., La théorie du système d'information organisationnel,
     Informatique et gestion, novembre 1978 à mars 1979.

(18) Le Moigne, J. L., The four flows model as a tool for designing the informa-
     tion system of an organization, Information systems and organizational struc-
     ture, Berlin 1976.

(19) Lorsch, J. W. and Allen, S. A., Managing diversity and interdependence, 1977.

(20) Lucas, H. C., The evolution of an information system : from Key-man to every person, Sloan management review, Winter 1978.

(21) Melese, J., Faut-il répudier le concept de système d'information, Les systèmes d'information des organisations, Aix en Provence, July 1978.

(22) Melese, J., Le système des représentations de l'organisation, Congrès AFCET 1977.

(23) Melese, J., Approche systémique des organisations, (Ed. Hommes et Techniques) 1979.

(24) Mumford, E., Hawgood, J., Land, F., Training the systems analyst of the 1980's four new design tools to assist the design process, Congrès IFIP 1979.

(25) Thompson, J. D., Organizations in action, Mac Graw Hill 1967.

(26) Campagne, J. P., Favrel, J., Petit, J. F., Méthodologie de conception et de mise en oeuvre de systèmes d'information dans les organisations : définition d'un axe de recherche, Colloque bilan A.T.P. "Informatique d'organisation", IRIA-CNRS Rennes, 25-27 avril 1978.

The Information Systems Environment
Lucas, Land, Lincoln, Supper (Editors)
North-Holland Publishing Company
© *IFIP, 1980*

THE MANAGEMENT INFORMATION SYSTEM :
AN INFORMATION PROCESSING VIEW OF ITS ENVIRONMENTS

Ph. DUMAS

University of Toulon
FRANCE

The organization in which an MIS is embedded, and the human
users of the system are defined as the main components of
the MIS environment. The organization and the individuals
are studied as information processors that have information
requirements and inherent information processing capabilities.
This approach results in de-emphasizing the importance of
the computer-based system for organizational information
processing, in improving reciprocal adaptation of the MIS and
its environments, and in reducing the gap of expertise
between users and information processing technicians.

INTRODUCTION

Information Systems (I.S.) theories more often than not consider the
environment of an information system as the outside of a "black box"
which is in charge of processing information (e.g. Forrester (1961),
pp14 ff). In this view, the environment is supposed to provide the
system with input data, to receive output data, and to place
requirements on these outputs. In some sort the environment is the
purveyor and the client of the I.S.. One implicit result of this
prevailing view is that the MIS of an organization tends to be taken
as the information processing system of the organization. This
conception eventually leads to ascribe the information systems
specialists a dominant role as unique specialists of information
processing. Relationship between "users" and "specialists" are based
on seemingly antagonistic interests like those of a vendor and a
customer.

We hypothesize that some fundamental problems of participative
approaches, like conflict resolution, are rooted in this conceptual
dichotomy between those who "utilize information" --say users or
managers-- and those who know how to process information --say
systems designers or analysts. We advocate in this paper the idea
that information is processed everywhere in the organization,
including and above all in the human mind. The formal I.S. or MIS is
only part of a larger information network. Enough evidence is
available, to support a theory of I.S. where the IS environment is
viewed as an information processor (or a collection of processors).

Several consequences can be expected from the information processing
approach to IS environment. First, it may be the basis for new and
saner relationship between users and information processing
technicians. The latter should relinquish the monopoly they have set
up with their expertise in information processing. Their
organizational role should shift from that of an expert to that of a
counselor. Conversely the manager should be recognized as qualified

as the system analyst to deal with communication channels. Second,
the information processing approach introduces a consistent viewpoint
throughout the organization : organization subsystems are
interconnected information processing systems. Thus, the engineering
concept of "coupling" is applicable to analyse connecting interfaces.
Third this approach places in perspective investment in computer-
based system as one possible manner to improve the information
processing capability of an organization. Other non-computer
resources can also be creatively utilized for that improvement.

MIS Environment or MIS Environments

Given the way environment has been defined in the literature on
"Systems Theory" (e.g. Ackoff (1971) p662), we should talk of a
system's environment in general. Yet the question of the environment
--like those of goals and boundary-- for complex, socio-technical
systems is not that simple. Because these systems are open and
recognized manifold, multipurpose, and evolving, their environment
is complex. Thus for an MIS we might consider the legal environment
including e.g. privacy laws, the scientific e.g. information science
advances, the professional e.g. career of EDP specialists, the
commercial e.g. the competition in computer industry, the sociological
e.g. general or trade-unions attitude towards automation, and so on.

Hence it is more accurate to speak of MIS environments. Yet it is the
discretionary choice of the inquirer (Churchman, (1971)) to select
the perspective in which significant environments are going to be
selected out of the infinity of possible ones. In the perspective of
organization theory (Dumas (1978)) we categorize MIS's into external
and internal environments. The external environment is that stemming
from a "macro-view" of an MIS embedded in an organization and in an
organization's own environment. The internal environment is that
which appears through a "micro-view" of an MIS interaction with an
individual, in that fuzzy area where data/information is transformed
into decision and action.

Scope of the Paper

The perspective in which significant external and internal
environments are selected is defined with respect to that essential
property of an MIS, the property to process information for managers
in an organization. In this manner the organization as an information
processing system, and the individual as another information
processing system with their respective information needs and
capabilities help describe the MIS.

It should be recalled that an MIS is an open system, so its boundaries
are essentially fuzzy. No attempt is made here to explicitely define
a boundary between an MIS and its organization, or the MIS and the
individual. Rather the properties at the limits are explored as
correspondences between inner and outer properties, all in
relationship with information transfers.

This paper is divided into two parts. The first one explores the
information requirements of the external environment,and emphasizes
that several strategies are possible to fulfill these requirements.
Following Galbraith (1973) MIS design and evaluation are placed in
the perspective of competing investments in the creation of slack
resources or other Organization Development strategies.

The second part of the paper explores the information requirements of

a manager in a problem solving situation. The basic principle of
human behavior based on a "representation", or "image" of the world
--a Weltanschauung-- is examined on operational grounds for the MIS
designer. The importance of the psychological or cognitive styles
of the manager is emphasized for accounting for the phenomenon of
information generation at the "coupling" of MIS with man.

THE EXTERNAL ENVIRONMENT : THE ORGANIZATION

It may seem contradictory at first to talk of an information
processing capacity of an organization, and to define an MIS as the
specialized part of the organization in charge of processing
information. So much so that MIS specialists often consider themselves
as "the" information specialists. The aim of this section is to
recall how an MIS must be charged with only a part of the task
of organization information processing and communications.
The requirements for information processing in the organization
depend on two factors : the uncertainty of the organization's
environment and the complexity of the task to be performed by the
organization. More information has to circulate within the production
department for coordination if the technology is comlex such as for
building an aircraft, than if the technology is mundane such as in
a shoe factory.

The tree factors (a) the information processing capacity of a social
structure, (b) the uncertainty of the organization's environment, and
(c) the complexity of the organizational task determine the
performance of the organization from an information processing
standpoint.

(a) Information Processing Capacity of a Social Structure

Coordination is identified by Thompson (1967) as the issue of making
a given organizational structure work. Coordination is an information-
processing related concept (Emery (1969)). Three types of coordination
standardization, plans, and mutual adjustments "place increasingly
heavy burdens on communication and decision" (ibid., p56) i.e. they
involve higher and higher volume of communications and information
handling.

Not only volume but other parameters of information processing are
affected by the structure of organizational interdependencies.
Leavitt's (1951) experiments have highlighted our knowledge of the
effects of communication patterns on group performance.

Several methods have been proposed to multiply lateral relations in
hierarchical organizations. Some of them are : committee meetings and
direct contacts between employees, liaison roles attributed to
individuals in a precise setting, task forces to resolve possible
conflicts in the accomplishment of a task, and finally matrix-type
organizations. Whether these methods are successful is not our
concern here. The point is simply that placing two persons in the same
office room or in two distinct ones is as much a problem of
information system design as planning a computer network.

(b) Uncertainty of the Environment

As noted by Simon (1957) : (1) decisions are based on incomplete
environmental information or (2) environment is uncertain are dual
aspects of our "bounded rationality". A definition of uncertainty can
be inferred from the preceding remark : it is the difference between

the information necessary to carry out a task and the information
possessed by the organization.

Two consequences stem from the importance of the concept of
uncertainty for MIS. First, uncertainty is not a trivial concept that
can be conveniently handled by the refinement of techniques, for
instance the use of O.R. techniques which have recently deceived so
many of our decision-makers. Second, and at least conceptually, the
amount of information needed in processing a task is related to the
degree of uncertainty of the environment.

(c) Complexity of Technology

Technology has long been proposed as a major factor influencing
social structure. Marx, and Mead, for example, have contributed to
the recognition of technology in anthropology and in sociology.
Consideration of technology in management theory dates back to Emery
and Trist (1960).

The complexity of the technology utilized by the organization depends,
after Thompson (1967), on the type of conversion processed by the
organization, and after Perrow (1967) on the number of exceptions
handled and on the nature of the search process. The nature of the
search is characterized by the absence or presence of analyzable
problems which determines to what extent search can be conducted in
a logical analytical manner.

It follows from these considerations that the more complex the
technology, the more information processing is needed everything else
being equal.

(d) The information System as a Function of Organization Structure, Uncertainty, and Complexity

For Galbraith (1973) the amount of information needed to perform a
task is (1) "a function of the diversity of the output as measured
by the number of different products, services, or clients, (2) the
number of different input resources utilized as measured by the
number of technical specialities on a project, number of different
machine centers, etc., and (3) the level of goal difficulty or
performance as measured by some efficiency criterion such as
percentage of machine utilization".

For instance, suppose, at a certain period of time, an organization
performs effectively and efficiently ; this performance occurs
through basic information processing capabilities. These capabilities
include (1) the rules and programs that provide a means for handling
routine situations, (2) the hierarchy that in this framework handles
exceptions, and (3) the subdivision of tasks that partly isolate
units. If task uncertainty increases because of greater uncertainty
in the environment, and/or greater complexity of technology, and/or
more difficult goals, then the number of exceptions will increase and
the information handling capacity of the organization will be
overwhelmed. Two ways are conceivable to adjust the system to new
emerging situations : either to increase information processing
capacity or to reduce the volume of information to be handled.
Galbraith recognizes four strategies of adjustment outlined in
Figure 1.

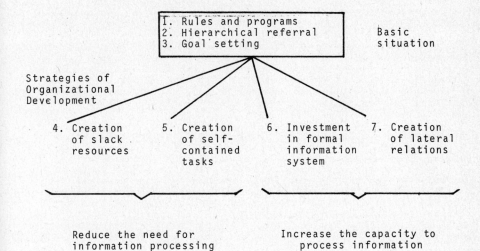

Figure 1   Organization Design Strategies (After Galbraith,1973)

Of utmost interest is the principle set by Galbraith (ibid. p19) :

> The organization must adopt at least one of the four strategies
> when faced with greater uncertainty. If it does not consciously
> choose one of the four, then the first, reduced performance
> standards, will happen automatically. The task, information
> requirements and the capacity of the organization to process
> information are always matched.

MIS in the Perspective of an Information Processing View of the Organization

The most salient contribution of the information processing view of
organization is that investment in information system is in
competition with oter strategies to improve organization effectiveness
and efficiency. The feasibility of a computer application has often
been evaluated on the basis of a cost reduction within the scope of
the application. The present approach emphasizes (1) the question
whether such a reduction really improves the efficiency of the whole
organization, and (2) the more deliberate and voluntary attitude
that other strategies like slack resources or lateral communications
deserve.

In a small industrial firm, a constant preoccupation of the controller
was to reduce inventories. Through successive improvements of
software, forecasting and modelling techniques, inventories were
reduced by 20 % in 1974, by another 10 % in 1976, and another 10 % in
1977. All decisions to implement the new systems were made on the
basis of profitable economic evaluations. The marginal costs of
systems improvement were compared with the marginal cost of capital
and storage facilities. In 1977 the firm incurred numerous problems
in job scheduling, and had costly delays in manufacturing. It was
then found that the inventory was buffering unforeseeable strikes in
the transportation system. In spite of the available technical

refinements, the size of inventories had to be set at the previous
level.

This serves as a warning against two kinds of practices. First, avoid
the tendancy to let the technician improve the technology of the
information system on the grounds that it has been successful at an
initial stage. Second, avoid the myth that marginal benefits from
eliminating slack resources, buffers or some sort of waste-generating
habits are always higher than the marginal costs for the whole
organizational system.

THE INTERNAL ENVIRONMENT : THE INDIVIDUAL DECISION MAKER

Passing from the macroscopic view of MIS in its organizational
environment to the microscopic focuses attention on the human being
who composes the environment. This view implies some understanding
of human behavior in a problem-solving situation. A model has been
proposed and developed in the past two decades called the human
information-decision processing model, or the cognitive approach to
human behavior. Newell and Simon (1972) synthesis of the research in
cognitive psychology will serve as a basis for discussion.

The Newell and Simon model of an Information Processing System (IPS)
and their findings indicate that the human IPS in particular :
(1) Processes symbols, which are symbolic in as much they have a
sensory referent or are a combination of other symbols.
(2) Utilizes a two-level internal memory, a long term and short term
memory . The long term memory has unlimited capacity but slow access
of the order of tens of seconds ; the short term memery has very
small capacity (five to seven symbols) and memorization in short
term memory needs rehearsal.:
(3) Features serial processing of symbols.
(4) Has elementary processing times of the order of fifty milli-
seconds.
(5) Implies the existence of a problem-space within the limits set by
the task-environment.

The task-environment is the problem as it exists in the real world.
The problem space is an abstraction of the real world conceived by
the IPS in order to work on it. The problem space is a representation
of the task-environment. It can be equated with the concepts of
"image", "plans", or "Weltanschauung" proposed by other authors.

Newell and Simon's model gives new insights into the concept of
individual bounded rationality, a concept which should be central in
a theory of information systems. Boundaries to fully rational
behavior are a combination of limitations due to low speed of access
to data, sequential processing, small size of short term memory, and
the reduction and simplification of the real world achieved by
problem spacing. Comparisons in size and speed between human and
electronic information processors are now quantitatively estimated :
the order of magnitude is one to tens, thousands or millions. A human
mind works on a problem space to reason with a simplified model of
reality. However, a rational solution for the simplified model may
not be rational in the real situation.

Consequences

When information system designers conceive a system that should be
used by the human IPS, they should remember the performance limits of
the human. These limits lead to the filtering of information so as

not to overwhelm processing capacity, provide feedback to ease
processing, adapt codes and system inputs to the limited span of
recall of the short term memory --"seven +or - two" according to
Miller-- and the like.

Besides Newell and Simon's experiments on human problem solving, or
Tversky and Kahneman's (1974) on the poor ability of the intuitive
human statistician, other research indicates how cognitive
capabilities vary from an individual to another. These researches
have generated the concepts of "cognitive styles" (McKenney and Keen
(1974)) or of "psychological profiles for information evaluation and
information perception" (Mason and Mitroff (1973)).

The important point is :

> What is information for one type will definitely not be
> information for another. Thus, as designers of MIS, our job is
> not to get (or force) all types to conform to one, but to give
> each type the kind of information he is psychologically attuned
> to and will use most effectively (Mason and Mitrof (1973) p478)

MIS is an Organizational Image-producer

While individual man is supposed to obtain information relevant to
his representations (problem space) directly through his senses, this
does not hold for the organization man. Organizations are specifically
devised to deal with problems that are beyond individual capacity.
Consequently information with regard to those problems circulates
through multiple channels and reaches an individual after multiple
steps and transformations. Among the transformations are the
measurement process and the substitution of "surrogates" for
"original information". How does the production control clerk know
the weight of a traction engine produced by his firm ? Not by direct
observation. Instead it is derived from a complex weighing machine
which he must trust or by personally adding the weights of the
components.

A decision made by an individual is a function of his own image of
the world, and this image is evoked in organization man through a
"system of information". Building individuals' images is a multistep
process in time and space. The information system contains a
"blueprint" of individuals' images : it is an image-producer.
Figuratively, MIS plays for organization man's eye a role similar to
an optical instrument. MIS extracts from the real world an image to
be provided to the manager who forms his own image on which problem
solving and decision are based. What is in practice the system
"blueprint" of the manager's image ? It is the data base including
the nature of data stored, the logical storage structure and the
models which are used to manipulate data. Following an empirical
approach, Alter (1977) has arrived at the conclusion that systems
presently used in management are data-oriented, or model-oriented.

By "extracting data from the real world", an MIS is not a passive
system, but instead an active one. Not all possible data can be
formally processed, stored, and transmitted by MIS, since the
variety of organizational environments tends to be infinite. MIS
selects data voluntarily or not; there is no neutral information
system.

If an MIS is not explicitly designed according to a representation
or a theory of the management system in which it is embedded, a

representation will exist implicitly anyway that may bias the image
produced by the system. Semantic validation of the system assures
that the representation actually stored in the system is a match to
the problem space of the decision maker.

MIS-MAN Coupling

A common way to view the relationship between MIS and decision maker
is to depict them as two systems whose boundaries are set at the
physical exchanges between "effectors" and "receptors" (i.e. the
output and input interfaces). Some improvement in the model is gained
by considering MIS and its long term memory as the external memory
for human decision maker.

Yet there is still a much more integrated scheme where relationships
are considered at each stage of the reasoning process (Pascot (1975)).
The engineering notion of <u>coupling</u> then applies to the process itself
and not only to the physical entities man-machine. MIS is viewed as
the amplifier of human reasoning (McKenney and Keen (1974)). Such a
conception implies the interactive sharing of image and processes in
addition to the fit between respective interfaces. This concept is
illustrated in the Figure 2.

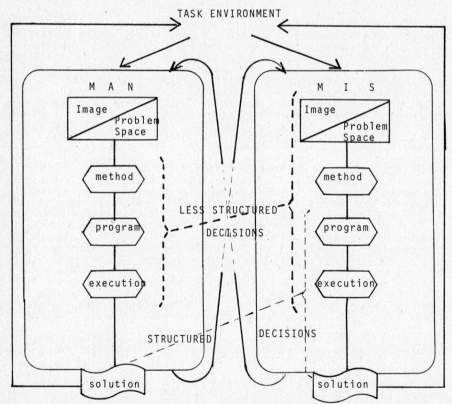

Figure 2   Some Types of Elaborate Coupling Between MAN and MIS
            (After Pascot, 1975, p 158)

This schematic is interpreted as follows. When management decisions are structured, the whole process from data gathering to the final solution can be carried out by the machine. The image, the program stored, and the method are imposed by the designer on the solution. When decisions are less structured and arrived at by a manager assisted by a computer-based system, the manager must be able to modify, to enrich the image stored, to adapt methods and programs, to improve both his and the machine's common output.

SYNTHESIS

The tendency to concentrate on the formal information system of an organization leads to an imbalanced relationship between technicians and managers or users. If one agrees to develop closer interaction between technicians and others, and to facilitate dialog, then conceptual grounds are needed that de-emphasize specialization and concern over the technology.

We have proposed here to recognize that any organizational structure not only imposes requirements on information processing system, but also possesses inherent capabilities for information processing. In that view, an MIS both competes and augments information processing capabilities of organizations. Therefore investment in MIS's should be placed in perspective with other possible investments in Organization Design, an issue that should definitively not be left to information systems designers.

On the other hand, there are differences in the way every individual converts data into information. Limits as well as advantages to the utilization of MIS's end-product are set by human information processing. Adequately coupling man to the MIS should be a major concern for future systems designers.

These conclusions can be interpreted as lessons of modesty for many systems analysts, and a call for less specialization, or at least/for consideration of "side effects" in information processing.

It is thought that the more balanced relationship between MIS users and designers implied in a general information processing view of MIS and its environments should ease the dialog and reinforce participative design.

REFERENCES

Ackoff, R.L., "Towards a System of Systems Concepts", MS, vol 17, (1971), n° 11, July, pp 661-671.

Alter, S, "A taxonomy of Decision Support Systems", SMR, vol 19, (1977), n° 1, Fall, pp 39-56.

Churchman, C.W., The Design of Inquiring Systems , New-York, Basic Books, (1971).

Dumas, P.J., Management Information Systems : a Dialectic Theory and the Evaluation Issue, PhD Dissertation, The University of Texas at Austin, Sept. 1978.

Emery, J.C., Organizational Planning and Control Systems, N.Y., Mc Millan, (1969).

Forrester, J.W., Industrial Dynamics, Cambridge, The MIT Press, (1961).

Galbraith, J., Designing Complex Organizations, Reading, Addison-Wesley, (1973).

Leavitt, H.J., "A collective Problem-solving in Small Groups", Journal of Abnormal and Social Psychology, vol XLVI, in Alexis & Wilson (1967), pp 40-56.

Mc Kenney, J.L. & Keen, P.G.W., "How Managers' Minds work", HBR, May-June, (1974), pp 79-90.

Mason, R.O. & Mitroff, J.I., "A Program for Research on Management Information Systems", MS, vol 19, n° 5, Jan.(1973) pp 475-487.

Newell, A. & Simon, H.A., Human Problem Solving, Engl. Cl., Prentice-Hall, (1972).

Pascot, D., Systèmes Interactifs de Planification Budgétaire, Unpubl. Thesis, Université d'Aix-en-Provence, (1975).

Perrow, C.B., "A Framework for the Comparative Analysis of Organization", Amer. Sociological Review, vol 33, (1967), pp 194-208.

Simon, H.A., Administrative Behavior (2nd ed.), N.Y., The McMillanCy, (1957), and N.Y., The Free Press, (1965).

Thompson, J.D., Organization in Action, N.Y., Mc Graw Hill, (1967).

Tversky, A. & Kahneman, D., "Judgement under Uncertainty : Heuristics and Biases", Science, vol 185, n° 27, (1974), sept., pp 1124-1131.

The Information Systems Environment
Lucas, Land, Lincoln, Supper (Editors)
North-Holland Publishing Company
© *IFIP, 1980*

ON A CONTINGENCY FRAMEWORK OF
COMPUTERIZED INFORMATION SYSTEMS

Agneta Olerup

Lund University and Örebro College
Sweden

In this paper a conceptual model of the environment of computerized information systems is developed. The purpose of
the model is to describe computerized information systems
in relation to contextual factors of the organization. It is
proposed that the characteristics of a computerized information system can be classified first in terms of data base,
reports or processing, and second in terms av time orientation or complexity.

INTRODUCTION

The relation between information systems and information technology and organizational structure and context is important. This topic can be broken down into a
number of segments. One important subset is the relation between organizational
structure and information technology, particularly computers. Empirical studies
suggest strong relationships between the use of computers and certain structural
features, e.g. increasing degrees of centralization, specialization and standardization (Elizur 1970, Mumford & Banks 1968, Stewart 1971, Whisler 1970)

Another important subset deals with the relation between the context of an organization and its information system. The evidence here is scarce, but nevertheless
consistently points to a relationship between the characteristics of information
and information systems and contextual factors (Gordon & Miller 1976, Macintosh &
Daft 1978, Whisler 1975).

The main purpose of this paper is to discuss ways of describing computerized information systems suitable to organizational contexts. A general model of information systems will not be pursued. The requirements for detailed specification of
data and information to be collected, stored, processed and distributed mean that
computerized information systems are generally formalized.

SOME MODELS OF INFORMATION SYSTEMS

A survey of relevant literature revealed a number of models of information systems,
particularly computerized ones. They are listed, and grouped, in Figure 1. Only
some brief comments on the models are offered.

Policy variables proposed in the models include timing which refers to the frequency of decisions, and scope which refers to the ability of an information system
to give access to information not only on local events, but also on more remote
ones (Carroll 1967, Galbraith 1973). Other suggested policy variables are frequency
of reporting which is a subdimension of timing, and degree of centralization
(Gordon & Miller 1976). The degree of centralization refers to the number of information systems with similar functions.

MODELS Author(s)	MAIN CONCEPTS
Policy variables	
Carroll 1967 Galbraith 1973	timing scope pf the data base degree of formalization capacity of decision mechanisms
Gordon & Miller 1976	frequency of reporting information load degree of centralization
Components	
Nahapiet & Banbury 1974	data processing system model interface
Losty 1971	data base information elements decision models
Coupling	
Losty 1971	active passive
Damodaran et al 1974	dominant active passive
Interaction	
Eason et al 1975	medium mode user support
Interface	
Edström 1973	information support
Mason 1975	boundaries of the information system
Data processing	batch or direct processing interactive decentralized (distributed) systems

Figure 1.   Some Models of Computerized Information Systems

Mahapiet and Banbury (1974) and Losty (1971) identify three components of a computerized information system, though as used by Losty (1971) they are more re-
strictive. Further Losty (1971) and Damodaran et al (1974) suggest different types
of coupling between a user and a computerized information system. They are the
dominant coupling, where the user is requested to follow a specific set of procedures for handling data (e.g. data input); the active coupling, which produces
reports without any measures by the user; and the passive coupling, which produces
reports only on request. Closely related to coupling is interaction which can be
described according to medium, mode and user support (Eason ⌄ al 1975).

Edström (1973) suggests that different phases of the decision process need different forms of information support. Thus it is obvious that the point where the
information system terminates and the decision maker begins varies (Mason 1975).

The last group of models furnished by the data processing field refers to typical
situations appearing in pairs. The distinction between batch and direct processing
depends on the respons or turn-around-time and the frequency of reporting. Interactive and non-interactive systems are distinguished on the basis af the delays
in manipulating data. A third pair is decentralized or distributed systems and
centralized ones, which refer to the number of points (e.g. terminals) where
access can be made to the data base.

In summary the models vary from the general to the very specific. Each approach
concentrates in an aggregate manner on one particular aspect of an information
system. Some models refer to formalized computerized information systems. Others
refer to the organization as an information system.

There are several difficulties with these models of information systems because
they refer to different kinds of problems, hence they belong to different frames
of reference. This paper proposes a contingency approach to computerized information systems. The models reviewed are insufficient for the purpose of describing
computerized information systems in relation to contextual factors because they
are not related to a contextual framework.

THE CONTEXT OF INFORMATION SYSTEMS

When analyzing the characteristics of a computerized information system, we will
discover several characteristics related to the context of the organization. Accordingly if we want a computerized information system which will support the
organization in dealing with its environment, then a contingency approach appears
necessary.

First it is not hard to find examples of computerized information systems which
were not successful because of insufficient recognition of organizational context.
Second there is the case of the firm which spent several man-years in designing a
computerized production-planning system and successfully used the system until
inventories started increasing dramatically. A last case is the computerized information system which was never used, or not used by certain groups, in spite of
its being technically well designed.

Explanations for cases like those above have identified several factors, e.g. the
cognitive style of decision makers, the change strategy used. An additional hypothesis, receiving increasing interest suggests the importance of contextual
factors.

In the first case above the computerized information system may have been designed
for products whose markets suddenly disappeared. In the second case the situation
changed from one where demand exceeded capacity to one where capacity exceeded
demand. Instead of utilizing machinery efficiently the firm needed to minimize inventory. Both of these exemples deal with the influence of sudden environmental

	COMPLEXITY	TIME-ORIENTATION
DATA BASE	11 Globalness Centralization Completeness Integration Information reference	12 Frequency of collecting Storage period Collection delay
REPORTS	21 Variability Mode of presentation Value reference	22 Frequency of reporting Period reference Life-time of report-type Distribution delay
PROCESSING	31 Program origin Operations Segmentation	32 Processing delay Ordering delay

Figure 2. Characteristics of a Computerized Information System.

changes on the computerized information system.

This paper is, however, based on the assumption that relationships between contextual factors and computerized information systems can be found also in less drastic cases than those above. It is obvious that a framework for analyzing computerized information systems which considers the contextual factors of the organization is important.

A review of the literature on contingency theory reveals that there are basically two approaches to the isolation and definition of contextual factors, either a given collection (e.g. consisting of environment, technology and size) is used or a determination of the relevant factors is part of the analysis. The framework proposed in this paper is based on the first approach.

The framework is limited to two contextual factors of the organization which are assumed to influence its computerized information system: environment and technology. It is, however, beyond the scope of this paper to isolate variables, components and dimensions which refer to either environment or technology. The characteristics of computerized information systems will be discussed in the next section.

A PROPOSED MODEL OF COMPUTERIZED INFORMATION SYSTEMS

A computerized information system has several characteristics. These may be classified first in terms of data base, reports or processing, and second in terms of time orientation or complexity. Time orientation and complexity refer to dimensions of uncertainty, while data base, reports and processing refer to the functions of an information system.

Information has been defined as something which reduces uncertainty (Ackoff 1958, Galbraith 1973, Whisler 1975), hence information systems are means for coping with uncertainty. Information systems, therefore, assist in collecting, storing, processing and presenting information about an organization and its environment. Uncertainty and the functions of an information system are fundamental.

In order to perform the functions noted a computerized information system can be seen to have characteristics that refer to collecting, storing, processing as well as presenting data. The characteristics of a computerized information system are classified in terms of data base, reports och processing. Characteristics referring to a data base are related to collecting och storing data, while characteristics referring to reports are related to presenting data to a user. Finally characteristics referring to processing are related to the processing of data, i.e. rules for manipulating or processing data.

In the framework suggested in this paper environment and technology are sources of uncertainty. Two dimensions of environmental uncertainty have been identified: the simple-complex dimension and the static-dynamic dimension (Duncan 1972). Similarly two dimensions of technological uncertainty have been identified: the number of exceptions and the analyzability of search procedures (Perrow 1970). The number of exceptions obviously depends on complexity, while the analyzability of search procedures is a dynamic dimension. The dimensions of environment and technology are identical, hence two dimensions av uncertainty can be identified: the degree of complexity and the degree of dynamism.

In order to correspond with the dimensions of uncertainty a computerized information system can be seen to have characteristics that refer to the degree of dynamism and the degree of complexity. The characteristics of a computerized information system are classified according to either complexity or time-orientation. First it is hypothesized that characteristics referring to the time-orientation of a computerized information system will primarily be influenced by the degree of dynamism of uncertainty. Second it is hypothesized that characteristics referring to the complexity of a computerized information system will be related to the degree of complexity of uncertainty.

Using the classification-schemes, Figure 2 lists the characteristics of a computerized information system (the boxes in Figure 2 are denoted as matrix-components). The characteristics are classified in terms of complexity and time-orientation, and cross-classified in terms of data base, reports and processing. The basis for identifying the characteristics is their power for discriminating among computerized information systems. Next the characteristics will briefly be described, though definitions and operational measures of individual characteristics are not discussed.

In terms of the complexity of a data base (box 11) we need to explore different aspects of the scope or extension of a data base, with regard to functional or product orientation as well as internal or external orientation. The relevant characteristics are globalness, centralization, completeness, integration and information reference.

In terms of the time-orientation of a data base (box 12) the focus is on the age of information. The relevant characteristics are frequency of collection, collection delay and storage period.

In terms of the complexity of reports (box 21) we regard the combination and presentation of information. Information may be combined in fixed ways or in variable ways, by the use of e.g. report generators; it may be presented in tabular, graphical or other forms; it may be used for comparisons between e.g. actual and expected results. The relevant characteristics are variability, mode of presentation and value reference.

In terms of the time-orientation of reports (box 22) the focus is on time-intervals and the currency of information. Reports may cover periods of variable duration as well as have different life-times. The relevant characteristics are frequency of reporting, period reference, life-time of a report-type, and distribution delay. Frequency of reporting is closely related to frequency of collection.

In terms of the complexity of processing (box 31) the rules and operations for manipulating information come into focus. Manipulating data will mostly require a combination of operations. The relevant characteristics are program origin, operations and segmentation.

Finally, in terms of the time-orientation of processing (box 32) the focus is on timpe-aspects of processing, e.g. turn-around-times and waiting-times. The relevant characteristics are processing and ordering delay. Both these characteristics are closely related to collection delay (box 12) and distribution delay (box 22). Together the four delays account for different portions of the time-interval between event occurence and the presentation of data about the event to a user. Delays influence the currency and availability of information.

SOME PRELIMINARY FINDINGS

The framework proposed in this paper has been used in an exploratory study of computerized information systems in a number of manufacturing organizations of the same size. Their computerized information systems have been described using the characteristics listed in Figure 2. These characteristics have then been related to contextual factors, primarily environment and technology.

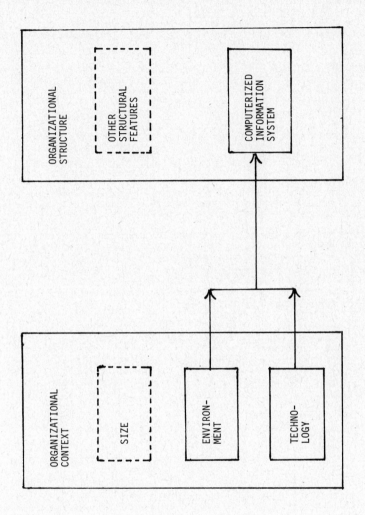

Figure 3.   Main factors Influencing the Characteristics of a
Computerized Information System.

It has been suggested in this paper that a computerized information system is influenced by the context of an organization. A proposed framework is depicted in Figure 3 with particular emphasis on factors considered. (These are indicated by solid boxes and lines. Factors and relationships, which are either not indicated or indicated by dashed lines, have been ignored. However, this does not mean that they are unimportant, only that they are outside the scope of this paper.)

It has been stated previously that only technology and environment are considered in organizational context. Size is thus ignored, or more precisely restricted. There are two reasons for this limitation. First it has been found that the relation between size and structure in organizations changes at a level of ca 1000 employees (Child 1977). Thus organiztions can be dichotomized into two groups, consisting of smaller and larger firms. Second it has been found that use of computers is more common among larger than among smaller firms (ADB och arbetskraften 1973, 1975). Hence by choosing organizations of approximately the same size it is possible to control for the influence of size on computerized information systems.

Groups of organizations having similar environments and tecknologies can be formed and the characteristics of the computerized information systems described for each group. Then it seems justifiable to assume that differences in the characteristics of computerized information systems depend on the influence of environment or technology.

It is beyond the scope of this paper to discuss every characteristic listed in Figure 2, only tentative results concerning frequency of collection and frequency of reporting will briefly be presented.

In the organizations studied the frequency of collecting was continuous or daily in organizations having complex technology and working in a complex and unstable environment. Information was collected more rarely (with lower frequencies) when the environment was relatively more dynamic (daily or weekly collection) or when technology was relatively less complex (daily or weekly collection).

Frequencies of reporting show a similar pattern. There is, however, in addition a greater range of frequencies of reporting, particularly in organizations having a relatively complex technology and working in an environment that is relatively complex and unstable.

Thus organizations need to collect and report information frequently when the environment is complex and unstable, and similarly when the technology is complex.

CONCLUSIONS

This paper has considered the relation between the context of an organization and its computerized information system. A framework for studying computerized information systems has been suggested. The framework attempts to relate characteristics of computerized information systems to the environmental and technological factors of the organization.

A review of a number of models of computerized information systems indicated that they were insufficient for this purpose. A model of computerized information systems has been proposed as part of the framework. This model consists of characteristics of a computerized information system which are classified in terms of complexity and time-orientation, and cross-classified in terms av data base, reports and processing.

The work reported here belongs to the initial phases of an exploratory study of computerized information systems in some manufacturing organizations. The computerized information systems in these organizations were examined with regard to environmental and technological factors. The results suggest that organizations need to process data more frequently in a dynamic or technologically complex environment.

REFERENCES

(1) Ackoff, Russel L., Towards a behavioral theory of communication, Management Science 4 (1958) 218-234

(2) ADB och arbetskraften - verkstadsindustrin (Information i Prognosfrågor/SCB, Stockholm 1973)

(3) ADB och arbetskraften - industrins ADB-förhållanden (Information i Prognosfrågor/SCB, Stockholm 1975)

(4) Carroll, Donald C., On the structure of operational control systems, in: Pierce, J.F. (ed), Operations research and the design of management information systems (New York 1967)

(5) Child, John, Organization - a guide to problems and practice (Harper & Row, London 1977)

(6) Damodaran, L., Stewart, T.F.M. and Eason, K.D., Socio-technical ramifications of forms of man-computer interaction, paper presented to the ALTORG-conference, Sweden (july 1974)

(7) Duncan, Robert B., Characteristics of organizational environments and perceived environmental uncertainty, Administrative Science Quarterly 17 (1972) 313-327

(8) Eason, K.D., Damodaran, L. and Stewart, T.F.M., Interface problems in man-computer interaction, in: Mumford, E and Sackman, H (eds), Human choice and computers (North-Holland, Amsterdam 1975)

(9) Edström, Anders, Conceptualization of the design problem for management information systems, Jrnl. of Management Studies 10 (1973) 118-132

(10) Elizur, Dov, Adapting to innovation (Jerusalem Academic Press, Jerusalem 1970)

(11) Galbraith, Jay, Designing complex organizations (Addison-Wesley, Reading 1973)

(12) Gordon, Lawrence, A. and Miller, Danny, A contingency framework for the design of accounting information systems, Accounting, Organizations and Society 1 (1976) 59-69

(13) Losty, P.A., The structure of MIS, in: Goldberg, W. et al. (eds), Management Information Systems. Selected papers from MIS Copenhagen 70 - an IAG-conference (Studentlitteratur, Lund 1971)

(14) Macintosh, Norman B. and Daft, Richard L., User department technology and information design, Information and management 1 (1978) 123-131

(15) Mason, Richard O. jr, Basic concepts for designing management information
     systems, in: Rappaport, A. (ed), Information for decision-making
     (Prentice-Hall, Englewood Cliffs 1975)

(16) Mumford, Enid and Banks, Olive, The computer and the clerk
     (Routledge & Kegan Paul, London 1968)

(17) Nahapiet, Janine and Banbury, John, Computer system characteristics and the
     design of organizations, paper presented to the ALTORG-conference, Sweden
     (July 1974)

(18) Perrow, Charles, Organizational Analysis (Tavistock, London 1971)

(19) Stewart, Rosemary, How computers affect management (Macmillan, London 1971)

(20) Whisler, Thomas. The impact of computers on organization (Praeger,
     New York 1970)

(21) Whisler, Thomas, Man, organization and computer - a contingency analysis,
     in: Grochla, E. and Szyperski, N. (eds), Information systems and organiza-
     tional structure (Gruyter. Berlin 1975)

PARTICIPATIVE DESIGN TECHNIQUES

The Information Systems Environment
Lucas, Land, Lincoln, Supper (Editors)
North-Holland Publishing Company
© *IFIP, 1980*

PROBLEMS OF CONSENSUS DESIGN IN COOPERATIVE
INFORMATION SYSTEM DESIGN PROJECTS

Friedrich Winkelhage
Jürgen Marock

Gesellschaft für Mathematik und Datenverarbeitung
St. Augustin
Germany

Consensus Design is being proposed by a number of
researchers as an effective type of user participation in the design of information systems. On
the other hand, a growing proportion of computer
based information systems will be developed in
joint projects by several cooperating organizations. Drawing on observations of different forms
of user participation in a number of cooperative
information system design projects, the paper
identifies potential problems of applying Consensus Design in such situations. Intensified research on cooperative Consensus Design is advocated to determine if the problems anticipated do in
fact arise, and to develop guidelines and tools
for the application of Consensus Design in cooperative systems design projects. Elements of a research program addressing these questions are outlined.

CONCEPTS OF PARTICIPATIVE SYSTEM DESIGN

User participation in the design of computer based information systems or, to use a more general term, participative system design
has been advocated as one particular aspect of the organizational
implementation of information systems. The term organizational implementation (Kolf et al. (1978)) denotes a complex strategy for the
design of information systems; it aims at providing an optimal integration of structure, tasks, people and technology, Leavitt´s (1965)
classical dimensions of organizations.

Initially, the research on organizational implementation focused
primarily on information systems for managerial planning and decision-making. For the success of these systems, a close fit between
the requirements of the tasks, the needs and capabilities of the
user and the computerized system was regarded as particularly important. With the advent of office automation and the increasing number
of interactive systems for routine administrative functions, there
is a growing awareness that these systems require a much better integration of structure, tasks, people and technology than was
achieved in the development of first generation, batchoriented information systems. Thus, organizational implementation will come to
play an important role in the design of new systems for the lower
echelons of organizations, too.

User participation still is a fuzzy and evolving concept. The term is used to describe a wide range of motivations for bringing the users into the development of information systems, and encompasses a variety of forms of user involvement. Mumford (1979) lists four principal arguments in favor of participative system design:

(1) it conforms with basic societal values and legislation concerning co-determination and industrial democracy,

(2) it helps to secure user acceptance of the system under development,

(3) it gives access to the users detailed knowledge about work content and procedures, which the professional systems designers do not have,

(4) it acts as a motivator for more effective and productive work with the new information system.

Participative system design can be implemented in a number of ways. Mumford distinguishes three typical levels in the scope and intensity of user involvement.

Consultative Design

The users provide information about problems and inefficiencies of the present system, determine major areas of improvement, and set the objectives for the new system, whereas most of the design decisions are still made by the professional system designers.

Representative Design

The design team is composed of users elected to represent all prospective users of the new system, and of professional system designers. Here the user representatives are responsible for the major design decisions, while the professional designers concentrate on the technical aspects of the system.

Consensus Design

Consensus design involves all prospective users in a process of discussion and decision-making about alternative concepts for the information system and the form of organization in which it will be embedded. These concepts are worked out by a design team of user representatives and professional system designers, who are also responsible for the implementation of the design after it has been approved by the users.

Looking at Consensus Design in particular, Mumford identifies a number of problems which were encountered in two projects in which this type of user participation had been implemented, and she mentions six major benefits of Consensus Design:

(1) the correspondence with broadly accepted values of industrial
    democracy and co-determination,

(2) the commitment of the users to the new form of organization and
    the embedded information system,

(3) the shared understanding of the objectices, functions and proce-
    dures of the organizational unit involved, and sufficiently de-
    tailed knowledge of the information system,

(4) increased job satisfaction of the users,

(5) improved efficiency of the new organization and the information
    system ,

(6) an optimal integration of the organizational variables techno-
    logy, tasks, human needs and organizational objectives.

It seems plausible to assume that in a large number of projects
these benefits could in fact be achieved through a well implemented
Consensus Design approach, and that this approach will produce better overall results than design strategies with a lesser degree of
user involvement or no user participation at all. Thus one might
feel inclined to recommend a broad application of the Consensus Design type of user participation as part of the effective organizational implementation of information systems. There are, however,
three negative arguments which could be leveled against a Consensus
Design approach:

(1) it is a time-consuming and costly process,

(2) due to a number of problems, a Consensus Design will require ex-
    tensive assistance by experienced consultants in most cases,

(3) in its present form, it appears to be applicable only to the de-
    sign of tailor-made systems with a clearly defined small group
    of users.

The third criticism points to a discrepancy between the domain where
a Consensus Design approach could be implemented, and the way in
which the majority of information systems will be designed in the
future. In view of the potential benefits of a Consensus Design approach it would be desirable to make it as widely applicable as possible. Some of the problems which may arise when Consensus Design is
applied to new forms of information system design projects will be
discussed in greater detail in this paper.

TRENDS IN THE ORGANIZATION OF INFORMATION SYSTEM DESIGN PROJECTS

The price/performance ratio of the hardware for information systems
is still decreasing at a dramatic rate. In spite of substantial research in all areas of software engineering, in the near future no
similar trend can reasonably be expected for software. The production and maintenance of application software will continue to require a highly qualified staff. Though small organizations now

could afford the hardware, the high cost of software could become an effective barrier against a widespread use of computers in small organizations.

One way to overcome this barrier is to distribute the development effort among several organizations, a practice followed for a number of years in the public sector in Germany. In the Bundesländer legislation was passed to set up elaborate schemes of cooperation among local authorities. With financial assistance of the Federal Government, several large scale development projects are under way for information systems which will eventually be used by agencies in all Bundesländer.

A similar tendency can be observed in the private sector. While the traditional standardized application software marketed by hardware vendors and software houses has not been widely accepted, there are now a number of examples of small companies cooperating in the development of application software that will fit the organizational requirements of these companies. For technological and economic reasons we will see many more of these cooperative system design efforts in the future.

In joint development projects with several cooperating organizations, information systems are designed for large, non-homogeneous groups of users and for diverse organizational settings and requirements. This poses a number of serious problems for a Consensus Design approach. Viable solutions to these problems must be worked out quickly if we want to implement cooperative Consensus Design in order to improve the quality of cooperative system development efforts and to avoid widespread disappointment with the results of these projects.

PROBLEM AREAS OF COOPERATIVE CONSENSUS DESIGN

In the last five years, the Federal Ministry of Research and Technology has funded a number of major cooperative information system design projects. In these projects, different forms of user participation have been implemented. While none of these could be regarded as a Consensus Design in the strict sense of the term, we can draw on the experience gained in these projects to identify some of the problems likely to be encountered in a cooperative Consensus Design. For the purpose of demonstration and analysis, these problems can be grouped under three different headings:
(1) qualification of users and user representatives,
(2) organization of cooperative Consensus Design projects,
(3) instruments for cooperative Consensus Design.

Qualification of Users and User Representatives

One severe limitation to a Consensus Design approach lies in the number and qualification of prospective users in the small organizations which join in cooperative development projects. Typically, a particular function for which a computerized information system is to be developed is performed by a very small group of staff. The staff does not have much experience in processes of planned organizational change and knows little about information technology. Due to the small number of prospective users, it is difficult for the organization to designate even one of them as a user representative on a joint design team. In most cases it is unfeasible to hire additional staff on a temporary basis, so it will be necessary to work out organizational solutions and to reduce the amount of time the users have to spend in the design process.

To improve the knowledge of the prospective users about information technology and about organizational change processes, some form of education and training will be necessary. Here, too, the small staff makes it difficult for prospective users to attend seminars and training courses. To achieve maximum efficiency in educational measures, guidelines and instruments should be developed to determine what kind of knowledge and experience a user or a user representative should have to effectively play his or her role in a Consensus Design. In addition, an educational program should be developed which is integrated in the design process and provides the necessary knowledge and experience without prolonged absense of the users from their organizations.

Some initial work on these problems will be done in two recently begun research projects, which will make the results of the project PORGI at BIFOA available for widespread application and will develop a series of seminars and tutorials on organizational implementation.

Organization of Cooperative Consensus Design Projects

The cooperation of small organizations in joint system design projects adds a new dimension of complexity to Consensus Design. The additional complexity may be attributed to the small size of the organizations, to the diversity of the size or the structure of the cooperating organizations, to their regional distribution or even to the fact that organizations performing different functions within a complex interrelated service system are cooperating in the joint system development.

The additional complexity of cooperative Consensus Design makes it necessary to examine whether currently available recommendations for the organization of Consensus Design processes still lead to effective user participation.

Motivation to Participate

One important aspect which should be studied is if and how groups of prospective users should be induced to participate in a Consensus Design process. It cannot reasonably be assumed that in all organizations which join in a cooperative system design project, management and prospective users will spontaneously agree to implement a Consensus Design process. Presently we do not know whether, in cooperative system design projects, Consensus Design in some organizations could co-exist with more traditional approaches in other organizations, which leave the design decisions to professional system designers. Should such a co-existence prove to be difficult or impossible, would it then be advisable to motivate users to agree to a Consensus Design, and how could this be achieved? Today, very little empirical evidence is available to answer these questions.

Allocation of Functions

A second aspect which should be examined is the distribution of functions and responsibilities among prospective users, user representatives, and professional system designers. In a cooperative Consensus Design, user representatives who come from different small organizations are even more at a disadvantage against professional system designers than are users who come from one department within a larger organization. Due to the small size of their organizations prospective users might be less knowledgeable and experienced as far as system design is concerned. Furthermore, user representatives will have to work out solutions to the various conflicts of interest among their organizations. This effort might require a great deal of assistance from outside consultants, or it could produce a shift of responsibility onto the professional system designers. In the latter case, the user representatives might even cease to work as full members of the design team; they might be reduced to a liaison function between the professional designers and the prospective users. As an extreme, this liaison function might even be performed by professional system designers or by outside consultants.

Presently we can only speculate about the consequences on the overall quality of the system design which this or similar departures from the Consensus Design model might produce. We hope, however, to obtain some information about these consequences from a joint system development project of about twenty textile companies which started in 1978.

Synchronization

The management of a cooperative Consensus Design project may also pose some problems to which innovative solutions must be found. One of these problems is how to synchronize the processes of organizational learning and change that take place in the individual organizations. How much pressure to speed up their internal discussions and decisions-making could be put on the organizations which cooperate on a voluntary basis, and what would be the best way to exert such pressure? On the other hand, should design decisions which some organization may already have communicated be binding or open for revision while other organizations are still contemplating their decisions?

These questions may seem trivial, but the procedure that is adopted could have considerable influence on the time it takes to complete the project and even on the viability of the cooperative system design.

Resolution of Conflict
================

A problem of similar importance is to find rules and procedures to
work out a consensus in the case of conflicting interests and decisions. Today, these rules and procedures are typically included in
the contractual agreement to join a cooperative information system
design project. They are usually drawn up by lawyers and may not be
best suited to encourage learning processes within the cooperating
organizations or within the design team. Modified rules and procedures should be devised and tested which provide sufficient flexibility for essential learning processes and still are a solid basis
for a major investment of time and resources on the part of the organizations.

INSTRUMENTS FOR COOPERATIVE CONSENSUS DESIGN

Consensus Design can be characterized as a set of interrelated personal and organizational learning processes. One essential element
of these learning processes is communication about user needs, organizational requirements, organizational and technical aspects of design alternatives. In a Consensus Design which involves one group of
users in one particular organization, much of this communication
will be on a face-to-face basis and it will be facilitated by reference to shared experiences within the present situation. In a cooperative Consensus Design, however, much of the communication will
be of a more formal nature, because the cooperating organizations
may be regionally dispersed, differ in size, organizational structure, or current level of automation, and because some kind of formal consensus about the design of the new information system has to
be reached. Thus, instruments to assist in this communication will
be of great importance for the success of cooperative Consensus Design projects.

The type of communication aids that would be required is certainly
not available off the shelf today. It is not clear what form these
instruments should have and what level of qualificaton could be set
as a prerequisite for their effective utilisation. If we accept the
assumptions that were made above about the qualification of the
prospective users and about variations in the allocation of functions, it would seem desirable to give highest priority to a set of
tools which assist user representatives in their dual communications
function.

Looking at the communications between user representatives and professional system designers, this could mean, for instance, that a
set of tools should interface with languages for requirements definition. For the communications between user representatives and
users, these instruments should be able to describe organizational
variables beyond the immediate realm of the computerized information
system. Among others the following dimensions might be considered
for inclusion:

- physical layout of the offices,

- division of tasks among the users,

- frequency and topics of task-related communication,
  . face to face
  . through technical media,

- control structure and performance criteria,

- time structure of the task,

- qualifications and performance required,

- degree of autonomy of (groups of) users.

Particular attention must be given to the problems of making the descriptions of the different dimensions consistent. Furthermore, these tools have to be easy to use in order to encourage the prospective users to draft alternative designs and to assess their likely consequences. This approach could help to simulate an iterative, stepwise process of learning and change from a prototype of the information system through successive interim versions to a relatively stable fullfledged system. In this way, one could hope to incorporate some of the elements and benefits of a Prototype Design process (Bally, Brittan and Wagner (1977)) in a cooperative Consensus Design, which today, for economic reasons, is essentially a linear design process.

ELEMENTS OF A RESEARCH PROGRAMM

Consensus Design has been proposed as an effective type of user participation in the design of information systems. It has been pointed out that increasingly information systems will be developed in cooperative projects of several organizations. A number of problems were identified which have to be solved before Consensus Design can be applied in cooperative projects as part of the organizational implementation of information systems. To work out solutions, a combination of two research strategies appears to be appropriate:

(1) We should attempt to implement a Consensus Design approach in several cooperative system design projects. Each of these projects should be studied individually to determine if the problems identified in this paper do in fact exist, and how they can be solved under the conditions of the particular project. Additionally, these projects should be examined in a comparative evaluation of different solutions to the organizational and technical problems which are encountered in cooperative Consensus Design processes.

(2) Research projects should be initiated to develop tools and educational programs which are tailored to the requirements of cooperative Consensus Design projects in small organizations. Conceivably, the research on Petri Nets (Petri, Brauer and Randell (1979)) could provide a formal basis for some of the tools for a multidimensional description of organizations and information systems. To develop and to substantiate this formalism, a great deal of research work will be necessary which integrates and re-

fines the various aspects and elements of organization theory.
This research should be planned and carried out in close cooperation with the system design projects, whose functions would be
to define requirements and objectives and to provide a realistic
and demanding environment to test the tools and educational programs.

So far, the problems of participative system design have received
only marginal attention in the three consecutive Data Processing
Programs of the German Federal Ministry of Science and Technology.
There is some indication that this might be different in future programs and we hope that the Gesellschaft für Mathematik und Datenverarbeitung will be able to contribute to the solution of a few of
the problems identified in this paper.

References

[1] Kolf, F., Oppelland, H.-J., Seibt, D. and Szyperski, N.,
    Instrumentarium zur organisatorischen Implementierung von rech-
    nergestützten Informationssystemen, Angewandte Informatik 20
    (1978) 299-310

[2] Leavitt, H.J., Applied Organizational Change in Industry.
    Structural, Technological, and Humanistic Approaches, in:
    March, J.G. (ed.), Handbook of Organizations (Rand McNally,
    Chicago, Ill. 1965)

[3] Mumford, E.: Consensus System Design: An Evaluation Of This
    Approach, in: Szyperski, N., Grochla, E. (eds.), Design
    and Implementation of Computer Based Information Systems
    (Sijthoff & Noordhoff, Alphen a. d. Rhijn 1979)

[4] Bally, L., Brittan, J. and Wagner, K.H., A Prototype Approach
    to Information System Design and Development, Information &
    Management 1 (1977) 21-26

[5] Petri, C.A., Brauer, W. and Randell, B. (eds.), Course Material
    for the Advanced Course on General Net Theory of Processes and
    Systems (Gesellschaft für Mathematik und Datenverarbeitung,
    St. Augustin 1979)

The Information Systems Environment
Lucas, Land, Lincoln, Supper (Editors)
North-Holland Publishing Company
© *IFIP, 1980*

SOCIO-TECHNICAL METHODS
FOR INFORMATION SYSTEMS DESIGN

Adriano De Maio

RSO-Istituto di Ricerca Intervento
sui sistemi organizzativi, Milano
and
Politecnico di Milano, Milano
Italy

This paper demonstrates the convenience and the
necessity of using methods based on the socio-
technical approach for the design of computer-
based information systems. The so-called
"traditional" methods of analysis are considered
to detect their most significant features and
limits.
Conversely, the main characteristics and theoretical assumptions of methods based on a socio-
technical approach are discussed.
Finally, two classes are identified of design
methods based on a socio-technical approach, and
their main objectives and characteristics are
explained.

"TRADITIONAL" METHODS AND TECHNIQUES

Major Characteristics

Automated information systems analysis and design methods and
techniques[1] were first developed by computer manufacturers. The prime
user has always been the so-called "system analyst", and obviously
everyone assumes that the end point has to be the computerization of
some part of the information flow (we will refer to these methods as
"traditional"). These methods:

a) Pay little attention to organizational facts, because they consider
   them as marginal and of no influence on the results of the analysis and on the major characteristics of the design.

b) Define an ideal operating model of a general business by describing the so-called "processes" - considered as a system of
   activities to be carried out in order to reach the business'
   objectives - leaving the organization completely out of the analysis.

c) Do not refer explicitly to any theory or organizational approach.

d) When at analysis or design time the organization is considered
   (for example, when the information flow structure is to be defined: who intervenes and with what role), dimensions other than
   formal organization are disregarded.

e) Finally, they assume that any organization may be "adapted" in the
   most appropriate way. In other words, once the information system
   has been planned - regardless of organization - they begin assessing the consistency between the system as defined and the exist-

ing organization, i.e. structure and formal procedures. If a
difference exists, action is taken to change the organization.

Similarities to Other Types of Design

Compared to say the design of production technologies, there are some
peculiarities of information technology we would like to emphasize.

a) The other technologies feature initial design data and technical
   specifications consistent with the user's language and culture.
   When automated information systems are involved quite often the
   suggested and imposed frames of reference - both conceptual and
   cultural - languages, and participation modes are at variance with
   the user's way of going about things.

b) The organizational factor intervenes at two different levels. The
   first refers to micro-organizational variables, such as: (a) job
   satisfaction - in all its dimensions, from psychological aspects
   to problems connected with professionalization; and (b) group
   dynamics, which turn into different levels of motivation and
   consequently into different ways of accepting, suffering, refus-
   ing, contrasting, and trying to modify technology. The first
   level is not typical of information technology applications,
   whereas on the contrary it is a characteristic of the second level.

Table 1 shows the similarities and difference between information and
other technologies.

INFORMATION TECHNOLOGY	OTHER TECHNOLOGIES
OBJECTIVES AND DESIGN SPECIFICATIONS ASSUMED AS DATA (A FEEDBACK IS PRESENT ONLY IN THE EVENT OF UNFEASIBILITY)	
DESIGNER'S ROLE (MAKING SURE THAT SPECIFICATIONS AND OBJECTIVES ARE CLEARLY DEFINED)	
SOCIAL SUBSYSTEM VARIABLES INTERVENE IN THE FINAL DESIGN STAGES IN MANY CASES THE ADOPTED PHILOSOPHY CONSISTS IN ADAPTING ORGANIZATION TO TECHNOLOGY (FEEDBACK ONLY IN THE EVENT OF UNFEASIBILITY)	
TECHNICAL FRAMES OF REFERENCE, LANGUAGE, AND CULTURE ARE VERY DISTANT FROM THE USER	THE USER IS IN CULTURAL POSSESSION OF SPECIFICATIONS AND TECHNICAL REFERENCE AS A WHOLE
THE SOCIAL SUBSYSTEM INTERVENES DIRECTLY AT TWO LEVELS: MICRO-ORGANIZATIONAL AND MACRO-ORGANIZATIONAL	THE SOCIAL SUBSYSTEM MOSTLY INTERVENES DIRECTLY AT MICRO-ORGANIZATIONAL LEVEL, AND INDIRECTLY AT MACRO-ORGANIZATIONAL LEVEL

TABLE 1 - Comparison Between Information Technology and other Technologies

Limitations to Traditional Design Approaches

The considerations above enable us to detect limitations in the
information systems design methods that follow an approach mainly
oriented to technical-economic aspects.

The limitations that in the case of information systems design appear
to be the most important are:

a) The cultural predominance of systems designers over users and
   their mostly implicit frame of reference;

b) The few possibilities users have of influencing technology.

c) The fact that as far as information technology is concerned the
   specialist-to-user relations have up to now been rather different
   when compared to other technologies. In fact, in other cases the
   user often manages the machine himself, which is why he learns to
   "master" the machine quickly and well although his scientific
   knowledge is not that of a specialist. In the case of information
   technology, however, the "technological system" is always managed
   by the specialist.

d) EDP specialists sometimes substitute for other company functions
   and powers, thus tending to maintain their own power by preserving
   and strengthening the previous model of user separation from
   technology.

e) Information technology appears to be much more _rigid_ than the
   majority of other technologies. It is clear that, in the majority
   of cases, automation tends to make some processes more flexible.
   In a pure information engineering field, it is not uncommon to see,
   for example, that automation permits the use of the same data base
   for different applications, which results in high flexibility. The
   more automation increases, however, the more operating procedures
   are bound to the way automation itself was designed. In other
   words, _flexibility is entirely contained and should be planned_
   completely within the design. We refer to rigidity in the sense
   that _the rigid link is between actual procedures and procedures_
   planned at design time.

Analysis of Systems Failures[2]

Problems and failures with systems are increasing in number which
explains why studies conducted with a view to identify the reasons
and to design corrective measures are becoming more and more frequent.

As stated in some well-known studies (Bostrom and Heinen (1977),Lucas
(1975[a]),Mumford and Sackmann (1977), Mumford and Pettigrew (1977),
Whisler (1970), Legge and Mumford (1978), Mumford, Land and Hawgood
(1978), De Maio (1980), De Maio and Zanarini (1980), Argyris (1977)),
the primary cause of problems and failures of computer-based
information systems is the inadequacy of the conceptual frame of
reference of information systems analysts/designers. In particular,
such a conceptual frame of reference can be analyzed through the
following seven "conditions" or characteristics:

- the implicit organization theories assumed by the designer;

- "responsibilities" the various participants take on for themselves
  at design time, and what is meant by responsibility;

- the "non-systemic" approach to design, as only variables relevant
  to the technical-economic "subsystem" are considered, while those
  relevant to the social subsystem are omitted;

- the resulting focus on a limited objective, namely the optimization
  of the technical-economic subsystem;

- the lack of care devoted to the proper composition of the design
  group, resulting in its failure to identify the user;

- the adoption of a mostly rational and static outlook of systems
  development;

- the inadequacy of designers' "cognitive technologies"[3] (mainly
  quantitative methods for decision making and resulting mathematical
  techniques, that is, all disciplines usually included in the
  umbrella term "Management Science and/or Operations Research").

The design "Philosophy" of Traditional Methods

We think that the major cause of problems and failures of computer-
based information systems is the way the design problem is approached as a whole. Our interpretation of the cause of failures is based
on the inadequacy of the analysis and design philosophy adopted by
traditional methods.

The following three points specify in detail the inadequacy:

a) In most designs a non-systemic approach is used. That is true at
   two levels. First of all, the aspects of the "social" subsystem
   are not considered enough. Secondly, the approach is non-systemic
   because it gives inadequate consideration to the process dynamics.
   In fact, when the effects of an application are analyzed - seldom
   if ever - two facts that no "systemist" should neglect are usually disregarded:

   - as a rule, interactions are complex. In other words, subsystems
     regarded as "isolated" when considered from a static point of
     view, in many cases are highly interactive and related;

   - the behavior of the various elements making up the system under
     consideration is non-linear and cannot be linearized, and some-
     times is highly dependent on past "history".

b) A principle is often adopted whereby it is possible and suitable
   to base analysis on a "purely rational" abstract organizational
   model. In fact this is a tendency or a wish that many people who
   have been concerned with organization issues at different levels
   and with different responsibilities have shown.
   The creation of an "ideal operating model" to be used as a
   reference is still present in most practical organization changes.
   In theory, one may refuse an ideal operating model - described as
   "mechanistic" - but in practice an approach philosphy of this
   kind is usually used.
   Consequently, the fact that several traditional methods make an
   "a priori" listing of the main corporate functions in respect to
   the design of an "Integrated Management Information System",
   irrespective of the organization involved, is perfectly consistent
   with such an approach. It is not by chance that also within a
   particular application - a functional subsystem or, more in detail,
   in a single procedure - a similar abstraction process is adopted

c) Finally, the problem of establishing who is the user of the
   information system is disregarded in traditional design processes.
   Sometimes the user is identified with the commissioner[4], or more
   often, the user is defined through the requirements established by

the formal organization - in terms of role, tasks, functions, and relations. That means that the organization is usually analyzed in an oversimplified manner through what the formal organization prescribes (or through what the commissioner - or more generally what the project organization manager - perceives).

To summarize, these three characteristics all emphasize the fact that the design philosophy of traditional methods tends to level the organization in the sense that all problems are only considered in the light of the logical consistency between different procedures, data, and information.

Failure - Diagnosis

The interpretation of failures and the consequential actions proposed are rarely organized in a conceptual systematization within the EDP culture. In fact, they are usually episodic and fragmentary.

Our interpretation of these failures is outlined in Figure 1.

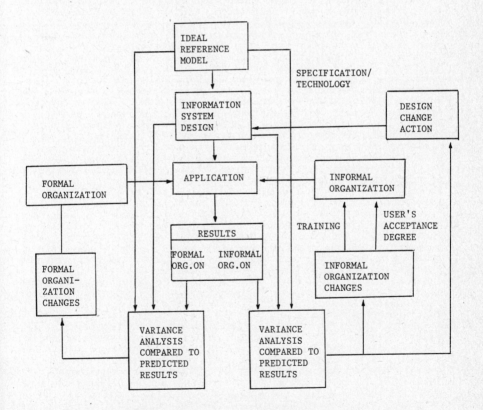

FIG. 1 - Interpretative diagram of Traditional Corrective Actions

This diagram highlights the following facts:

a) The diagnosis of failures is based on two assumptions. First, no
   feedback on the initial model can exist because it is ideal by
   definition. Investigations and changes may be made, though not as
   a result of an analysis of specific applications but by a more
   accurate theoretic examination.
   Secondly, the organization is viewed as consisting of two parts:
   the "formal" part that reflects or should reflect the abstract
   ideal model, and the "informal" part that takes interpersonal
   relations and human behavior into account.

b) Consequently, corrective actions have to affect the formal
   organization on the one side (tasks - jobs - responsibilities -
   procedures) and the informal organization on the other side. These
   actions are illustrated in the diagram as feedback loops made up
   as follows: measurement of the effects caused (analysis),
   comparison with predicted results (diagnosis of variances), and
   change in the situation (alternatives to be implemented)[5]. The
   feedback on the "formal" organization is immediate. It only needs
   to be related to functions, tasks, and responsibilities emerging
   while the computer-based information system is being designed.
   The feedback on the "informal" aspect is more complex and so far
   has led to very broad-spectrum and contradictory policies. The
   first action may consist in reducing the negative effects of
   discretionary power cannot be brought to acceptable levels. The
   most usual way of implementing such a reduction is offered by
   training, through which the user learns ideal mode for the
   organization. The training also extends the acceptance degree of
   a new system as it adjusts the user's language to the technician's
   language. Another very important aspect is acceptance. As a matter
   of fact, in many cases what is diagnosed is that this is the
   cause of the success or failure of an application.
   Acceptance by user may depend either on subjective facts (the
   change being viewed generally as a negative fact) or on
   "objective appraisals" (the new technology being considered not
   up to the user's needs). In both cases a solution to this problem
   is the involvement of the user at design time; who, with what
   role, and in what ways is a problem that all traditional methods
   have tackled by now. The need/opportunity to induce the user to
   shoulder precise responsibilities is manifest by now. Likewise, an
   increasing number of methods have established the opportunity of
   also including organization analysts in the design stages in
   order to prevent, from the beginning, possible variances with the
   existing formal organization from occurring.
   The feedback loop, however, also affects the technical specifications and may even lead to the adoption of one technology in place
   of another. The so-called "distributed EDP" is a case in point.
   The "filter" function played by the end user both at the input (as
   a data supplier) and at the output (as a user of results) is
   easier to control if the user also utilizes for his own specific
   purposes processed data he entered himself. Distributed EDP makes
   a design of this type easier to carry out and, what's more,
   immediately and actually visible. Also this new technological
   development, however, does not seem to be able to automatically
   overcome the limitations and problems described before. On the
   contrary, it appears to decrease technological constraints and to
   render some design procedures more feasible.

To summarize; we might say that even who ever accepts a traditional
approach to the design of information systems has become aware of
the existence of an adverse effect that brings about inadequate
results compared to those predicted.

Conclusions

In this section the so-called traditional information system analysis
and design methods have been described. We contend that the present
objectives are not always reached. On the contrary, when a review of
the applications is made, failures are quite numerous. We also notic
ed that designers following the traditional methods have become aware
of this, and have modified their approaches accordingly. In our
opinion, however, this change is not sufficient in that it does not
question the design philosophy as a whole. Actually, we believe that
most failures are due to the way traditional methods tackle organiza
tion problem.

THE ORGANIZATION AS A SOCIO-TECHNICAL SYSTEM

Contrary to the approach of traditional methods, we regard the
organization as a socio-technical system. Such an approach is
illustrated very schematically in Figure 2.

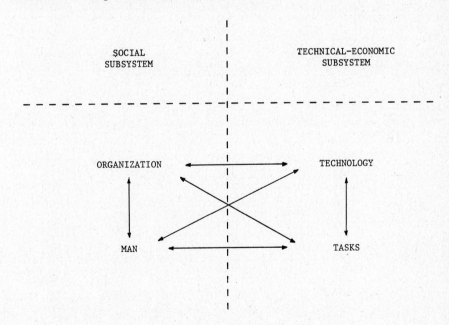

FIG. 2 - Socio-technical System Variables

As this diagram shows, a design only considering the technical-economic sybsystem yields poor results because:

a) it entirely neglects the elements making up the "social subsystem";

b) it does not consider that these elements interact with technical-economic variables in both directions, i.e. as influenced and also as influencing elements. This does not mean that de facto in a purely technical-economic design social subsystem variables are neglected, but an interaction model is assumed implicitly between these and the technical-economic variables, and this is assumed to be a one-way interaction. The consequences are extremely negative because the model, besides being inadequate is not made explicit and cannot be easily appraised and consequently changed;

c) even more, it does not consider the dynamics of the complex relations intercurring between all the diagram variables. Thus it tends to oversimplify the processes attendant to the introduction or development of automation. The emerging problems are often considered to be the mere consequence of the user not being "willing" to accept the automated information system.

For all these reasons, the results of the design are not only partial, but also turn out to be wrong due to their inadequacy in the actual situation.

The Actual Organization

Compared with the hypotheses about organizations adopted by traditional methods, the following are our interpretations and assumptions (see Boguslaw (1965), Greiner (1967), Davis and Taylor (1976), Cooper, Leavitt and Shelley (1964), Butera (1979), Lupton (1975)) :

a) Making reference to an abstract ideal model is surely consistent with a theory considering only technical-economic variables but not with an organization model based on a socio-technical system. In fact, while in the first case a general definition of functions, tasks, and coordination mechanism is possible relative to detailed and little changing technical-economic objectives, in the second case the organizational definition of functions and their interaction modes depends on specific situations and is greatly influenced by dynamic aspects.
Moreover, the information system mainly refers to coordination and control activities viewed collectively. But such coordination and control activities may change with situations. As extreme cases, one could think of a system based on centralized programming in which information flows toward a single point and decisions flow through all organization branches in a hierarchical way. This structure is opposed to a decentralized and participative programming system in which information flows to the various levels and decisions follow an articulated negotiation process.

b) If we just consider the formal organization, we notice that it is not defined univocally because a distinction must be made between "prescribed organization" and "perceived organization".
Perception may vary with the organization level, and sometimes with time, giving rise among other things to different prescriptive systems. All that defines the task and the job is articulated

in a formal way, but still does not explain the real nature of the
organization. At any rate, a difference certainly exists between
what is prescribed, what is perceived, and what happens in reality.
But "what happens" cannot be regarded simply as a combination of
formal and informal aspects. In fact, most times it proves to
reflect a definite logic and organizational model - sometimes
complementary to and sometimes conflicting with both logic and
formal models - whereby it is appropriate to speak of a "real
organization". If the project takes just the formal organization
and, frequently, only what the hierarchy prescribes and perceives
as a reference, it will be easy to find that a global loss of
knowledge could affect the design, and that the design itself
could be inconsistent and at variance with reality.

If this consideration is linked with the previous ones, it is easy to
assess how a mutual intensification of negative effects occurs. The
acceptance of an abstract, rationality model tends to give prominence
both to the formal aspect of the organization and to the interpretations of top management as the truthful representative of the general
objectives of the organization itself. On the other hand, the formal
organization in turn quite often relates to a "technical-economic"
job and task identification, assignment, and coordination model thus
giving prominence to the abstract rationality model suggested by
traditional methods. That results in an increasingly wider gap
between the frame of reference for the design and reality.

A very partial, but apparently very significant example is provided
by the redundancy of data. Usually an automated information system
aims at reducing or even eliminating redundant data. On the contrary,
whoever studies organizations considers redundant information flows
as a basic condition of effectiveness.

These remarks can be summarized with reference to Figure 3 which
stresses that, at different organization levels, the main active role
with regard to processes to be controlled is played by the organizational memory and by the input to such a memory (see De Maio (1978)).

What results from the interpretation of this diagram is:

  i) the real organization model cannot be viewed as the mere super-
     imposition of formal and informal aspects. Actually, it considers
     in a complex way all socio-technical variables. Memory collects
     and integrates knowledge and behavioral hypotheses related to
     the technical subsystem and to the social subsystem at the same
     time. A decision is made on the grounds of different kinds of
     objectives and constraints originating from different levels
     within the organization;

 ii) the organizational memory is spread across organizational levels,
     and not concentrated in one;

iii) what flows into memory is:

       . technical/economic facts,
       . social facts,

     viewed as:

       . objectives to be reached,
       . constraints to be respected,
       . attained results (effects),

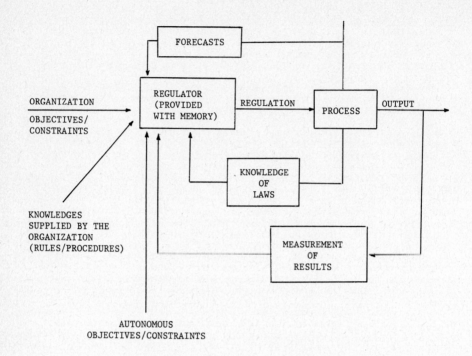

FIG. 3 - Process Control Diagram

and the whole is synthesized in the formulation of hypotheses on the expected process behavior, and in a set of possible alternative actions;

iv) frequently such a model is neither transmitted nor codified; nevertheless, it is fundamental for the overall operation of the organization;

v) sometimes man surpasses any machine in processing ability as he operates on highly complex synthese rather than on detailed analyses;

vi) this way of acting is particularly powerful when behavior is considered in the light of emerging variances to be controlled. On the contrary, if an operation "to rule" is assumed, these operating procedures can be hampered by the formal organization to a considerable extent.

As a result, interpretative diagrams and consequently design procedures are particularly important if poorly foreseeable, highly dynamic, and heavily interconnected situations are to be tackled.

ACTION STRATEGIES

If it is true that, based on the previous diagnosis the general
approach philosophy of the traditional automated information systems
analysis and design methods must be changed, this change may possibly
result from two complementary action strategies.

Training

The first action consists in changing the conceptual frame of
reference not only of systems analysts - as Bostrom and Heinen
maintain - but also of those who are concerned to a various extent
with different roles and problems connected with the design and
development of computer-based information systems. It is therefore a
training action that usually proves effective in the medium-long run
as its primary goal is the creation of a globally fertile ground
instead of sparse peaks of specific professionalism. The more it is
a matter not only of integrating but mainly of replacing a prevailing culture, the longer training taken.

New Analysis and Design Methods

Another action strategy consists of developing analysis and design
methods based on an approach considering organization as a socio-
technical system, and suitably integrating traditional methods.

In that connection, actions would not start from scratch. On the
contrary, reference should be made to the many and proven experiences
in the field of organization analysis and design.

a) Both the analysis and the design take the existence of technical-
   economic social factors into consideration.

b) Any organization is examined in all its dimensions, and in
   particular the existing decision taking levels and their existing
   interactions are pinpointed. Thus procedures are not analyzed from
   the standpoint of their abstract rationality, but from that of the
   way they interact with and interconnect different organization
   units at the same or at different levels.

c) As the emphasis is placed on the social system, it is clear that
   the use of an ideal model is impracticable because the specificity
   of the single situation is given due prominence.

d) Eventually the socio-technical approach always gives prominence to
   how participation in the analysis and change design process takes
   place.

Some Problems with the Socio-technical Approach

There are several drawbacks to socio-technical design:

a) When such an approach is adopted, analysis and design time and
   costs generally are (or rather could be) much higher than those a
   traditional approach would require. There are at least three
   reasons for this. First of all because the analysis and design
   process obviously require a greater effort; as the scope of the
   analysis is wider.

Secondly, because user participation - not only with a purely
"covering" function but as a real involvement - makes the process
slower and, time being equal, more expensive as more resources are
employed.
Finally, the approach tends to give prominence to, rather than to
omit, any conflicts and disagreements at all levels between users,
hierarchy and specialists, between different user groups, and
within the same group of users. Time is required to discuss and
resolve the conflicts.

b) The presence of EDP specialists from the initial stage, onwards as
   planned by some methods, aims at facilitating the transfer or
   requirements, objectives, and constraints defined at the end of
   analysis as technical specifications self-consistent with the EDP
   language. Such a transfer, however, is by all means more difficult
   that with traditional methods.

c) The systems designers' culture (or conceptual frame of reference)
   is, as Bostrom and Heinen put it, "a very complex process that is
   not completely under the conscious control of the persons. This
   fact also implies that the analysts are not always aware of the
   content of their conceptual frame of reference".

d) Almost every traditional method includes an "organization analysis"
   in the initial stages. It would be easier to persuade the
   commissioner of the need for such an analysis than to suggest
   directly a method based on organization theories and methods.

METHODS BASED ON A SOCIO-TECHNICAL (STS) APPROACH: A CLASSIFICATION

So far, very few methods based on a STS approach have been expressly
prepared for the analysis and design of information systems. In most
cases they either are socio-technical designs in which the process to
be analyzed and designed is represented by the data processing system
(consequently it is a systems design for the EDP unit) (Taylor (1979))
or an analysis (and design) of a change is carried out for a given
organizational subsystem within which there are some activities having something to do with information handling (De Maio and D'Andrea
(1980), Butera and Bartezzaghi (1979)).

Another quite interesting sector includes studies and applications
conducted by computer science scholars, which somehow introduce STS-
type concepts and techniques into analysis and design methods (see
for example Gilb and Weinberg (1977), London (1975), Lucas (1975[b],
1978[a], 1978[b]).

Methods based on a socio-technical approach have been established by
groups of people concerned with organizations who, starting from
organizational design and analysis techniques and methods, tried to
create "ad hoc" methods for the design of information systems. A
basic difference exists with regard to the objectives and the object
of the analysis and the objectives and object of the design.

Methods based on a socio-technical approach belong to two classes:

- the "participative" methods;
- the information requirements identification methods.

Participative Methods

This method (see Mumford, Land and Hawgood (1978)) has,as the author state, "two objectives related to the management of change. First, it seeks to legitimate a value position in which the future users of computer systems, at all organization levels, play a major role in the design of these systems.
The second objective is to persuade groups concerned with the design of computer systems to set specific job satisfaction objectives in addition to the usual technical and operational objectives".

In our opinion, the objectives actually attained by such a method are much wider than those stated by the authors because, in suggesting techniques made to take the human factor into account, some instruments are in fact supplied which prove very interesting also for the definition and attainment of technical and economic objectives. Consequently, the starting point of the whole method is participation considered both as a value per se, and as a means of reaching a higher efficiency/effectiveness level.

Effectiveness is achieved because the method sets out explicitly (thus rendering attainable) traditionally disregarded objectives, and at the same time sets a change process making objectives more easily achievable at a globally lower cost (efficiency).

The first problem to be tackled and solved is participation in the analysis and design process, particularly:

. who is the user

. what type of participation should be implemented (consultative representative or consensus participation) related to the various analysis and design stages and to the user involved.

The method suggests using, during the initial analysis stage, techniques typical of the STS approach. The authors made a significant contribution from the view-point of analysis techniques, through the proposal of two implements: (a) "future analysis" to identify significant opportunities and development goals, and (b) benefit assessment for system change to compare the desirability of alternative courses of action.

The first procedure was formulated in order to design a system which meets the future as well as the present requirements of an organization. If carried out correctly, the effectiveness of such a procedure as far as global cost reduction is concerned, is self-evident.

The second procedure, BASYC (Benefit Assessment for System Change) consists of a multi-objective, multi-criteria decision making approach based on the following principles:

- that all those affected by system change should play a part in identifying goals

- that all those affected are permitted to declare their own appraisal of the different goals

- that tangible (directly accountable) and intangible (not directly accountable) values be treated compatibly by replacing money values as a yardstick for decision taking by utlity values

- that it permits the use of subjective as well as objective methods.

The procedure consists of the following steps:

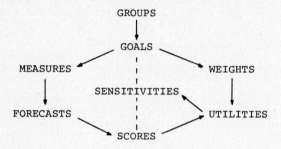

Information Requirements Identification Methods

The second class of methods starts from the following assumtpions:

a) One of the major causes of computer-based information systems
   failures consists in correctly identifying the initial design
   specifications, which in its turn results from interpretative
   modes adopted with regard to organization. A design objective is
   to find a method affording a more correct identification of
   initial design specifications through a three-stage logic process.

   1. Identifying the objectives to be reached and constraints to be
      respected with regard to a specific set of problems.

   2. Identifying the set of structured information required for the
      preset objectives to be reached in compliance with constraints.
      Such a set of information is called the "information require-
      ment".

   3. Translating information requirements to be handled through a
      computer into design specifications.

   We believe that the third stage is suitably included in traditional
   methods whereas the other two are not developed as they should be.
   Here a highly significant implication attendant to the identification of how design specifications are defined must be emphasized.
   If a method allows information requirements to be identified in
   the aforesaid manner, user training in information technology
   principles and methods will not be necessary anymore. As a matter
   of fact, the user will be able to assess the adequacy with respect
   to his own needs without needing to know that particular technology.

b) As the objective of the method thus consists in identifying
   information requirements, we have to see how that objective can be
   reached. It does not apply to the whole class, on the contrary it
   is strictly dependent on assumptions made within a specific method
   with regard to the way of interpreting the organization. The
   assumptions can be summarized in the concept of real organization
   on the one hand, and on the other, in the necessity to analize the
   actual transformation process through the examination of behavior
   (analysis of the variance control system) to succeed in identifying the real organization.

As traditional methods in a sense start from the identification of information requirements too, the methods included in this class compare with them much more directly than the methods of the previous class.

The method we deal with is discussed in De Maio, Bartezzaghi and Za-narini (1979) and in De Maio et al. (1980).

Participation is viewed in information requirements analyzes as a factor necessary to carry out the analysis, thus there is no need for a judgment on its value. The method does not say explicitly very much about participative forms and relies more on an evaluation by the user of the method according to the circumstances. Generally speaking, all three forms of participation have been used in the applications performed as yet as the case and the steps required.

The method includes seven steps:

. identifying the object of the analysis

. procedure analysis

. evaluation of problems and procedures

. variance analysis

. evaluation of control circuits

. variances and effects map

. identifying goals and constraints of the information system.

The key points of the method are:

a) To identify the object of the analysis means to define the boundaries, the input and the output of the system and generally the expectations linked to change.

b) Procedures analysis is carried out with reference to the real organization: the problems a real organization is faced with and the actual way it solves them.
Such a procedure analysis is far from the same step present in many traditional methods. Consequently the participation of all those involved in the problem solving process is absolutely necessary for a correct execution of the procedure itself. From the examination of procedures key variances[6] also emerge.

c) From the variance analysis the effects likely to be produced by a variance either in a direct way (if inadequately controlled) or indirect way (just because it is controlled) can be found.
By selecting these effects, i.e. considering the more significant ones (both social and technical) the variances and effects map can be drawn, which in a sense is the supporting element of the method. As a matter of fact, by means of this map it is possible, starting from effects to be reduced or eliminated, to see which alternative actions could be executed and which would be the effects resulting from said actions (simulation or change).

d) In that way it is possible to keep the change process under control and to perform any suitable corrections during the process itself.

The main benefits over other methods based on the STS approach are the short time and limited cost this approach requires. So far, for each application not more than 5 calendar months and 40 days/man for external experts have been necessary. Another benefit results from the utilization of some techniques usually adopted in the field of information technology. For example, in the procedure analysis step of the last version of the method Petri's networks have been used. The key open problems concern the need for a better formalization of some steps and for a link with specifications. In fact it should be observed that this too is not a method devoted exclusively to the analysis and design of information systems.

CONCLUSIONS

In conclusion we would argue that the benefits of methods based on a socio-technical approach so far have largely overcome their drawbacks. We are inclined to believe that it is only the beginning and that many opportunities are open. The first and most important one relates to the integration of these methods with one another and with other methods with a different background. For example, strong integration is possible between the two methods described herein. Both future analysis and benefit assessment would be used quite profitably within the analysis of the variances and effects map. Similarly, the procedure adopted in the second method for variance analysis could replace the traditional technique employed by the first method. Still greater integration could be obtained through other approaches. We are firmly convinced that social sciences and organization sciences would also greatly benefit from such an integration.

FOOTNOTES

(1) The terms "method" and "technique" are used here interchangeably.

(2) In agreement with the current literature, a "failure" occurs either when the actual results of the application diverge decisively from the predicted values and this is not due to technical reasons, or when the application generates problems that reduce the performance of the organization.

(3) By "cognitive technologies" we mean the wealth of knowledge that translates into specific techniques to identify and solve a given problem.

(4) The commissioner is the individual who originates the study.

(5) These corrective actions do not concern the specific project where the failures have been found, but future projects (e.g. redesigns of the same system).

(6) A "key" variance is identified as a variance requiring the implementation of a stable well-known set of activities that can be interpreted as a "real" procedure, even if it is not written nor formally defined.

REFERENCES

Argyris, C., Organizational Learning and Management Information Systems, Accounting, Organizations and Society, 2 (1977) 113-123.

Boguslaw, R., The New Utopians: a Study of the System Design and Social Change (Prentice Hall, Englewood Cliffs, 1965).

Bostrom, R.P. and Heinen, J.S., MIS Problems and Failures: a Socio-Technical Perspective, Part I and II, MIS Quarterly, 3 (1977) 11-28.

Butera, F., La Divisione del Lavoro in Fabbrica (Marsilio, Venezia 1977).

Butera, F., Lavoro umano e prodotto tecnico (Einaudi, Torino 1979).

Butera, F. and Bartezzaghi, E., R & D Department: A Socio-Technical Analysis, RSO Working Paper, Milan (1979).

Cooper, W.W., Leavitt, H.J., Shelley, M.W. (eds.), New Perspectives in Organization Research (Wiley, New York 1964).

Davis, L.E. and Taylor, J.C., Technology, Organization and Job Structure, in: Dubin, R. (ed.), Handbook of Work, Organization and Society (Rand McNally,Chicago 1976).

De Maio, A., Decision and Coordination Processes: the Role of Computerization, RSO Working Paper,Milan (1979[a])

De Maio, A. and Zanarini, G., Socio-Technical Perspective and Systems Designer's Frame of Reference: Engineering Models Revisited, Studi Organizzativi 3 (1980[b]) forthcoming.

De Maio, A., Interazione fra Informatica e Sistemi Organizzativi, Studi Organizzativi, 1-2 (1978) 233-240.

De Maio, A. and D'Andrea, R., Maintenance-Production System Analysis and Design, RSO Working Paper, Milan (1977), in Italian.

De Maio, A., Bartezzaghi, E. and Zanarini, G., A New System Analysis Method Based on the STS Approach, in: Schneider, H.J. (ed.), Formal Models and Practical Tools for Information System Design (North Holland, Amsterdam 1979[b]).

De Maio, A., Bartezzaghi, E., Brivio, O. and Zanarini, G., Ricerca per la definizione di un metodo socio-tecnico di analisi e progettazione dei sistemi informativi (Angeli, Milano 1980[b]).

Gilb, T. and Weinberg, G., Humanized Input (Winthrop, Cambridge 1977).

Greiner, E.L., Patterns of Organizational Change, Harvard Business Review, 5 (1967).

Legge, K. and Mumford, E. (eds.), Designing Organizations for Satisfaction and Efficiency (London 1978).

London, K., The People Side of Systems (McGraw Hill, New York 1976).

Lucas, H.C., Why Information Systems Fail (Columbia University Press, New York, 1975[a]).

Lucas, H.C., Toward Creative System Design (Columbia University Press, New York 1975[b]).

Lucas, H.C., Information Systems Concepts for Management (McGraw Hill, New York 1978[a]).

Lucas, H.C., The Implementation of Computer Based Models, National Association of Accountants (1978[b]).

Lupton, T., Efficiency and the Quality of Worklife: the Technology of Reconciliation, Organizational Dynamics, 2 (1975) 68-80.

Mumford, E. and Sackmann, H. (eds.), Human Choice and Computers (McGraw Hill, New
York 1977).

Mumford, E. and Pettigrew, A., Implementing Strategic Decisions (Longmans, London
1975).

Mumford, E., Land, F. and Hawgood, I., A Participative Approach to the Design of
Computer Systems, Impact of Science on Society, 3 (1978) 235-253.

Whisler, T.L., The Computers in Organizations (Praeger, London 1970).

The Information Systems Environment
Lucas, Land, Lincoln, Supper (Editors)
North-Holland Publishing Company
© *IFIP, 1980*

DEVELOPMENT OF AN INFORMATION SYSTEM
IN A SELF-MANAGEMENT ENVIRONMENT

Vladislav Rajkovič

Jožef Stefan Institute
Edvard Kardelj University of Ljubljana
Ljubljana, Yugoslavia

In this paper, fundamental concepts of a self—management environment in
Yugoslavia are explained. Their reflection on information system requirements
is discussed, together with some design considerations and practical results.

INTRODUCTION

The main characteristic of our self—management (SM) philosophy is a right and duty of every
individual to decide his personal and collective interests in the organizations of associated labor,
local communities and other self—management organizations and communities. This requires
direct participation of the people in problem solving and especially decision making, not only
in factories and institutions but also in their broader social life.

There are several organizational levels in our SM system. The whole system of associated labor
is founded on basic organizations of the associated labor (BOAL) which are one of the two
basic elements of the whole socio—economic and political system. The other element is the
local community.

A BOAL is a unit of work organization which makes up a working whole (e.g. a plant, a
technological unit, etc.) in which the results of joint labor can be expressed in terms of value,
either on the market or within the work organization concerned. The BOAL is the basic form
of associated labor in which workers, directly and on equal terms, realise their socio—economic
and other self—management rights and decide on other questions concerning their socio—
economic status.

A local community is the basic territorial unit, i.e. is the basic self—management community
organized by working people and citizens living in a settlement. They try to realize their
common interests and satisfy their needs associated with the physical improvement of their
settlement and with matters concerning other spheres of life and work.

On the next level, local communities are assembled into a commune and BOALs are assembled
into an organization of associated labor, and at a higher level into a composite organization of
associated labor. The assembly functions on the basis of the delegational system. The delegational system ensures direct presence by the working people in the assemblies, and ensures
functional linkage of short— and long—term interests of individual sections of society and of
society as a whole. The system is institutionally new and is a special kind of link between SM
and government (Toplak (1978), Tanović (1977)).

It is obvious that information is a dominant economic and socio—political category. The field
of information has always been and will be the field of class struggle and confrontation of
different social interests. Because information is fundamental to govering, it is understandable

123

that the control of information represents the basis of techno-bureaucratic influence and manipulation.

Starting from the constitutional provision that informing workers is essential for the realisation of their SM function. The law treats that position in a double sense: as the right of the workers and citizens to be informed, and the duty of SM organs and responsible individuals in the organizations and communities to inform people (Džinić (1977)).

Therefore it can be concluded that the SM environment imposes complex and demanding information requirements. This results in some special features of information system (IS) design and functioning within work organizations and territorial units.

INFORMATION SYSTEM REQUIREMENTS

In the broadest sense an appropriate IS has to support development of man as producer, consumer and manager, on the basis of goals such as: carrying out socio—political activities, expression of personality, job satisfaction, social security, education, etc. There are at least two major questions: (1) what kind of information is needed, and (2) how to present the information in a readable form.

The governing organs are obliged to inform workers and citizens about the following: the entire functioning of the organization and commune, the material-financial situation, distribution of the revenue and utilization of the funds, the results obtained by integrated work and funds, the activities of SM organs, realization of SM workers' control, and other questions relevant to work and management (Džinić (1977), Kavčič (1977)).

Besides, there are possibilities for other information requirements, which are not commonly prescribed. They are stated within work organization or community by the users — workers and citizens. The requirements can differ from one work organization or community to another. These requirements are usually very dynamic in nature as well. From one point of view it may seem to produce total anarchy in the IS requirements, but from another point it leads to IS which people really need and want. Within the framework of reasonable limitations there are "personal ISs" for a working organization or community with a common prescribed part which ensures a common basis for connecting ISs together at the higher levels of SM. It offers a possibility for common understanding and comparison of information from BOAL and community up to the level of government.

Another important requirement is that an information picture which is a basis for SM activities should be simple and clear, containing all necessary information but no more. It looks like a desired goal only, but the goal can be and should be approached by participation of users stating their requirements on such an information picture.

In practice such an information picture is usually semantically and syntactically structured. General information which gives an overall picture is physically separated from detailed information. For example, general information is given first on a separate form. After that users may ask for some further details if necessary.

Having a simple and clear information picture does not mean only to be informed for required decision making. It means also to be protected from information pollution and manipulation, e.g. it implies a certain degree of self—protection against being misinformed. And to be properly informed is an important basis for every society.

The stated requirements for somehow "individual", simple, clear and secure information may not look special (Land (1974), Langefors and Sundgren (1975), Mumford (1977)) unless we recall that these requirements are somehow obligatory, regarding SM rights stated in our constitution.

This places demanding requirements on system designers from the human point of view as well as from the technological point of view. The fit between man and technology seems to be very important and has to be reflected in appropriate IS development techniques.

DESIGN CONSIDERATIONS

If the SM is adopted as our life philosophy it is logical to treat it also as a system design philosophy. This means that participation in IS design should be a natural part of the normal activities of the users. Because of the complex requirements stated in the previous section, participation of the people in the whole life cycle of IS seems to be the only possible methodology.

As stated by Lundeberg (1979), suitable circumstances are required for participation. Following our experiences in the framework of circumstances, the most important is the motivation of users. The SM circumstances (SM rights and duties) are a motivating factor on their own, where the identification and verification of appropriate information pictures can be especially emphasized. Besides motivation, education in a broader sense is also required (Rajkovič (1978)). Up to now, formal regular education seems to be insufficient, therefore the whole participation process should be treated as an educational (learning) process. It can be also stated that among circumstances, an appropriate method for participating in system design lays an important role.

We started with well—known, more or less classical system analysis and design techniques (Benjamin (1975), Lucas (1976), Taggart and Thorp (1977)). These techniques are still on in wider practice with some modifications towards participation. At "J.Stefan" Institute, a technique based on ISAC methodology (Lundeberg (1979)) and approach described in (Efstathiou and Rajkovič (1979), Hawgood, Land and Mumford (1978), Land (1974)) is being used now with reasonable success. The technique includes a simplified version of the description language of ISAC. The reason lies in the participation of non-professional users who should not have many problems with learning the new language necessary for system development. Therefore, some details are ignored, components of natural language are introduced and inseparable utilities are used in making decisions during a development process (Efstathiou, Hawgood and Rajkovič (1979)).

The technique was used in some projects, such as development of IS for stock control or internal accoutancy in BOAL. We found our users' involvement in the specifications of IS on three levels (change analysis, activity study and information analysis) very useful. Information analysis is usually also divided into several levels, each with a given problem and different types of users. The use of natural language (verbal measures) for quantitative description results in a better fit between people and technique. With this approach the possibility of making mistakes by, for example, forgetting important factors is reduced. It was also noticed that users' ability for abstract thinking was increased during the design process.

Let us consider the question of the role of the system analyst in the participative approach. He should act not only as a catalyst but also as a "teacher" and the person concerned with implementation. It may happen that he obtains the impression of wasting his time in partici- pative work, but the benefit is in the decreasing possibility of designing a "wrong" system, a system which is not desired. Of course he shares the responsibility with users participating in the design process.

CONCLUSIONS

It can be stated that in self—management society, workers and citizens have to express a high degree of consciousness about information. An appropriate information picture is needed for realization of self—management rights and duties. Therefore, we are highly motivated to get the right information in right time and this is a general climate among people and not only among managers. Active fit between people and information system is something natural. There is no need to convince anyone to participate in system development it is everybody's right and duty. This general thinking which is incorporated in self—management life philosophy, is an advantage for the development of information system in our environment. It provides favorable circumstances for system development.

General consciousness about information results in the active participation of system users in the system development process from the very begining. Here, however arise some educational problems and usually a problem of information system requirements which are often too demanding. Therefore the development process is demanding and time-consuming. Consequently an appropriate development technique seems to be essential. As previously mentioned serious attempts have been made to develop an adequate technique. It is possibly true that the benefits of self-management circumstances have not been used to their full advantage in the field of IS development. Further work should be done to incorporate self-management philosophy better into the effective IS development techniques as well as into the whole life cycle of IS.

REFERENCES

[1] Benjamin, I.R., Control of the information system development cycle (J. Wiley, 1975).
[2] Džimić, F., System of communication in the associated work: the Yugoslav case, Proc. Proc. of 2nd Int. Conf. on Participation, Self-Management and Workers Control (Paris, 1977).
[3] Efstathiou, J. and Rajkovič, V., Multi-attribute decision making using a fuzzy heuristic approach, IEEE Transactions on Systems, Man and Cybernetics, 9 (1979) 326—333.
[4] Efstathiou, J., Hawgood, J. and Rajkovič, V., Verbal measures and inseparable multi-dimensional utility in system evaluation, Proc. of IFIP WG8.1 Working Conference, Formal Models and Practical Tools for Information System Design (Oxford, 1979).
[5] Hawgood, J., Land., F.F. and Mumford, E., A participative approach to forward planning and system change, in: Goos, G., Hartman, I. (eds.), Lecture Notes in Computer Science (Springer—Verlag, 1978).
[6] Kavčič, B., The success of self-management, Proc. of 2nd Int. Conf. on Participation, Self-management and Workers Control (Paris, 1977).
[7] Land, F., Criteria for the evaluation and design of effective systems, Proc. of Int. Symp. on Economics of Informatics (Mainz, 1974).
[8] Langefors, B., Sundgren, B., Information system architecture (Petrocelli, 1975).
[9] Lucas, C.H., The analysis, design and implementation of information systems (McGraw—Hill, 1976).
[10] Lundeberg, M., An approach for involving the users in the specification of information systems, Proc. of IFIP WG8.1 Working Conference "Formal Models and Practical Tools for Information System Design" (Oxford, 1979).
[11] Mumford, E., Job satisfaction: a study of computer science (McGraw—Hill, 1977).
[12] Rajkovič, V., On the role of computer—science subjects at the secondary school level, in: Moneta, I. (ed.), Information Technology (North—Holland, 1978).

[13] Taggart, W.M. & Thorp, M.O., A survey of information requirements analysis techniques, Computing Surveys, 9 (1977) 273–290.
[14] Tanović, A., Contradictions of value orientation in socialistic self–management, Proc. of 2nd Int. Conf. on Participation, Self–management and Workers Control (Paris, 1977).
[15] Toplak, L., The Yugoslav legal system (ČGP Delo, TOZD Gospodarski vestnik, Ljubljana, 1978).

The Information Systems Environment
Lucas, Land, Lincoln, Supper (Editors)
North-Holland Publishing Company
© *IFIP, 1980*

USER PARTICIPATION - WHY IS DEVELOPMENT SO SLOW?
The Dynamics of the Development of End User Control

Rolf Höyer

Chalmers University of Technology
and University of Gothenburg
S- 412 96 Gothenburg, Sweden

The general interest in developing industrial democracy in the Scandinavian countries has influenced the philosophy and practice of information systems development. Legislation, agreements and new cultural norms relating to working life have made it necessary continuously to redefine the role of end users in the systems development process. There is still a gap, however, between general intentions and current practice. Implementation of an effective "systems democracy" is experienced as a long and cumbersome process by many systems professionals and end-users. Many feel frustrated when they realize that good intentions are difficult to integrate into current practice and have therefore raised the question: Why is development so slow?

This article explores the dynamics of this important change process in industry, emphasizing the implied change of basic organizational ideologies relating to codetermination. Finally some practical obstacles for further development are discussed.

A HISTORICAL PERSPECTIVE

There are, indeed, many different conceptions of the role of the end user in the systems development process. These differences are displayed on all levels: - within the company, between companies - and one may also observe general dissimilarities between different countries.

This paper is based on the assumption that these different conceptions are strongly related to basic beliefs, values and norms regarding principles of organization and management. In short, it is a matter of different organizational *ideologies*. I am going to use this concept in an explanatory model of current practice and conceptions of the end user role. In particular, I will focus on the conflict of ideologies within a company, emphasizing the potential ideological differences between the systems designers and the user community. This ideological interface will probably illuminate the dynamics of the current development of the end user role within most companies.

In general, I am referring to the development in Scandinavia in this decade, during which the development has been rather dramatic. Here, the interest in the role of end users may be categorized into three areas:
1)   Social and humane *considerations*,
2)   User involvement and *participation* in the design process,
3)   *Codetermination*, the right to be consulted and decide upon the properties of the new systems.
These areas are not independent and they may be ranked on different types of scales, each indicating a perspective upon historical development. Immediately, one may think of a time scale, mapping different groups according to when the interest became a reality. Another interesting scale, of ordinal type, is associated with the degree of end users' real influence in the design process.

Figure 1 combines these two scales to indicate the growth in real influence and

power of the user community during the Seventies. This figure also shows the most
significant events and factors which have contributed to this growth. The figure
reflects the development in Norway and Sweden which are rather similar in this respect. Now, let us have a closer look at the three areas of interest in the end
user role identified above.

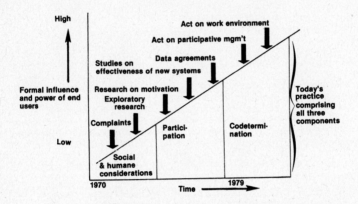

Figure 1:   Changes in the End User Role during the 70's.

The first area, *social and humane considerations*, is mainly based on extensive ex
post facto investigations of the consequences of data processing systems for job
content, work environment and organization structure. Using this knowledge, the
systems designers may adjust their development practice to prevent the consequences they consider undesirable. Here, the end users have no formal influence or
power. Some influence is, however, possible through informal joint consultations
which may take place within the narrow framework of this practice.

The area user *participation* has two directions - one based on pragmatic considerations and one based on formal agreements. Pragmatically based participation, probably the most common today, is founded upon the belief that participation is useful and profitable. Comprehensive work research has long shown that change processes are generally easier to manage and create less resistance to change, if those
affected are engaged into planning and implementation-changes. This is also regarded as more or less a truism among thoughtful practitioners. Furthermore, both
research and practice indicate that information systems may be qualitatively improved when experienced users participate in the systems development process.
Current interest in this area is focused upon methods of project organization, formal tools for systems description and communication about system properties etc.
Within this framework, user influence may be considerable, being controlled by
more or less efficient steering groups and the implicit obligations of the participation process.

Furthermore, we have user participation which is based upon formal agreements. The
most prominent example is the "data agreement" established 1975 in Norway between
the national representatives of workers and employers. This main agreement is often supplemented by local agreements as needed.

Typical for this kind of participation is that end user influence is channeled
through special elected representatives of the trade unions, called "data shop

stewards". By its nature, this implies a participation by formal representatives.
However, the main agreement includes a recommendation stating that the employees
immediately affected by new systems as far as possible should be engaged in their
development work. The rationale for these provisions is mainly pragmatic. The national agreement is somewhat unclear regarding the content of the formal influence and power in this participation system. On important issues it contains only
loosely formulated recommendations, such as the following concerning a central objective: "...[shop stewards shall be able to]....further their points of view as
early as possible and before the decisions of the company are carried into effect."
Nevertheless, the agreement is regarded as an important and powerful tool for the
improvement of the formal influence and control of end users.

Finally,the third area, *codetermination*, must today be seen in connection with
specific Scandinavian legislation, such as e.g. the Norwegian Act relating to Worker Protection and Working Environment and the Swedish Act relating to Codetermination. This legislation provides end users with the legal right to participate
during systems development and to decide upon the properties of new systems. However, we will also have a de facto state of codetermination when mutually binding
Organization Development projects include data systems development and when the
participative procedures of the trade union agreement are supported by broad actions among employees.

Codetermination may be looked upon as an extension of both the humane considerations and participation areas, and necessarily includes the potentials of both.
What is genuinely new within the legislative framework is that employees are given
the right to improve their working conditions, both in the physical and psycho -
social area, during any change process. The Norwegian Act on Working Environment
provides employees with the right to demand that proper considerations are given
to environmental questions in systems development projects. It also provides employees with the right to participate in order to promote their own objectives.
Another significant characteristic of the legislation is that it is explicitly aimed at a more democratic work environment and a more meaningful job for each employee, and not based upon pragmatic considerations.

The formal influence and power of end users are significantly increased in the
area of codetermination. What is genuinely new with respect to the two former
areas is that:
1) implied participation is supported by strong and unambiguous rights. It is not
   attached to pragmatic considerations towards the technical and economic aspects
   of the systems design
2) the right to participate is given all employees affected by new systems. Participation is not limited to a narrow representative system, which most present
   practice frequently degenerates into.

PROBLEMS IMPROVING PRESENT PRACTICE

Neither Labor-Management agreements nor legislation has yet dramatically changed
established practice. Although most companies have implemented the required legal
forms, one has the impression that the real content of new and more potential participation options develop at an unsatisfactory low rate. At the Scandinavian data
processing conference summer 1979, the question was formally raised:Why is progress so slow?

The various efforts aiming at democratization and participation are partly imposed
upon the companies from outside, and only partly emerge from an internal, voluntary desire for change and development. Above all, it is important to realize that
those matters imply ideological changes.

Planned change within work organizations, in particular of ideologies, is always
a very problematic task. Generally, the development of change processes results
from interaction between the *pressure for change* and the change *capacity* of the organization. The problems associated with implementation of extensive codetermina-

tion practices according to law and agreements may be illuminated by using this simple model.

The pressure for change comprises the ambitions, will and competence among the change agents who desire to give formal, legal constructions a meaningful content. Change capacity is influenced by the desires generally within the organization regarding codetermination and democratic practice, what the people generally care enough about to apply.

Those matters are to a large extent a question of organizational ideologies. Types of such ideologies will be discussed separately below.

PRESSURE FOR CHANGE: MOTIVES AND ATTITUDES

The concept "pressure for change" is far too complex to be made operational. Instead, we shall narrow our scope, looking at motives and attitudes among the people responsible for implementation of participative practices in connection with systems development. To a large extent, this includes mainly professional systems designers.

Data on motives are not easily available. Motives are seldom clearly formulated and are often deliberately kept hidden. We can, however, identify at least four major types of motives which frequently are found in discussions. Below they are ranked according to their potential for development of meaningful efforts towards codetermination practices:

1) *Idealistic motives:* Every employee has a democratic right to decide upon his daily environment. This right reflects common ethical and ideal values in society, and is independent of legislation and labor-management agreements.

2) *Legal motives:* The participative constructions prescribed by law and contracts are to be implemented and operated as defined. Special appointed boards and authorities must decide upon the efficiency of the resulting practice. It is not a problem for the professional systems designers.

3) *Pragmatic motives:* In the long run, it is probably most practical and even profitable to implement democratic practices.

4) *Personal or situational motives:* Involvement in participative efforts and support of these, may be exploited for personal benefit to obtain career advancement and power positions within the organization.

These motives are found in different combinations in different companies, shaping the pressure for, and content of, developing participation practices. In many companies, one finds a heavy ideological conflict about legitimacy by exposing motives of type 1 above.

While motives are more or less hidden, attitudes are more easily identifiable; they are at least clearly observable through open actions. Below is a list that attempts to categorize the most common attitudes exposed in practice:

1) *Technocratic:* Systems design is a part of engineering science. The task of the designer is to develop systems as ordered and unambiguously described by others. How those specifications are arrived at is not within his field of responsibility and interest.

2) *Manipulative:* User codetermination and democratic practice is nothing new. Generally it only implies an unnecessary formalization of previous good and conscious practice. Participation and codetermination are most efficiently arrived at by utilization of informal networks within the organization. Generally, the users do not know their own best interest, and need to be taken care of.

3) *Passive formalistic:* Codetermination will be taken care of by the formal bodies prescribed by laws and agreements, and by the official steering committee for each project.

4) *Progressive*: The systems designer is professionally and personally responsible for the real content and outcome of the codetermination processes. He is
conscious of the premises of end users, and he is more oriented towards the
underlying intentions of legislation and agreements than strictly following
the formal written text.

In order to arrive at efficient participation practices, the potential available
in technology and project design must be identified and adapted. End users seldom
have the resources to achieve this alone. The attitudes of the professional systems designers are therefore the most important factor shaping the pressure for
change. A rapid development of codetermination will probably require a general
progressive attitude among the designers. Motives and attitudes are here used as
indicators of the ideological content of the pressure for change. This pressure
will encounter general organizational ideologies within the company. Those two
different sets of ideologies may be in concordance with each other, or they may
be in conflict. Let us therefore explore the dynamics of this interface.

THE CHANGE CAPACITY: ORGANIZATIONAL IDEOLOGIES OF THE COMPANY

Although all members of an organization have their own conceptions and ideals concerning the shaping and operation of the organization, they will be influenced towards some common norms. To a large extent, this process will converge towards
the established order. Efforts to change procedures and policy are moulded and a-
dapted so as to differ only incrementally from existing norms. Illustrative for
this process are Lindblom´s formulations in his theory of "Muddling-through":
"Attempts at understanding are limited to policies that differ incrementally from
existing policy". (Hirschman & Lindblom, 1962). If this process of adaption is not
successful, the change effort will be beaten down or abandoned.

The Muddling-through-model implies a process of interaction and mutual adaption
between the new ideas and the prevailing ideology, the latter usually being the
far strongest. This mutual process of adaption is theoretically described by
Philip Selznick. Introducing the term organizational *cooptation*, Selznick states:
"Cooptation is the process of absorbing new elements into the leadership or poli-
cy-determing structure of an organization as a means of averting threats to its
stability or existence". (Selznick, 1948).

Cooptation as described by Selznick, originates from situations where formal control is not in concordance with commonly held beliefs and norms regarding right
and wrong ("A hiatus between consent and control"). The organization will respond
to this lack of concordance or hiatus by a process of adaption and equalization -a
process of cooptation.

There are formal and informal mechanisms of cooptation. When formal cooptation is
applied, control methods are modified so that they formally look acceptable. But
this formal cooptation is more directed towards equalization of the formal issues
of power and influence than towards real, exercised power.

The informal cooptation is carried out by means of more sophisticated and hidden
methods.

These concepts are directly applicable in our context. Introduction of new codetermination practices is of course an attempt to modify the control system of the organization. The question is then: Is the ideological content within the new practice in accordance with commonly held beliefs and norms within the organization?
If a hiatus is identified, the organization may respond with formal cooptation,
which is frequently seen in practice. Ingeniously performed cooptation has manipulated many codetermination efforts into meaningless constructions of empty formal democracy.

Organizations may also respond with informal cooptation. This implies that influence and power, and even policy, are changed or modified within the existing formal
framework. For example, a troublesome shop steward can be neutralized by promoting him into a managerial position. Or, a pressure group can be neutralized by

134   R. HÖYER

officially meeting a few of its most important demands, or simply giving lip service only. In our context, the pressure group may be a trade union, a project
steering committee or a systems department. The cooptation process may be directed toward the behavior of an individual or his attitudes, applying means ranging
from threats to formal training. Or it may be more drastic, for example changing
members of committees and project groups.

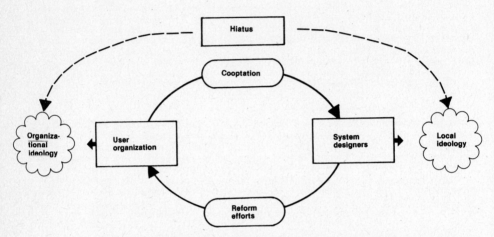

Figure 2:   Attempts at Reforming Participation Practice
and Organizational Cooptation.

The progressive systems designer trying to act as a change agent may quickly realize that he is involved in a mutual process of cooptation in relation to the
surrounding organization.. The strength of the cooptation process will of course
be reflected by the size of the hiatus between the new ideas and the existing
ideology. Or more specifically, - the ideology of the systems project as interpreted from the suggested procedures for codetermination, and what the user organization finds relevant and desireable as working procedure in systems design
within the company, which of course will be a reflection of organizational ideology. See Figure 2.

THE DYNAMICS OF END USER CONTROL

We are now equipped with a framework suitable for describing the development of
meaningful and efficient codetermination practice within industry. Within each
company, the development will emerge from the interrelationship between the ideology applied in systems projects and the related ideologies of the total organization. Or to be more specific: it will depend on the relationship between what
the systems designers actually practise, and what the organization generally expects. These two parties may have very dissimilar ideologies regarding the promotion of extensive and real codetermination practices. Future developments within
a company will probably be determined by this actual combination of ideologies.
Diagnosis of present state and forecasts for future development is visualized
in the model shown in figure 3.

In the elements along the main diagonal, there is concordance between the implied
ideology in current systems projects and the ideology behind the expectations of
the organization. Element 1.1 displays a situation which probably will not be very
fruitful for future development of codetermination practices.

Figure 3: The Dynamics of the Development of End User Control

| | | IDEOLOGY OF THE ORGANIZATION | | |
		NEGATIVE	INDIFFERENT	POSITIVE
Ideology of the systems designers	NEGATIVE	1.1 HARMONY No development. Change potential low.	1.2 RELAXED Codetermination is not considered an objective in itself	1.3 CONFLICT Formal cooptation activated
	INDIFFERENT	2.1 RELAXED Systems designers produce the systems they think the organization deserves	2.2 FORMAL DEMOCRACY working and satisfies expectations	2.3 LATENT POSSIBILITIES General OD-activities will influence systems design practice
	POSITIVE	3.1 CONFLICT Informal cooptation activated. Frustrated system designers	3.2 AREA OF POSSIBLE Reforms are initiated by systems designers. Progress is slow	3.3 PROGRESS Experiments and learning takes place. Knowledge and tools searched for

Element 3.3 of course displays the best situation for development of the present practice. Here, the issue under discussion is not whether or not one shall engage into a codeterminative practice, but rather how to do it in an effective way.

In the corner elements 1.3 and 3.1 there will be active mechanisms of cooptation. Systems designers in element 3.1 will probably be those who most frequently raise the question why there is such poor progress, while their colleagues in element 1.3 will have the perception that development in this area is far too rapid to manage properly. They will probably be more inclined to warn against inherent dangers of the democratization process, e.g. that it may endanger the future survival of the company and create managerial difficulties, than to contribute as a professional to develop, for instance, better methods and tools for communication and project organization, which are necessary to increase user participation to a level of real codetermination.

In both the latter examples the ideology of system development professionals is not shared by the general user community. Hence, cooptation mechanisms will be active in order to close the gap between consent and control. A typical informal cooptation would be quiet, but effective, using delay and obstruction aiming at passifying progressive change efforts. A typical formal cooptation would take the shape of heavy formalization, for example, introducing an excessive number of committees, construction of bureaucratic rules and procedures etc.

The model introduced above provides a comprehensive picture of the manifold, dynamic situation of present and future development of participation and codetermination practice. Hopefully, the model will provide a useful framework for local diagnosis and discussions on more powerful strategies for future development.

PRACTICAL OBSTACLES

Problem Areas

The development of participation and codetermination is of course not only a question of organizational ideologies, although the ideological issue probably is the most important and hidden factor. Obviously, it is also a question of resources, knowledge, insight, as well as practical procedures and tools. Fortunately, these

are all of a more easily recognizable nature than the process of ideological change in organizations and in society.

However, these factors are to be developed and put into practical use. If not, the
development of workable systems democracy will end as a grounded dream, even in
organizational settings as indicated in the lucky bottom-right corner of the matrix in Figure 3. Five of the most dominant problems frequently encountered in
current practice, being related to the factors mentioned above, are briefly summarized in the following.

1) *Erroneous Focus of Codetermination and Participation.*

Information systems seldom appear as an independent phenomenon per se in the consciousness of the end user. Instead, he will look at them as *part of a totality.*
He will perceive them on background of his immediate work setting. Hence, information systems are understood, interpreted and evaluated according to their interaction with the job and the work structure.

On the other hand, the systems designer perceives the information system as the
main issue, loosely connected to the work organization. Consequently, he will tend
to believe that the codetermination efforts should be focused upon the data systems development process in a rather narrow sense. This erroneous focus has frequently led participation and codetermination efforts into a confined and unmoti-
vating situation, ending up with bored and disappointed end users and frustrated
systems designers.

A development process aiming at codetermination should instead focus on the job
of the individual employee and its relations to the work organization in which it
is embedded. The main objective of the development process may then be derived
from this focus - how to develop and improve the actual work situation, and how
new information systems may contribute to this.

This axiom has a particular bearing on the development and implementation of on-
line terminal systems. During the analysis and design stages of the system itself,
participation may at best only take place through a very limited number of user
representatives. Because such systems often are going to be used by some hundreds,
and sometimes thousands, of end users, direct participation is of course totally
impossible. Furthermore, both research and practical experience have shown the in-
efficiency of codetermination through user representatives. Consequently, one may
believe that sociotechnical design based on general codetermination is not meaningful in such situations.

Field experiments by the author, see for instance Höyer (1979), have however documented that democratic based development of work environment in connection with
implementation of such systems is possible. A fundamental prerequisite for this
approach is that the concept of systems development is expanded to encompass both
the data systems itself and the surrounding work organization. The experiments
have clearly shown that the most significant decisions regarding the change process are related to the modeling of the surrounding work structure, and not so
much oriented towards the actual design properties of the technical system.

When using this expanded concept of systems development, one will probably in most
cases discover that technology has many more degrees of freedom than one will expect when focusing only on the systems design process. In this way, the change capacity of technology may be exploited to good purpose in order to achieve social
objectives arrived at through a democratic based organization design process.
This insight is the background of the formulation of *the theory of organizational
turbulence*, suggested by the author:

> "Organization Development efforts may be powerfully enhanced by exploiting the
> disturbances to the stable organization caused by the process of technological
> change" (1975).

Application of this theory will, however, require that the focus of the codetermi-

nation practice is placed upon the actual organization setting of the new information system, and not only on the system itself.

2. *Intangibles and Demand for Hard Resources.*

The best way of minimizing direct costs related to systems development, will be
to apply good old-fashioned autocratic management practice. Unfortunately to some,
this peculiar practice will acquire considerable indirect costs and often conflicts.

One has to realize that attempting to develop participative practice and codetermination implies an increased demand for resources in the form of time and money.
Analysis and design will be more complicated and consume more time, and may even
lead to an increased demand for technical equipment. An upgrading of flexibility
in the work structure, is for example often associated with an increased demand
in the number of terminals when implementing an on-line system. No effort should
be made to hide this fact.

The price incurred may therefore be calculated in time and money. The benefits
are on the other hand usually hard to measure. They involve intangibles such as
motivation, innovation potential, flexibility, service level etc. And contrary to
the debit side, the intangibles are never provided with a guarantee.

It is a prerequisite for success that intangibles are defined as far as possible,
prior to the systems development, and then in later stages compared to the results
obtained. It is important to realize that further progress in this area depends
upon *learning*, which in turn requires an evaluation process. Furthermore, social
objectives may very easily be disregarded if they are too loosely formulated, because "hard" data always will tend to supress "good intentions" and "soft" data.
This fact is strongly emphasized by the Norwegian Act on Working Environment,
which declares social objectives to be of equal importance to technical ones.

This problem may be illustrated by a management phrase sometimes encountered in
current practice:"Participation and codetermination shall take place, but must
not, of course, endanger efficiency of the daily work". Combined with an unwil-
lingness to provide adequate resources, this managerial philosophy will effectively block any progressive effort.

3. *Adequate Tools.*

User involvment implies a communication process. The communication quality is dependent on many factors, all of which may be significantly improved by proper
training and tools. The communication quality within a project group may be improved by applying common group development schemes and consultation. Communication on systems properties may be more comprehensible to the end users when selecting adequate description techniques - several promising ones are readily available. Finally, the quality of the learning environment within a systems development project may be improved by applying a systems development model which takes
elementary pedagogical considerations into account. Many well known accepted models
are very unsatisfactory according to this criterion.

Adequate tools and procedures are slowly penetrating into current practice and
will   potentially support participate efforts.

4. *The Belief in Policies - a Naive Superstition.*

Many progressive systems designers frequently complain about the reluctance of
most companies to declare and follow up powerful and unambiguous policies and expressions of will in those matters. Some even argue that further progress is un-
thinkable without the existence of such policies.

They will be disappointed. Top management is, and will remain, rather loosely committed to the progress of user participation within the company. Furthermore, experience shows that when top management for some reason formulates and signs such

a policy, this will tend to have very little immediate effect upon practice. Policies are generally very easily reformulated and intepreted so as to confirm present procedures and thinking, without significant modification of the latter.See
the theory of Muddling-through.

In any company, policies develop and spread as a result of initiatives and practice of vigorous individuals and interest groups. In other words, policies should
be regarded as an internal political issue. Policies of a general nature formulated by top management may only marginally influence upon this internal process
of policy-making.

Consequently, policies on user participation mainly emerge from the daily interaction between systems managers and representatives of the user community. The rules
and structure of this continuous policy-determining power game seem to be complicated and are generally very specific to each local environment. However, it seems
that the individuals possessing the keys to technology have a far more influential
power base than generally realized, or admitted by themselves. Therefore, progressive systems professionals should strongly and openly implement their intentions
in their daily practice instead of being paralyzed by a felt lack of policy from
the echelons above.

Policies are generally invisible to most people until they are directly readable
from current practice. If real codetermination is experienced to be embedded in
the management of actual systems projects within the company, then a true and
meaningful change of policy is accomplished, and will eventually be accepted by
top management. Corporate policy-making is an integral part of general management,
possessing one of its main characteristics - pragmatism.

5. *A Continuous Process of Organizational Learning.*

Development of meaningful codetermination practice is basically a question of
broad organizational learning for all those effected by new systems. But learning
processes cannot be switched on and off, in the same way as systems projects traditionally have been activated and deactivated. Organizational learning processes
must be of a continuous character and steadily be kept alive. They must be an integral part of organization and management practice. Therefore, real codetermination processes will only be a faint dream among progressive systems designers if
codetermination is suddenly called for within the narrow and limited framework of
a certain systems project, without any continuity and attachment to previous organizational policy and practice. This is the dilemma of progressive systems people of today. And probably this will answer the general question; why is development so slow?

Contemporary research and thinking on the role of information in work organizations,
quite independent of the democratization issue, indicate that systems development
generally should be conceived of as a learning process for the company. This process should include as many of the end users as practically possible. This approach is perfectly identical with the basic prerequisites for general development
of a democratic work environment as prescribed by legislation and general political development in the Scandinavian countries. Those two innovative activites may
therefore powerfully support each other, - but they will also be mutually restric-
tive.

REFERENCES:

[1.] Lindblom C.E. & Hirschman A.O., Economic Development, Research and Develop-
    ment, Policymaking 1962, in Emery, F.E (ed):Systems Thinking, London, 1969.

[2.] Höyer R., Systems Design and Social Reality; Formal and Informal Aspects of
    Administative Control, Personnel Review, No 1, 1976, pp 5-12.

[3.] Höyer R., Information Systems Supporting Organization Development, In Samet,
    P.A.(Ed): Proceedings Euro-IFIP 79, North-Holland, Amsterdam, 1979.
[4.] Selnick P.,Foundations of the Theory of Organization,1948.Reprinted in Litte-
    rer,J.A(Ed):Organizations:Structure & Behaviour,John Wiley,New York,1963.

The Information Systems Environment
Lucas, Land, Lincoln, Supper (Editors)
North-Holland Publishing Company
© *IFIP, 1980*

THE INFORMATION SYSTEM DESIGNER AS A
NURTURING AGENT OF A SOCIO-TECHNICAL PROCESS

Jean-Claude Courbon
Marcel Bourgeois

Institut d'Administration des Entreprises
Université des Sciences Sociales
Grenoble
FRANCE

The process of Information System design is one of coupling a
technical process, moving from Analysis and Design to Implementation, and a parallel social process, moving from consciousness about the system to building norms of behavior with
it. Given the emerging trends of people values, organizational reality and technological capabilities, it is argued that
information system designers have to cope with a large variety of situations, and instead of only being asked to apply appropriate methods correctly, have to rely more and more on
their ability to monitor fuzzy processes. In the case of managerially-oriented systems, designers will have to be more
nurturing agents than change agents.

INTRODUCTION

The field of information systems has been recently invigorated again after the
disillusions caused by the exaggerated claims for MIS in the early ' 70 s. Researchers and practitioners recognize the growing importance of non-technical matters
in information system design and implementation (Keen and Scott-Morton (1978)).
These considerations have led to a view of an information system as the product of
people, with their roles and behavior, of an organization with its rules and objectives, and of communication and technology. The process of Information System
design is one of coupling a technical process, moving from Analysis and Design to
Implementation, and a parallel social process, moving from consciousness about the
system to building norms of behavior with it. Given the emerging trends of people
values, organizational reality and technological capabilities, it is argued that
information system designers have to cope with a large variety of situations.
Instead of only being asked to apply appropriate methods correctly, designers have
to rely more and more on their ability to monitor fuzzy processes. In the case of
managerially-oriented systems, they will have to be more nurturing agents than
change agents.

NEW CONSIDERATIONS IN INFORMATION SYSTEM DESIGN

People as Part of the Information System

More attention is being given to the fact that information systems have to deal

with people ; the increase of productivity in the mechanics of collecting, generating and processing of information is not the only reason for user interest. One
knows that at the level of clerical work however, total or partial automation can
create more problems than it can solve. Moreover, it is recognized that information system design cannot be reduced to computer intervention in recording, memo-
rizing or processing transactions. Emphasis is being placed on the contribution
of the information system to the management of an organization. But this was already the claim behind the ideas of MIS in the early ' 70 s which failed, causing
information systems specialists to become very cautious about the idea of contributing to decision processes in organizations. Among the reasons for these failures, one can put forward the longing for integration, the excessive confidence in
and emphasis on technology and the lack of knowledge of organizational reality and
human behavior. Fortunately, researchers and practitioners are dealing with this
particular role of information systems, but with renewed ideas deeply rooted in
human and organizational realities.

Melese (1979), for example, speaks about information "desires" as opposed to information needs. Obviously systems analysts have felt more comfortable with expressed needs which can be fitted to computer systems. Methods tend to confine
managers to this formulation of needs. But people in organizations are in informational situations involving desires, and this plays down the role of the computer while enlarging the concept of information systems,making it more relevant.

In the same way information system must be able to allow managers to form their
own understanding and interpretation of situations : this can be done by having
managers take an active attitude about information, consider it from different
standpoints. Managers should avoid "optical illusions", which make their "needs"
unpredictable and difficult to satisfy. The emergence of personalized systems and
the recognition of the importance of the learning process (people must learn about
systems, but also about their problems) illustrate the fact that information systems can indirectly contribute to the organization's effectiveness by helping people first. This notion contrasts sharply (or complements ?) the accepted view of
information systems serving first the organization by requiring people to "behave"
correctly. The consequence for the designer is that he must participate in the
manager's problems, whereas the common view was that the managers were those who
had to participate in the analysis and design problems.

Information System Design and Organizational Reality

Much has been said about the organizational implications of information systems
design. Some aspects will be emphasized here. First, the survival of an organization is conditioned by its ability to adapt. This adaptation requires the capacity
to effectively perform three types of activities :
- in short-term management of operations, an efficient utilization of present
  resources which will provide the necessary slack resources for tomorrow's
  renewed activities ;
- in long-term planning, an effort to invent new types of actions, to grasp
  new opportunities and to forecast economic, political and social changes ;
- the middle-term task for management is that of change, i.e the path from a
  short-term satisfying situation to the future state aimed at the long-term
  vision.

These activities are implemented by individuals and groups with their skills and
own particular objectives. Power plays take place inside the rules (or for altering)
these rules) accepted by the organizations (Crozier and Friedberg (1978)). In this
picture the information system is not passive or neutral.

In the short-term the organization attributes languages to individuals and groups :
the information system has to help them to speak their own language better and
then to facilitate negotiation between them. The information system has also to

put order in the knowledge state about operations and transactions. Up to now, the
latter role has been fairly well played, although too many organizations do not go
further.

Indeed, in long-term activities, the information system has to put some kind of
disorder : the necessary slack, fuzziness and informal information from which tomorrow's order will emerge (Hedberg and Jonsson (1978)). New ideas are usually
produced by individuals and then have to be assumed by a group. Thereafter other
groups need to interpret, assimilate, modify or appropriate the idea. The information system, particularly the communications component, has an important part to
play in these phases of invention, promotion and consolidation of novelty.

A MODEL OF THE INFORMATION SYSTEM DESIGN PROCESS

There is a technical aspect in the process of designing an information system. This
aspect is clearly recognizable and has been up to now the focus of concern. To put
it simply, this process goes from Analysis to Implementation.

Figure 1   The Technical Process of IS Design

But in parallel,there is another process going on in the organization where the
new information system is being constructed. Call this a social process in which
people and groups become aware of what is going on, talk about it, interpret what
is being said (or not said) ; in short people become conscious of a change. Pro-
gressively, these people form some expectations, cristallize attitudes, as a general rule develop norms of behavior about dealing with the end product.

Figure 2 The Social Process of IS Design

Most of the problems which have been encountered in IS Design have come from a lack of concern or from the ignorance of this social process. This condition leads to a lack of congruence between the technically designed Information System to be implemented and the norms of individuals who will be concerned in the implementation phase.

Fortunately, there is now a recognition that these two parallel processes do occur and that they have to be coupled in some way for a success in the information system design process. This coupling can be done in different ways described now.

The Technocratic Approach

In the technocratic approach, the coupling - as illustrated by the solid arrow in Figure 3 - is accomplished by trying to manage the sequence of the technical process followed by the social process :

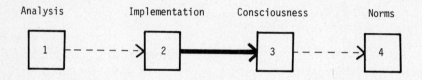

Figure 3   The Technocratic Approach

Relying on the quality of the technical design, one tries to delay any discussion about the system after it is working. There is a heavy commitment to information, education and even manipulation in order to have people develop norms congruent with the technical object which will not be altered except for cosmetic improvements. Conditions for the success of this approach are rarely met, although it can be used in certain circumstances.

The Traditional System Analysis Approach

Another way of coupling these two processes is the opposite of the technocratic, i.e having the social process precede the technical one.

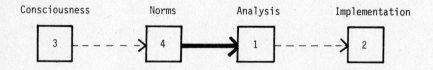

Figure 4   The System Analysis Approach

Future users are asked to express themselves about the new system and their norms are transformed into specifications which will be transformed into the final system during the technical phase. This approach supposes that designers can freeze the norms as long as the technical process takes place, that is, they can avoid the social process to continue system development.

The Participative Approach

Since it is difficult, or not desirable to have future users removed from the technical process, one may want to manage through participation the parallel coupling of the social and technical processes, as illustrated Figure 5.

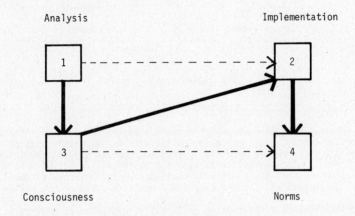

Figure 5   The Participative Approach

Users are involved early in analysis, participate in design, and are active all along. Hopefully user norms will be in accordance with the implementation of the information system. The participative approach, as described here, couples the two processes in a linear way, i.e. moving from a starting point continuously to a final product , the new information system. The participative approach has been advocated usually for large transactional systems highly dependent on clerical workers.

The Evolutionary Approach

In contrast with the preceding approaches which follow a linear path in coupling the processes, it is possible to accomplish coupling in a cyclical way, as illustrated in Figure 6.

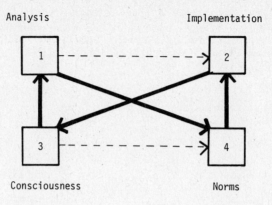

Figure 6   The Evolutionary Approach

Here, the information system is built in small steps, incrementally. At each cycle in systems development, users are able to live with a new, usable version of the system (box 2). Users derive from this active use the feeling and the desire for improvement (box 3), conceptualize it with the designer (box 1) who will build a revised version on which the users will develop expectations (box 4) about the new use (box 2) which then will be the base for a new life cycle of the system.

For managerially-oriented information systems this evolutionary process is isomorphic with Kolb's model of the learning process (Kolb (1974)). Indeed, Figure 6 illustrating the evolutionary approach to information system design can be placed in the following equivalent form.

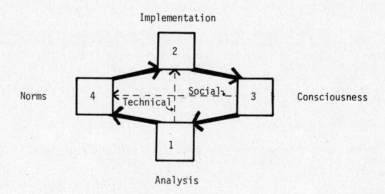

Figure 7   The Evolutionary Approach

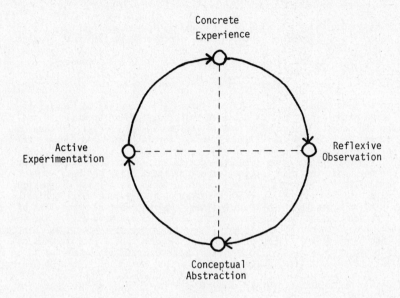

Figur 8   Kolb's Model of the Learning Process

Figures 7 and 8 are identical if one equates experience with implementation, observation with consciousness, abstraction with analysis and experimentation with norms.
The representation of the evolutionary approach is, in fact, a learning model. But
why should one be interested in the fact that building an information system might
(or should) follow a learning process ? In the case of managerially-oriented information systems, one can answer that an information system is the system by which
individuals and the organization become informed, which means acquiring knowledge :
learning is the process by which one acquires knowledge. But knowledge is an additive and synergistic construction and only the use of an information system (not
the information system in itself) produces cumulative knowledge. In this type of
information system, the designer has to be aware of this dynamic learning process
which has to be translated into a design of implementation strategy.

Following and accompanying the learning process of managers and of the organization
imposes a strong challenge for information systems designers.

IMPLICATIONS FOR THE DESIGN OF MANAGERIALLY-ORIENTED INFORMATION SYSTEMS

The information system is an integral part of an organization (in the sense of an
organized human construct). Systems analysts have for a long time considered the
organization as an automaton. In this picture, the designer's role was to formalize

needs, inputs, outputs and processing. Formalization was accomplished through the use of methods, models or frameworks.

What has been said above adds a vision of the organization as an organism, i.e an interacting, adapting and evolving living system. Therefore, systems must present the following qualities :
  - be individualized (at the level of a person or a group, for autonomy),
  - be simple and easy of use,
  - be flexible.

Present formal methods to design information systems are too rigid to provide these qualities. Formal methods rest upon a detailed analysis, leading to well defined specifications and careful design. The time to implement systems easily exceeds one year. These formal methods are useful and necessary for important and complex transactions processing systems. The life cycle of other systems will, in many cases, be a lot shorter. This point can be illustrated with the industry of air transportation. On the one hand, the transactional aspect of the airline business implies long life cycle systems : aircraft with a life of 10 to 20 years (with progressive adaptations on a basic model) or reservation systems with the same characteristics. On the other hand, the management of this business implies constant remodeling of services offered from season to season, from one market to another, etc... The information systems departments will also have these two types of systems, as pointed out by Ness and Hurst (1978) . They differentiate between type P (for processing) and type S (for support) systems. Type S systems will increase in number and in importance, will have short life cycles and will be very different from each other.

Will formal design methods be useful for S systems ? In the view of the characteristics of these systems, it can be hypothesized that methods will be less important than the ability of the system designers to manage the process of implementation.

It is apparent that for the management of organizations, the use of Operations Research or Management Science formal models will lessen and emphasis will be placed on action, either by relying on man or waiting to manage events when they happen (see as an example, among many Hall (1975) .The same phenomenon is appearing with information systems applications : operational and functional managers find themselves uncomfortable with the constraints and delays imposed by rules from the information system departments, and / or disappointed by results. At the same time, all the ingredients are here for strongly challenging information system department's traditional modes of action (Canning (1978)). Mini and micro-computers, distributed processing, networks and easily accessed software make it feasible for managers to build their own information systems support.

What is happening is that managers are becoming less and less impressed by computer technology and more aware of the multiplicity of possible uses of the technology. At the same time, managers are in a position to question the methodologies which were imposed on them by information system departments whose status in the organization has coincidentally been lowered. Managers know that a too strong a link between information and decision is an error and that top down approaches miss their real problems. Managers also know that they cannot (and do not want to) be reduced to tasks and functions in the organization : the tools brought to them by bottom-up approaches are too closely related to this limited view of their roles from which they want and need to escape. For them, the word Decision is mythical : managers cannot have a clear view of what they decide, when nor how. They are very conscious of the importance of their information system, but the way they become informed is multifaceted and continuously evolving. The formalized and technologically supported part of this information system must therefore be flexible and balanced.

The challenge to MIS departments is important. Their expertise in technology (not only computer) will be taken for granted. Applying well-defined methods for designing and implementing applications will not be enough because designers will be

asked for other additional skills, actually the ones needed to monitor fuzzy processes. The dynamic aspects of information system applications have been recently
emphasized. The designer is involved in a change process (Alter and Ginzberg
(1978)), a political process (Keen and Gerson (1977)), a socio-technical process
(Mumford and Pettigrew (1975)) and a learning process (Argyris (1976)). All this
research indicates that the designer's role as a change agent is becoming paramount. But this role is mostly related to large and complex transactions processing systems which are viewed by the organization as unavoidable and whose analysis, design and implementation has to be conducted as smoothly as possible.

It is argued here that a new breed of designers will emerge for managerially-oriented systems. More than being change agents, they will have to be nurturing agents.
This means that designers will be involved in the whole information environment
managers. Designers will follow managerial learning processes, support the manager's continuous adaptation to constantly changing situations and help in intelligence building. This view also obliges information system departments to adapt
their modes of intervention. Designers will be "sent" close to managers or operational / functional departments and act like craftsmen in very small teams or
alone. Some organizations are already following approaches based on these ideas
(Courbon, Grajew and Tolovi (1979) ; Earl (1978)). The purpose is to allow the
creation of the necessary variety (in Ashby's sense) of the organization's information system which obviously creates a major challenge for the designer.

The answer to this challenge may create the conditions necessary for the revival
of MIS ideas.

148   J.-C. COURBON, M. BOURGEOIS

REFERENCES

(1) Alter, S. and Ginzberg, M., Managing uncertainty in Mis implementation, Sloan Management Review. (Fall 1978).
(2) Argyris, C., Double loop learning in organizations, Harvard Business Review. (September-October 1976).
(3) Canning, R., Get ready for major changes, EDP Analyzer. (November 1978).
(4) Courbon, J.C., Grajew, J. and Tolovi, J., Conception et mise en oeuvre des systèmes interactifs d'aide à la décision : l'approche évolutive, Informatique et gestion. (Janvier 1979).
(5) Crozier, M. and Friedberg, E., L'Acteur et le Système (Seuil, 1978).
(6) Earl, M., Prototype systems for management information and control, Accounting Organizations and Society. 2 (1978) 161-170.
(7) Hall, W.K., Why risk analysis isn't working, Long Range Planning. (December 1975).
(8) Hedberg, B. and Jonsson, S., Designing semi-confusing information systems for organizations in changing environment, Accounting Organizations and Society. 1 (1978) 47-64.
(9) Keen, P. and Gerson, E., The politics of software decision, Datamation (November 1977).
(10) Keen, P. and Scott-Morton, M., Decision Support Systems : an organizational perspective (Addison Wesley, 1978).
(11) Kolb, D.A., On management and the learning process, in : Kolb, D.A., Rubin, I. M. and Mc Intyre, J.M., Organizational Psychology, (Prentice Hall, 1974).
(12) Mélèse, J., Analyse Systémique des Organisations (Hommes et Techniques, 1979).
(13) Mumford, E. and Pettigrew, A., Implementing Strategic Decision (Longman Group Limited, 1975).
(14) Ness, D. and Hurst, G., Characterizing Type-P and Type-S Systems, Working Paper 78-03-01, the Wharton School, Pennsylvania Univ. (1978).

The Information Systems Environment
Lucas, Land, Lincoln, Supper (Editors)
North-Holland Publishing Company
© *IFIP, 1980*

FRAMEWORK FOR PARTICIPATIVE SYSTEMS LONG RANGE PLANNING

Markku Sääksjärvi

Helsinki School of Economics
Runeberginkatu 14-16 A
00100 Helsinki 10
Finland

A participative methodology for systems long range planning is
presented, the aim of which is to satisfy the ever growing need
for more formal long range planning procedures of information
systems.

Analysis of user needs is a central activity during the
planning procedure. We discuss methods for involving
different user groups in planning to fit systems objectives
with overall objectives.

The paper is based on methods development for the Finnish
state administration.

INTRODUCTION

There seems to be a major pitfall in the common approach of developing computer-
based systems on the basis of independent applications. In spite of the fact
that the price of hardware has dropped very rapidly, there is a growing need for
more formal planning and design methods for total information systems architecture.
This need exists because the systems are becoming more complex, take longer to
develop, involve multiple departments, have a greater impact and change the
organization and work systems.

Conventional technical systems design methods are not very suitable for long
range planning. One major reason is the great need to communicate actively both
with top management and system users to obtain priorities for development
activities. A participative approach to planning should be developed which
provides procedures that allow for the varying needs of the different division
and on integration of top management and user objectives. A framework for such
a technique has been developed in Finland to be used and implemented in the State
administration. This paper presents the main principles of a methodology called
METO.

WHY A LONG RANGE PLAN ?

The time delays in application software development are long. Normally, the
freezing of automated functions for a period of about ten years results from the
decision to implement a new system. A long range EDP plan is really needed and it
should be prepared with care. It is also possible to get major savings from a
better coordination of resource use. For that reason, some preliminary design is
needed to define the main files, data flows, systems and subsystems and the
connections of data processing to word, image and voice processing.

The fundamental questions to be answered by the planning procedure are:

a. How does the information service contribute to the overall success
of the enterprise (organization)?

b. How could the contribution be developed better: what kind of
applications and services are needed?

c. What type of technology is to be used in the future?

d. What type of management, staff and new work positions are to be
developed?

e. What is the impact of planned development on the host organization,
the professional milieu and job satisfaction?

NEED FOR PARTICIPATION

The typical long range planning procedure currently used is the top-down, bottom-up procedure. General objectives are formulated by top management and transmitted to divisions, which in turn prepare divisional plans. The plans are then presented to top management for review and approval. But does this process work for systems development planning?

In most cases top management is not aware of the details and problems of departmental EDP systems. EDP management and users for their part are often more interested in modifying existing systems to meet new requirements or to utilize new technology. It is difficult to get an overall top-down picture of information systems architecture and its contribution to business. Without an extensive collection of facts about the current situation it will not be possible for management to formulate concrete objectives for systems development.

On the other hand new theories and experience concerning user issues in participation have put much emphasis on the interface between systems specialists and different user groups. As the analysis stage of designing information systems seems to be more and more important, the participative approach should also be started during early planning phases.

Both of the above factors force us to develop a methodology which includes a systematic way of collecting facts, of analyzing current problems and the contribution of information systems to the enterprise, of designing a new system to support the future major activities and of improving the effectiveness of information systems.

It is also of great importance to improve the communications between top management and the EDP department as well as between EDP specialists and the users of EDP systems. This may be successfully accomplished by organized cooperation and participation during a formal, long-range systems planning procedure.

We think that the lack of feedback from existing systems is one of the major pitfalls in the current practice of project-oriented, technical systems development. The systems long-range planning procedure forces one to collect user's opinions and their experiences and to analyze them (˜superiteration˜ principle).

METHODOLOGY

A framework for MIS strategic planning has been proposed by McLean and Soden (1976). For practical work a more detailed methodology and working rules should be given. Further, participative activities should be carefully designed to provide means for real consensus and formal ways of applying the many new proposals included in the socio-technical systems design approach. For these reasons we have developed a participative method for systems long range planning.

The main aims of the method are:

> a. To mesh the systems objectives with host organization's objectives.
>
> b. To priorize and balance the user's needs and demands before final systems development goals are fixed.

The formal method consists of four main steps. For each step a group of central activities is defined by their role, their documentation, their participative procedures and their working tools (Sääksjärvi (1979)). In the following we discuss only the key points and from the participant's point of view.

Major Steps of The Method

The major task of strategic systems planning is to provide knowledge for a rational judgemental allocation of company resources to achieve stated goals. To achieve this the following steps should be carried out:

> a. Identification
> -Survey of major functions, their goals and the measures of effectiveness,
>
> -Identification of problems in achieving the goals and an estimate of the value of solving these problems,
>
> -Survey of current information systems, their contribution to the major functions, their costs and service level;
>
> b. Analysis
> -Analysis of the match of systems with current and future major functions, analysis of the problems identified and generation of systems development objectives;
>
> c. Construction and evaluation
> -Construction of new system proposals and alternatives, their main architecture, subsystems, files and information flows, generating the projects needed to transform the current systems into the new one, estimating the costs, benefits and other impacts and deciding on priorities;
>
> d. Collecting the final plan
> -Collecting of the ranked project proposals, translating them into a time-phased profile of activities, collecting the total resource requirements and fixing the final goals.

The main steps are decomposed into a detailed project network with activity descriptions (Sääksjärvi (1979)).

User Groups and Their Roles

The success of data processing depends very much upon the degree of satisfaction of user needs. Actually, the users are the only reason for the existence of systems. For long-range planning purposes we use the following classification:

> a. Top management
> -Responsible for the overall objectives and goals, initiation and financing of systems,

    b. Middle management (intermediate end-users); (Dolotta, Bernstein, etc
       (1976))
       -Responsible for decision making and operation of object systems,
       -Users of information generated by systems,

    c. Direct end users
       -People using systems in their work,

    d. Systems specialists (mid-users)
       -People who are responsible for practices and methods of systems
       development and production.

It is apparent that the main interest of these groups are very often nonparallel.
Thus, the systems long-range plan will be unbalanced if only one of the above
groups - e.g. top management - is involved in the planning procedure.

Participative Procedures

There are no direct routes from business goals to systems objectives and goals.
In our method the generated list of problems forms a needed link between goals and
systems objectives. But different user groups have perhaps even conflicting
opinions about the value of solving the problems and the weights of the objectives.
Thus, when designing new system proposals and projects, different groups would
like to allocate resources in different ways. Therefore, it is of importance to
communicate the varying needs of the user groups and also to try to balance them.
For that reason some participative procedures are needed.

The major participative activities and their character are the following:

    a. During identification a consultative project team collects facts
       about organization, business functions and systems by interviewing
       top management, middle management and key end users and by reviewing
       existing documents. The needed bottom-up approach to collect
       information about existing routines and systems can be well organized
       by letting the departments describe their routines by themselves using
       the V-graph technique of the ISAC-group (Nissen-Andersen (1977)).
       These graphs help the end users in defining problems and give valu-
       able facts about data volumes, time delays, resource needs, etc. We
       have seen that it is very motivating and useful to involve some key
       users in this type of cooperation work during the identification.

    b. During analysis we have successfully implemented a two-stage manage-
       ment seminar in order to generate systems objectives. First there
       is a top-management seminar to review collected facts, to rank the
       problems and to generate overall systems objectives from business
       objectives and goals. Then, a series of departmental seminars with
       team work will be arranged to handle the detailed lists of problems.
       Representatives of key end users are also involved in these seminars.
       Besides the collected written documents and lists of problems several
       tools can be utilized, e.g. matrices relating the systems to functions
       or problems to systems, productivity trends, cost trends, cost and
       manpower indices, V-graphs, etc.

    c. During construction, after the design of overall system proposals
       and the generation of projects, a major participative activity is
       needed to estimate the relations of projects to problems and to
       describe the impacts of new systems. For ranking projects a multi-
       value analysis is needed where the various user groups provide esti-
       mates for the projects and communicate them to other groups. In an

iterative procedure the project proposals will then be collected into
balanced sets of projects which will be translated into a time
phased profile establishing the final systems development goals.
Several tools and methods can be used in the multi-attribute analysis
(e.g. Hawgood (1974) and Land (1975)). The use of interactive
gaming also seems promising.

The role of documents in such a participative planning procedure is not that of
end products. More important than to produce paper is to help individuals learn
by doing. The participative process is important in itself. However, for
further development good documentation is needed; it also serves to prepare for
participation.

SUMMARY

Unfortunately, EDP long-range planning requires a rather considerable effort.
This effort is even greater if a proper and necessary participation by consensus
is to be realized during planning. Nevertheless, we believe that this effort
should be made at quite regular intervals and that, if properly carried out, is
of great value:

1. Planning provides a concrete way for management to manage the
   development of information systems and to be sure they contribute
   to business functions.

2. Utilization of advanced technology on a cooperative basis and
   coordination of software procurement can result in dramatic
   reductions in development costs.

3. A participative approach results in better motivation, in a
   reduction of uncertainty and isolation, and in better effectiveness and utilization of computer-based systems.

But it is good to remember that:

"Good formal planning must complement, but cannot replace, the political sensitivity, entrepreneurship, conceptual contribution and basis business leadership
required of the successful MIS executive" (McLean and Soden (1976)).

It should also be remembered that a long range plan is dynamic, not static. The
plan should be developed into a more detailed operational plan and budgets for
each successive year. The project proposals undergo normal systems development
phases with more detailed analysis, design and implementation. If participation
has begun during the earliest planning phases, there should be a better chance of
real participation in coming detailed design phases.

REFERENCES

[1] McLean, R. and Soden, J.V., Strategic Planning For MIS - A Conceptual Frame-
    work, in: AFIPS Conference Proceedings, AFIPS Press 1976, 425-432

[2] Sääksjärvi, M. (ed), Tietojenkäsittelyn kokonaistutkimuksen menetelmät, Hel-
    singin kauppakorkeakoulun ja valtiovarainministeriön kehittämisprojekti,
    Valtion painatuskeskus 1979

[3] Nissen, H.E. and Andersen, E.S., Systemering - Verksamhetsbeskrivningar
    (Studentlitteratur, Lund 1977)

[4] Hawgood, J., Quinquevalent Quantification of Computer Systems in: Friedlink

(ed),Economics of Informatics, (IBI-ICC International Symposium, Mainz 1974)

[5] Land, F.F., Evaluating of Systems Goals in Determining a Design Strategy For a Computer Based Information Systems, the Computer Journal, 19, no 4, 290-294

[6] Mumford, E. and Henshall, D., A Participative Approach To Computer Systems Design (Associated Business Press, 1979)

[7] Ciborra, G. and Gasbarri, G. and Maggioli, P.G., A Participative Approach to Systems Analysis: An Action Research In the Local Government,in: Lockemann (ed),Proceedings ECI-78 (Springer Verlag, 1978)

[8] Naor, J., Planning by Consensus - a Participative Approach to Planning, Advanced Mmgt Journal, 43 (1978), no 4, 40-47

[9] Sääksjärvi, M., Balancing User Needs in Systems Long Range Planning, Working Paper (Helsinki School of Economics 1979)

[10] Dolotta, T.A. and Bernstein, M.I., etc: Data Processing in 1980-85, (John Wiley & Sons 1976)

The Information Systems Environment
Lucas, Land, Lincoln, Supper (Editors)
North-Holland Publishing Company
© *IFIP, 1980*

A PARTICIPATIVE APPROACH

TO SYSTEMS DESIGN

PAUL BLOKDIJK

IBM NEDERLAND N.V.

This paper presents a description of a design procedure which
attempts to achieve an improvement in system design and to
maximize user participation.

The design is divided in two major steps: the Logical design,
and the Technical design, that is the translation of the first
step into software.

The Logical design, is done in steps, each of which uses a
graphical notation with two or three symbols. The result is
a top down analysis of the new system and the needed information,
a conceptual (relational) Data Base, and structured procedure
descriptions.

These methods were used on a 15 manyear project, in which an
experiment was performed with user communication during the
Logical design.

During detailed design, participation changed from concensus
design in the beginning to consultative design at the end
(Mumford, 1976).

THE REASON FOR INTENSIVE COMMUNICATION WITH USERS

The development of Information Systems (I.S.) is of interest
to a large number of DP professionals. The reason for this is:

1. The success of structured programming techniques in the
   programming area leads to an assumption that the same
   kind of approach is possible in the design area.

2. The increasing complexity of proposed DP applications
   and the increasing influence they have on the organization
   and behaviour of companies.

3. The failure or near failure of projects which use project
   management type of design techniques. These techniques
   expose what is to be done, not how.
Therefore the formula:

     EFFECT OF I.S. = QUALITY X APPRECIATION

was used as a base for the selection of new techniques
developed in this area.
Quality means not only good working programs and reliable
computer usage, but also programs which produce the results
the user needs and expects. Appreciation is somewhat more
complex. It includes a sense of happiness with the new
situation, a feeling of improvement.

Good user knowledge of the system is needed. This
knowledge is hard to gain, at least at the start of a new
situation, without having the user intensively involved
in the design process. Only participation during the design

will give users the system they want and the "do-it-yourself"
satisfaction required for good appreciation.

To facilitate communication between designer and user, a
language is needed. This language must fit into a method that
supports the solution of both users 'and designers' problems.
The designer faces such problems as: Complexity,

Consistency,

Completeness.

While users problems are: Imagination,

Overview,

Check the developed design.

Communication Pattern

The normal communication between users and DP personel
normaly has a fixed pattern: (see Figure 1)

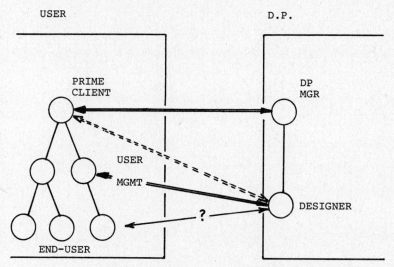

Normal User - DP Communications Pattern

Figure 1

The DP manager maintains the contact with the Prime Client.
The Prime client is the manager in whose responsibility area
the new system will be installed, but his personal situation
will not necessarily be changed.

The Prime client is mostly interested in the boundaries of
the system and delivers the "Change Motives", the most important reasons for the change. Together with the DP manager
she or he initiates the change and controls the progress of
the project. The Designers contact the Prime Client in the
beginning of the project, but after a while these contacts
will have a decreasing frequency. The Prime Client is not
interested in details.

The main source of information for the designers is user
managers, in most cases first line managers. These managers
are very much involved in the change. Their responsibility
area or their position in the organization may be changed.
This means that they have a changed bargaining position for
resources, an other influence in other parts of the
organization; the change may reduce or increase the work load
of their departments.

These users need a large amount of imagination, to understand
and think through an abstract model of the future organization.
Later, they have the problem of conversion. Are they able to
bring everything to the new organization without losing control
of the work that is at hand?

The End User is hardly ever involved in the design. However
he or she is subject to a complete change. Most managers are
still managers after the change, but in many cases the end user
has a complete different job. This job may be significantly
improved, or, on the other hand an extremely boring job may be
created.

The jobs are in most situations however completely design dependent. It is in this respect very odd that designers hardly
communicate with the end-users.
Research by Mumford (1974), among others, who have found that
the ideas and attitude of Information System Designers about
the jobs of the end-users, are very much in conflict with the
ideas of the end-user themselves.

The system designers are probably not the best job designers for
the end user possible. However in most cases the jobs are
designed and implemented without any communication with the
end users.

A SYSTEM ANALYSIS & DESIGN METHOD

The proposed procedure starts with Objective and Change
Analysis (Land, 1977).
A new working method is designed in the form of an Object
System. A top down model is constructed to describe systems;
the modelling must be Top Down to check its completeness.
With modelling dimensions are changed or they are even left
out. In the model in Figure 2 the timing and quantity aspects
are omitted: only in- and output, transformations and their
connections are shown.
This method, developed by the ISAC-group of the University
of Stockholm, managed by Lundeberg (1978) produces easy-to
understand graphs. Where Objective and Change Analysis together
with the Object System design can be handled by consensus,
Information analysis leads to a more representative system.

160   P. BLOKDIJK

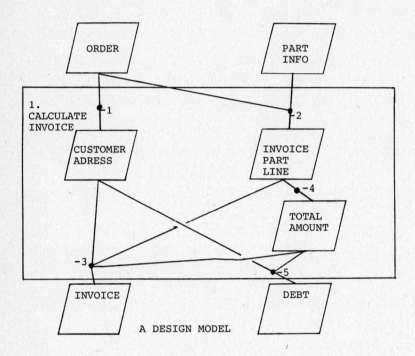

Figure 2

The final results of Information Analysis included Information
Elements or Elementary Messages. An Information Element contains
an object or entity identifier, one (and only one) attribute
name, and the time the attribute value is true. These Information
Elements are the input for component analysis and data base (DB)
design.

Data Base Design

To design a data base the association between identifier and
attribute is analyzed. Three assocation types are considered:

1.   Simple associations, e.g. a child has one and only one
      mother.

2.   Conditional associations: A man has one and only one
      wife, but he may be a bachelor.

3.   Multiple associations: A woman may have none; one or
      many children.

This analysis is done with consultation between users and
designers.

If an attribute of an identifier, is an identifier in an other
information element, a network of identifiers and attributes
can be built, into a conceptual schema (an example is given in
Figure 3).

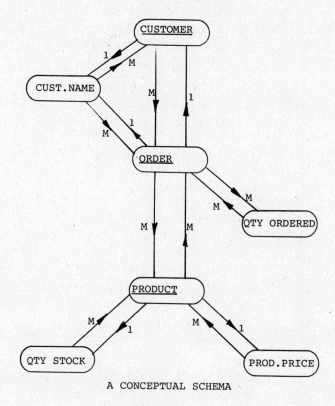

A CONCEPTUAL SCHEMA

Figure 3

To be able to store this information without difficulties this
schema is normalized to develop a data base following the
standards of relational data bases. Storage anomalies and
data redundancy are prevented.

For the normalization procedure the method of Vetter (1977) is
used. The active construction of the data base is done by the
designers without any participation by users.

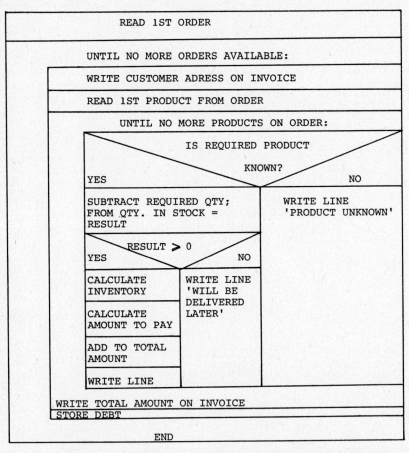

FIGURE 4   NASSI-SCHNEIDERMAN FLOWCHART

Process Analysis

Nassi Shneiderman (1973) flowcharts are used to describe
processes. They allow only 3 control patterns:

- Sequential (See 'write customer adress on invoice' followed
    by 'read 1 st product from order' Figure 4)
- If-then-else (See 'result   0' and 'yes' and 'no' blocks,
    Figure 4)
- Do while of Do until (See 'until no orders available',
    Figure 4)

From the graphical notation:

1.   The control structure is shown in another language
     as "production" activities, so the structure is
     easy to read and to understand.

2.   Processes are only described in a well structured
     way so programmers do not have te rewrite or redesign
     the process.

For Dialogues a start is made in a rough dialoque overview,
in which showa only an undisturbed sequence. (For an example:
see Figure 5).

Then screens are designed. Based on the screens user options
can be developed, as there are breakouts returns, jump
aheads etc. and with this information the detailed flow of
the screens is noted and checked. Due to the large number of
descriptions and the limited availability of users, this part
of the design is conducted with consultation.

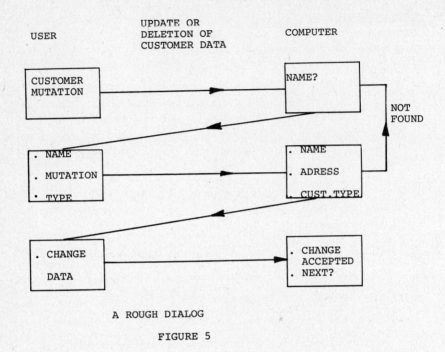

A ROUGH DIALOG

FIGURE 5

THE PROJECT

After a pilot project in which the design methods were tested,
a real project was started in February 1977.
In this project about 150 people were involved; about 25% of
the company assets are handled by the system.

In September 1977 the decision was made to work with a part-time
group of representatives of end users, instead of having an end
user representative on the project team. Part time was chosen
because it was impossible to assign a group of end users due to
capacity problems.
A presentation was given to all of the interested parties in
which included:
1.   Objectives and system boundaries of the new system,

2.   The object system sketch, as agreed upon by the
      steering committee,

3.   A motivation and request to begin a selection of
      an end user group to work in a participative design
      environment.

After these meetings, the group of user managers came to the
designers and asked for a second group so they could participate
in the design too.

In November 1977 both groups were installed. The end user group
contained 5 persons and the managers group 6. No one in either
group had any experience with DP, not even as users!
Meetings required was half a day a week.
A basic education course of 4 sessions was held to explain:

−   Basic Design principles as
     −   Top Down
     −   Object System Design
     −   I/A and N.S. graphs
In June 1978 the Logical Design was finished and the groups
were discontinued.

FINDINGS ON COMMUNICATION
The normal design approach consisted of having one user
representative in the project group. The designers felt that
working with the groups of representatives was far better
as with one user representative on the project group.
The reasons are:

1. After a while the representative has accepted the objectives
    of the group: to create a DP system in one way or another.
    He of she loses resistance against unfriendly design decisions.
2. The connections between the group and the rest of the users
    are too dependent on one person. After a while contacts
    become worse because users think that their representative
    is betraying them. Therefore in most cases this represen-
    tative can not return to the user department.

Only in situations where the design group is managed by and
constructed by users and a DP representative, can this effect
be reversed.
However in most situations this is impossible because the people
can not be spared or the design takes too long.

The main problem with working with this group was the imagination
of the users. The IA graphs and NS graphs are readable and
logical, but it is still hard for them to picture their personal
situation for a non-existing system, and to see if it is what they
want. It is not a fight against the logic of the system, these
problems are solvable, but against hidden problems being overlooked.
Simulation tools are very much needed. The next time at least
the dialogues will be simulated on-line, so that the screen
lay-outs and sequence can be changed easily.

THE OPINION SURVEY

In August 1978 an opinion survey was completed to find the
reactions of the participants. Ten of the 11 group members filled
in the questionaries. The opinion survey was the same for both
groups and anonymous, but it was known from which group the answers
were recieved.

The results are:

%

	positive	neutral	negative
- What has it done for you?	100	0	0
- How do you judge your impact on the design?	100	0	0
- Did you like the way we organized it? Other suggestions?	80	20	0
- Did you think the frequency of the meetings was right? (The 30% thought that only a meeting was to be held if the designers thought it necessary)	70	0	30
- The quantity of the information?	100	0	0
- The contents of the design information? (30% had problems with the language used in the design, 10% missed good minutes of the meetings).	60	40	0

P. BLOKDIJK

THE OPINION SURVEY

In August 1978 an opinion survey was completed to find the
reactions of the participants. Ten of the 11 group members filled
in the questionaries. The opinion survey was the same for both
groups and anonymous, but it was known from which group the answers
were recieved.

The results are:

%

	positive	neutral	negative
- What has it done for you?	100	0	0
- How do you judge your impact on the design?	100	0	0
- Did you like the way we organized it? Other suggestions?	80	20	0
- Did you think the frequency of the meetings was right? (The 30% thought that only a meeting was to be held if the designers thought it necessary)	70	0	30
- The quantity of the information?	100	0	0
- The contents of the design information? (30% had problems with the language used in the design, 10% missed good minutes of the meetings).	60	40	0
- Education in the design graph's?	100	0	0
- Education in the computer possibilities (10% missed the meeting in which the education was given)	80	10	10
- How did you think about the designers reactions on your comments	90	10	0

In our opinion the results for this first experiment are very positive, especially as one takes into account that none of the members had any experience with D.P. before. The most important aspect the designers learned from the experiment was that their knowledge of the social aspects of organizations and should be incorporated in their education.

Also the DP organization has to adjust to support the new approach. In summeray the participative approach performed with Information Analysis and other design tools was very effective in this case.

REFERENCES

1) E. Mumford, Computer Systems and Work Design: Problems of
   Philosophy and Vision, Personnel Review vol 3 no. 2 spring 1974

2) M. Lundeberg, A Systematic Approach to Information Systems
   Development - Part I:, Introduction, General Report,
   TRITA - IBADB- 4223 University of Stockholm, Dept. of Informa-
   tion Processing, 1978

3) M. Vetter, Principles of Data Base Systems, paper presented at
   the International Computing Symposium (ICS 77/ACM) Liege,
   Belgium.

4) I. Nassi-
   B. Shneiderman, 'Flowchart Techniques for structured
   Programming', SIGPLAN notices '73, Dept. of Computer Science,
   State University of New York, Stony Brook.

5) E. Mumford, Industrial democracy and system design, 8
   Computer Bulletin 1976

6) F.F. Land, Evaluation of system goals in determining a design
   strategy for a computer based information system, The computer
   journal vol 19 nr. 4.

METHODOLOGIES AND TOOLS

The Information Systems Environment
Lucas, Land, Lincoln, Supper (Editors)
North-Holland Publishing Company
© *IFIP, 1980*

SYSTEMS REQUIREMENTS ANALYSIS -
METHODS AND MODELS.

Leif B. Methlie

Institute for Information Systems Research
Norwegian School of Economics and Business Administration
Bergen, Norway

Two perspectives on information systems development are discussed.
The first perspective, the datalogical, takes the information requirements as given by the existing data flows in the organization
and the objective of the systems development task is to improve
efficiency. The infological perspective, on the other hand, looks
for an effective information system for the organization. The
datalogical approach seems to be dominating in current systems work,
and some reasons for this are discussed. A methodology based on the
infological approach is presented. It consists of four tasks, boundary analysis, functional specifications, systems requirements analysis, and information processing modeling. This paper discusses
the functional architecture of systems, but emphasis is on a systematic approach to establish goals and constraints and information
requirements.

THE PROBLEM

Two perspectives on Information Systems Design

Information requirements can be studied on the level of individuals in an organization; how they interpret and utilize data. An information system is then
viewed as an interconnected network of users and data flows. On the other hand,
information can be studied on the organizational level; what are the information
needs of the organization to perform its tasks. In this case task uncertainty
and functional division of tasks determine the communication pattern, and thus,
the information system of the organization. The greater the task uncertainty,
the greater the amount of information that must be processed to achieve a given
level of performance.

In this paper we shall look at the information system requirements from an organizational point of view. Design choices for information systems will be discussed
and a model to describe organizations, here called object systems, will be presented. Designing information systems from organizational needs leads to effective information systems.

Faced with the problem of changing information systems in organizations, two
approaches or perspectives can be taken:

(1) a datalogical perspective

(2) an infological perspective.

The datalogical perspective regards the existing data flows as satisfactory representations of the information needs in the organization. The aim of a change task
is to find more efficient ways of processing the existing data. A common solution
is to computerize manual procedures and data files. The benefits of this approach

are primarily of the cost-savings type. This perspective is the traditional computer application view and is still common in current systems work. The problem is defined as a technical one and system development is a matter of designing an efficient computer application. In recent years the influence of technology on the working environment has been much in focus. Thus, the datalogical perspective has been extended to encompass behavioral aspects as well as technical aspects.

The infological perspective of information systems design looks at the organization as an information processing system. Communication and control aspects are in focus. Information is the knowledge communicated between individuals and groups needed to perform organizational tasks. The focus of this perspective is to find an effective information systems for the whole or part of the organization to which the information system is to give service. Task uncertainty and inter-task dependencies become the primary sources of information requirements. These requirements cannot be determined without analyzing the tasks structure of the organization. While the datalogical perspective accepts the existing data flows as an adequate representation of the information requirements, the infological perspective regards these flows as a construct of a previous design and not necessarily a good basis for a new design. When applying new technologies the communications pattern may change. The infological view treats the problems of information system design more fundamentally. The kind and amount of information is determined from the task uncertainty and intertask dependencies. Data structures and data processing requirements are determined on the basis of semantic aspects.

It is often said that design and implementation begin before the problem is really defined and the real needs and system functions are fully known. The difference between the datalogical and the infological approach is not that the problem is unstated, but rather there is a difference in the aims of the system development task and in problem definition. The datalogical view can be said to be more process-oriented; that is, computer technology is applied to data processes where improved efficiency can be obtained. Therefore, the methodology applied is process-oriented. Flow charts are used to document processes, data flows and data storages. Design issues are applied to sub-processes and users are mostly involved in technical aspects and behavioral aspects at man-machine interaction points.

The infological approach, on the other hand, is more product-oriented, i.e. output-oriented. Here, we concentrate on the outputs of the information system and how the information is used in the organization. Only by having clearly defined and understandable system outputs can an effective information system be designed. A systems approach can be applied to systematically analyze the information needs and system functions. By decomposing a system into its components, communications requirements due to task uncertainty and intertask dependencies can be specified. Diagrams more than flow charts are used to discuss with the users and management the system requirements and the problem statements. Infological approaches to systems development can be found in Ross and Schoman (1977), Methlie (1978) and Langefors (1973). Structured development is a term much used currently. However, applying techniques like HIPO (IBM (1977)) or Warnier diagram (Orr (1977)) do not necessarily give an infological perspective on systems development.

Why does current systems work take the more narrow approach to systems design even though the literature has emphasized the need for more comprehensive problem definition before design issues are addressed? Problems are not unstated in the datalogical approach, but they are limited to technical problems of efficiency in data processing. We can list some factors to support the datalogical approach:

(1)   Proposals for changes in the information systems very often emerge in the data processing department.

(2)   The data processing department is primarily staffed with computer technologists.

(3)   The scope of the design task is in the outset limited to technical aspects (efficiency).

(4)   Because of the technical nature of the task, management is less concerned and their participation is limited to approvement of proposals on the basis of some kind of cost-benefits analysis.

(5)   Changes restricted to data processing efficiency aspects have little impact on management. Thus, they will approve a more narrow scope on the the task.

(6)   Impatiance by system designers to get on with building systems more than "waste" time on analysis of system requirements.

(7)   Problems of systems requirements analysis are more abstract in nature than design of computer programs and files.

(8)   The actual benefits of a more extensive analysis task are intangible. It may seem that a more comprehensive systems analysis delays the project and increases development costs.

(9)   No established methodology exists for an infological approach.

(10)   Systems analysts are not educated for the wider perspective on the problem.

Technical and Political Issues in Systems Design

In crude terms we can divide the system development task into three sub-tasks: (1) requirements analysis, (2) technical development (design and programming) and (3) implementation. It would be easier if these tasks could be performed in distinct phases following each other in the above sequence. However, one of the most difficult aspects in development is determining when system development is "finished" and whether or not the system meets the predefined specifications.

Due to changes in the organization which are not under control of the system development task group, new requirements may be imposed on the system continously during development. Furthermore, specifying requirements is a learning process for the users who will have difficulties in discussing "paper" solutions. As they learn from the system they may identify new opportunities and needs. In these situations it is rather difficult to determine if what was intended has been accomplished. When criteria for success are ambigous and lack a simple measure, decisions on systems specifications appear arbitrary from the perspective of different groups.

Due to these aspects a school of thought emphasizing political and behavioral aspects in systems design has emerged in recent years. Keen and Gerson (1977) criticize the more formalized engineering approach to systems development and says:

"Thus, the value of recent techniques for involving users in the design process (structured "walkthroughs", prototype development, IBM's HIPO procedures etc.) is that they encourage the emergence of potential conflicting goals. If conflicts are left unidentified and unresolved, they may emerge later when the systems development effort is most vulnerable to changes, withdrawal of support or loss of momentum".

Resolution of potential conflicting goals are an important part of the requirements analysis irrespective of a datalogical or an infological approach. In both approaches users should be involved; in the datalogical perspective socio-technical issues are raised particularly around man-machine interaction points. In the infological perspective the whole range of organizational, behavioral and socio-technical issues are addressed. Is a muddling through process the only way to reach systems specifications or can a methodology based on more analytical approaches be developed? An analytical approach requires a firm statement of the problem. Conflicting goals can also emerge from misunderstandings about what the system will do.

> "The inability to set clear, measurable goals would be funny if it weren't so common. Human beings seem to want to do anything other than think through the problem. This unfortunate tendency means starting on details before the important work of setting goals and objectives has been completed. And getting started to early on the wrong thing leads in turn to a variety of dead ends. We will discuss some of these dead ends, but without a doubt the single largest cause of systems failure is not defining clear, understandable, and measurable goals at the outset". (Orr (1977)).

We believe that systems work can be improved if systems requirements can be determined from the organizational needs. Effectiveness is not obtained by setting some (and often conflicting) goals in an ad hoc manner. Only by a systematic approach, where goals, constraints and information requirements are determined simultaneously, can an effective information system be designed.

SYSTEM REQUIREMENTS

System requirements must encompass everything necessary to lay the groundwork for subsequent design. Requirements analysis is a careful assessment of the needs that a system is to fulfill. It must say why a system is needed and what system features will serve and satisfy these overall needs. When we use the term "system" we have to be careful with what we actually mean. System is a recursive concept, that is, a system can be decomposed into subsystems each of which can be decomposed into new subsystems etc.. We can look at the organization as a system. The system will then encompass different kinds of flows, money, orders, material, information etc.. Forrester (1961) observed that industrial organizations are strongly characterized by closed-loop structures.

> An industrial organization is a complex interlocking network of information channels. These channels emerge at various points to control physical processes such as the hiring of employees, the building of factories, and the production of goods. Every action point in the system is backed up by a local decision point whose information sources reach into other parts of the organization and the surrounding environment.

The information system is a subsystem in the organization. It is designed to give services to this organization by initiating and controlling actions, by supporting decision-making and coordination and by motivating behavior. It is in the organization that the actual needs for information can be identified. Thus, in an infological perspective, requirements analysis must deal with the organization. We shall call that part of the organization for which we want to design a new information system, the object system. The subject areas of system requirements analysis are:

(1)   boundary analysis;
(2)   functional specifications;
(3)   systems requirements analysis;
(4)   Information processing modeling.

A brief description of these subject areas will be given below. Emphasis is put on area 3. However, later we will return to a model in which we can specify the functional architecture of the object system.

Boundary analysis: Conditions calling for an information system change task must
be stated followed by a statement of the problem and an analysis of boundary conditions of the object system. Analysis of boundary conditions consists of defining
components in the system environment and their relationships with the system. The
results of the boundary analysis are: delineation of the object system from its
environment and the overall functional properties (sometimes termed external properties) of this system.

Functional specifications: From the external properties we can decompose the system into functional processes; that is, the essential decisions and actions required to manage and operate the object system in order to produce the required
output. Functions combine resources and processes into structures of actions,
decisions and data processing working on resources like material, capital, information etc. (see Figure 1). An object system decomposed into functions and functional relationships we call the functional architecture of the system. Note that
functional architecture is not to be confused with the existing organization structure. Each function can be decomposed into a number of sub-functions, which in
turn involve any number of decisions and actions. An example is an order processing function consisting of the sub-functions: customer-service, inventory and
accounting (see Figure 4).

Functional specification of an object system provides a comprehensive understanding
of .how the system accomplishes its objectives. We shall separate management control from transaction processes and production processes (the processes to be controlled). We will use a control perspective to analyze and understand information
needs. Control-information flows into action-points and feed-back information is
transmitted back to the management system. Furthermore, information is used to
process orders (transaction processing). Functional specifications of an object
system are founded on a generic universe of resource-objects and processes. Hence,
the functional architecture of our object system is both modular and hierarchic.
Information requirements can now be determined from the end-use of information at
actions and decision points. This end-use of information is sometimes called
terminal information from which information precedents and processing requirements
can be determined. This we shall deal with in subject area four.

Systems requirements analysis: Above, we have determined the tasks to be performed
by the object system in terms of functions. Information flows as well as material
and transaction flows are identified. Information requirements are closely related to uncertainty in performing tasks. If we are faced with a certain event,
no information is needed. For instance, in the case where we know exactly how
much and at what times our customers need their products, no order processing would
be necessary. This is seldom true and therefore companies have order processing
systems. However, we can affect the amount of information processed in a number of
ways, e.g. by introducing discount rates to increase order-sizes and thereby reducing the number of orders. The greater the task uncertainty, the greater the
amount of information processing needed to perform tasks on a given level of performance. Perfect information is the amount of information needed to eliminate
uncertainty. Uncertainty is therefore, the core concept upon which the functional
architecture of our object system is based. The amount of information required to
perform a task is related to:

(1)   task complexity, e.g. the number of different products increases
        the complexity of the customer order entry function;

(2)   intertask dependencies, e.g. credit authorization, shipment order and
        billing are related tasks in an order entry function;

(3)   level of performance, e.g. increased delivery time reduces the need
        for accurate information about stock-on-hand.

Systems requirements analysis encompasses the task of determining operative goals
and constraints and the ultimate information requirements. An example will illu-

strate how interconnected these variables are. A common ad hoc goal for an order
processing system is to "reduce the number of rush-orders". We can address this
problem in a number of different ways, some of which do not affect the information
processing requirements. First, we can increase the safety stock level (create
slack resources). Second, we can reduce order-processing time (by a computer processing system) and decrease the use of a particular procedure for handling rush-
orders. Third, we can eliminate the category "rush-orders". In systems work we
must avoid these kinds of operative goals and instead analyze requirements from
the more basic concept of task uncertainty.

There is a set of mechanisms with which we can change the information processing
capacity of the organization or change the needs for information. Effectiveness
is the function of matching capacity with needs. If there is a gap we can obtain
a fit in either of two ways: (1) by increasing the capacity or (2) by reducing
the needs.

From general systems theory we known that interrelationships between systems (or
tasks) can be reduced by hierarchic organizations and by decoupling (slack, buffer
stocks, standards). On the other hand, we can increase information processing
capacity by developing formal information systems or by organizing for lateral communications. Formal information systems may, for instance, enable increased planning frequency and thus reduce the need for slack and buffer stocks.

The point to make here is that before we can determine information requirements, we
have to establish the functional architecture of the object system and use this to
analyze task uncertainty. Furthermore, formal, integrated and rigid information
systems are only one of several mechanisms by which we can affect the information
processing capacity or needs of an organization. The design strategy chosen has
tremendous effect on the information processing system to be developed. From the
above, we can see how analysis and design problems have to be solved concurrently.

The aspects of task uncertainty and information processing have been treated more
comprehensively in organization theory. Here we have extracted some aspects of
particular interest to information systems design. For more detials the reader is
referred to Galbraith (1977) and Tushman and Nadler (1978). We shall return to
applications of this subject below.

Information processing modeling: The aim of this step is to expand the information
network defined by the functional specifications into such detail that processing
requirements can be described in terms of information items, precedence relations
and procedure-descriptions (process-logic). We shall not deal with this task in
this paper. The reader is referred to Methlie (1978) for further information.

A MODEL

Need for Formalism in Requirements Analysis Work

In discussing the problems of systems design we concluded that software systems
development encompasses political as well as technical aspects. Political aspects
are concerned with the influence of systems on power structures in organizations
during the development task and after implementation; on working conditions of the
individuals, and on the influence of learning on changing requirements. Diagnosis
of these aspects is important. The behavioral theory, however, is a descriptive
theory and in systems work we need prescriptive theories, i.e. methods and techniques.
The design of a complex software system has no definite solution, and no analytical
model exists of the design process. However, we need a methodology based on theory
and models to:

(1)   understand the fundamental problems,

(2)   guide the progress through the problem solving process,

(3)   enable communications between people involved,

(4)   ensure improvements in methodology.

We shall look at one model to describe the functional architecture of an object system and which enables us to study interrelationships of subsystems (tasks) in relation to task uncertainty.

Requirements on an Organizational Model for an Infological Approach

The model must describe the elements of an object system (OS) relevant to a study of information requirements and information processing systems. The model must enable the information system to be extracted from the object system for further analysis and modeling. We can formulate the following more specific requirements:

(1)   information requirements must be determined from the tasks (actions and decisions) executed in the organization, i.e. the tasks have to be identified before information requirements can be specified;

(2)   a system approach should be applied, i.e. the model is a hierarchic ordering of subsystem-models;

(3)   the functional architecture of the system should be determined by successive increase in detail;

(4)   the process of establishing the model must be an "open" problem solving process, i.e. communication between users and analysts must be part of the development process.

Structural Elements of the Model

The basic elements of our model can be found in Figure 1. In discussing the tasks of systems requirements analysis we found that a functional specification of our object system was required. Functions combine resources and processes into structures of actions, decisions and data processing. The flows of resources are governed by these structures. We can say that a resource can be any kind of flowing objects, physical or abstract, such as material or information. A process is the conversion of a set of inflowing resources into a set of outflowing resources. Compound processes consisting of processes of different kinds, e.g. actions and decisions, we call functions.

We distinguish between three kinds of flows: (1) materials, (2) transactions and (3) information. Function is the entity acting upon these flows, and the functional architecture of the system is the functions and their interrelationships determined by the connecting flows.

It may sometimes be difficult to differentiate between transactions and information flows. We shall use information to control actions and transactions. A transaction is an action in the object system that initiates a set of processes in the information system, e.g. customer orders. The control perspective is important and the model must describe information-decision-action relationships. By looking at the organization as a complex communication network controlling transactions and material flows, information requirements can be determined from a management control point of view. Furthermore, various communications pattern can be evaluated according to uncertainties in the environment and intertask dependencies. This is in contrast to determining information requirements by asking the individual user of his or her needs and formulating some ad hoc goals for the design task.

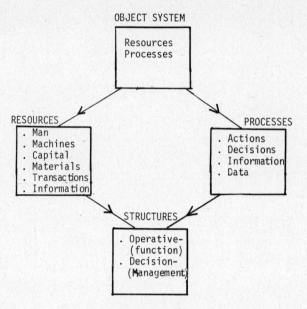

Figure 1
Elements of an Object System

A Graphic Language

Above we defined the concepts needed to describe an object system. We shall now look at a graphic language to represent an object system model. The graphic language provides a limited set of primitive constructs from which analysts and designers can compose orderly structures of any required size. The primitive constructs are boxes, rhomboids and arrows. Boxes represent processes, compound processes like functions or more elementary processes. Arrows represent flows of objects between processes. Rhomboids are used together with arrows to specify functional properties, i.e. the kinds of resources flowing into and out of a process. A system diagram represents "wholes" and is composed of boxes, rhomboids and arrows, and certain other notations which we will not detail in this paper.

To emphasize the control aspects in the model we make the following distinctions:

(1)   flows acted upon enter the system from the left and leave to the right of the diagram. Furthermore, we separate transactions flows from material flow.

(2)   information to control actions enters at the top of the diagram, and feed-back information leaves the system at the bottom.

An OS-model is an organized sequence of system diagrams. The first diagram is an overview of the total system which is to be studied. Each lower level diagram models a subsystem; i.e. a function of the organization. Furthermore, each lower level diagram connects exactly into higher portions of the model by components relationship for resources and processes. Thus, the logical relationship of each component to the total system is preserved. An OS-model is a graphic representation of the hierarchic structure of a system. It is structured so that it gradually exposes more and more detail.

The process of structuring the object system into subsystems starts with the
functional properties of the total system; that is, the relationships with its
environment. These relationships (resources) may be decomposed into components
and a subsystem structure to process these components can then be found. This
determines the functional properties of each of the second-level systems.

Figure 2 shows a simple system diagram of an object system. General object systems
concepts are used to show the syntax of the graphic language. We can think of the
diagram as representing a flow of customer orders (transactions) with product
deliveries (material flow) from inventory. Management control (control information)
may be servicing policies and feedback information could be processing times for
orders.

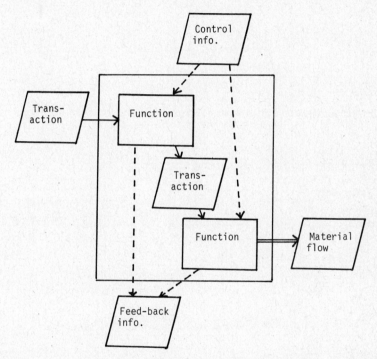

Figure 2
A Conceptual Model of an Object System

Systems Requirements Analysis - An Illustration

The system diagrams give a description of the functional architecture of an object
system. They specify the basic tasks to be performed which determine the ultimate
information requirements. The systems requirements analysis should be based on
the mechanisms available to (1) change the capacity of the organization to process
information or (2) reduce the requirements to meet the capacity. These mechanisms
have been presented above. The kind of analysis to be done can best be explained
by an example. We will therefore, apply the methodology on a customer order entry
function.

Figure 3 shows a very simple model (an overview diagram) of an object system encompassing the order processing function. We will not decompose this system, but use this level of detail to discuss aspects of information requirements and task uncertainty.

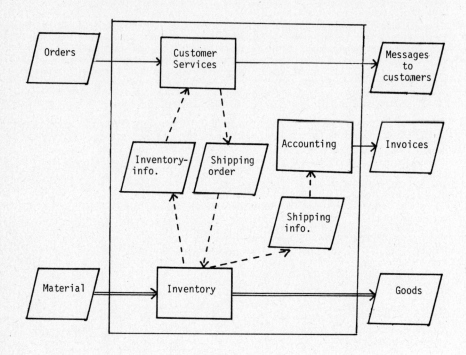

Figure 3
Object System Model - Basis for Analysis (Descriptive Model)

What kinds of problems can be posed on the basis of this model?

1.   Changing Environment: We can study each information set passing the system boundary to or from its environment and evaluate the kind of uncertainty it represents. For instance, let us look at customer orders. Orders represent a kind of perfect information in the sense that they eliminate uncertainty about what the customers want and at what time. We can change the coupling between customers and our business in a number of ways. One way to decrease the information processing load is to introduce discounts which will increase order-sizes. If this is our decision we must insert discount rates into the model as a new information set controlling order processing (see Figure 4).

2.   Intertask Dependencies: Can we change the functional architecture, and particularly the communication pattern, of our system? Let us look at task uncertainty again. In our descriptive model of the system (Figure 3) billing is made on the basis of actual shipped items, information about which is passed from "inventory" to "accounting". This approach is sometimes called post-delivery billing. However, we know that this leads to delays in billing the customers causing accounts receivable to increase. This information system is based on uncertainties to what extent orders can be processed in quantity and time from the inventory.

If, on the other hand, exeptions from orders are limited we may change our billing procedure. Billing can be made on the basis of ordering information and not shipping information. This is called predelivery billing. A communication channel between "Customer Service" and "Accounting" is established as shown in Figure 4.

3.   Creation of Slack: If the number of exceptions of shipments from orders increases we can reduce exceptions by introducing slack. First, we can extend delivery dates until the number of exceptions are within the information processing capacity of the system. Second, we can increase safety stock levels to reduce exceptions caused by being out of stock of the particular item ordered. The strategy of using slack resources has its costs. Increasing the time span from order date to shipment date has the effect of delaying customer receipts of the products. Delay may lead to introduction of prioriy-rules or special rush-order procedures. We have inserted priority-rules (control information) in Figure 4.

4..   Degree of Self-Contained Tasks: One method of reducing the amount of information processed is to make our system functional with regards to outputs (products). For instance, it could be appropriate to organize the customer service department into groups on the basis of products or markets. This organization gives the order processing staff opportunities to know customers and markets better and some decisions may be decentralized. This design choice is not utilized in our example, and thus, no effect of this is shown in Figure 4. A further decomposition of the customer service function would have been necessary to illustrate the effect of self-contained tasks.

5.   Formal Information System: A global database for customer order services may be established. This database can be accessed from customer services, accounting and stock management. It may also give information to management on sales-statistics, stocks etc.. In Figure 4 we can see the effect of such a global database on the communications patterns.

Above, we have described some of the design choices we have and illustrated these by examples. They will all have an effect on the ultimate information requirements and on the information processing system to be designed. In a systematic way we are able to establish systems requirements. Our new system diagram, which can be thought of as a normative model of the object system, is shown in Figure 4. We have only shown one step towards the specification of the functional architecture and the systems requirements. In successive steps we can perform analysis and evaluation on subfunctions until we reach a desired level of detail from which we can extract the information system and proceed with detailed information processing modeling.

CONCLUSION

What can be achieved by the use of this conceptual framework and the method proposed? First, information requirements are determined from organizational needs. This approach implies that the functional structure of our organization is not taken as given. Design choices have been introduced by which information processing requirements and capacity can be changed. Task uncertainty is the core concept for these choices. Second, goals and constraints for the information system design task follow from a discussion of task uncertainty on the organizational level. The graphic models help us to visualize the communications pattern of existing organization as well as the effect of design choices.

Current systems development work seem to be dominated by efficiency issues and oriented towards computerization of existing data flows. Some reasons for this datalogical approach have been given above. For certain applications this may be an adequate approach. However, data flows should be regarded as a construct designed to facilitate communications in the existing organization structure.

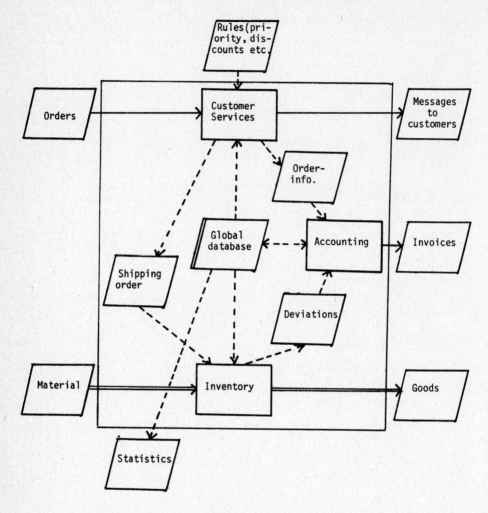

Figure 4
Object System Model with Alternative System Requirements (Normative Model)

Changes in the information system impose changes in the organization. In the datalogical approach changes in the organization follow from consequences of a changed
information system.

This paper proposes a method to reverse the datalogical process by starting with
an analysis of the need for changes in the organization followed by the design of
an information system that supports these organizational changes.

REFERENCES

[1] Forrester, J.W., Industrial Dynamics, Cambridge, (The MIT Press, 1961).

[2] Galbraith, J.R., Organization Design, (Addison-Wesley Publ., 1977).

[3] IBM, Improved Programming Technologies, IBM GE 19-5086-2, Third Edition,(1977).

[4] Keen, P.G.W. and Gerson, E.M., The Politics of Software Systems Design, Datamation, Nov. (1977).

[5] Langefors, B., Theoretical Analysis of Information Systems, (Studentlitteratur/ Auerbach, Third Edition, (1973).

[6] Methlie, L.B., Information Systems Design. Concepts and Methods, (Universi- tetsforlaget, Norway, 1978).

[7] Orr, K.T., Structured Systems Development, (Yourdon Press, New York, 1977).

[8] Ross, D.T. and Schoman, K.E., Structured Analysis for Requirements Definition, IEE Transactions on Software Engineering, Vol SE-3, No. 1, (January 1977).

[9] Tushman, M. and Nadler, D.A., Information Processing as an Integrating Concept in Organizational Design, Academy of Management Review - (July 1978).

The Information Systems Environment
Lucas, Land, Lincoln, Supper (Editors)
North-Holland Publishing Company
© *IFIP, 1980*

THE INCORPORATION OF OBJECTIVE AND SUBJECTIVE ASPECTS
INTO THE ASSESSMENT OF INFORMATION SYSTEMS*

Janet Efstathiou

Computer Science Division
Department of Electrical Engineering and Computer Sciences
and the Electronics Research Laboratory
University of California, Berkeley
Berkeley, California 94720 U.S.A.

The evaluation of Information Systems poses the problem of how to combine the assessment of both objective and subjective aspects in a structured decision-making framework. Previous methods derive from number-based techniques, such as cost-benefit analysis, and the operational research tradition. These methods tend to emphasize and measure the numerical weighting of the system and its impact. Some procedure for aggregation of utilities is adopted to provide a means of discerning the most suitable alternatives.

A new approach will be proposed, involving the use of some elementary fuzzy subset theory. The need to establish a common language for every attribute is removed, together with the aggregation procedure, by mapping directly from the "attribute space" onto "utility space" by means of a user-defined relation. Each attribute is described using a vocabulary best suited to it. The user-defined relation is expressed in natural English statements. The technique may be used to predict a preference ordering of the proposed alternatives. By reiterating over the earlier stages, a decision-maker may gain better understanding of his decision-making process. The emphasis is placed upon the human, subjective assessment of systems and the encouragement of participative decision-making.

INTRODUCTION

The evaluation and selection of an information system is an example of a multi-attribute decision-making problem. The organization or decision-maker has to fulfill a set of objectives which may be conflicting, and seeks to choose the alternative which will best fulfill the objectives. The evaluation of information systems poses, in particular, the following problems:
1) The measurement and combination of objective and subjective aspects of the system and its impact,
2) The forecasting of future events with their inherent uncertainty,
3) The reconciliation of the opposing points of view of different interest groups,
4) Communication with non-technical groups.
There is no simple solution to these problems, but they must be clearly recognized. This paper proposes a means of tackling these problems by arguing for a shift in the emphasis of past decision-making techniques.

A CHANGE OF APPROACH

The first problem is that of combining objective and subjective criteria in the evaluation of system change. Previous attempts have been derived from numerical

187

techniques, such as cost-benefit analysis, and from the operations research tradition. (See Efstathiou (1979) for a review and references.) These methods follow
a pattern of separating out the aspects of the system and assigning to each a
financial value and/or a numerical weight. Each aspect is measured separately and
the weights and measurements are combined to give an overall rating to each alternative for the final selection. These methods emphasize the numerical aspects of
weighting and measurement and the mathematical methods of aggregation.

In practice, two problems arise with these methods. First, the strict conditions
which must be met for additive combination are difficult to satisfy and time-consuming to test. (See Fishburn (1970) and Keeney and Raiffa (1976) for their deri-
vation and use, and Efstathiou (1979) for a discussion.) Second, the assessment
of subjective aspects becomes problematic because of their imprecision. How does
one measure prestige or trust on a ten-point scale with the same precision as the
size of CPU store? By their very nature, subjective aspects are imprecise, and
numerical assessments of their value can only produce spurious impressions of
accuracy, which may be compounded as the calculations proceed. Subjective aspects
are important in the successful implementation of new systems, but they tend to be
ignored because they cannot be measured objectively.

These difficulties mean that the only objectives which can be handled satisfactorily are those which are quantifiable, such as turnaround, frequency of breakdown and cost. Those aspects of any system which impinge directly upon the quality of life of the people involved are often relegated to a "second division" simply because they cannot be easily measured and not because of lesser importance.
In fact, their very subjectivity may indicate a deeper relevance. So, objectives
involving good working relationships, job satisfaction, a pleasant environment and
prestige, etc. are used to resolve the finer points of decisions made according to
the quantifiable objectives, when in effect ignoring such qualities could lead to
the premature downfall of apparently impeccable system designs.

To solve the problem of combining both objective and subjective aspects in the same
procedure, cost-benefit analysis sought to convert all measurements to a common
financial unit. Recently, these procedures have encountered opposition (Leitch
(1978), Self (1970)). The complex mathematics involved leaves most of the
affected parties baffled, bewildered and alienated. While it is reasonable and
possible to forecast deaths, injuries and increased noise levels, etc. which will
be caused by the construction of a new road or airport, to place monetary values
on these emotive aspects is repugnant and unreal to many people. Cost-benefit
analysis, despite some success, has been inadequate for coping with the subjec-
tively valued issues which affect people's lives.

Methods apart from cost-benefit analysis have tried to scale everything to a
common dimensionless unit, but still require the numerical expression of subjective aspects. (See, for example, Hill (1968), Mumford, Land and Hawgood (1978),
Dujmovic (1977) and Efstathiou (1979) for further references.) Ideally, it should
be possible to devise a method which allows objective aspects to be expressed in
numbers and subjective aspects to be expressed in their most appropriate language
of words, removing the need to translate artificially into numbers, and moving
away from the emphasis on measurement and precision for their own sake.

The mathematical processes of aggregation to produce a final rating may be criticized on a number of points. These processes assume general techniques may be
applied to each particular problem. In other words, the aggregation of values in
every case follows a particular pattern which is neatly described by mathematics.
Such methods may also be unable to take account of sudden deviations from smooth
combination caused by critical changes in the level of the attributes. If an
aggregation rule is shown to be correct over a local region, this rule is sometimes extrapolated over the entire, global space, perhaps ignoring catastrophic
deviations at extreme values. Many techniques do not allow for asymmetry about

the status quo in the weighting of attributes and complex trade-offs involving more than two attributes at different levels.

The second problem of forecasting events can also be relieved of the number-based tradition. In attempting to assess the relative likelihood of various events, the decision-maker is encouraged to place numerical values of probability on the complete set of possible events, so that the sum of these numbers equals unity. These numbers are not objectively testable and will reflect the decision-maker's attitude towards risk, i.e. how much he is likely to win or lose (Phillips and Edwards (1960)). These numerical values of probability are used in conjunction with the numerical measurements, perhaps to estimate the "expected utility". If one can eliminate the need for the numerical measurement of aspects, then numerical estimates of probability or relative likelihood will also become unnecessary.

This paper argues against the emphasis on numerical techniques, and their arbitrary constraints, such as the removal of emphasis from subjective aspects and the inappropriate language it imposes upon them. In the consideration of some systems, or subsystems, subjective attributes might play no role at all. Such systems might be the computer control of factories operated by robots where alternative systems may be evaluated entirely on financial grounds. But, as the boundary of the system is drawn ever wider, the human element will eventually be included bringing a different set of objectives and a different value system. Thus, the boundary of the problem is important when a decision is to be made. It might be possible to draw the boundary in such a way as to permit exact, numerical assessment of the alternatives, but as the problem becomes wider the human factor is more likely to become important making precise assessment and aggregation less appropriate.

The assessment of information systems must include the human factor, because the success of such systems depends strongly on the people who operate and use them. This implies that numerical assessment techniques become inappropriate because of their lack of emphasis on the human aspect.

THE ADVANTAGES OF A FUZZY APPROACH

In order to alleviate the problems of numerical techniques, this paper proposes a method based on the use of words or numbers as appropriate, giving objective and subjective aspects equal prominence. Words are the natural means of expressing an opinion or "measurement" of a subjective aspect, but they have been difficult to handle consistently, or to include in a computer-assisted decision aid. One method of doing this is to use some elementary fuzzy subset theory and fuzzy logic which allows a numerical representation of words, rendering them amenable to mathematical manipulation (Zadeh (1973,1977)). However, the numerical representation need not be revealed to users, so that their experience remains based on words. A brief description of fuzzy subset theory and a simple example of the technique follows.

For each aspect set up an appropriate vocabulary of description, which may be a group of adjectives, e.g. (good, medium, poor), or a range of numbers. The aspects define an "attribute space" and each alternative is a fuzzy region of that space. Omit the mathematical aggregation procedure and use instead a user-defined relation to map from this attribute space onto "utility space". This user-defined relation will consist of statements describing verbally (1) the relative importance of the attributes, (2) the trade-offs which exist between them at certain levels, and (3) those levels which are intolerable or ideal. Using this relation, a preference ordering of simple, trial alternatives may be predicted. This preference ordering is presented to the decision-maker who may choose to amend the relation, include more aspects, change statements or trade-offs or reconsider other points. The output of this procedure is a set of aspects relevant to the system which are relevant to the decision-maker and a set of rules which should describe the means whereby his preferences are made. This procedure has been described elsewhere (Efstathiou (1979), Efstathiou, Hawgood and Rajkovic (1979), Efstathiou and Rajkovic (1979)).

As a result of this process, the decision-maker should acquire a deeper insight into his own decision-making process and learn more about the problem he faces. It is probably true that with many decisions the process of analysis and study may make the eventual decision obvious, without going through the formal mathematics of the process. The decision-maker must be convinced that the outcome of the decision technique is right, otherwise he cannot fully commit himself to its implementation. This commitment must come from a learning process, an understanding of the aspects of the problem. By giving the decision-maker a method of learning about the environment together with his internal assessment of it, greater commitment and better decisions should result. To assist and encourage this learning process, the decision-making technique should be as easy and as natural as possible. It seems that a method involving natural language could achieve this.

Consider now the other two problems mentioned at the beginning of the paper, i.e. the reconciliation of opposing points of view and communication with non-technical groups. So far, the decision-maker has represented one opinion, but many groups have to be considered in any real-life problem.

Because the groups have conflicting objectives, the designer must seek out those areas of compromise and build upon them. One group may be willing to tolerate an alternative which is less than the best available for them if they see it as beneficial to a group which they recognize as less advantaged. The user-defined relations can produce a preference-ordering of alternatives, but at a higher level, these orderings can be modified as a result of the preferences of other groups, via a further user-defined relation. In a spirit of participation and cooperation, hopefully groups may be willing to discuss trade-offs at two levels: (1) among the aspects of the alternatives, and (2) among the preferences of different groups and themselves.

Non-technical groups have objectives which are different from those of groups closer to the problem; they may be groups of users, shareholders or politicians. These people may not be directly interested in the hardware behind an information system, but will need to know in plain language how well the alternative systems match their objectives. Having argued throughout for a de-emphasis of the numerical aspects, the information which such groups require need not be overladen with statistics and figures. Once they have obtained the information necessary to take the decision, such groups can use a non-mathematical decision technique to assist them in the process of rating alternatives, and not be excluded by the use of overly mathematical methods.

AN INTRODUCTION TO FUZZY SUBSETS AND A SIMPLE EXAMPLE

Before considering a simple, hypothetical example which is intended to illustrate some features of the proposed method, the reader requires an introduction to fuzzy subset theory.

Fuzzy Subsets

Traditionally, a subset of a set is defined by choosing which elements of the set belong or do not belong to the subset. The characteristic function is restricted to the values 0 and 1. For a fuzzy subset, the characteristic function can take any value in the interval [0,1]. See Figure 1. The scale or horizontal axis represents the set of which A is a fuzzy subset. This 'superset' is known as the "universe of discourse". The values of the characteristic function are

INCORPORATION OF OBJECTIVE AND SUBJECTIVE ASPECTS   191

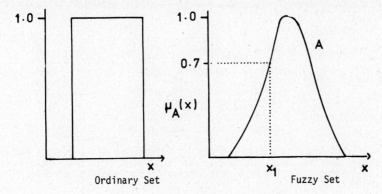

Figure 1
Comparison of Ordinary and Fuzzy Sets

interpreted as truth-values. In Figure 1, x_1 belongs to the set A with a truth-value of 0.7, written as

$$\mu_A(x_1) = 0.7$$

These non-integral truth-values also occur in multiple-valued logics.

The fuzzy subsets may be used to define such concepts as 'tall' or 'heavy', which are well-understood but defy the precision of ordinary set theory. The set of 'tall men' does not have a crisp boundary in the sense that it is impossible to choose a precise height, such that all men who are just short of this height are not tall, and all men who are just above this height are tall.

A basic vocabulary may be defined along the scale, e.g. (short, about average, tall), but this is not enough on its own. The vocabulary may be extended by introducing modifiers and a simple grammar. The most common modifiers are words like 'very', 'fairly' and 'not', together with the connectives 'and' and 'or'. These may be given the following definitions, but other definitions may be chosen:

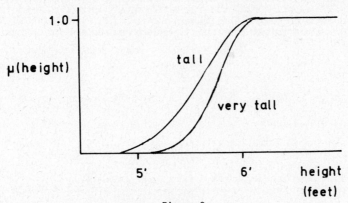

Figure 2
The Fuzzy Sets 'tall' and 'very tall'

$$\mu_{very\ tall}(x) = \mu^2_{tall}(x) \qquad \text{VERY TALL} \subset \text{TALL}$$

$$\mu_{fairly\ tall}(x) = \sqrt{\mu}_{tall}(x) \qquad \text{TALL} \subset \text{FAIRLY TALL}$$

$$\mu_{not\ tall}(x) = 1 - \mu_{tall}(x)$$

$$\mu_{tall\ and\ not\ very\ tall}(x) = \mu_{tall}(x) \wedge \{1 - \mu^2_{tall}(x)\}$$
where $\wedge$ is the min operator

$$\mu_{fairly\ tall\ or\ not\ tall}(x) = \sqrt{\mu}_{tall}(x) \quad \{1 - \mu_{tall}(x)\}$$
where is the max operator.

Here, 'very' is understood to modify a fuzzy set by squaring the grades of membership and 'fairly' modifies by taking the square root. Note that the $\wedge$ (min) and $\vee$ (max) operations reduce to the usual definitions of intersection and union when applied to ordinary non-fuzzy sets.

We may define relations between fuzzy sets. The following matrix defines a relation between a car's maximum speed and the utility thereof. (This potential car-owner does not like a car which can go too fast!) The universe of discourse for top speeds is

$$S = \{40,60,80,100\}$$

and the universe of discourse for utility is

$$U = \{1,2,3,4\} \qquad 1 = \text{low}, 4 = \text{high}$$

$$R = \begin{vmatrix} 1.0 & 0.3 & 0 & 0 \\ 0 & 1.0 & 0.7 & 0 \\ 0 & 0 & 0.8 & 1.0 \\ 0 & 0.6 & 1.0 & 0.3 \end{vmatrix}$$

Suppose we have a particular car whose maximum speed is 70 mph. This may be given the fuzzy set

$$C = 0.7/60 + 0.7/80$$

since '70' does not appear in the discrete universe of discourse S. This notation means that 60 has a truth-value of 0.7 and 80 also has a truth-value of 0.7. The elements 40 and 100 both have truth values of 0. The '+' signs indicate union and not arithmetic addition. One may use 'max min' composition to find the utility of a vehicle with this top speed. This is very similar to matrix multiplication, except that the multiplication operation is replaced by min and addition is replaced by max. This is written as

$$U_c = C \circ R$$

or

$$\mu_{U_c}(u) = \max_{s_i}\{\min \mu_C(s_i),\mu_R(s_i,u_j)\}$$

where U_c is the utility of C, $s_i \in S$ and $u_j \in U$. This yields

$$U_c = 0.7/60 + 0.7/80 \circ \begin{vmatrix} 1.0 & 0.3 & 0 & 0 \\ 0 & 1.0 & 0.7 & 0 \\ 0 & 0 & 0.8 & 1.0 \\ 0 & 0.6 & 1.0 & 0.3 \end{vmatrix}$$

$$= 0/1 + 0.7/2 + 0.7/3 + 0.7/4$$

This may be interpreted as meaning 'generally good', because of the spread of possibilities over the upper elements of U.

There are some problems involved in 'discretising' continuous variables in order to allow relations such as these. These problems may be overcome by using inter-polative techniques or by increasing the number of intervals to match the respon-dent's perception of the scale. In the above example, 5 mph divisions would have probably been enough, because utility will not vary significantly with 5 mph, although it will do so across a range of 20 mph

We may use such a relation with many more dimensions. If there are n variables, we require an n+1 dimensional relation. Hence, if the n+1 dimensional relation is denoted by Φ and the set of measurements describing a particular alternative is denoted by A_i, then we may calculate the utility ν_i:

$$\nu_i = A_i \circ \Phi$$

This is the model used in the proposed technique. A simple illustrative example follows.

An Example - Choosing a Typewriter

This example is intended to demonstrate the first phases of a decision-making task. The problem of selecting a typewriter has been chosen because this is a standard piece of office equipment and the problem is a small-scale version of the type of decision which is likely to be encountered.

Eight alternatives are available and are described in Table 1. At this first stage, only three aspects have been used, i.e. price, downtime and special fea-tures. There are many features which differentiate between the typewriters, but those which are relevant to the decision-maker have been grouped together and assessed jointly, for the sake of simplicity. The data on the alternatives was obtained from Library Technology Reports (1978) which is biased towards office and library use. To represent a different user viewpoint, the alternatives will be assessed supposing the user wishes to type long passages of text and has selected the special features accordingly. Of the many features which could have been chosen, e.g. weight or length of typing line, some have been rejected because they are of no interest to the decision-maker and the others because they have no powers of discrimination among the alternatives.

Table 1. Description of the Alternatives

Alternative	Price	Downtime	Special Features
A	$520	moderate	poor
B	$895	low	poor
C	$680	low	poor
D	$455	moderate-high	very good
E	$675	low-moderate	very good
F	$660	low	good
G	$430	low	good
H	$875	moderate	good

A relation to map from this three-dimensional decision space onto utility is pre-sented in Table 2. The table was obtained using heuristics of the following kind:
(a) If the downtime is high and the special features are at least good, the price will be very important in determining utility.

J. EFSTATHIOU

Table 2. The Utility Relation

Price	Downtime	Special Features	Utility
≤ $400	low	poor	good
		good	good
		very good	ideal
	moderate	poor	medium
		good	good
		very good	very good
	high	poor	poor
		good	good
		very good	good
≈ $600	low	poor	medium
		good	medium-good
		very good	good
	moderate	poor	medium-poor
		good	medium
		very good	medium
	high	poor	intolerable
		good	poor
		very good	poor
≥ $800	low	poor	poor
		good	medium
		very good	medium-good
	moderate	poor	very poor
		good	very poor
		very good	poor
	high	poor	intolerable
		good	intolerable
		very good	poor

(b) If the special features and reliability are good, then the price will not be so important.
(c) Most importantly, the machine should be fairly cheap and have a low downtime.
(d) An ideal machine would cost under $400, have a low downtime and possess very good special features.
(e) If the special features are poor and it costs over $600 and has a high downtime or if it costs over $800 and has even a moderate downtime then in either case it is intolerable.

The universes of discourse in use are:

Price = {≤ $400, ≈ $600, ≥ $800}

Downtime = {high, moderate, low}

Special Features = {poor, good, very good}

Utility = {intolerable, poor, medium, good, very good, ideal}

To obtain the fuzzy description of each alternative on these coarse universes of discourse, the following formulae are used:

$$\$y = \le \$400 \qquad\qquad\qquad y \le 400$$

$$= \frac{(600-y)}{200}/\le\$400 + \frac{(y-400)}{200}/\approx\$600 \qquad 600 \ge y > 400$$

$$= \frac{(y-600)}{200}/\approx\$600 + \frac{(800-y)}{200}/\ge\$800 \qquad 800 \ge y \ge 600$$

$$= \ge \$800 \qquad\qquad\qquad 800 \le y$$

'moderate high' is interpreted as .5/moderate + .5/high. The fuzzy description of alternative D, for example, consists of 4 n-tuples combining $\le$ \$400, $\approx$ \$600 with moderate, high in all combinations. The 'min' rule is used to pick the composite grade of membership. Thus,

$$D = \$455 \times \text{moderate-high} \times \text{very good}$$

$$= (.725/\le\$400 + .275/\approx\$600) \times (.5/\text{moderate} + .5/\text{high}) \times \text{very good}$$

$$= .5/(\le\$400, \text{moderate, very good}) + .5/(\le\$400, \text{high, very good})$$

$$+ .275/(\approx\$600, \text{moderate, very good}) + .275/(\approx\$600, \text{high, very good}) \ .$$

The utility of each alternative is calculated using Table 2, and is presented in Table 3 with a linguistic approximation where needed. A preference ordering is shown in Table 4, together with that for the library/office users, as obtained from Library Technology Reports (1978). In places the rank ordering is vague and one must not be too confident in asserting firmly that A is preferred over E, for example. This vagueness is reasonable because of the vague information supplied. If further cycles are carried out, the number of variables can be increased, the utilities of Table 2 may require correction or the universe of discourse may be amended.

Table 3. Fuzzy Utilities of the Alternatives

Alternative	Utility	Linguistic Approximation
A	.4/medium + .6/medium-poor	'slightly below medium'
B	poor	'poor'
C	.6/medium-good + .4/medium	'slightly above medium'
D	.5/very good + .5/good + .275/medium + .275/medium	'good but not very good'
E	.5/good + .5/medium + .375/medium-good + .375/poor	'about medium'
F	.7/medium-good + .3/medium	'medium but not good'
G	.85/good + .15/medium-good	'good'
H	very poor	'very poor'

From Table 4 it seems that, interestingly, alternative D which is the favorite model of the text-typing user is the least preferred for the office or library user. This is due to different attitudes toward the trade-off between price and downtime which also accounts for the difference in preferences for alternative B. If a machine must be shared by these users, alternatives F or G would stand closer scrutiny by both parties acting cooperatively, or any of A, E or C in the next instance.

So far, the procedure described above has been partially implemented in a real situation to test the assumptions involved and user reactions. See Efstathiou (1979), chapter 9.3.

Table 4. Rank Ordering of the Alternatives according to Predicted Preference
(Bracketed alternatives have no strong preference difference.)

Rank Order	Text Typing User	Office/Library User
1	D	B
2	G	F
3	F	⎫ G ⎫
4	⎰ A ⎱	⎪ A ⎪
5	⎱ E ⎰	⎬ E ⎬
6	⎱ C ⎰	⎭ C ⎭
7	B	H
8	H	D

CONCLUSION

To conclude, traditional methods of decision-making have been founded on a cult
of numbers which has imposed unnatural and unnecessary constraints on methods of
structuring the human decision-making process. These constraints have resulted
in a loss of emphasis on the subjective aspects of system design and an over-
emphasis on precision. Objective and subjective aspects gain equal footing via
fuzzy set theory and fuzzy logic. By emphasizing the learning process prior to
decision-making, one can achieve an approach to systems evaluation which is more
natural and less frustrating to non-technical groups. Such an approach gives
freedom of choice to each group and encourages dialogue and inter-group
preference trade-offs.

REFERENCES

[1]   Dujmovic, J.J., The preference scoring method for decision-making: survey,
      classification and annotated bibliography, Informatica 1 (1977) 26-34.
[2]   Efstathiou, H.J., A Practical Development of Multi-Attribute Decision-
      Making using Fuzzy Set Theory, Ph.D. Thesis, Dept. of Computing, Durham
      University (1979).
[3]   Efstathiou, J., Hawgood, J. and Rajkovic, V., Verbal measures and insepara-
      ble multidimensional utility, in: Schneider, H.J. (ed.), Formal Models and
      Practical Tools for Information Systems Design (North-Holland, Amsterdam,
      1979).
[4]   Efstathiou, J. and Rajkovic, V., Multi-attribute decision-making using a
      fuzzy heuristic approach, IEEE Trans. Syst., Man and Cyber. SMC-9 (1979)
      326-333.
[5]   Fishburn, P.C., Utility Theory for Decision Making (John Wiley & Sons, New
      York, 1970), chps. 4, 5.
[6]   Hill, M., A goals-achievement matrix for evaluating alternative plans,
      Jrnl. Amer. Inst. Planners 34 (1968) 19-29.
[7]   Keeney, R.L. and Raiffa, H., Decisions with Multiple Objectives (John Wiley
      & Sons, New York, 1976).
[8]   Library Technology Reports 14 (1978) 555-614.
[9]   Leitch, Sir G., Report of the Advisory Committee on Trunk Road Assessment
      (Her Majesty's Stationery Office, London, 1978).
[10] Mumford, E., Land, F.F. and Hawgood, J., A participative approach to the
      design of computer systems, Impact of Science on Society 28 (1978) 235-253.
[11] Phillips, L. and Edwards, W., Conservatism in a simple probability
      inference task, Jrnl. Exp. Psych. 12 (1960) 346-354.

[12] Self, P., Nonsense on stilts: cost-benefit analysis and the Roskill
     Commission, Political Quarterly 41 (1970) 249-260.
[13] Zadeh, L.A., Outline of a new approach to the analysis of complex systems
     and decision processes, IEEE Trans. Syst., Man and Cyber. SMC-3 (1973)
     28-44.
[14] Zadeh, L.A., A Theory of Approximate Reasoning, Memo UCB/ERL/M77/58, Dept.
     of EECS, Univ. of California, Berkeley (1977).

FOOTNOTE

*This research was performed at the University of Durham, Department of Computing,
England and was supported by a postgraduate scholarship awarded by the Northern
Ireland Department of Education. Research was also partially supported by
National Science Foundation Grant ENG78-23143 and Naval Electronics Systems
Command Contract N00039-78-C-0013.

The Information Systems Environment
Lucas, Land, Lincoln, Supper (Editors)
North-Holland Publishing Company
© *IFIP, 1980*

ON INFOLOGICAL RESEARCH INTO THE SYSTEMEERING PROCESS

Pentti Kerola

Institute of Data Processing Science
University of Oulu
Linnanmaa, SF-90570 Oulu 57
FINLAND

The basis, objectives and restrictions of the infological
research into the systemeering process are defined and
described in the framework of the PSC systemeering model.
The major problem of the infological approach is how the
people involved in planning and decision-making define,
form, store and process knowledge about the reality with
which they interact. The infological results provide the
basis for datalogical design and implementation. The reality for this research is the process of information systems
development itself.

INTRODUCTION

The main purpose of the paper is to define and describe the general
methods and models needed when the infological approach is applied
to the information systems development process itself. Specifically
the Scandinavian researchers (see e.g. Langefors (1973), Langefors-
Sundgren (1975), Lundeberg & al (1976,1978), Sundgren (1973), Høyer
(1976)) have established the concept and term "infological", but the
same type of approach has been studied and emphasized by the
researchers in many other countries (e.g. Davis (1974), Grochla
(1970), Land (1976), Lucas (1975), Mason-Mitroff (1973), Mumford &
al (1978), Le Moigne (1977), Singer (1976), Stamper (1977), Taggart-
Tharp (1977), Wedekind (1976), Welke (1977)). In the first and
second parts of the paper we discuss the major concepts and their
historical development in order to establish the basis for the
objectives of the research.

The infological approach stresses the investigation of organizations
utilizing information and especially value criteria in decision
making. Therefore the third part of the paper gives a synthesis of
the selected systemeering model and its extension to the general
model of information systems development. Because of the subject
scope, only the development and definition of the models have been
described. The fourth part is a summary of the concepts and research
procedures. The main content concerns the definition of different
groups of people in systems work based on the general model, and the
value criteria used in the selection of information and data system
models developed in the process.

INFOLOGICAL VERSUS DATALOGICAL APPROACH

A data system is a system composed of people, data processing and
transmitting equipment and functional instructions intended for the

processing of data. Such a system may be employed in various sectors of society in order to produce amounts of data requiring repeated and/or complicated processing in a systematic and purposeful way. The development of computers in the last 25 years has opened up enormous opportunities, but it has also caused almost "revolutionary and chaotic" situations to occur in data production, i.e. in information technology and its utilization.

This development can be viewed internally, from the standpoint of the computers and the software needed, or more extensively, externally in terms of the construction of data systems and the adaptation of their use. In the scientific sense, a new science has been born which investigates the general regularities in the processes of gathering, storing, transmitting and transforming data. It should be noted that such research is not based on the existence of the computer, it is not focused on the content or meaning of the data, but only on methods and techniques of defining its content and meaning.

So far, the dominating trend in this science has been datalogical, "computer science", which is computer-centered, as its name would suggest. In the last few years an opposing, infological trend, "data or information processing science"[1], has started to gain a foothold among researchers, and especially among users of data systems.

The infological approach would stress the investigation of
- people and organizations utilizing information,
- criteria for the utilization and usability of a data system,
- measurement of the value of data,
- the influences of the data system on its environment,
- the total function of a data system during its life cycle,
- the construction of a data processing system.

The major effort is directed at the identification of information, the evaluation of its influence and the logical definition of its content regarding the methodology and techniques used. The appropriate research methods are closer to those used in the social and behavioral sciences and in economics than those employed in the "exact" sciences, which in turn are best suited for datalogical research.

OBJECTIVES AND ASSUMPTIONS OF INFOLOGICAL RESEARCH

Historical Synopsis

As far as the development of the theory of information systems development is concerned, the historical trends in the field have caused many problems. At the beginning, the exclusive existence of large, expensive computers gave impact to the use of a number of very practical, organization-based constructional models - the "phase models". At the same time the use of data processing systems was restricted to the small number of basic routines of administrative data processing in organizations. The role and properties of the human being as an interactor and a data processor were neglected or underestimated. As the computers became smaller, cheaper and more modularized, the possibilities for choice in the constructive design of data systems increased enormously, and a need arose for improved methods and techniques. The general theoretical basis was weak, however, and the terminology used was badly defined. Thus the late

1960's saw the emergence in a number of countries either of higher
theoretically oriented research groups, or else of projects aimed
even at the automation of the analysis and design processes.

The greatest problem in theoretical research has been the difference
in the basic nature and level of the terminology between the sciences
investigating the various components of the data system and its
development, and the resulting problems of coordination. Internation-
ally speaking, the results so far have been diffuse. A number of
local coordinating publications do exist, but the generally accepted
basis for the theory and terminology is very limited. The automation
projects have produced suitable software for solving partial problems, but the overall aims have not by any means reached fulfillment.
In Scandinavia the basic term "systemeering" has been established as
a synonym for "systems analysis and design"[2], but even the content
of this concept is unclear.

The research and development work started at the Universities of
Oulu and Tampere in 1973 is mainly concentrated on producing a
uniform terminology and a systemeering model based on general systems
theory, cybernetics and semiotics (Ackoff-Emery (1972), Ahmavaara
(1974), Eco (1976), Mesarovic & al (1970), Nauta (1972)). As far as
information processing science is concerned, the scientific results
of Professor Langefors' team in Sweden have had a great influence on
the work. The empirical background of the research has mainly been
the practical systems work carried out by the senior members of the
group in Finnish industry during the period 1960-1973. The main
objective of the basic work has been normative: how to formulate a
conceptual systemeering model in which the infological and datalogical points of view are balanced one with another. The concept
"systemeering" is defined in the model

> as a hierarchical entity of tasks
> composed of the following actions:
> study, design, construction and
> testing of operationality, focusing
> on the goals, content, structure
> and operation of a data system.

The main results have been expressed as a set of constructs by means
of which we have developed the PSC systemeering model and its modifications (Kerola-Järvinen (1975-1979), Iivari (1978), Kerola & al
(1979)) which are described briefly in the following section.

Infological Research into Systemeering

In this research under consideration the major idea is to look at
the systemeering process itself as a potential utilizer of the
results of systemized or form-bound information production defined
by infological analysis. Regrettably, there is no well-known and
accepted theory for the systemeering process, although many different
models exist. Thus the research plan is mainly based on the PSC
systemeering model developed. The major purpose and objectives are:
-    to obtain new defined[3] and organized information and knowledge
     on the object systems[3] involved in the different phases of the
     systemeering process, i.e. concerning the elements (objects)
     and the relations between them,
-    to obtain test information on the validity and generality of
     the PSC systemeering model,
-    to understand better the different roles and intercommunication

of people involved in the systemeering process,
- to create a well-defined basis for the data processing systems which support systemeering activities,
- to apply semiotic theory to the development of systemeering theory.

THE PSC SYSTEMEERING MODEL AND ITS MODIFICATIONS

The theoretical basis of the systemeering model concerned is in the general systems theory, cybernetics, information theory and semiotics.

Basic Constructs and Development of the Model

The fundamental principle in the development of the model has been to divide the whole imperceivable phenomen - information systems development - into basic perceivable structures i.e. constructs with which we build up the different levels of the model. The most important constructs are:
- main aspects,
- structure of control and design function,
- structure of learning and knowledge basis,
- subsystem structure of data system,
- main functions of purposeful system,
- discontinuity of process.

The main aspects

The definition of a data system is based on the following system theoretical main aspects.

The pragmatic aspect studies the purposeful system[4] Z as an element in its environment, paying attention to the needs of those having an interest in the outcomes of Z and to the effects of the outcomes of Z upon its environment.

The input-output aspect studies the external behavior of the purposeful system Z, i.e., the outcomes provided by Z and its environment and the resources necessary to achieve these.

The constructive aspect examines the purposeful system Z as a system of functions and of the resources responsible for the realization of these functions.

The operative aspect studies the internal behavior of the purposeful system Z.

Each main point of view defines a system model of Z, these being known as the P, I/O, C and O models of Z respectively.

When Z is an information or data processing system the I/O aspect especially studies the semantical relations between Z and the real or abstract phenomenon about which the systematic information is considered to convey. We call this aspect as S aspect. Very often in the development work we have different people with different interests and backgrounds concerning the studies about the main aspects. The usual exception is with the last two ones and therefore we call them together shortly as C aspect. So PSC refers to the combination of pragmatic, semantic and constructive main aspects[5].

Structure of Development and Control

The second construct is based on partition of the development function. The simplest partition will be between design (D) and test (T). By combining these two constructs we obtain the hierarchical PSC structure of Figure 1.

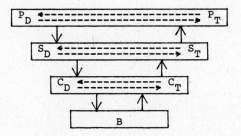

Figure 1
The Hierarchical PSC Structure

The continuous lines in Figure 1 refer to the sequence of performance in a succesful case, and the dotted lines to feedback loops.

The hierarchical PSC structures can be presented in sequence form by the following way:

(I) $P_D S_D C_D B C_T S_T P_T$

According to the sequence I, we have the following tasks:

P_D = pragmatic design

S_D = semantic design

C_D = constructive design

B = implementation of elements

C_T = constructive test

S_T = semantic test

P_T = pragmatic test,

in this order. The testing tasks will be performed in the opposite order from the design task, for the natural reason that it is not sensible to test the semantic features of the result unless the construction of the result is feasible. Nor is it profitable to test if the result has the desired benefits (P_T), unless it is semantically feasible.

Structure of Learning and Knowledge Basis

The information or data processing system during its life cycle is all the time under the different kind of management and control. The development process can be seen as the information production to those decision makers in order to add their knowledge basis- so it is

<u>a learning process too</u>. This means that we make decisions concerning the studies about the aspects P, S and C in this order and at the same time sequence I is iterated:

$$\underset{\text{aspect P}}{\text{decision of}} \qquad \underset{\text{aspect S}}{\text{decision of}} \qquad \underset{\text{aspect C}}{\text{decision of}}$$

$$(II) \quad \left[P_D S_D C_D B C_T S_T P_T\right]^{n_P} \left[P_D S_D C_D B C_T S_T P_T\right]^{n_S} \left[P_D S_D C_D B C_T S_T P_T\right]^{n_C}$$

where n_P, n_S and n_C are the numbers of iterations of subsequences before decision making.

The main activities in sequence II are P_D from the aspect P, S_D from the aspect S and C_D from the aspect C. The activities S_D, C_D and B from the aspect P will be performed preliminarily in order to determine whether it is potentially possible to build up a data system fulfilling the pragmatic objectives and requirements. Regarding the level of his knowledge basis the decision maker can iterate the subsequence. Also the decision to interrupt systemeering can be made after the tasks of the first subsequence of II.

Considering the transfer from first subsequence of II to the second one, we can conclude that it has been found at the end of the first subsequence that the design of the new data system fulfill the pragmatic requirements (P_T). After that we should again carry out pragmatic design (P_D), now within the aspect S. For the reason stated above, we shall ignore that task here, and by the same arguments we shall also ignore P_D and S_D from the aspect C.

By applying to the subsequences of the P, S and C decisions in connection with sequence II the terms <u>P, S and C main phases</u>, and by denoting them with upper indices, we obtain sequence III:

$$(III) \quad \left[P_D^P S_D^P C_D^P B^P C_T^P S_T^P P_T^P\right]^{n_P} \left[S_D^S C_D^S B^S C_T^S S_T^S P_T^S\right]^{n_S} \left[C_D^C B^C C_T^C S_T^C P_T^C\right]^{n_C}$$

P main phase   S main phase   C main phase

This sequence is characterized by stress on the production of decisions and information. Each main phase produces suitable information for some decision maker on the data system under development. Simultaneously, iterations at the two highest level are realized in this construct combination. It must be seen that this model is totally independent of organizations, and that a person or organizational unit can be engaged in more than one activity on the relation with the data system under development.

We found above that final implementation was not accounted for in our model of systemeering. After the addition of this and the corresponding testing tasks C_T, S_T and P_T with possible iterations to sequence III, we obtain our final sequence with the implementation main phase included:

$$(IV) \quad \left[P_D^P S_D^P C_D^P B^P C_T^P S_T^P P_T^P\right]^{n_P} \left[S_D^S C_D^S B^S C_T^S S_T^S P_T^S\right]^{n_S} \left[C_D^C B^C C_T^C S_T^C P_T^C\right]^{n_C} \left[B^B C_T^B S_T^B P_T^B\right]^{n_B}$$

Subsystem Structure of Data System

The partition into subsystems is crudely presented in Figure 2.

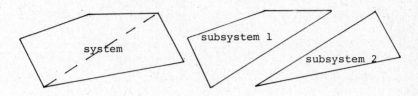

Figure 2
The Partition into Subsystems

The partition process demands that the subsystems together should have the same external properties as the original system. A system is often divided into subsystems because the system itself is imperceivable, i.e. too large to comprehend, and that the "smaller" subsystems can therefore be mastered more efficiently. Generally the subsystems are connected with each other in ways that are not included in the external properties of the original system. The "external properties" of a system refer to the relationships between the system and its environment.

Let us suppose now that in the systemeering task C_D^P we perceive it profitable to divide the data system into two subsystems. The hierarchical PSC structure, sequence I, is then applied to both subsystems. Sequence IV is then extended as follows:

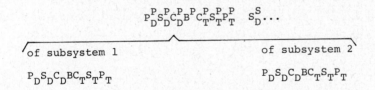

Task P_D of subsystem 1 represents its pragmatic design. Subsystem 2 is then allotted to the environment of subsystem 1 and can exercise certain pragmatic demands upon it. The other possible tasks also have to be interpreted in a corresponding way; i.e. subsystem 1 is now regarded as a system subject to design and testing. In due course the same also holds for subsystem 2.

It is possible that while performing the subphases C_D we may notice that either subsystem 1 or subsystem 2 (or both) are not yet perceivable. Supposing, for instance, that we cannot positively deduce "what parts subsystem 1 is made of and how it works", we could then divide it into three subsystems, indexed by 11, 12 and 13 respectively. Sequence IV would then be extended as follows:

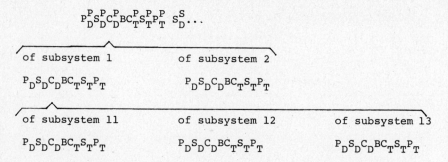

$P_D^P S_D^P C_D^P BC_T^P S_T^P P_T^P \; S_D^S \ldots$

of subsystem 1   of subsystem 2

$P_D S_D C_D BC_T S_T P_T$ $P_D S_D C_D BC_T S_T P_T$

of subsystem 11   of subsystem 12   of subsystem 13

$P_D S_D C_D BC_T S_T P_T$ $P_D S_D C_D BC_T S_T P_T$ $P_D S_D C_D BC_T S_T P_T$

Our implication is that subsystems have to be divided sufficiently deeply in the C_D tasks, and that the sequence I ($P_D S_D C_D BC_T S_T P_T$) has to be applied <u>simultaneously</u> and <u>repeatedly</u>.

The division into subsystems depends greatly on the person who carries it out. The more relationships there are between the subsystems, the more clarification and description work the systemeerer has. Therefore <u>the partition into subsystems should be carried out in such a way that each subsystem has as few connections with its environment as possible</u>. Partitioning into the subsystems can be exercised up to the different levels of abstractions and details.

MAIN PHASES with iter. / LEVELS OF DETAIL	P-PHASE with iter.	S-PHASE with iter.	C-PHASE with iter.	B-PHASE with iter.
P-SYSTEMEERING levels of detail { = = =	$P_D^P \quad P_T^P$	P_T^S	P_T^C	P_T^B
S-SYSTEMEERING levels of detail { = = =	$S_D^P \quad S_T^P$	$S_D^S \quad S_T^S$	S_T^C	S_T^B
C-SYSTEMEERING levels of detail { = = =	$C_D^P \quad C_T^P$	$C_D^S \quad C_T^S$	$C_D^C \quad C_T^C$	C_T^B
LEVEL OF OPERATIONS -implementation	B^P	B^S	B^C	B^B

Figure 3
Two Dimensional Structure of the PSC Systemeering Model

A two dimensional picture summarizing the PSC systemeering model appears in Figure 3. The column headings identify the main phases and their iterations. The rows in the Figure list four abstraction levels formed by three systemeering types and the operational level. Every level of abstraction has many levels of detail. The systems work proceeds through the main phases from left to right and in every main phase from top down and up again. On every abstraction level, the degree of detail increases when we move from one main phase to the following one.

On the General Model of Information Systems Development

Main functions and discontinuity of process

A systemeering process can be regarded as a purposeful system which always possesses certain main functions. In Järvinen-Kerola (1977) we partitioned a purposeful system into eight main functions: γ, μ, α, π, λ, ε, ι and ρ functions. The functions μ, α and π together define the logistic function and λ, ε, ι and ρ the supporting (resource) functions, which are a set of activities for the acquisition, attendance, maintenance and development of the long-term physical resources (λ), man-power resources (ε), information resources (ι) and financial resources (ρ) needed by the purposeful system. The γ function is a set of control activities for the whole system, and also takes care of its own maintenance and development. The partition process is described in Figure 4.

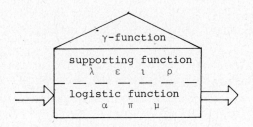

purposeful system

Figure 4
Partition of a Purposeful System

As the PSC and other systemeering models show, systemeering is not a unique process, but consists of different subprocesses or tasks which can also exist iteratively and/or recursively. In general, production processes can be classified as either continuous or discontinuous. The systemeering process is clearly a discontinuous one. Discontinuous processes differ from continuous ones in that they always require some initiating and terminating effort preceding and following the essential process (Figure 5).

By replacing the essential process in Figure 5 by the partition in Figure 4 and using the same term "activity", we obtain a model for a discontinuous process (Figure 6).

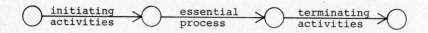

Figure 5
Initiating and Terminating Activities Surrounding
an Essential Discontinuous Process

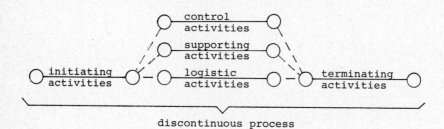

discontinuous process

Figure 6
Model of a Discontinuous Process

The PSC systemeering model is now appended to the general model of information systems development (systems work) by applying this construct to the whole process, the main phases and minor phases, the "logistic activities" being replaced by the sub-processes of the model in the sequence IV or Figure 3. At the beginning, for example, there are the first initiating tasks for the whole process, secondly the initiating tasks for the main phase P ($P^P_D S^S_D C^C_D B^P C^P_T S^P_T P^P_T$) and thirdly the initiating tasks for phase P^P_D. The initiating tasks for the whole process contain: 1. organization of the control subsystem, 2. formation of the supporting subsystems λ, ε, ι, ρ, and 3. organization of the essential project group for the systemeering and/or implementation process.

The model developed and described in general terms above does not imply that every effort in the information systems development must contain all the main phases. It depends on the level of knowledge and objectives of the different decision makers and the level of the model descriptions concerned and/or their implementation. The starting point may be the beginning of any main phase, the whole process then comprising the set of logically consequent main phases by the assumption that the documents from the earlier phases are available. If not, those must be prepared.

The other conclusion to be drawn from this discussion is that it is not possible to give a fixed model, applicable to every case of

information system development. The model presented can be thought
as a metamodel or framework model which is flexible and can be
applied according to situation. The latter point argues in favour of
the view that there is no reason for learning the task list of sequences by heart, but one should rather try to adopt the construction principles behind it. Then one would be able to develop models
suitable to each particular development project.

THE INFOLOGICAL RESEARCH METHOD

Basic Concepts

Partly because of their complicated nature, the results of infological research have not received the attention they deserve. The
research does not yet appear to possess a sufficiently clearly-
defined conceptual framework, and thus the concepts and terms are
continually being elaborated upon, and differ in usage from one
researcher to another. Thus it is difficult to interpret the results.
The framework set out below as a background to infological research
is based on semiotics.

Semiotics, which dates back to the turn of the century, is that
branch of science concerned with signs and symbol systems, and as
such its models have spread to many other branches. The structures
recognized by semiotics include the division of information into
pragmatics, semantics and syntax, and the recognition within semantics of a physical, a conceptual and a linguistic level.

In Figure 7 we have a summary of the basic set of concepts needed in
this research. It is impossible here to give the complete definitions of the concepts, but this simply gives an idea of the approach.

Figure 7 contains a semiotic analysis of the knowledge associated
with a subject-object pair and a definition of the objects of infological examination and the basic concepts required for this. The
subject is divided up into a subject system, and it is the informational relationship between this and the object system which is the
real point of interest. This general examination may then be applied
to the project for constructing an information system and the object
systems contained in this. The most essential parts of this are
depicted in the lower part of Figure 7.

Decision Makers and their Choice and Quality Criteria

The PSC systemeering model used as a starting-point here is depicted
in the form of a decision-making process in Figure 8.

The research examines the construction of a data system from the
point of view of the form-bound information production required by
the decision-makers. The persons or roles responsible for the decisions fall into four groups:
- (P) pragmatic-level decision-makers, responsible for the influ-
      ences created by the functional units of the whole information
      system,
- (S) semantic-level decision-makers, responsible for the information
      content produced by the data system,
- (C) constructive-level decision-makers, responsible for the

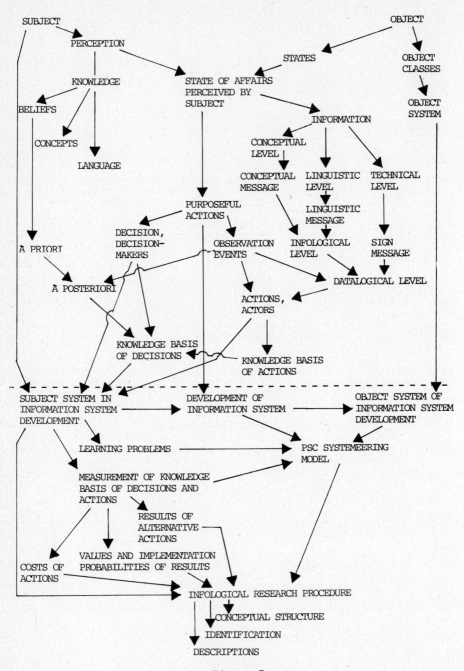

Figure 7
Set of Basic Concepts

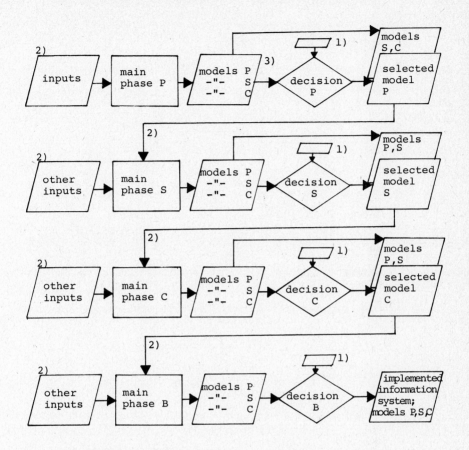

The alternative descriptions for the information system to be constructed, which are produced as the results of the application of
each type of systemeering in each main phase of the PSC systemeering
model, are termed the models P, S and C. The decision-making process
at the end of each main phase selects that model which represents
the result of the most essential designing unit of the phase within
the construction process. The selected models P, S and C then form a
description of the implemented information system after the last
main phase.

1)   Information held by the decision-makers not obtainable from the
      systemeering process.

2)   Input information required for the formation of the models P, S
      and C in the respective main phases.

3)   The models also appear in physical and linguistic form in this
      connection.

Figure 8
Decision Process

constructional solutions concerning the data system,
- (B) <u>operative-level decision-makers</u>, responsible for the production and use of the data system.

Each group may be composed of all the potential decision-makers, or
persons chosen by or representing them. The decision-making subjects
form a hierarchy in the above order, with the decision-making knowledge of each subject groups being based on criteria particular to
that group, so that the production of additional evidence presupposes
the corresponding main phase. <u>Each main phase may be seen as a
process of information production as far as that decision-making
group in concerned.</u> The <u>action subjects</u> are those persons who perform
each type of systemeering and the tasks of implementation - the P, S
and C systemeerers and implementers. Their actions and increasing
knowledge are governed by the corresponding criteria as those applying to the decision-makers. The work of the various individuals
involved in constructing a data system is viewed as a process of
cooperation and interaction, even though we restrict it here to
<u>exclude directive information from our sphere of interest and concen-
trate on defining and producing knowledge concerning the final outcome, the data system itself</u>.

The problem of the selection of a data system is defined to be in
general of the form (Emery (1974), Iivari-Koskela (1979)).

Search for a model or set of models such that the object
function

$$\sum_{S_i \in \sigma} P(S_i) [\sum_{o_k \in 0} P(o_k|S_i)V(o_k) - \sum_{c_k \in C} P(c_k|S_i)c_k]$$

is maximized, where

S_i = alternative premises

o_k = results

$V(o_k)$ = yield, i.e. value of the results

c_k = costs

$P( )$ = probabilities of realization of the premises, results
and costs

and where certain limiting conditions are met.

The decision-maker must then ensure, in accordance with the structure of the selection criteria, that he possesses knowledge concerning
-     the set of models from which to choose,
-     the set of initial assumptions or premises, and the probabili-
      ties $P(S_i)$ of its elements being realized,
-     the results obtained by each model, measured by the quality
      criteria $V(o_k)$, and the probabilities of realization of these
      results under different premises $P(o_k|S_i)$,
-     the costs c_k implied in each model, and their probabilities of
      realization under different premises $P(c_k|S_i)$.

Certain special features of the selection criterion parameters for
the models P, S and C defined in Figure 8 are illustrated in Figure 9.

	MODEL P	MODEL S	MODEL C
LIMITING CONDITIONS	CONCERN QUALITY CRITERIA	CONCERN QUALITY CRITERIA SELECTED MODEL P MUST BE REALIZED	CONCERN QUALITY CRITERIA SELECTED MODELS P AND S MUST BE REALIZED
s_i	POSSIBLE EXPLOIT-ABLE DEVELOPMENT MODELS OF THE UTILIZING SYSTEM	POSSIBLE ACTION MODELS FOR USER IN RESPECT OF THE INFORMATION	POSSIBLE RESOURCES AND THEIR ACTION MODELS
$v(o_k)$	EFFECTIVENESS - COMPONENTS	USER SATISFAC-TION - COMPONENTS as the "sum" of all users	-
c_k	ALTERNATIVE COSTS		
SELECTION	EFFECTIVENESS/ COSTS	USER SATISFAC-TION/COSTS	COSTS

Figure 9
Selection Criterion Parameters

It follows from the Figure 9 that

1.   Net value criteria based on effectiveness and costs of the information system during its life cycle are employed for the selection of the model P.

2.   Net value criteria based on user satisfaction and costs of the information system during its life cycle are employed for the selection of the model S.

3.   The cost of the information production serve as the selection criteria for the model C.

These effectiveness, user satisfaction and cost criteria are known as the quality criteria for the data system. In practice, of course, each has its own hierarchical structure of lower level criteria, but it is not possible to examine these in detail here (see for example Iivari-Koskela (1979)).

Research Procedure

The main steps in the procedure are the following:

1.   The decision-making subject is the starting point for each main phase, and information production takes place in coopera-tion with the action subject.

2.   Research is focused first upon the conceptual level, i.e. a conceptual structure is created, by means of which the subject attempts to understand phenomena concerned with the object

system.

3.   The conceptual structure is described at the linguistic level
        by the tree.

4.   Within the conceptual structure an examination is made of the
        choice criteria used by the decision-maker and of the object
        system under observation.

5.   All the elements of the trees are described at the linguistic
        level by the information identification matrices, where the
        columns are the selected quality and choice criteria and the
        rows different characteristics of the object element concerned.
        The matrix values give the existence of potential relation
        between the columns and rows.

The research operates principally with units of the conceptual level.
The analysis concentrates upon identification of the components of
the object system and in part on the evaluation of the significance
of information concerning the components in relation to the quality
and choice criteria used by the decision-maker. Some examination is
also made of the logical rules of information formulation. The
procedure is illustrated in Figures 10 and 11.

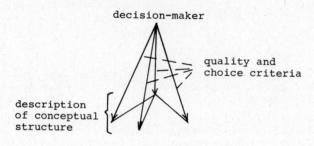

decision-maker

quality and
choice criteria

description
of conceptual
structure

Figure 10
The Research Objects

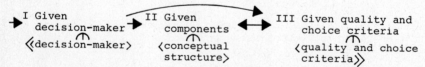

I Given
   decision-maker
《decision-maker〉

II Given
   components
〈conceptual
structure〉

III Given quality and
    choice criteria
〈quality and choice
criteria》

I   One decision-maker at a time is selected from the set of deci-
    sion-makers defined in the research.

II The decision-maker selected determines what conceptual structure
    components are to be the topic of interest in each case.

III The decision-maker selected and the components to be examined
    determine the relevant quality and choice criteria, which in
    turn enable the conceptual structure to be examined from the
    viewpoint of the decision-maker.

Figure 11
The Research Process

CONCLUSION

This paper has presented the outlines of infological research into the systemeering process. Research has been recursive in nature, because the infological approach also is an essential part of the systemeering process. The emphasis has been on the definition and description of the models and methods needed in the research. For the following steps, every main phase is analyzed by this same research procedure. The first results of the analysis are now available as working papers. This systems and information analysis of the development process offers a better and deeper understanding of the different roles and communication among people involved in the systemeering process, and of the development of computer assisted information systems which support systems work.

ACKNOWLEDGEMENTS

Because of the summary nature of this paper, many earlier papers have been used. The development of the PSC systemeering model and its infological research has been based on the excellent team work among several researchers and senior students. Especially I would like to express my gratitude to Pertti Järvinen, Juhani Iivari and the members of DISCO project team. I have also gained valuable insight from discussions with the participants of systemeering research seminars at Tampere and Turku.

FOOTNOTES

1   This tendency is also reflected in the terms for computer science in other languages, e.g. French "informatique" and German "Informatik".

2   See the analogy with the term "programming" regarding the content of the concept in the general sense and in the specific sense concerned with computers.

3   The term is used in a different meaning from that normally assumed in systems analysis and design.

4   Defined by Ackoff (1972).

5   Welke (1977) has given very similar perspectives accordingly: systelogical, infological and datalogical.

REFERENCES

Ackoff, R., Emery, F.E., On purposeful systems (Aldine-Atherton Press, Chicago, 1972).

Ahmavaara, Y., The cybernetic theory of development (Tammi, Helsinki, 1974).

Davis, G.B., Management information systems: conceptual foundations, structures and development (McGraw-Hill, New York, 1974).

Eco, A theory of semiotics (Indiana Univ. Press, Bloomington, London, 1976).

216 P. KEROLA

Emery, J.C., Cost and benefits of information systems, IFIP 74.

Grochla, E., Die Wirtschaftlichkeit Automatisierter Datenverarbeitungssysteme, Betriebswirtschaftlichter (Verlag Dr. Th. Gabler, Wiesbaden, 1970).

Høyer, R., System design and social reality: formal and informal aspects of administrative control, Personnel Review 1 (1976).

Iivari, J., Pragmatic control in the development of data processing function, Lic. Thesis, Inst. of DP Science, Univ. of Oulu (1978) (in Finnish).

Iivari, J., Koskela, E., Choice and quality criteria for data system selection, EuroIFIP 79, London (1979) (to be appeared).

Järvinen, P., Kerola, P., Notes on research in systemeering. Ann. Univ. Turkuensis, Ser A.1.175, Turku (1977).

Järvinen, P., Kerola, P., Systemeering I - Practice in data system development (Gaudeamus, Helsinki, 1979) (in Finnish).

Kerola, P., On hierarchical information and data systems in data systems life cycle, Systemeering 75 (Studentlitteratur, Lund, 1975).

Kerola, P. & al (eds.), Summary report of the systemeering research seminar of Tampere 21.-24.8.1978, Finnish Data Proc. Ass., Helsinki (1979).

Kerola, P., Järvinen, P., Systemeering II - System theoretical and cybernetic model of data system development and use (Gaudeamus, Helsinki, 1975) (in Finnish).

Land, F., Evaluation of systems goals in determining a design strategy for a computer based information system, Comp. Journal, Vol.19 4 (1976).

Langefors, B., Theoretical analysis of information systems (Studentlitteratur, Lund, 1973).

Langefors, B., Sundgren, B., Information systems architecture (Mason/ Charter Publ., London, 1975).

Laundry, M., Le Moigne, J-L., Towards a theory of organizational information system - A general system perspective, IFIP 77, Toronto.

Lucas, H., Why information systems fail? (Columbia Univ. Press,1975).

Lundeberg, M., Some propositions concerning analysis and design of information systems, Specialist Report, TRAITA-IBADB-4080, ISAC (1976).

Lundeberg, M., Goldkuhl, Nilsson, Information systems development - A first introduction to a systematic approach, ISAC Group, Univ. of Stockholm (1978).

Mason, Mitroff, A program for research on management information systems, Mgmt Sc., Vol.19 5 (1973).

Mesarovic, M.D., Macko, D., Takahara, Y., Theory of hierarchical multilevel systems (Academic Press, London, 1970).

Mumford, E., Land, Hawgood, A participative approach to the design of computer systems, Impact of Science Society, Vol.28 3 (1978).

Nauta, D., The meaning of information (Mouton, Hague, 1972).

Singer, C.A., A methodology for the determination and communication of requirements for an information processing system, PHD Thesis, Purdue Univ. (1976).

Stamper, Semantic aspects of information systems, Crest Course, Man. Inf. Syst. (July 1977).(to be published).

Sundgren, B., An infological approach to data bases, Statistiska Centralbyrån, Skrifts no.7, Stockholm (1973).

Taggart, Tharp, A survey of information requirements analysis techniques, Comm. of ACM (1977).

Wedekind, H., On the parametric specification of data base oriented information systems, Mgmt Datamatics, Vol.5 (1976).

Welke, R.J., Current information system analysis and design approaches: Framework, overview, comments and conclusions for large-complex information system education, in: Buckingham, R.A. (ed.), Education and Large Information Systems (Nort-Holland, Amsterdam, 1977).

The Information Systems Environment
Lucas, Land, Lincoln, Supper (Editors)
North-Holland Publishing Company
© *IFIP, 1980*

PARTICIPATIVE DEVELOPMENT OF INFORMATION
SYSTEMS

METHODOLOGICAL ASPECTS AND EMPIRICAL
EXPERIENCES

H.J. Oppelland and F. Kolf

In order to realize economic and social benefits
in the design and implementation of computer-based
information systems we must recognize the interests
of potential users. Passive "user-involvement" is
insufficient because the success of systems development depends on socio-psychological phenomena. User
interests are primarily oriented toward the organization and procedures of the development process
and the design of system components. In this paper
we present several exisiting approaches to integrating user interests in design. We focus on the PORGI-
concept of planning for organizational implementation,
which aims at operational tools to support the recognition and integration of user interests from
the start of an OR/MS-project. The paper reports
some empirical observations and discusses some conclusions.

METHODOLOGICAL BACKGROUND OF PARTICIPATIVE SYSTEM DESIGN

In this paper - like some previous work (e.g. Kolf et al. (1978);
Kolf and Oppelland (1979); Kolf and Oppelland (1980) - we stress the
importance of participative system development for computer-based
information systems (CBIS). If the participative approach for system
development is claimed to be more than what we can call normative,
we have to clarify what contribution we can expect from participation
of those concerned in system development, implementation and evaluation.

To evaluate alternative approaches, strategies and procedures in information system design we need to define the aim of system development, the expected result of system design activities. A final aim
in system development is to reach satisfactory results for the process of system development and system use in economic and social
terms.[1] It is clear that this goal implies an effective and

---

[1] As to our knowledge there exist two explicit (and methodical supported) participative approaches to information system design:
ABACON (including BASYC and ETHIC) and PORGI, see e.g. Mumford et
al. (1978) and Kolf et al. (1978). PORGI is an acronym for "planning tools for the organizational implementation of computer-based
information systems". The PORGI-approach is developed since 1975
at the "Betriebswirtschaftliches Institut für Organisation und Automation (BIFOA)" at the University of Cologne, Germany.

efficient combination of the technical, organizational, and personal parts or elements of an information system. But the equalization of social aims with economic ones results in some considerable consequences for the way in which those concerned are to be involved in system design. Beside a real necessity to consider special knowledge and experiences of those qualified there is a demand for consideration of interests, goals and needs of individuals and the groups in organizations which are concerned with system development.2)

But what is the background to support this understanding? Realization and implementation of CBIS for strong formalized information processes involve well known technical problem solutions. Extending CBIS for more unstructured decision processes leads to other kind of problems, which require a new broader understanding of system development as a process of change (Ginzberg (1975)). Experiences show that explication and modelling of task procedures, problem solutions, and decision processes requires adequate cooperation between task experts and dp/system experts to overcome problems of different occupational training, cognitive styles (Barkin (1974); Bariff and Lusk (1977); Benbasat and Schroeder (1977)), attitudes (Churchman and Schainblatt (1965); Dyckman (1967); Lucas (1975)), and values (Hedberg and Mumford (1975)), and even different expectations to system design results.
The degree of organizational and social change arising from system development lead to structural and motivational (or emotional) barriers. These problems can not be solved only through some organizational modifications or user training, but often make necessary a far extending system revision (Oppelland et al. (1977)). Some experiences with the application of PORGI instruments show that those concerned tend to evaluate system development and its changes more emotionally and uncritically if they are not involved in active system design, but only receive information about it (see below). On the other hand it seemed that active participation enables those concerned to develop better understanding of problems and create helpful system design contributions.

Heterogenity and number of organization members which are affected or concerned by systems development, their interests, goals, and needs are another relevant problem causing aspects of complex system development processes. These aspects make necessary adequate organizational and social rules for interaction, interests balancing, and decision making. If, for instance, based on organizational or other reasons, not all those affected can be involved in system design activitis and therefore have to be represented by selected representatives, the rules for representative selection and adequate compensation for being less involved become very important points. We have to stress here, that passive involvement in system design has proven to be inadequate to stimulate motivation, acceptance, and identification for successful system use.

---

2) Another wellknown but somewhat narrow term for "those concerned" or "those affected" is "user" (enduser).

The PORGI Approach of Participative System Design

PORGI is the name of a research project[3] involving a concept of participative system design and organizational implementation of information systems. The PORGI approach focusses on two objectives of system development

. system fit and

. process fit.

The system fit means that a system is designed so that all parts of the system fit together. This approach implies consideration of not only the technological aspects of a system, for example hardware and software features, but attention on integrating task, men, organizational structure and (information) technology[4] into a view or concept of information system as a whole.

This integrated design of information systems for system fit requires:

. Adequate diagnosis of the actual state of system use,

. Intensive analysis of problems in actual system use and their possible causes,

. Clear definition of system design objectives including consideration of innovation (step) feasibility,

. Careful and repeated tuning of all system components during the design process.

The more people involved with different roles, interests, and professional education and knowledge, the more we need careful management of the system development process. We argue that system fit can not be guaranteed without attaining process fit. The process fit means that the planning and managing of the system design process is so good that all those affected accept it as satisfactory[5] technologically, economically, and socially. Users are satisfied for themselves, their department, and the organization as a whole.

This successful management of information system design process for process fit requires:

. Clear organizational structure, task and responsibility definition for project groups and committees for steering, decision-making, or controlling,

. Thorough structuring and documentation of the substantive and temporal systems design (project phases),

. Adequate rules for organizational and social interaction of those organizational members to be involved into system design,

---

[3] The PORGI-project has been realized from 1975 to 1979 at the "Betriebswirtschaftliches Institut für Organisation und Automation (BIFOA)" at the University of Cologne and has been granted by the government.

[4] These differentation stems from Leavitt (1965).

[5] We differentiate "satisfactory" from "optimal" because of the human aspects of (individual) evaluating.

. Acceptable consideration of users'/specialists' personal and task-
oriented needs for participation in system design.

The Methodical Framework of the PORGI Approach

The PORGI approach is based on empirical experiences and theoretical
knowledge related to problems of information system design and process management (Oppelland et al. (1977)). The first step of our research has been to discover those characteristics of information system design and implementation which have caused problems leading to
system failure or at least to negative side-effects. The results of
this empirical analysis is a descriptional framework and a pool of
implementation problems.

The Descriptive Framework (DF) can be seen as a systematic, hierarchi-
cally structured description of principal terms of system design and
implementation situations which are related to possible problems. It
is the background for the design and application of PORGI tools as
methodical instruments for situational analysis and diagnosis. The
descriptive framework can serve to check the PORGI tools in order to
complete, reduce, or alter them in another way for adequate applications.

To decide which states or characteristics of an actual system design
and implementation situation are to be seen as problems requires information about

(1) the actual states or characteristics of the situation,

(2) What kind of situations have created problems[6]

The need for information about the actual states and characteristics
of a systems design project lead to the development of the PORGI-
tools. They can be seen as Methodical Instruments (METH) for situational analysis and diagnosis.

The PORGI-tools are checklists, questionnaires, and tables for gathering, presenting, and analyzing those data necessary for adequate management of the system design process. These checklists and questionnaires focus on aspects of system design and process management relevant for attaining system fit and process fit (see Tables 1 and 2).
They attempt to obtain information about the actual state of system
fit and process fit and can refer to either departments' or individuals' attitudes, statements, or views.

---

[6] As to our knowledge there does not exist any theory of system
design and implementation up to now, which can help to explain
problem rise.

Name	Scope
. SITUATIONAL ANALYSIS (SIT)	Actual state of system use, "history" of system development until the present
. PROBLEM ANALYSIS (PROB)	Intensive analysis of problems in actual system use, possible problem causing elements
. ORGANIZATION ANALYSIS (ORG)	Determination of existing formal and informal organizational structures
. OBJECTIVES DEFINITION (OBJECT)	Definition of system design objectives, including determination of information requirements and consideration of innovation (step) feasibility
. SYSTEM TUNING (TUNE)	Tuning of system components in design and implementation phases

Table 1: PORGI Tools for System Fit

Name	Scope
. ANALYSIS OF CONCERNS (CERN)	Analysis of kind and degree of concerns in system development
. PARTICIPATION ANALYSIS (PART)	Analysis of desired versus experienced kind and degree of participation in system design and implementation
. ORGANIZATION OF SYSTEM DESIGN PROJECT (ORSYS)	Analysis of existing and required organizational structure for project groups and committees, and rules for organizational and social interaction

Table 2: PORGI Tools for Process Fit

System Design Activity \ Situational Diagnosis	with PORGI Tool ...							
	CERN	PART	ORSYS	SIT	PROB	ORG	OBJECT	TUNE
(1) Problem description	X	(X)		X	X	X		
(2) Problem analysis	X	X		X	X	X	X	
(3) Feasibility study	X	X	(X)	X			X	
(4) Project organi-zation	X	X	X					
(5) Coarse concept	(X)	X	X					X
(6) Detailed concept	(X)	X	X					X
(7) Realization	(X)	X	X					X
(8) Test				(X)				X
(9) Introduction	(X)	X	X					X
(10) Use		X	X					

Table   3: Synopsis of PORGI Tool Application During
         the Design Process

The pool of Implementation Problems (IP) can help to identify actual or possible future problems, because it contains a set of empirically and theoretically based problems of system design and process management. These problems are correlated with insufficient system or process fit. Analyzing the information gathered by PORGI tools and comparing them with the set of prior implementation problems suggest potential problems in a given implementation effort.

In order to support the system designer, project manager, etc. in attaining system fit and process fit we present proposals of experts in system design and project management. These proposals are appropriate for avoiding expected problems, reducing their possible consequences, or handling unexpected problems. These design proposals and general design principles are joined to form a pool of Design Concepts (CON). They can be seen as problem solving examples which have been confirmed by practice.

By a Procedural Scheme (PROC) we describe a sequence of ten well-known system design activities (phases). For each of these system design activities special procedures are specified for organizational implementation (O.I.) to attain system and process fit. In addition for all these organizational implementation activities, the procedural scheme contains references to the PORGI tools available to support them. Thus the procedural scheme can be seen as the regulation part of the PORGI concept, which aids in selection and application of PORGI tools.

The procedure of PORGI tool application can be determinded by the following steps (see Figure 1 for an overview):

(1) Identification of the actual stage or phase of the system design process and location in the Procedural Scheme (PROC);

(2) Selection of the appropriate PORGI tools, which for this system design phase are available in the pool of Methodical Instruments (METH);

(3) If necessary, adapt the selected PORGI tool to actual circumstances through features of the Descriptional Framework (DF);

(4) Application of the PORGI tool for data gathering and presentation; analyzing the data obtained for discovering possible problems (METH);

(5) Comparing actual problem profiles with the problem descriptions documented in the pool of Implementation Problems (IP);

(6) Critical checking of proposed problem solutions or system design proposals which are assembled in the pool of Design Concepts (CON);

(7) Realizing appropriate design actions, go on to the next step or phase of system design, and starting a new cycle of PORGI tool application.

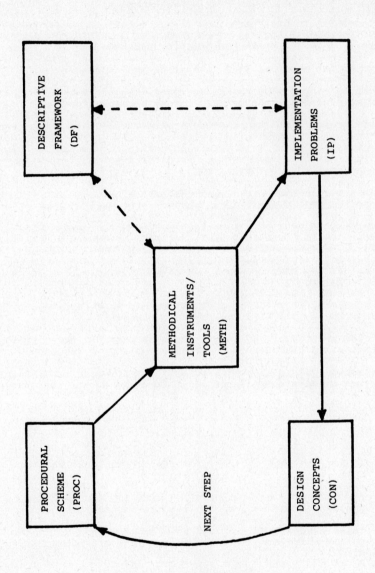

Figure 1:Steps of PORGI Tool Application

EMPIRICAL EXPERIENCES WITH THE PORGI TOOLS

The second part of this paper discusses some of our experiences with the practical application of PORGI tools in two computer-based information systems development projects in German companies.

The studies focus on

(1) process fit diagnosis in a large-scale electrical engineering company and

(2) system fit diagnosis in a medium-size pharmaceutical company.

This studies will be followed by some critical conclusions regarding the application of such tools.

An Electrical Engineering Firm

We started practical tests of PORGI instruments in a wellknown large-scale company in the German electrical industry. Their department for data processing has been willing to cooperate with us in the application of methodical instruments in system development for a new cost accounting and evaluation system (CAES). The new system will replace existing subsystems. The system development implies little technological innovation but much standardization of procedures. Directly concerned with system application are about 2oo project leaders (the users) - with perhaps 2ooo subordinates indirectly concerned - and a project-group of six members concerned with system design (the designers). The user project-groups belong to different sub-departments for hardware and software research and development, organizational development, maintenance tasks, and others. They are a heterogenous group of users with different demands and interests. The designers are members of the sub-department for organization and data processing and were partly supported by members of the sub-departments for accounting and software development. We joined this project (CAES) in a phase called "planning phase I", which is completed with a coarse version of the systems design.

Step (0.1): Situational Diagnosis

Preliminary information which was given to the PORGI-team indicated that it would be helpful to make an extensive diagnosis of implementation. For this diagnosis we use the special checklist PORGI-SIT, which enables us to review the project history up to the present. PORGI-SIT is a combination of other PORGI checklists and questionnaires and was especially designed for ex-post check up. It is very valuable when PORGI is applied in the middle of the systems development process. Responses from the CAES project group on age, degree of concern and participation to date were placed in a summary table. This summary table may be used in all diagnoses performed during the design process - starting with rough information about the initiating phase (as in our case) and continuing with proposals for adequate participation. The table also aids in demonstrating the changes in design process organization and increases in process fit. Diagnosis with PORGI in this case led to the conclusion to concentrate the application of PORGI-tools mainly on aspects of design process organization, on some aspects of tuning system components and on consideration of organizational consequences.

PARTICIPATION	ratifi-cation	responsible performing	cooperation consultancy	receiving information	not involved
1. What kind of participation have you experienced in the past phase of system development ?					
2. What kind of participation would have been appropriate to you ?					
3. What kind of participation do you desire for the future phases of system development ?					

Please note reasons, when experiences kinds of participation differ from the appropriate desired ones:

ELECTION OF REPRESENTATIVES	hierarchy	qualifi-cation	available time	co-worker proposal	other
4. On what kind of criterion are elections of representatives for system design participation based ?					
5. On what kind of criterion do you think that elections should be based ?					

Please note the reason for your desire, if it differs from your experience :

Table 4: Part of the PORGI-based Questionnaire CAES-Q

Step (O.2): Selection and Compilation of PORGI tools

PORGI tools are designed to supply instruments which are to be selected, compiled and, perhaps, modified as necessary for application.
In this case we decided to apply a special combined questionnaire
composed of different sets of questions from different tools to
supply information needed to organize the design process so that the
interests and needs of those concerned could be met adequately. The
questionnaire focused on the following aspects:

. Function and competency of those concerned with system usage, e.g.

   .. supply of input

   .. preparing alternatives

   .. operating the system

   .. ratification of the results

   .. receiving output

. Expected or known changes for task-oriented aspects of work resulting from system development and their importance for those concerned, e.g.

   .. task assignment

   .. work flow

   .. decision autonomy

   .. responsibility

   .. information

   .. quality of own work

   .. work loads/stress

   .. control by others

These first aspects are aimed at the identification of concerns and
their degree; the following concentrate on the kind of participation experienced and its evaluation for past phases of system design, the desired participation in future phases, the experiences
and desired rules for the election of representatives of a user
group, identification of members who cannot participate at all, and
the experienced and desired kind of information exchange in represented groups. Some of these items are shown in the selected part
of our questionnaire (see Table 4).

In order to support the use of system components and the interpretation of questionnaire results we added some questions which refer
to the evaluation of system concepts, personal and organizational
consequences of system implementation, proposals for preparing and
managing the system introduction, and personal data (age, sex, education, professional experience).

Step (1): Tool Application I

The designed questionnaire CAES-Q was applied first during a session
for presentation and tuning the coarse version of the CAES concept
at the end of planning phase I. It was answered by the representation of the involved subdepartments. The following points emerged:

. In no case is experienced participation evaluated to be too
intensive.

. Only 25 % of those concerned called their experienced kind of
participation unconditionally satisfactory, 75 % desired more
intensive participation.

. Active cooperation in systems design by giving suggestions, consultancy etc. and participation in decision responsibility is evaluated to be positive or ideal compared to any more passive kind of
participation.

. The more important expected or known changes are for those concerned, the more they desire an intensive and active participation
in system design.

. Intensive participation of those concerned clearly corresponds
with their ability
  .. to realize the extent and importance of personal and organizational consequences of system implementation,
  .. to consider possible problem solutions and to create constructive proposals for organizational changes.

. The attitude towards system development of those concerned is
rather positive, their evaluation is more critical but also diffe-
rentiated if they have experienced more intensive participation.
Much too little participation tends to result in an emotionally
influenced distance from system development or neglect of its
impact.

These statements confirm the importance of process organization.
They led to the following proposals referring to PORGI design concepts (CON):

. To increase openess and transparency of system design process by
more intensive information about it, beginning with the feedback
of questionnaire results,

. to document an individual's participation in system design activities in writing, protocols, circulars etc., in order to consider
his self-assessment and self-confidence, but also to achieve clear
responsibility,

. to consider competence of user department's representatives by
paying special attention to their hierarchial status and the cri
teria of representative elections,

. to ask those concerned (or their representatives) what kind of
participation they desire in the next phase of system dssign.

The CAES-project group accepted these proposals and the underlying ideas. Feedback of questionnaire results were given together with a protocol explaining the critical aspects and a short additional questionnaire regarding participation demands. All these questionnaires were filled out completely and returned to the CAES-group. Organization of participation in the planning phase II of CAES was altered due to the results of this questionnaire.

Step (2): Instrument Application II

At the end of the so called planning phase II the modified questionnaire CAES-Q was used to check the detailed version of the system concept for adequate design. CAES-Q was sent to the representatives of the departments involved, 2/3 of the questionnaires were completed and returned.

The evaluation of the answers in comparison to those of the previous questionnaire application led to the following problems:

. The degree of participation of those concerned had increased, but not in all cases. Therefore evaluation of perceived participation had been impaired.

. By better knowledge of the changes intended through system implementation or resulting from it the participants felt impressed and were able to point to some crucial aspects of system realization and implementation.

Our proposals for the following phase of system realization were:

. If one has called for a need to participate in system design, one has to satisfy it - or problems could become more difficult.

. The more participants changed during systems design, the more the judgement and competence of new participants are uncertain and unreliable for design decisions.

. The more participants learn to express their needs and to evaluate perceived system design the better they are able to help the system specialist in designing an adequate system and preparing the organization for successful system implementation and efficient system use.

A Pharmaceuticals Company

The application of tools and instruments for planning the system fit is illustrated by a CBIS-project in a medium-sized pharmaceuticals company. The main focus of this study was on the transition from the pool of methods (METH) to the pool of implementation problems (IP). The study describes how we proceed from the information gathered by the use of PORGI checklists and questionnaires to the analysis of the situation and the identification of possible problems and solutions.

The pharmaceuticals company is organized in functional divisions (finance, marketing, production etc.). The PORGI-team became involved after the company had decided to implement a standard software package from a large software supplier. The objective of the CBIS-project was to implement a corporate financial planning model for

a five years planning horizon. Some of the initially stated requirements were:

- To simulate different alternatives regarding sales volume, prices,
  costs etc.,

- To state the consequences of these alternatives for the profit and
  loss statements and balance sheet of the next five years,

- To set up a five year financial plan,

- To develop a procurement plan for raw materials,

- To perform sensitivity analysis for specific groups of costs,

- To develop a capacity and investment plan.

The first activity of the PORGI team was the completion of the
initial situational diagnosis by the use of the PORGI checklist SIT.
From that initial situational diagnosis we were able to identify
those members of the organization who were strongly affected by the
new system and should therefore be participants in the phase "problem definition/analysis". The problem definition and analysis was
performed by the use of the PORGI checklist PROB and will be used
as an example to demonstrate the interaction between the different
types of PORGI instruments.

We assume that a CBIS-project is initiated to solve a specific problem by designing a new socio-technical solution. With the term "problem" is associated "the difference between some existing situations
and some desired situations"(Pounds (1969)).
The objective of problem analysis/definition is therefore to describe
an unsatisfactory situation in a way which gives a picture that is
accepted by all those affected.

The use of the checklist PROB in an interview or (group)discussion
follows those steps:

  . Inform the participants about the objective of the
    interview/discussion,

  . Describe design activities performed up to now,

  . Discuss the planned procedure of the interview/discussion,

  . Discuss the items on the checklist and whether they can
    be identified as being problems in your specific
    situation or not.

The right column of the checklist ("possible problem causes") may
serve as examples for stimulation of the discussion.

By checking the items and associated problem causes PROB serves as a
guide for the discussion and interviews with all those who have been
identified in the initial situational diagnosis. As an example some
of the items of PROB regarding the planning task to be supported by
the new system are shown in Table 5. Additionally the system components "man", "organizational context" and "information technology"
are covered in the same way.

Characteristics of the situation	Possible problem causes
TASK:	
<u>Time structure of task</u>	
· Planning horizon	Too short Lack of long-range perspectives
· Length of planning process	Too long Insufficient possibility to answer Changes in market conditions appropriately
· Initiative for planning process	Unsystematic ad-hoc planning
<u>Level of task</u>	
· Problem-level	Only operative plan-ing, no integration with strategic planning
· Considered units	Isolated unit plan Inclusion of additional organizational units Integration with other units insufficiently handled Planning process is crossing lines of authority but no unit for coordination available

<u>Table 5:</u> Part of the PORGI Checklist PROB for Problem Analysis

(1) Interpretation of diagnosed problems

   All of the information regarding each individual item of PROB
   has to be checked if a significant number of people have identified that respective item to be a problem descriptor.

(2) Interpretation regarding the people involved

   For each member of the organization involved in the planning
   task under consideration (or relatively homogenous groups of
   people) items have to be analyzed which individuals have identified to be problem descriptors.

One of the major findings of PROB application in this case study was
that the CBIS-project was primarily initiated by the vice-president
of finance and that this division had dominated all design activities
up to now. But the new system would be an integrated system covering
all company functions. Furthermore the organizational analysis with
PROB showed that the organization structure did not have any unit
(staff, committee, rules etc.) to handle an integrated planning process.

Analysis of this situational profile leads us to the problem of planning a system which crosses lines of authority, one of the problems
discussed and documented in the pool of implementation problems (IP).

   A planning system is called "crossing lines of authority"
   if it supports activitis in more than one organizational
   function.

The interests of different organizational units with different managers have to be considered and coordinated if lines of authority are
crossed. In these situations very often one finds competitive situations, sometimes of highly explosive nature.

Regarding the specific problem there are detailed descriptions of
possible solutions drawn up in the pool of design concepts (CON)
which take into account the specific situation of a CBIS-project,
e.g. general style of cooperation in that company etc. In the case
of the pharmaceuticals company we identified the problem of realizing
an integrated, line crossing planning process without having adequate
organization structures or rules for the coordination of different
interests or requirements. The results of the organizational analysis
with PROB made clear that the company used to practice a rather informal style of cooperation which is seen as sufficient for such planning problems.

We proposed an interdepartmental working group consisting of five
members (one representative of each concerned function) which should
be managed and coordinated by a member of the central services department. Furthermore we suggested the idea of not setting up a new
department or establishing a permanent working group, but organizing
the working group to get together if problems call for coordination.

The members of that working group were identified by our initial situational diagnosis by use of SIT (see above). Currently this working
group is performing its first tentative steps in the direction proposed by the PORGI team.

CONCLUSIONS

In the proceeding parts we have presented some results of the application of some PORGI tools in real CBIS-projects. This concluding
part focusses on relevant experiences about the PORGI tools themselves and problems applying such instruments. Under methodological
aspects we would like evaluate these instruments regarding the following issues:

(a) General applicability, that is, the instruments shouls not be
    tailored to one specific case. In our experience we have deve-
    loped a general set of instruments consisting of questions,
    items and procedures which are generally applicable in CBIS-pro-
    jects which have the objective to design and implement informa-
    tion systems for the support of planning activities. Additional-
    ly it may be necessary to tailor some of the instruments accord-
    ing to the individual terminology of the company or the specific
    CBIS-project (especially regarding the types of organizational
    units involved or the names of units of project organization).
    The checklists and questionnaires are aimed at covering the whole
    relevant ground, therefore some parts may be irrelevant for a
    special case. Therefore in our experience a certain creative ef-
    fort by the individual project manager, implementor etc. is in-
    dispensable to ensure the effective and efficient use of PORGI
    instruments.

(b) Valid description of the situation, that is, the situations which
    are described and analyzed have to be valid. In all situations
    in the two CBIS-projects it could be stated that the main char-
    acteristics of the respective situations were judged by the par-
    ticipants as being valid. This holds true also for those situa-
    tions where we diagnosed specific problems existing between dif-
    ferent departments.

(c) Relevant aspects of the situation; our aim in describing and an-
    alyzing implementation situations is to diagnose early in the
    process potential problems and to take corrective actions. There-
    fore the evaluation criterion for our instruments is whether our
    tools were able to translate our diagnostic results into action
    plans. Until now we have enough evidence to prove that our diag-
    nostic results were sufficiently exact and operational to form
    the basis for planning specific actions. In case 1 the project
    team of the electric company changed the participation pattern
    after our first analysis and planned the participation for the
    next phases in using the PORGI criteria. In case 2 the partici-
    pation pattern initially intended by the DP managers of the
    pharmaceutical company was changed completely according to our
    propositions. Specific organizational design activities were ini-
    tiated parallel to the technical design activities as a result
    of our problem analysis.

(d) According to our objective of being able to have some kind of an
    early-warning-effect in order to take corrective actions before
    the problem we have to stand the criterion of early warning. We
    were able to initiate necessary organizational design activities
    in one case in the problem analysis/definition phase when the
    project team was initially not involved in a project plan - dom-
    inated by technical considerations.

(e) <u>Economic aspects</u> of applying PORGI tools, that is, the use of
    our instruments should not demand such an amount of manpower,
    time etc. that the results are not worthwhile. At this point we
    only can give some impressions of the efforts we have experienced.
    The questionnaire CAES-Q in case 1 took approximately 2o minutes
    per person, the individual tailoring of PORGI tools to that sit-
    uation, the analysis and interpretation of about 3o question-
    naires and discussion of results took approximately two man-
    weeks. The activities with SIT and PROB in case 2 took approxi-
    mately 2 hours per interview, the analysis and interpretation of
    the results and discussion with the participants took approxi-
    mately 2.5 man-weeks. In both cases the members of the respec-
    tive project teams agreed that this was a reasonable amount of
    time with respect to the outcome which was judged in both cases
    as very important.

From these preliminary experiences we can conclude the PORGI tools
are evaluated positively on the above-mentioned criteria. But we
have to add some critical aspects of applying such tools like PORGI
in real profitmaking social systems:

(f) Participative approaches of socio-technical system design imply
    an understanding of system development as an organizational
    change process. It is true that such change processes need active
    support by responsible management.

(g) The application of such instruments increases the transparency
    of systems development processes: it makes it possible to dis-
    close technological, organizational and personal problems and
    conflicts in systems design. This problem disclosure and ana-
    lysis demands a good deal of neutrality and independence, which
    possibly only an external consultant may have. We do not know
    how to avoid disclosure of such problems or conflicts that can-
    not be solved or handled adequately because of either lack of
    appropriate procedures or organization members' insufficient
    willingness or capability to solve such conflicts.[7]

(h) Application of such instruments is critical for the individual's
    need for participation. Applying questionnaires without provid-
    ing feedback and a critical discussion of answers is not worth
    the trouble and will result in a negative impact.

---

[7] In the above described cases of PORGI instruments application we
tried to anticipate problems potentially disclosed in the analysis,
discuss available problem solutions and possible consequences of
either the conscious solution of the problem or the conscious
"not-solution" of the disclosed problem or neglection of possibly
existing latent conflicts. In every case the client organization
resp. its management has to take the responsibility for the application of PORGI instruments. Thus we are rather sure only to disclose problems or conflicts which could be solved, but are not sure
to disclose all existing problems, which should be solved for economic and social satisfactory results of system development.

(i) Questionnaire application can help to realize participation, but
does not create it automatically.

. Insufficient participation results in a lack of satisfaction
  and motivation to support system implementation and use,

. Passive involvement in systems design hinders an individual's
  identification with the design results, and increases change
  resistance and negative attitudes toward the system.

As a final statement we want to stress our opinion that many project
managers or system designers may be able to manage a systems design
project as well without methodical support, but they will have to
bear less risk using methodical instruments like PORGI tools.

REFERENCES:

(1) Bariff, M.L. and Lusk E.J., Cognitive and personality tests for
     the design of information systems, Management Science 8 (1977)
     820-829.

(2) Barkin, S.R., An Investigation into Some Factors Affecting In-
     formation System Utilization, Ph.D. Thesis, University of
     Minnesota (1974).

(3) Benbasat, I. and Schroeder, R.G., An experimental investigation
     of some MIS design variables, Management Information Systems
     Quarterly (March 1977).

(4) Churchman, C.W. and Schainblatt, A.N., The researcher and the
     manager: a dialectic of implementation, Management Science 4
     (1965) B69-B87.

(5) Dyckman, Th.R., Management implementation of scientific research:
     an attitudinal study, Management Science 10 (1967) B612-B621.

(6) Ginzberg, M.J., A Process Approach to Management Science Imple-
     mentation, Ph.D. Thesis, M.I.T. (1975).

(7) Hedberg, B., Mumford, E., The design of computer systems, in:
     Mumford, E. and Sackman, H. (eds.), Human Choice and Computer.
     Amsterdam, 1978).

(8) Kolf, F., Oppelland, H.J., Seibt, D., Szyperski, N.,
     Tools for handling human and organizational problems of com-
     puter-based information systems, in: Information Systems Meth-
     odology. Proceedings in the 2nd Conference of the European
     Cooperation in Informatics. Venice, Oct. 10-12 (1978) ed. by
     G. Bracchi and P.C. Lockeman (Springer, Berlin, Heidelberg,
     New York, 1978) 82-119.

(9) Kolf, F., Oppelland, H.J., Berücksichtigung von Benutzerinter-
     essen bei der Entwicklung von Informationssystemen, in:
     Hansen, H.R., Schröder, K. and Weihe, H.J. (eds.), Mensch und
     Computer. Zur Kontroverse über die ökonomischen und gesellschaft-
     lichen Auswirkungen der EDV (München, 1979) 307-325.

238 H.J. OPPELLAND, F. KOLF

(10) Kolf, F., Oppelland, H.J., Guidelines for the organizational
     implementation of information systems. Concept and experiences
     with the PORGI implementation handbook, in: Bjørn-Andersen, N.
     (ed.), The Human Side of Information Processing. Proceedings
     of the Copenhagen Conference on Computer Impact-78, October
     25-27, 1978 (North-Holland, Amsterdam, 1980).

(11) Leavitt, H.J., Applied organizational change in industry.
     Structural, technological, and humanistic approaches, in:
     March, J.G. (ed.), Handbook of Organizations (Skokil, Ill.,
     1965) 1144-1170.

(12) Lucas, H.C.jr., Why Information Systems Fail (New York,
     London, 1975).

(13) Mumford, E., Land, F., Hawgood, J., The ABACON-approach 1978:
     A participative approach to forward planning and system change
     (ABACON Ltd., Durham, 1978).

(14) Oppelland, H.J., Kolf, F., Claus, J., Dokumentation der Ergeb-
     nisse einer Expertenbefragung zur Entwicklung und Einführung
     rechnergestützter Informationssysteme. PORGI-Projektbericht
     Nr. 5 (BIFOA, Köln, 1977).

(15) Pounds, W.F., The process of problem finding, Industrial
     Management Review 4 (1969) 1 -19.

The Information Systems Environment
Lucas, Land, Lincoln, Supper (Editors)
North-Holland Publishing Company
© *IFIP, 1980*

TRAINING THE SYSTEMS ANALYST OF THE 1980s:

FOUR ANALYTICAL PROCEDURES TO ASSIST THE DESIGN PROCESS

Frank Land, Enid Mumford and John Hawgood

INTRODUCTION

The conventional systems life-cycle approach concentrates on the sequence of
activities and decisions which take place between the decision to
examine the possibility of changing a system (or changing the supporting
technology) and the actual implementation and operation of the changes. These
activities and decisions are described in terms of tasks to be carried out by
designated functionaries - analysts, designers, users, programmers, database
administrators, operators and project controllers. The organizational framework
in which the activity takes place is frequently taken as given.

However, experience suggests that it is the organizational framework which
determines the relationship and roles taken by the various participants in the
process of analysis, design and implementation of the system. The success of the
process is determined to a considerable extent by the way these relationships
operate. Hence it is important to make the correct decisions regarding the
organization of the various individuals and groups who will be concerned with the
life-cycle process. Recognizing this complexity, many people involved in the
design of computer systems are today looking for new inputs to what have
become conventional design philosophies and procedures.

First, they recognize that systems design is not merely a technical process that
involves the choice of hardware and the development of appropriate software, but
appreciate that it requires the insertion of a set of new computer-based procedures into a surrounding organizational framework that includes a network of
people carrying out a variety of tasks, engaged in different roles and having
individual relationships and job satisfaction needs. In most cases the introduction of the computer system requires a redesign of the function and tasks people
are expected to perform. The design process is therefore much larger and more
complex than was envisaged when early training programmes for systems analysts
were conceived. It requires of the systems analyst an ability to identify and
specify both organizational and social needs, and to create a socio-technical
system that facilitates the achievement of these needs.

By 'socio-technical' we mean a system which on the one hand is regarded as
efficient in the sense of productivity and quality, co-ordination and control, and
its ability to permit the organization to develop and adapt to changing requirements. On the other hand, it provides group and individual efficiency and motivation by promoting an environment for work in which people can achieve personal
development and satisfaction. The design of a new computer application therefore
requires the ability to create a system which uses the technology to assist in the
attainment of efficient operating procedures, together with human effectiveness
and satisfaction throughout the organization as a whole and at inter-departmental,
intra-departmental, work group and individual employee levels.

Second, there is increasing interest in methods for involving users in the design of their own systems. The reasons for this interest are many. They can originate in a philosophical belief in the right of employees to influence changes in their own work environment. This belief is now expressed in the legislation of a number of countries.[1] There is also a recognition of the fact that users possess a great deal of knowledge concerning the objectives, functions and problems of their departments and that this knowledge should be incorporated into the systems design process.

Systems designers are now aware that the conventional tools for requirements analysis and fact finding cannot overcome the communication gap between user and computer specialist, and that alternative methods for capturing the knowledge of the user have to be found.

There is a management view that more participation today means fewer industrial relations problems tomorrow, and a trade union view that participation can assist greater employee control at the lower levels of the organisation. The systems analyst may subscribe to some or all of these views but perhaps the most important factor for him is that he wants a user who approves of the system - a satisfied user. He may argue that if he shares the design task with the user then the system that emerges from such co-operation will produce this satisfaction.

Third, experience with many existing computer systems suggests that they are short-lived, having to be replaced by redesigned systems before the planned benefits from them have been realized. Systems have to be replaced for many reasons - because new technology becomes available, because of changes of attitudes, because they do not operate effectively within the particular organizational framework, because of changes in economic environment and because of changes within the organization itself. Designers have recognized the need to design systems within the confines of a planning horizon, and with the use of systematic methods to assess the impact of future changes on the system. These methods are themselves dependent in part on the socio-technical and participative design approach.

Fourth, designers have noted that new computer systems often behave in unexpected ways and result in unanticipated effects within the organization. Some of these unexpected effects are connected with the efficiency of the technical system - they show themselves by low performance in terms of accuracy, reliability and turn-round. Others are demonstrated by the non-use or mis-use of computer produced reports. Designers realise that the behavior of innovative systems cannot be predicted with precision and that the design process must involve a variety of experimental techniques, such as model building, simulation, controlled experiments and pilot schemes.

A broader definition of the systems design process to include organization and work design, the involvement of users, the planning for long-life systems and the use of an experimental approach to design, requires the development of a new set of design tools. These must be comprehensive enough to provide a means for analyzing organizational and human needs and simple enough for users to learn and apply.

This paper offers four analytical procedures that contribute to both of these objectives. The professional systems analyst who accepts a wider design role may wish to acquire them for his own use. If he favors a participative design approach he will also want to teach them to users and assist the user group

---

[1]
See, for example, The Norwegian Act relating to Work Protection and Working Environment. Order No. 330, 1977.

to apply them. Designers have of course been using ideas similar to these since
systems design began, but in this paper they are presented as part of a formal
methodology.

Diagnosis, design, evaluation and implementation activities require the creation
of a facilitating group structure for those who are involved in these processes.
This will include deciding on the membership of control, design and implementation
teams and on the responsibilities of each of these groups. It will also require
decisions on the amount and nature of user participation and on the kind of group
structures that will encourage such participation.

DESCRIBING THE SYSTEM PRIOR TO ITS REDESIGN

The computer literature is full of analytical tools for the professional systems
analyst but most of these focus on the technical and procedural aspects of the
system and few assist description and diagnosis of wider organizational needs. We
suggest that the four analytical procedures set out below will provide a useful
methodology for the professsional designer by enabling him to widen the scope of
his analysis, and a simple methodology for the user who wishes to make his own
diagnosis of needs.

Before moving an organization from state A to a new state B, it is important to
obtain knowledge of, and describe in detail, essential or requisite requirements
of the unit that is to be redesigned. By essential requirements we mean those
activities which the unit must undertake if it is to perform effectively the
functions for which it exists. It is also necessary to have a good understanding
of the actual procedures that are in use in the pre-change situation. This
information will provide a conceptual model of basic system needs together with a
description of what is actually happening. Analytical tools 1 and 2 provide the
means for making these descriptions.

ANALYTICAL PROCEDURE 1

Describing the Essential Organizational System[2]

Nature of the problem

Specify in detail the nature of the *presenting problem* or opportunity: why does
an existing system or systems need redesigning?

Boundaries of the system

Define the *boundaries* of the system with which the design exercise is concerned.
A simple I/O model can be of use here showing what inputs enter the system and
where they come from, and what outputs leave the system and where they go.

---

[2]
By "essential" organization is meant those functions which a system must
include if it is to achieve its principal goals.

If the system is an information one which will cross many functional boundaries a tracer approach which identifies the paths taken by information and the senders and recipients may be a useful preliminary.

Objectives

Specify the *primary objectives* of the system - the principal reasons for its existence. It is important to establish that there is a consensus view on primary objectives before proceeding further.

Unit operations

Identify principal *unit operations* (subsystems) associated with each objective or set of objectives. By unit operation is meant an integrated set of activities which are attached to a major system function. This set of activities is separated from other sets of activities by some kind of boundary - a change of input, time, location etc.

For example, the unit operations associated with the treatment of coronary patients in a hospital would be:

a) Receiving a message that someone has had a heart attack and despatching an ambulance to the patient. Bringing the patient into hospital.

b) Crisis treatment to prevent death occurring.

c) The maintenance of a state of non-crisis once this has been established.

d) Restoring the patient to health.

e) Steps to prevent a second coronary.

Each of these unit operations can be logically separated from the others. See Figure 1.

Variance analysis

Describe those problems or variances which are prone to occur because of the nature of the systems objectives or principal activities. <u>These must ideally be avoided, or rapidly corrected if they occur.</u>

A variance is defined as a tendency for a system or subsystem to deviate from some desired norm or standard(s). These problems should be described in the following way: in terms of the systems *sensitivity* to the problem; i.e., the problem is likely to be expensive or difficult to correct. Its occurrence will cause a major disturbance in the functioning of the unit operation. At this level of analysis only variances which tend to occur because of the nature of the systems goals or essential functions should be recorded. Variances which are a result of an existing set of procedures or organization of work will be examined later.

An example of a variance to which the system is sensitive in unit operation a) is communication with ambulances. Poor communication greatly increases the time a casualty has to wait before transportation to hospital.

Problems to which the system is most sensitive are 'key' variances. Feedback loops between one key variance and another should be noted.

Coronary Treatment Example

Figure 1

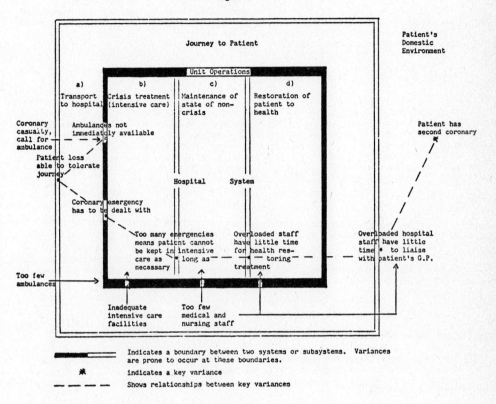

Describing the Essential Human System[3]

The human system is defined as the network of roles and relationships necessary to achieve system objectives and the job satisfaction needs of the people filling the roles and involved in the relationships.

Roles and relationships

This analysis requires the specification of necessary roles and relationships but *without, at this stage, making any allocation of tasks to groups or individuals*. Each role and relationship should be described in terms of its function and the kinds and levels of knowledge and skill required to handle it.

Roles can be placed in the following categories.

3

  The essential human system covers those roles, relationships and attitudes that must be associated with the essential organisation if the system is to achieve its principal or goals.

244   F. LAND, E. MUMFORD, J. HAWGOOD

Operational roles

These are the roles associated with producing the product, service or other output
which is the essential function of the system. Some of these roles may require a
high level of skill, others may be semi- or unskilled. In the coronary intensive-
care ward these will include roles concerned with the daily care of patients; e.g.,
providing routine treatment, comfort and nourishment.

Problem avoidance or correction roles

This covers the roles associated with solving problems or preventing the occurrence
of problems. Here again different kinds and levels of skill and knowledge will be
required: handling medical or technical crises once they occur; taking steps to
ensure that they occur as infrequently as possible.

As most operational roles have a problem-solving component and vice versa, these
two categories can usefully be combined and described as roles with a small or
large responsibility for problem avoidance or correction.

Co-ordination roles

These are roles associated with co-ordinating different activities. Many of these
will cross system boundaries and therefore involve ensuring the successful interaction of the system with other adjoining systems, ensuring that treatment decided
on by doctors is implemented by nurses, ensuring that when the patient is ready to
leave the intensive-care unit a bed is available in the normal ward.

Development roles

These roles are associated with assisting the system to improve its output or
methods and enabling it to respond to changes in its environment. Many of these
roles will also cross system boundaries and role holders will be concerned with
obtaining information from the system environment, e.g., developing new forms of
treatment for coronary patients, or more advanced cardiac monitoring technology.

Control roles

Control roles are those associated with ensuring that key objectives are achieved
and that the total system fits together and works as an effective unit. These can
be designated supervisory roles, although this does not necessarily mean that they
will be undertaken by managers or supervisors.

Part of the later design task will be to assemble clusters of roles so that they
provide logical and challenging sets of activities for groups or individuals.
Vertical integration is a good design principal, with an attempt being made to
incorporate a number of role levels into each group or individual's job responsibility (1).

A description of *relationships* requires a recognition of which role activities
have a dependent relationship with other role activities and cannot function in
isolation. These should be recorded. In the coronary ward doctors cannot easily
function without nurses and vice versa.

Job satisfaction needs

Job satisfaction needs and expectations must be made explicit as part of the system description. This involves each individual associated with the system specifying the kinds of satisfaction he would ideally like to receive from his work environment. Unless a very small group is involved this information is best collected by asking system users to complete questionnaires and using the data collected in this way as a basis for small group discussion on how job satisfaction needs and expectations can best be achieved.

Job satisfaction, defined by Mumford (2) as the 'fit' between what an individual or group is seeking from the work situation and what they are receiving, is seen as being achieved when three kinds of need are met in the work situation. These are:

> Personality needs
> Competence and efficiency needs
> Needs associated with personal values.

Needs associated with personality

Knowledge needs: How, ideally, would each individual or group forming part of the system like their existing skills and knowledges to be used? What opportunities would they like for these to be developed further?

Psychological needs: What are their needs for responsibility, status, esteem, security and advancement and how do they define these needs?

Needs associated with competence and efficiency in the work role and the successful performance of work activities.

Support/control needs: The kind of support services which users at every level believe would enable them to carry out their work responsibilities more efficiently. These support services will include the information and materials necessary to work at a high level of competence as well as supervisory support and good working conditions.

The kind of control systems that users believe would assist their motivation and efficiency. The level and structure of wages and salaries is an important part of any control system.

Task needs: The kinds of task structure that different groups of users will find motivating, interesting and challenging. For example, to what extent do users want jobs that include elements of all our five system levels, i.e., opportunities for self management, for developing new methods, services or products, for co-ordinating their own activities and taking organizational decisions, for solving their own problems and monitoring their own progress, as well as the first level tasks of producing a product or service.

Needs associated with employee values

Ethical needs: How do users at every level want to be treated by management? Do the organisation's policies on communication, consultation and participation meet employee expectations? Do other kinds of policy also meet these expectations?

ANALYTICAL PROCEDURE 2

Discrepancy analysis

Once system essentials have been described following the analytical model above, it is useful to establish the extent to which existing organizational arrangements are meeting or failing to meet efficiency and job satisfaction objectives and needs. This provides information on the extent to which the existing system diverges from the required or 'closer to ideal' system. A warning is needed here, however. Too great a concentration on the weaknesses of the existing system may lead to a superficial remedying of these weaknesses via a minor reorganization plus the intervention of a new computer system. A more fundamental re-thinking of organizational needs is required so that any redesign is based on a clear identification of organisational objectives and purposes, and an analysis of staff job satisfaction needs which incorporates a philosophy of personal development and is based on what can be made to happen rather than on an improvement of what happens now. (3)

Discrepancy analysis covers an identification of *variances* which are a product of existing procedures and organisation of work, or availability of resources. Many of these kinds of variance will interact with each other and travel through the work system. A variance matrix will show the pervasiveness of a problem (i.e., if it occurs it leads to or interacts with, other problems in the unit operation or adjoining systems). An example is set out below in Figure 2.

It can be seen, for example, how variance 1 (an ambulance not being immediately available) effects variance 3 (a deterioration in the patient's condition); this in turn affects variance 4 and so on. The other variances have a similar pervasive impact on the system.

a Bring patient to hospital	1					Ambulance is not immediately available		
		2				Ambulance has long journey to collect patient		
	1	2	3			Patient's condition deteriorates through waiting		
	1	2	3	4		Resuscitation prior to journey to hospital is difficult and partial		
	1	2	3		5	Journey is a hazardous event, patient's condition deteriorates		
b Crisis treatment to prevent death	1	2	3	4	5	6		Limited hospital resources are strained by arrival of emergency case
	1	2	3	4	5	6	7	Treatment of less serious cases is delayed
	1	2	3		5		8	Patient dies
Unit operations	Bring patient to hospital a			Crisis treatment to prevent death (b)				

Note: Variances are numbered 1, 2, 3, etc in the right-hand boxes with the nature of the variance written at the right-hand side. The numbers in adjoining boxes are those variances which interact with the right-hand side variances.

Example of a Variance Matrix (unit operations a and b of earlier examples)

Figure 2

Discrepancy analysis will also involve an examination of existing task structures
and work flows to establish the extent to which there is a good or bad fit between
these and efficiency requirements, and a survey of the extent to which existing
organisational arrangements are meeting employee job satisfaction needs. This job
satisfaction information can be collected in the same questionnaire as that used
to establish the kinds of satisfaction that employees would ideally like to
receive from their work situation. Both 'fact' (now) and 'preference' (the future)
questions can be included (4).

Discrepancy analysis will assist an identification of systems areas where there is
already a good fit between efficiency and job satisfaction needs, and work organization and technology. It will also help identify those areas where the fit is poor
and the variances or dissatisfaction are prone to occur. It should only be used
as a guide to areas which do not require redesign because they are working effectively if the existing system is clearly geared to achieving efficiency and job
satisfaction goals in these areas.

ANALYTICAL PROCEDURE 3

Future analysis

Decisions to implement systems changes are often based on assumptions about the
minimum time that is expected to elapse before the system is subjected to further
major changes. Typically the evaluation would be based on an expected system's
life of five to seven years. While some major systems have provided adequate
returns on investment in much less time, there are also many cases where the system
has failed to survive for a time sufficient to yield a return on the investment,
or the cost of maintaining the system in the face of continuous requests for change
have totally destroyed the economic basis on which the original decision to proceed
was taken.

Members of a systems design team have to plan the expected life-span of the system
(the system's planning horizon) on the basis of their forecasting horizon - that
is on how far into the future they can plan with sufficient certainty to be confident that the system will be capable of meeting the needs of the organization.
The greater the flexibility or adaptability of the system, the more it should be
capable of long life. The greater the uncertainty regarding relevant aspects of
the future, the more important it is to plan systems with a relatively short
expected life-span. The design team may be faced with a trade-off between
designing very flexible costly systems (development costs and operational costs)
versus short-lived, less adaptable but possibly cheaper systems. In practice we
frequently see attempts, by brute force and highly expensive systems-maintenance
techniques, to prolong the life of a non-flexible system in an attempt to meet
original life-span objectives.

Figure 3 shows the relationship between the planned life-span of the system,
the extent to which the designer utilizes techniques which make the system more
flexible and the perceived uncertainty.

The curve AB represents the frontier of technical possibilities with regard to
flexibility techniques. The curve is shown as rising because over the lifetime
of the system it could be expected that such techniques would improve even in
respect of a system designed at an earlier time.

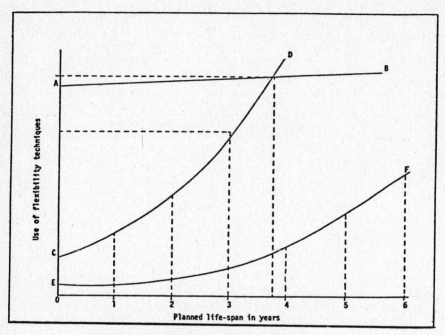

Relationship Between Planned Life-span and Flexibility
of the System, and Perceived Uncertainty

Figure 3

The curve CD represents the 'amount' of flexibility that has to be built into the
system for each possible life-span of the system under conditions of considerable
uncertainty about the future. To achieve a life-span of three years the designer
has to make the system very flexible. He cannot quite achieve a life-span of four
years with currently available technology. The forecasting horizon for the system
is just under four years.

The curve EF represents the 'amount' of flexibility needed to achieve different
life-spans under conditions of relative stability. The forecasting horizon for
this system lies beyond the end of the diagram and it is therefore not relevant
in determining the planning horizon for the system.

The systems design team has to decide what kind of life-span it should design the
system for, and the extent to which it should give the system a 'flexibility'
capability. To help them we suggest that the following guidelines may be useful.
The analysis can be carried out in four stages.

The first stage is concerned with an attempt to discover the kinds of change which
may have an impact on the system under consideration. There are two broad classes
of change the design team has to consider:

    Changes which may affect the logic of the system

    Changes in the 'traffic' the system has to cope with - changes in volumes, in
    frequencies, e.g., peaks, numbers of elements etc.

Changes also need to be classified as:

Transient or short-lived

Permanent or long-lived. Note should be taken of how frequently the changes
occur over the lifetime of the system.

Changes can be classified into a number of major categories, and the design team
has to consider the system in relation to each of these categories. The major
categories are:

Changes in available technology

The technology referred to may be information-processing technology such as computers in communication equipment, or it may be technology which is embedded in
the system itself, such as, machine tools, production processors and so forth.
In general, in times of very rapid technological change, the planning horizon for
a system would shorten, and the technology chosen would, as far as possible, be
modular and replaceable.

Changes in legal requirements

Many aspects of company law, tax law, industrial relations law and now privacy
laws, can have a profound effect on systems. A feature of changes required to
meet new legislation is that the changes are mandatory and have to be implemented
to a strict externally determined timetable.

Changes in economic and other environment factors

Changes in the economic environment have an impact on the rate of growth or decline
of organizations, and on their competitive place in the market. At the most
trivial level such changes can have a large effect on the level of activity and
hence movement of messages through a system, and on the peak traffic the system may
have to be considered. At a more profound level there may be major changes in
organisations, affecting the product range, the method of distribution, the policy
on stockholding, wages policy and questions relating to the ownership of the
enterprise iteself.

Changes in attitudes, expectations, tastes, or in climates of opinion

Attitudes towards technology, and in particular to computer-based systems, have
changed over the past decade and will continue to evolve. Attitudes toward the
role of government, industrial democracy, devolution work and many other
features of life are constantly undergoing change.

Most of the change categories discussed so far concern themselves with changes over
which the organization has no control. Changes are triggered by events outside
the organization, and the organization and the systems within it must respond
as best they can. But other categories are concerned with changes originating
within the organisation itself and therefore to some extent controllable by the
organization.

Changes within the organization

All commercial and administrative organizations have a tendency to change their structure and style of management. Organizations evolve because of external pressures and there is no doubt that changes in management techniques, in management style, in the control system and procedures, and in organizational structure can have large impacts on information systems.

The first task of the design team is to consider which category of change could be relevant to the system under consideration.

The second task is to identify the people most likely to contribute knowledgeably to a discussion of future trends in each relevant category. For an evaluation of technical change the discussions with the design team could involve:

    Suppliers of computer Equipment and software
    Members of computer or management services staff
    Members of the organisation's research or R and D department
    Outside consultants.

For consideration of the second category, legal changes, the important authorities to consult would include:

    The company secretary
    The chief accountant
    The personnel manager or industrial relations manager
    Officials of trade unions
    The organisation's legal advisers

The third category, changes in the economic environment, is perhaps broadest, and in many ways, the most difficult. Since many of the issues resulting from changes in economic circumstances are matters of highly confidential policy, for example, issues related to mergers or takeovers, it may be impossible to obtain information even where such information exists.

Those who should be involved in discussions may include:

    Top management representatives
    Corporate planners (if they exist)
    The chief accountant
    Marketing management
    Management services
    Outside consultants.

If the third category presents most difficulty, the fourth category, changes in attitudes and expectations, gives rise to the greatest uncertainty on the impact of such changes on the system itself. Those who may help to resolve the uncertainty include:

    Representatives of user departments
    The personnel or industrial relations manager
    Members of the management services staff
    Shop stewards and union officials
    Outside consultants.

The fifth category, changes within the organization, involves a great variety of different change types. Discussion on such changes could therefore be structured by levels in the organization. Strategic and control systems changes could involve:

Top management representatives
Heads of major departments
Management services
Senior trade-union officials
Consultants.

Changes in unit operations should be discussed by:

Departmental managers
Section heads
Member of unit operation staff
The personnel manager
Shop stewards or union representatives
Management services staff.

It should be noted that the change categories are not independent. A change in one category can trigger changes in other categories. A change in the attitude of the population at large to industrial democracy can trigger legislation which will lead to organizational change and a consequent change in the expectations of the people working in the organization. Hence the groups of people identified to help in forecasting the future should always be organised in such a way that such triggering effects could be traced.

The third task is to select appropriate analytical procedures to help in the future analysis. These procedures include some of the diagnostic methods discussed earlier. Job satisfaction analysis can help to give indications of attitude and expectation changes. These can be supplemented by other surveys designed to elicit attitudinal data. The identification of unit operations helps to define the areas where organizational changes may arise. Further techniques include statistical forecasting methods for extrapolating rates of growth or decline, changes in volumes, changes in frequencies; economic modelling of the economy and the organization itself to identify economic trends, and simulation methods to test the effect of various changes on the performance of the organization.

To summarise: *stage one* categorizes the types of change which could have an impact on the system under consideration, identifies those who can help in discussing future trends, and selects tools and techniques which can be used as an aid to forecasting.

In *stage two*, the design team has to try to assess the kind of future which the system under consideration will have to face. With respect to each change category, the team with the aid of the selected discussants and the use of the available tools, has to attempt to answer the following questions:

1 What changes are conceivable at the present time, and when may they occur?

2 What impact might such changes have on the system?

3 What is the probability of such changes actually occurring?

The chief methods employed in stage 2 are open-ended discussions between the design team and the people identified as capable of contributing to the discussion, using 'brain-storming' techniques, DELPHI methods, surveys, and a variety of forecasting and diagnostic tools. The extent of the future analysis would depend on the kind of system under consideration. If the system is central to the organization's existence and a failure of the system could imperil the whole enterprise, the future analysis must be very detailed. In such projects as the Apollo moon shot, the analysis of all possible contingencies was very elaborate indeed.

The outcome of stage 2 is:

1 A revised list of design objectives

2 A revised list of design objectives

3 A list of systems features which may need to have flexibility built into them.

Up to this point the design team has concentrated on the kinds of change the system may face in the future. However, there is no way in which a team can make precise predictions about the future, and even with the best possible future analysis, unexpected events will test the system. If the system is to be robust, a further diagnostic procedures needs to be invoked. In *stage 3* the design team has to systematically test the system under consideration to establish those systems features which are sensitive to any change in requirements, either in terms of the logic or the traffic. The team has to ask itself two questions:

1 What feature of the system is sensitive to changed requirements of traffic?

2 What will be the impact on the viability of the system as a whole if such changes occur?

The team has to consider the whole system - the computer subsystem and the manual subsystem. It has to establish the extent to which the proposed system could be modified to make it less vulnerable if changes were to occur however unexpected.

As a result of the *stage 3* analysis the design team can list those elements of the proposed system which are most sensitive to change, and those elements where such changes would have the greatest impact on the organization. A particular element in the system may be very difficult to change in response to a revised need, but the effect of not accommodating the need may be trivial as far as the organization is concerned. It may, for example, be possible for a manual procedure to be set up to cope with a new requirement which cannot be implemented on the computer system. The important list is the one which identified the elements which could have important consequences on the organisation if they cannot be amended quickly (or cheaply).

In *stage 4* the design team considers the output from stages 2 and 3 in order to make recommendations regarding the system's planned life-cycle and to decide how much flexibility to build into the system. To do this the team has to assess the possible damage to the organization from failure to adapt to changes and compare this with the cost of building in flexibility. To a large extent, the tradeoff has to rely on the judgement of the design team, since it is difficult to quantify precisely the cost of building in flexibility or of evaluating the damage from failure to adapt. It is important, however, for all concerned with the proposed system to be aware of the way the decisions have been arrived at and this can best be achieved by using the techniques of benefit assessment in participation described in the following section of this paper.

One further point needs to be noted. The extent to which a system responds to changes is not only a function of the way the system is constructed but also the type of organization in which the system operates. Some forms of organization are inherently more capable of responding to change than others. This applies to the organization responsible for the design implementation and operation of the information system and the organization of the enterprise itself. In considering the questions of life-span and flexibility, the design team has to be aware of any constraints imposed by the style of management and the structure of the organization.[4]

ANALYTICAL PROCEDURE 4

Setting Objectives and Evaluating Strategies

In describing the first analytical procedure we referred to the need to identify the primary objectives of the organization. The setting of objectives at that level and at the level of actual operation requires a formal procedure.

In the part of the design process described here we are concerned with design objectives intended to reduce discrepancies between the essential system as described above and the existing or predicted future situation. A problem is that each user group will tend to rate objectives which further its own interest as most important, and this potential conflict of goals must be recognised and dealt with. An ideal solution is to find a design which meets each group's most important objectives, but this is not always possible and conflict situations often arise. If these are brought out into the open early enough, they can be discussed by all concerned and it may be possible to reach agreement on priority objectives.

The procedure has also to help the design team to choose a strategy that will assist the attainment of priority objectives. One method is to assess first the extent to which each strategy contributes to the achievement of priority objectives and second, to identify the importance of sets of objectives to the interest of particular user groups.

John Hawgood has developed a diagrammatic aid to this process, which consists essentially of a rectangular plot of the predicted performance of alternative systems in respect to different objectives, against the relative importance of the

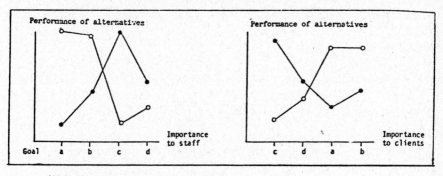

Aid to the Assessment of Alternative Policies

Figure 5

4

The work on 'future analysis' was greatly helped by members of the British Computer Society Specialist Group on Business Information Systems, who, in 1977, worked out methods for providing flexibility in systems. These were presented in a paper at the 1977 Datafair. Contributions were made in particular by George Clifton, Alan Garner, Elizabeth Somogyi, Arthur Tulip and Mike Herd.

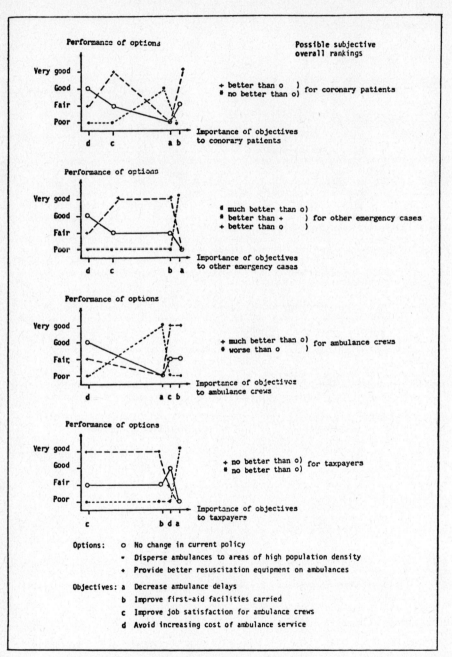

Ambulance Subsystem : Assessment of Alternative Policy Options

Figure 6

objectives to people involved. Figure 5 shows the plots for two different
groups when alternative policies o and . are being assessed. (The lines joining the
corresponding points have no meaning in themselves, but have been found helpful
as a visual aid). The horizontal scale can be labelled 'unimportant', 'fairly
important', 'important', 'very important', 'extremely important' (working from
left to right). The vertical scale may be different for each goal according to
what attributes are appropriate, but in each case the scales will work upwards
from numbers or words corresponding to 'poor' performance to those corresponding
to 'very good' performance. In the diagram above, policy . is clearly better for
staff, while policy o is better for clients; this would indicate a potential
conflict if either of these policies were adopted. The design team should seek
another policy which would resolve this conflict.

To make this approach more concrete, consider again the coronary treatment systemunit
and unit operation a (the ambulance subsystem). A design team might wish at an
early stage to consider the following objectives, all intended to contribute to the
overall aim of improving the treatment of coronary patients:

a   Decrease ambulance delays (measured in minutes).

b   Improve first-aid facilities carried (measured in words).

c   Improve job satisfaction for ambulance crews (measured in words according to
     the fit between preferences and actual work situation).

d   Hold expenditure within cash limits (measured financially).

An investigation of the relative importance of these objectives to the different
groups involved might give the importance rankings shown below (the group
'taxpayers' is put in to ensure that cost is considered as well as benefit).

Then a prediction of the performance of two possible changes to policy compared to
that for the existing policy, might give the graphs shown in Figure 6. A quick
look at the overall patterns suggests the subjective overall rankings of the three
polocies given to the right for the four groups. Taken together, these seem
to show a possible consensus on policy '+', which helps the ambulance crews' job
satisfaction by developing their skills and opportunities for teamwork as well as
benefiting coronary patients and other emergency cases. Clearly the design team
might also wish to examine some combination of the two changes.

The procedure described here is most useful in the early design stages when
possible alternative policies or systems are being explored, although it can be
applied again as a check once a design strategy has been selected and developed.
It is important to ensure a high degree of consultation so that group priorities
on objectives and the ranking different groups give to alternative strategies
become clear.

The ultimate purpose of the procedure is to guide the decision makers in their
choice of strategies and systems. The decision makers may have particular
criteria in mind when making such a choice. They may decide, for example, that
the solution chosen must be regarded as an improvement over the current system
by all participants even if another solution would show a higher 'return' to
some groups. The final choice of policies or systems may also take into account
factors other than those prescribed by the design team. For example, when there
is an unresolved conflict of interests between the different groups a 'political'
judgement may have to be made.

CONCLUSIONS

The four analytical procedures described in this paper all represent attempts to take account of the organizational context into which computer systems are introduced. This covers the essential functions and roles of the organizational unit where change is being introduced, existing procedures which may or may not be optimal in enabling the unit to function effectively, employee job satisfaction needs and the extent to which the unit is likely to experience change in the future.

These procedures are now being tried out in a number of firms and government departments and, in the authors' view, need to be incorporated into training courses for systems designers and users. Some attempt to do this has already been made. For example, The Manchester Business School holds regular one and two day courses on 'New Approaches to Systems Design'. These focus on designing the organizational context into which a computer system is to be introduced. Brunel University and the London School of Economics regularly hold courses called 'Successful Systems Design: The Human Element'. A book has recently been produced by Enid Mumford and Mary Weir which contains a number of exercises on the socio-technical design of computer systems. In addition most computer conferences today have papers on the organizational implications of systems design.

REFERENCES

1. Mumford, E., A strategy for the redesign of work, in: Legge, K. and Mumford, E. (eds.)., Designing organizations for satisfaction and efficiency, Gower Press (1978).

2. Mumford. E., Job satisfaction: a method of analysis, in: Legge, K. and Mumford, E. (eds.)., Designing organizations for satisfaction and efficiency, Gower Press (1978).

3. Mumford, E., Land, F. and Hawgood, J., A participative approach to the design of computer systems, Impact of Science on Society vol. 28, no. 3, pp. 235-253 (1978).

4. Mumford, E. and Henshall, D., A participative approach to the design of computer systems, Associated Business Press (1978).

The Information Systems Environment
Lucas, Land, Lincoln, Supper (Editors)
North-Holland Publishing Company
© *IFIP, 1980*

A SIMULATION BASED INQUIRY SYSTEM
FOR THE DEVELOPMENT OF
INFORMATION SYSTEMS

A. Bosman
H.G. Sol
Information Systems Research Group
University of Groningen, The Netherlands

It is our hypothesis that in the years to come the content of
man-computer interactions for decision making will be one of
the most important factors defining the relationships between
an information system and its organizational setting. Support
for this hypothesis can be found in Lucas (1975, 1978), Mitroff
(1974) and Mumford and Henshall (1979). We observe that until
recently computers in organizations have been entirely used for
the solution of well-structured problems. Langefors (1978)
recently discussed the differences in the contents and the role
of the notion of user needs for the development and the construction of an information system. These differences can be
related to different paradigms for the construction of models
organizational decision processes.
We postulate that attempts to apply computers for the solution
of ill- structured problems in organizations demand a redefinition and an extension of the methods and techniques for the
problem solution. Another approach for the design of information systems is needed for these ill-structured problems.

HUMAN PROBLEM SOLVING

Men solve problems using methods. The number of methods men can use is
enormous. We assume that the number of possible combinations of these
methods can be reduced if we postulate a certain procedure for the solution of problems. This assumption is, of course, not new. During centuries it was one of the main points of discussion in the field of epistemology and methodology. The procedures specifying combinations of methods are known as modelcycles. Different modelcycles can be distinguished and the differences between these modelcycles can be explained by
referring to two main factors:
    a. differences between paradigms,
    b. differences between methods.
We show that the differences between paradigms are especially relevant
for a discussion of human problem solving.

Mitroff et.al. (1973) introduced a general framework defining different
stages of a modelcycle, see Figure 1. The various stages in Figure 1 can
be transferred in a different sequence, specifying different modelcycles
(Bosman, 1978). The main cause for the differences between modelcycles
are different paradigms leading to different conceptual models and generally also to different models (see Figure 1). Starting from epistemology
it is possible to define a number of different conceptual models, see for
example Churchman (1971). Churchman denominates modelcycles as inquiring
systems that specify activities in a problem solving process.

The activity of conceptualization and especially its relation with the
activity of constructing a model, see Figure 1, is a neglected topic in
the literature on problem solving. We endorse the following statements on
this subject made by Sagasti and Mitroff (1973): "To a large extent, the
difference between "reality" and "conceptual model" would correspond to
that customarily made between "data" and "information"... The fact that
many conceptual models may correspond to a given problem situation poses
the additional problem of deciding how to build a "good" or workable
conceptual model, and how to propose rules on how to construct conceptual
models and/or provide criteria for evaluating alternative conceptual
models for a given reality". In the realm of problem solving, men need
models. For the construction of models two activities are necessary.
The activity of conceptualization assumes the existence of a world-look
or a paradigm. Given world-looks models, can be constructed through idealization and/or abstraction.

In the literature on human problem solving the well-known distinction
between well- and ill-structured problems is often used as a paradigm for
the construction of models of human thought processes, see e.g. Newell
and Simon (1972), Slagle (1971), Nilsson (1971) and Uhr (1973). To quote
Uhr (1973, p. 274) as "ill-formedness in problems seems to be closely
related to issues of vagueness, ambiguity, flexibility, and creativity
about all of which little is known". We regard this definition of ill-
structured problems as too vague and for that reason as not useful. If
one wants to distinguish between well- and ill-structured problems it is
suitable to refer to a distinction in Figure 1, between the activities of
conceptualization or creating correspondence and the test of consistency.
We define a problem as well-structured if the activity of conceptualization can be specified in a unique way, leading to a consistent model.
This means that it must be possible to define the set of alternatives or
possible solutions.Examples of well-structured problems are games like
chess, checkers and tic-tac-toe. It is incorrect to infer from this definition of a well-structured problem that it can always be easily and/or
quickly solved, e.g. think of the game of chess.
To regard all other problems as ill-structured is also not very useful.
We propose to subdivide the set of ill-structured problems to certain degrees of ill-formedness, see Bosman (1977). One of the most important
instruments for this subdivision is the availability of a conceptual
model meeting certain conditions.

Man as a problem solver has to deal with a number of cognitive constraints, see Newell and Simon (1972). To find solutions for the construction of a conceptual model man uses different procedures of a heuristic nature. In science a well known procedure is defined by the loop
conceptual model, model, solution and conceptual model in Figure 1. In
economics in this modelcycle the variables are generally defined through
idealization. For that reason this modelcycle is named the axiomatic one,
or in the terminology of Churchman (1971) a Leibnitzian inquiring system.
The main emphasis in this modelcycle is on finding a solution through the
specification of algorithms. Conceptualization as a separate activity is
missing. The inquiring system used is of a normative nature with its main
emphasis on defining all problems as well-structured ones. Procedures
necessary for the recognition and the specification of problems are not
available.

To summarize, it is our opinion that the cognitive constraints of men are
the main cause for the way we solve our problems. Science has delivered
programs for finding solutions taking these constraints into account.
These programs, with a few exceptions, use computers for the solution of
well-structured problems. On the threshold of the introduction of the
personal computer it becomes time for men and organizations to study the
redifinition of our programs. The first step in this process is to pay
more attention to the role and function of conceptual models.

ORGANIZATIONAL PROBLEM SOLVING

We define an <u>organization</u> as a set of human beings, procedures and means
of production - such as capital, raw materials and data - trying to
achieve goals in some kind of rational manner. To reach these goals decisions have to be made. We regard decision making in organizations as a
process of problem solving. As human beings operate as decision makers
organizations are confronted with the cognitive constraints of human
beings. This confrontation leads to differences in degree between human
and organizational decision making processes. The most important of
these differences are:
1. Decision makers in organizations can concentrate on certain problems
through a process of division of labor and a kind of specialization,
named functionalization.
2. As an organization can be regarded as a hierarchic ordered set of
functions, decisions are in one way or another interrelated. This interaction can be implemented in different ways.
   - Through an interaction of aspiration levels, in the form of goals
     and budgets.
   - Through an interaction of problem definition: planning procedu-
     res.
   - Through an interaction of data: data base procedures.
   - Through an interaction of control of the decision making process:
     budget procedures.
   - Through a combination of the mentioned interaction procedures.
In general one could state that the decision makers acting as problem
solvers in organizations in many cases are compelled to define the models
they use explicitly. As a hypothesis, we think that the fact that problem
solvers in organizations use explicitly defined models does not imply
that also more attention is paid to the process of defining conceptual
models.

To define a conceptual model of an organization use is made of the paradigm of rationality. Different notions of rationality can be distinguished. We mention two, see also Simon (1976).
1. Unbounded rationality requires an axiomatic, conceptual model of an
organization. It assumes a decision maker with perfect knowledge and no
cognitive constraints. It includes an assumption of the homo-economicus
which also assumes implicitly, a homo-informaticus. All decision problems
are well-structured problems in our terminology.
2. Unbounded rationality defines a yardstick in the form of an absolute
standard of rationality. <u>Bounded rationality</u> exists when one or more of
the assumptions of unbounded rationality are relaxed. The results of this
release are twofold:
   - bounded rationality becomes a dependent variable of the decision
     making process;
   - as bounded rationality is not an absolute standard anymore, one
     must distinguish different degrees of rationality.

We postulate that any prescription or design process of activities in an organization demands a notion like rationality. Therefore, any prescription needs a description of <u>how</u> a decision maker acts rationally. For the purpose of implementation the description must be based on the existing situation in an organization.

The description and analysis of the existing situations in an organization can be regarded as an ill-structured pro- blem. To find a solution it is necessary to take into account:
  a. the variables and relations specifying the decision problem;
  b. the algorithms applied to find a solution;
  c. the relations with other decision makers.
A specification can only be made if data are used for the construction of a model. For that purpose two groups of methods can be distinguished, econometrics and simulation.

Simon (1960) has introduced a distinction between programmed and unprogrammed decisions. He states: "I hasten to add that they are not really distinct types, but a whole continuum, with highly programmed decisions at one end of that continuum and highly unprogrammed decisions at the other end "(p.5). Generally in literature the distinction between programmed and unprogrammed is considered to coincide with the one between well- and ill-structured problems, see Brightman (1978). Referring to our definition of a well-structured problem we regard this identity as incorrect. The set of well-structured problems has less and not necessarily the same elements as the set of programmed decisions. The distinction between the two is a result of the fact that problem solvers can find solutions for ill-structured problems that can be programmed.

Regarding well- structured problems and programmed decisions as two of a kind has had a major influence on the way computers are used in organizations. We illustrate this hypothesis by showing that three stages in the development of methods describing user needs or user requirements can be distinguished. The distinction between these stages are explained referring to different views of the way human beings act as problem solvers.
1. In the first stage user needs are decribed using "process - or form driven methods", Davis (1974, p.420). Examples of these methods are SOP of IBM and ARDI of Philips. The main purpose of these methods is to define a relation between the given output and the data necessary to produce this output. The analysis is restricted to the design of a system of programs and collections of data (files) specifying this relation. The way problem solvers use output to solve their problems is not defined. Most of the EDP applications of computers are defined and programmed in this stage. For recent developments in this stage, see Davis (1978).
2. In the second stage of development special algorithms are used to solve ill-structured problems. Through the use of these algorithms the decision problem is regarded as programmed and user needs are specified through algorithms and the data necessary to apply this algorithm. Implicitly one assumes that the decision problem is transformed into a well-structured problem. Examples of this stage are the applications of operations research methods and the construction of integrated or total systems. The methods used in this stage are design oriented, the principles for the design of an integrated system are of management philosophical nature, see e.g. Blumenthal (1969) and BSP of IBM.

3. In the third stage a decision problem is regarded as an ill-structured
problem. To solve these problems attention is directed at the aspect of
defining the problem in the form of a set of relations between problem
solver procedures, and data. To define such a set of conceptual models
and a model describing the relations between problem solver and procedures, see Figure 1, are necessary. The developments in this third stage
can be regarded as an extension of the ones in the first and second stages. The first stage is directed at the relation between data and procedures, while the change needed in the second stage is the recognition
that ill-structured problems cannot be solved by algorithms only.
In this third stage the main emphasis is not on the computer, but on the
human problem solver who has to learn how to use computers to define
problems. He has to recognize the fact that the computer has abilities
that open new possibilities to adjust his cognitive constraints. Man did
so in the first and second stage in so far his abilities to perform calculations were concerned. Man in the third stage must try to use the
computer to increase his ability to solve ill-structured problems. He can
define these problems in such a way that more and better defined alternatives become available. To reach this goal we have to develop inquiry
systems using computers to solve organizational problems.

INFORMATION SYSTEMS

An information system (IS) is generally regarded as a concrete subsystem
of an organization. As we already remarked for the specification of user
needs the use of abstract systems in the form of conceptual models and
models becomes apparent. Of course, one way or another the abstract system must be translated and implemented in the organization as a concrete
system. To define this ill-structured design problem we make use of a
distinction made by Welke who extended the Scandinavian methodology
of Langefors (1966). Welke (1977) identifies the following problem areas.

- Systelogical problem: the generation of one or more information change
facilitated object system alternatives and the selection of that alternative which is better or best in either an efficiency or effectiveness
sense;
- Infological problem: given, by analysis, determination or assumption a
solution to the systelogical problem, determining and specifying the
information requirements (both elements and properties) and their mode
of presentation for those individuals associated with the object sy-
stem(s);
- Datalogical problem: given, by analysis, determination or assumption a
solution to the infological problems associated with the information
system related object systems, to generate alternative data processing
sequences and grouping necessary to satisfy these requirements, and to
select from among those alternatives that which is better or best in an
effeciency or effectiveness sense.
Although this tripartite distinction is generally acknowledged as relevant most of the attempts to find a solution begin at the infological
level. We argue that this is an incorrect procedure. One should start
trying to find a solution for the systelogical problem, as also Welke
suggests, otherwise the infological problem can only be defined using the
approach we described in the preceding section under the label "first
stage".

As we already remarked that the problem of designing an IS (in Scandina-

via named systemeering) needs for its solution an inquiry system. Generally this inquiry system is implicitly defined in the procedures the
designer uses. We regard this as incorrect, because a discussion about
the design is only possible if we know its foundations. The foundations
of design were bounded rationality as the basis for the description of
decision processes in an organization and the use of a modelcycle to
decribe these processes. This foundation allows one to define a design in
which relations between problem solvers, procedures and data are specified. The main question to answer is, of course, what is the context of
such an inquiry system? Before we go into detail in the next sections, we
will mention the main demands such a system should meet.

1. It must be possible to define the concepts of bounded rationality
   in the form of a conceptual model.
2. It must be possible to define variables, starting from concepts,
   that specify relations between a problem solver and the inner and
   outer environment of an organization.
3. It must be possible to specify the relations with data resulting
   in a model or models of the organzation, see Figure 1. Of course,
   these models generally specify only parts of organization. These
   parts can differ according to functions or levels in the organizations and according to the problem concerned.
4. It is of central importance that it is possible to define relations between the different models mentioned in point three.
5. It must be possible to conduct an analysis with these models. The
   structure of the model should not be restricted by the way an
   analysis has to be performed. For instance possibilities should
   exist to perform an analysis of discrete and continuous processes
   and processes of a stochastic or deterministic nature.
6. There should be facilities for experimental design, verification
   and validation.
7. It must be possible to use a computer in an interactive way. To
   be able to realize the other points the computer system must have
   data base facilities and a method bank with at least statistical
   packages.

A SIMULA(TION) BASED INQUIRY SYSTEM

An inquiry system is an abstract system that reflects the meta- theoretical premises of a modeller and that encompasses a methodology that makes
it possible to constrain a model of a problem. We use the term methodology a a set of methods to be used for the analysis of problems and not in
the sense of "science of methods". It is our opinion that an inquiry
system meeting the demands we made in the previous section must use the
methodology of simulation. In accordance with Shannon (1975, p.2) we
define simulation as: "the process of designing a model of a concrete
system and conducting experiments with this model in order to understand
the behavior of a concrete system and to evaluate various strategies for
the operation of the system ". We regard simulation as a separate methodology comparable for instance with the methodology of econometrics. We
prefer simulation as a methodology because,

- it offers possibilities to emphasize the activity of conceptualization;
- it has a relative great number of degrees of freedom for the identification and specification of different models;

- it offers a possibility for a combined emphasis on analysis and
design. The conceptual model is a basis for the construction of
various models and the analysis of these models can deliver different alternatives for design.

We choose as the basic concept for conceptualization and model construction the notion of an entity that is charcterizes by a set of associated
data-items, patterns, and by actions which may involve itself and other
entities, see Nygaard (1975). An entity can have one or more attributes.
An action defines a relation between the attributes of entities. The
notion entity is comparable to the notion variable. We prefer the use of
the term entity because this notion is broader than the commonly used one
of variable. A data-item can be a quantity that expresses the value of an
attribute, or a reference to another attribute or entity. A pattern can
be

- a type, giving the common properties of quantities belonging to
that type,
- a category pattern, given the characteristics of entities sharing
a common structure,
- a procedure, giving a rule for the execution of actions,
- a function, giving a rule for the evaluation of a value.

A system is a nested set of entities.

A framework for the simulation based inquiry of the problem of Systemeering is depicted in Figure 2. In Figure 2 the symbol ⬛️decribes an
acitivity, the symbol ◿ the outcome of an activity. We will discuss
the different activities following the sequence in Figure 2.
The activity of conceptualization consists of three different steps. The
first step is the formulation of a context for conceptualization where
the chosen meta-theory, methodology and application area are expressed in
entity-categories. As we want to specify the time-dependent character of
entities in order to make a dynamic exploration of their behavior possible, we have to choose the concepts of entity-categories. In this connection we have a choice of three concepts, an activity-, event-or process oriented structure of time dependent entities and their associated
procedures and actions. Based on the paradigm of bounded rational behavior we prefer the entity category "process". It has been found that
events are time-efficient, but processes are easier to program and debug.
Furthermore, efficiency of process-specifications can be improved by
changes in the algorithms for the scheduling and scanning of the sequen-
cing set. Another argument for the use of processes lies in the ability-
to specify and describe parallel processes, with or without interrupts.
The same argument can be found in discussions on modern programming
languages when the advantages of descriptions in terms of "petri-nets",
"functional networks", etc. are put forward. The methods to describe a
"process" can be discrete, continuous or a combination of both.
The resulting conceptual model is used in the second step to identify the
entity-categories specific to the problem situation.
In the third step, the specification, the identified categories are used
to generate a base model of the concrete system at hand.If we have applied a formal language for the specification a consistency check using
syntactical and semantical rules is possible. If a compiler exists for
this language, the checking can be done automatically.
The activity of simulation model construction comprises the following
sub-activities:

- the form of the relations between the entities have to be specified,
- possibly new entity-categories have to be introduced to make a
  translation of the conceptual model into a simulation model possible,
- the data necessary for the estimation of the parameters have to be
  collected,
- the data necessary for specifying the values of attributes have to
  be collected, perhaps after provision of entity-categories for
  input-data,
- an experimental frame has to be setup and provisions for output-
  data collection have to be established.

The activity of simulation consists of a series of time-dependent trac-
kings of the experimental setups, possibly on a man-machine interaction
controlled by statistical considerations. In the activity of evaluation
the experimental results are analyzed and validated. This may lead to
alternative conceptual models, simulation models and experimental setups.
After evaluation of the results the analysis phase is ended and the design phase starts. A simulation model can be regarded as a systelogical
target specification for technical construction and implementation. As
long as the target specification is not satisfactory, alternative conceptual models and/or simulation models can be explored.

As soon as a target specification is specified, we can enter the activities of infological analysis, datalogical design, technological design
and implementation. Various algorithms and simulation approaches exist
for conducting these activities. Pilot implementations and automatic code
generation become feasible. For a more extensive discussion we refer to
Sol (1978a, 1978b).

Looking at the framework again, we can ask

1. What entity-categories, together with semantics and application
   rules, are to be used in the distinguished activities?
2. What communication tools or language(s) should support it?

We have chosen the high level programming language SIMULA to support our
simulation based inquiry system for the following reasons (Birtwistle
1973; Dahl, 1970):

1. The 'class'-concept in SIMULA reflects the entity-attribute-
   action- model and thus has great opportunities for the description of bounded rational decision making. The 'hidden-protected'-
   feature (Palme, 1975) embodies the limited data-accesabiblity
   inherent in bounded rationality. On the other hand, only integer,
   real, boolean, text and character 'types' are defined, which has
   not lead to difficulties in practice.
2. Hierarchical systems can be build by 'prefixing' classes. So we
   are able to define a nested structure of entity-categories as a
   context which can be used as a starting platform for conceptualization, simulation model construction as well as solution finding
   by simulation.
3. A family of "contexts" is available for the conceptualization and
   model construction of systological, infological and datalogical
   problems, see Sol (1979).
4. The inquirer can define his own building blocks for conceptualization, simulation model construction and simulation. In Sol
   (1978b) we introduced a hierarchy of concepts for the simulation
   of information system in general.

A DESIGN PHILOSOPHY

The main function of an inquiry system is to be an instrument for describing problems and defining alternatives to find a solution. It can also
be used to formulate and try to implement different design philosophies.
In this section we discuss a philosophy for the design of an IS that
differs at several points from the philosophies "normally" used for that
purpose.

One of the greatest problems decision makers in organizations have to
deal with is the problem of co-ordination. It is our opinion that starting from the paradigm of bounded rationality the co-ordination problem
can only be solved if one acknowledges the fact that there is not one co-
ordination problem, but that there are many of these problems. Of course,
the set of these problems can be defined as the co-ordination problem. A
set, however, can only be defined if we know the feature that connects
its elements. Our design philosophy tries to define features to make it
possible to define a set of co-ordination problems. We shall discuss the
main features of our design philosophy and try to relate these features
to the function of the inquiry system and the possible use of computers.

We already sketched a general outline of decision making problems in
organizations. We postulated that men as problem solver behaved "more"
rational in an organization than outside. We gave a number of arguments
to support this hypothesis. There are, however, arguments that can be
applied to contradict our assumption. In relation to organizational problem-solving we think it is relevant to make in this respect a distinction between an inner and outer environment.[1] Problem solvers in an organization specify two different kinds of environments. The inner environment describes the relations with other problem solvers in the organization. The outer environment describes the relations of the organization
with its environment. Stated in other words, the outer environment is
described by problem solvers who make decisions that influence the environment of the organization. A problem solver can make these decisions in
a rational manner only if he knows or assumes to know how relevant or
effective these influences are. We postulate that problem solvers in
organizations solve problems with regard to the distinction between
inner- and outer environment in different ways and that they are inclined
to define problems in terms of the inner environment. This assumption is
confirmed through the outcomes of many research projects. To discuss the
differences between ill-structured problems with regard to inner and
outer environment we make a distinction between efficiency and effectiveness. A solution is efficient if one reaches a certain goal not using
more means than necessary. A solution is effective if one meets the
highest possible value of a goal with a given amount of means.

We can now reformulate our statement about the rational behavior of problem solvers in organizations. We postulate that human beings as problem
solvers within organizations act more rational than outside the organizations only as efficiency as an instrument for defining rationality is
concerned. Ill-structured problems are in many cases explicitly redefined
as well-structured ones through the use of efficiency oriented procedu-

[1] These terms are also used by Simon (1969) with a somewhat different
   meaning.

res, as those of planning and budgeting. Implicitly a redefinition takes
places by assuming effectiveness criteria. As the effectiveness side of
problem solving is ignored one cannot state that the co-ordination problem can be solved in a rational manner. It is for that reason that we
stress the importance of a solution for the co-ordination problem in our
design philosophy.

Next to the distinction between effectiveness and efficiency there is
another important feature of human problem solving in organizations. This
feature is directly related to man's constrained capabilities as a data
processing instrument, see Section 2. As man is not able to store and
retrieve large numbers of data he is inclined to simplify his problems
and to use aggregated data to specify them. In organizations aggregation
is conducted with the help of prices and/or time. When using prices one
can speak of a money veil. Co-ordination problems are therefore defined
in aggregated- and in money terms as variables giving solutions which
cannot be used for the co-ordination of decisions at other levels of an
organization . It is, therefore, necessary to define relations between
the elements in the set of co-ordination problems that in a consistent
way combines aggregation, co-ordination and data processing capabilities.
Our design philosophy, as the definition of these relations is concerned,
can be reflected in the following points, see Figure 3.
1. Instead of trying to define and solve the co-ordination problem
   through vertical defined subsystems (production, marketing, personnel and accounting) and horizontal defined levels of planning
   (strategic, administrative and operational) we propose horizontal
   defined subsystems that are connected by planning procedures.
2. These horizontal defined subsystems co-ordinate decisions at the
   same level of specification. We make a distinction between on the
   one hand local decisions and on the other hand aggregate decisions. This last category can be subdivided in decisions of different degrees of aggregation. Local decisions are defined
   through decision rules that are
   - of a relative simple nature,
   - circumscribed by variables specified in physical attributes,
   - used to direct and control the movements of parts and goods in
     the production processes of an organization,
   - in most cases directly related in one way or another to the EDP
     transaction processes,
   - aimed at efficiency,
   - not directly defined to solve co-ordination problems.
   Aggregate decision rules have as their main purpose the solution
   of co-ordination problems. The differences in aggregation are a
   result of the fact that we are not able to define the co- ordination problem taking into account aspects of effectiveness in one
   model.
3. Different planning procedures can and should be used at the different levels of horizontally defined subsystems. At the local
   level we generally use planning procedures with algorithms based
   on heuristic rules. At the lower level of aggregated decisions it
   is possible to use operations research algorithms that co- ordi-
   nate alternatives defined through variables with physical dimen-

sions and a goal function with parameters defined in monetary
terms. At the higher level of aggregated decisions one generally
uses simulation procedures to define alternatives and find a
solution, see Naylor (1979). Although we made a tripartite distinction in Figure 3 generally more than three levels must be
perceived to solve the co- ordination problem.
4. The planning procedures should be defined in such a way that
connection between a lower and higher level is established. This
can be realized through aggregation of the data used and an in-
terrelation of goals.

Our design philosophy opens possibilities:
- to enlarge problem solving abilities with the help of different
planning procedures and the availibility of data. To enlarge these
abilities an explicitly defined inquiry system should be used.
Different opinions about design philosophies and design principles
of an IS can only be debated if inquiry systems are defined;
- to construct an IS as e.g. defined by Mason and Mitroff (1974) in
which it is possible to integrate human decision making procedures
on the basis of bounded rationality trying to accomplish an efficient and an effective co-ordination;
- to integrate the EDP data transaction processes with the decison
processes. In this way one can prevent a situation in which two
different IS exist, one processing EDP programs, the other being
used for decision making. A situation that typifies the state of
many existing computer systems. Boulden (1975, p. 68) describing
this situation correctly remarks:"the elusive concept of a management information system is largely irrelevant to computer-assisted
planning systems and is thus not a condition for their accomplishment. ....In point of fact, the data collection system for most computer-based planning systems is manual, not computerized";
- to redefine the relations between files, data base, EDP data processing and data for decision making.
With regard to the topic of this conference we conclude:
a. the paradigm of bounded rationality makes it possible to specify
the relations between procedures - data - and the two environments decision makers deal with;
b. starting from the co-ordination problem an equilibrium can and
must be defined between the attention paid to the specification
of an inner and an outer environment;
c. the aspects of effective decision making can only be taken into
account if a data bound specification of the outer environment is
made;
d. for this data bound specification an inquiry system defining
relations with the help of a computer is a must;
e. possibilities should exist to specify scenarios describing possible future states (alternatives);
f. as far as defining the inner environment is concerned bounded
rationality opens possibilities to construct a multidisciplinary
approach to decision problems.

REFERENCES

(1) Abel, B., Problemorientiertes Informationsverhalten, (S. Torche-Mittler Verlag, Damstadt, 1977).

(2) Ackoff, R.L., Management Misinformation Systems, Management Science Vol.14, nr. 4 (1967).

(3) Birtwistle,G.M., et al, Simula Begin (Lund, Studentlitteratur, 1973).

(4) Blumenthal, S.C., Management Information Systems (Prentice-Hall, Englewood Cliffs, 1969).

(5) Boulden, J.B., Computer-assisted Planning Systems (McGraw-Hill, New York, 1975).

(6) Bosman, A., Systemen en toekomstonderzoek. Een methodologische beschouwing in: Systemen en toekomstverkenning, Broekstra G. en Knipscheer J.S. (eds.), (Stenfert Kroese, Leiden, 1977).

(7) Bosman, A., System Identification and Simulation,(IFIP-IAG, Proceedings of the Seminar Modelling in Business, Amsterdam, 1978).

(8) Brightman,H.J., Differences in Ill-Structured Problem Solving Along the Organization Hierarchy, Decision Sciences, Vol.9, nr.1. (1978).

(9) Churchman,C.W., The Design of Inquiring Systems, (Basic Books Inc. New York, 1971).

(10) Cyert, R.M. and March, J.G., A Behavioral Theory of the Firm, (Prentice Hall, Englewood Cliffs, 1963).

(11) Dahl, O.J., et al, Simula Common Base, (NCC, Oslo, 1970).

(12) Davis, G.B., Management Information Systems, (McGraw-Hill, New York, 1974).

(13) Davis, G.B., Evolution of Business System Analysis Techniques, in: Entwicklungstendenzen der Systemanalyse, Hansen, H.R. (ed.) (Oldenbourg, 1978).

(14) Langefors, B., Theoretical Analysis of Information Systems, (Lund, Studentlitteratur, 1966).

(15) Langefors, B., Analysis of User Needs, in: Information Systems Methodology, Bracchi, G. and Lockemann, P.C., (eds.) (Springer Verlag, Berlin, 1978).

(16) Lucas, H.C.,Jr., Why Information Systems Fail, (Columbia University Press, New York, 1975).

(17) Lucas, H.C., Jr., Information System Concepts for Management, (McGraw-Hill, New York, 1978).

(18) Mason, R.O., and Mitroff, I.I., A Program for Research on MIS, Management Science, Vol.19, nr. 5, (1973).

(19) Mathewson, S.C., et al, Draft Simula, Proceedings 4th Simula Users Conferense, (NCC, Oslo, 1976).

(20) Mitroff, I.I., et al, Dialectical Decision Theory: A Meta-theory of Decision Making, Management Science, Vol.19, nr.1, (1972).

(21) Mitroff, I.I., et al, On managing science in the systems age: Two Schemes for the Study of Science as a Whole Systems Phenomenon, Tims Interfaces, Vol. 4, nr. 3, (1974).

(22) Mumford, E. and Henshall, D., A Participative Approach to Computer Systems Design, (Associated Business Press, London, 1979).

(23) Naylor, Th.H., Corporate Planning Models, (Addison-Wesley, Reading, Mass., 1979).

(24) Newell, A., and Simon, H.A., Human Problem Solving, (Prentice-Hall Englewood Cliffs, 1972).

(25) Nilsson, N.J., Problem-solving Methods in Artificial Intelligence, (McGraw-Hill, New York, 1971).

(26) Nygaard, K., System Description and the Delta Language, (NCC, Oslo 1975).

(27) Palme, J., Hidden Protected, (NCC-SDG, Oslo, 1976).

(28) Sagasti, R.F., and Mitroff, I.I., Operations Research from the Viewpoint of General Systems Theory, Omega, Vol.1, nr.6, (1973), pp. 700 - 701.

(29) Shannon, R.E., Systems Simulation, (Prentice-Hall, Englewood Cliffs, 1975).

(30) Simon, H.A., The New Science of Management Decision, (Prentice-Hall, Englewood Cliffs, 1960).

(31) Simon, H.A., The Sciences of the Artificial, (M.I.T. press, Cambridge, 1969).

(32) Simon, H.A., From Substantive to Procedural Rationality, in: 25 Years of Economic Theory, Retrospect and Prospect, Kastelein,T.J., Kuipers,S.K., et al, (eds.) (Martinus Nijhoff, Leiden, 1976).

(33) Slagle, J.R., Artificial Intelligence: The Heuristic Programming Approach, (McGraw-Hill, New York, 1971).

(34) Sol, H.G., A Procedurally Rational Inquiry System for Systemeering, paper Information Systems Research Group, University of Groningen, (1978a).

(35) Sol, H.G., Simula Software for Systemeering, Proceedings of the 6th Simula Users Conference, (NCC, Oslo, 1978b).

(36) Sol, H.G., On the choice of Simula Simulators, Proceedings of the 7th Simula Users Conference, (NCC, Oslo, 1979).

(37) Uhr, L., Pattern Recognition, Learning and Thought, (Prentice-Hall Englewood Cliffs, 1973).

(38) Weick, K.E., The Social Psychology of Organizing, (Addison-Wesley, Reading, 1979).

(39) Welke, R.J., Current Information System Analysis and Design Approaches, in: Education and Large Information Systems, Buckingham,R.A., (ed.) (North-Holland, Amsterdam, 1977).

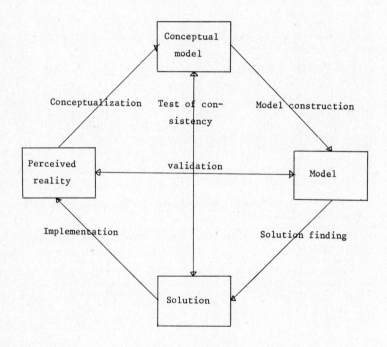

Figure 1. Modeling

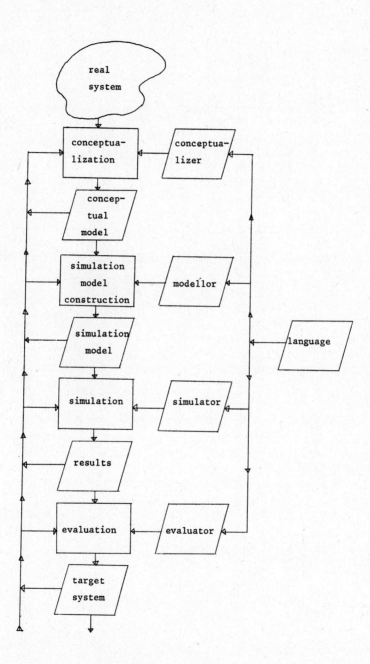

Figure 2. A Framework for Systemeering

272

A. BOSMAN, H.G. SOL

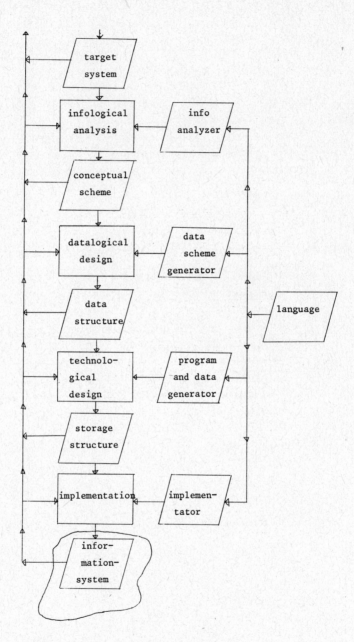

Figure 2. A Framework for Systemeering

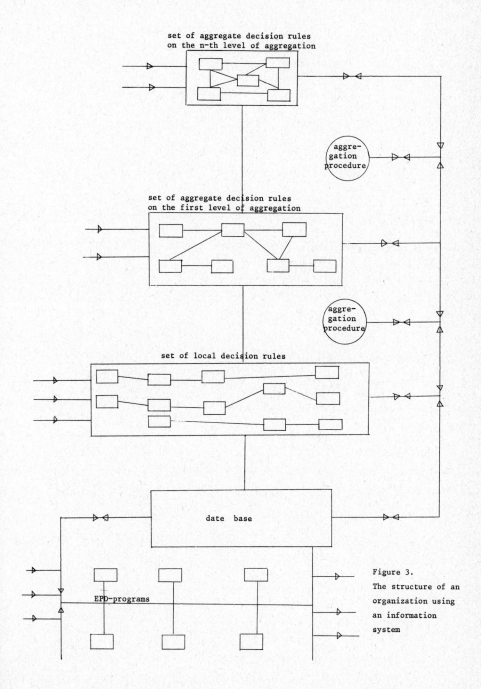

Figure 3.
The structure of an
organization using
an information
system

The Information Systems Environment
Lucas, Land, Lincoln, Supper (Editors)
North-Holland Publishing Company
© *IFIP, 1980*

THE INFORMATION SYSTEMS ARCHITECT
AND SYSTEMS DEVELOPMENT

E.A. Ben-Nathan

IBM UK Ltd
Information Systems Support Centre
Chiswick, London W.4
England

While formal information systems planning techniques have been sucessfully used to generate
executive management commitment to an applications
development plan involving integrated data base
concepts, the subsequent implementation quality
leaves much to be desired. It is suggested that
there is a gap between the strategic view developed at the I.S. planning level and the short term
view of the individual project leader; one loses
sight of strategic objectives during implementation. It is proposed here that a systems architecture function could bridge that gap, and some
techniques available to the architect are
outlined.

INTRODUCTION

This paper is concerned with the need for the function of an I.S.
Architect within systems development. It is recognised that the
concept of a systems architect could apply to other areas than
systems development, such as hardware and software strategy or
distributed processing and data strategy, but these are not considered here.

The architect's role in development is aimed at ensuring coherence
of individual information systems projects and their consistency
with overall information systems plans and strategies. With that in
mind the subject is discussed by reference to some formal methods
used in the planning of information systems and data bases, and
their relationship with subsequent application and data base design
techniques. The relationship between these two conceptual levels is
key to the role of the I.S. architect.

I.S. architecture is considered here to mean some form of overall
systems design covering main business functions, the associated
types of information required, information flows across system
boundaries, proposed or planned computer implementation sequence.
The architecture is refined to greater levels of detail as systems
are designed and implemented.

The purpose of the architecture is to ensure the integral nature of
the resultant systems developed, and to maintain a strong strategic
influence on application development. A key requirement for a
systems architecture stems from the desire to implement systems

founded on integrated data bases. Data base imposes a need to ensure
coherence of overlapping data requirements of differing systems.
Another key requirement derives from those systems which cross
organizational boundaries, particularly if those boundaries are also
national ones.

Information system planning techniques, such as IBM's BSP(Manual No.
GE20-0527), seek to derive from executive management identification
of and commitment to a set of prioritized computer application
projects which are aimed at enabling data processing to make an
effective contribution to the achievement of business objectives.
In order to implement the applications plan, individual projects are
established hopefully with well-defined objectives and completion
dates. These project characteristics mean that no project leader can
reasonably be expected to spend his project's resources on effort
not contributing directly to his own objectives.

However in planning to implement applications with strong
inter-relationships such effort is required. It is the author's
belief that the strategic and inter-system implications should be
managed by means of a systems architecture function.

At the lower, application development, level much effort has gone
into developing formal techniques for application design and development. Structured Design, IBM's IPT(Manual No. GE19-5086) are
reasonably well understood and accepted. In the data base area
relational analysis and Bachmann diagrams are examples of techniques
evolving to support the data base design process.

The problem addressed in this paper is the bridge between these two
conceptual levels (see Figure 1).

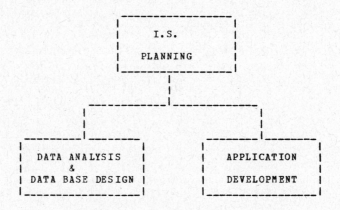

Planning and Application Development

Figure 1

Experience has shown that often a high level application/data base
development plan, over which many man-months or man-years of effort
may have been spent, may be misinterpreted during the application

design phase. The reasons are many:

1. The people that produce the high level plan are different from
    the application development teams, who may not understand the
    purpose or content of the high-level plan (except that it was
    responsible for the project's existence).   Also the people
    involved in the plan's production may no longer be available as
    a team or even individually.

2. The high-level plan is inevitably not detailed (as is the
    nature of planning documents) and consequently looses credibil-
    ity with the application development teams who discover incon-
    sistencies at the detailed level.

3. The prime source of information to the application development
    team is the end user and not the high level plan. It is the end
    user who is the main influence upon system functions and
    contents. This inevitably means that a parochial departmental
    view will be predominant over the strategic view established
    during the planning phase.

4. Possibly most importantly, conflicts arise between project
    schedules or resources and the plan, resulting in compromises
    in function or scope which impacts the achievement of strategic
    benefits. However good a project analyst may be, given project
    objectives to achieve the long term will inevitably be compro-
    mised for the short term.

Another factor leading to the difficulty in carrying through an I.S.
plan into development phases is associated with the relative scope
of the enterprise for which the planning activity takes place. This
influences the significance of the second problem above.

If the plan is for a small enterprise, say a merchant bank, then 100
or so business processes, or activities, such as 'Offer Loan', may
cover most of the important detailed procedures of the bank. Since
100 is a rough number that is manageable in terms of activities or
data types, the path from I.S. plan to development seems relatively
simple. (Experience of many I.S. planning studies has shown that
numbers of processes significantly in excess of 100 makes analysis
very difficult, although not impossible). Because the enterprise is
small the plan will be at a level of detail that is meaningful to an
individual project leader.

If, on the other hand, the plan is for a large, multi-divisional
enterprise, with many thousands of employees, then 100 or so processes will, of necessity, be at a high level of generality. The
alternative of planning to the lowest level of activity would result
in a number of processes, say 1000, which is too large to be dealt
with easily at one time. The problem then exists of translating
this high-level business model into terms meaningful to individual
project leaders.

I.S. PLANNING TECHNIQUES

Information systems planning is considered, here, to be the activity
of determining a plan of work for the I.S.   department over a

strategic (say 5 years) timeframe. The constraints on this activity
are the need for the I.S. department to make an optimum business
contribution to the enterprise, both in terms of the individual
projects comprising the plan and in terms of their mutual consistency and future extensibility.

Formal methods addressing this activity include the need to specify
the following characteristics of the enterprise:

1. The formal organization (disposition of responsibility and
    authority),

2. The processes or activities performed by each element of
    organization (e.g. "manage inventory" or "counsel employee"),

3. The data messages used by each activity or process,

4. The entity types involved in each data message-- entity types
    representing the information categories about which records
    must be kept such as customers, products, employees or cost
    centers.

These can also be cross-related, for example, to determine which
entity types are used in each process. See Figure 2 for a sample
matrix relating each of the above types of information. The matrix
describes the activities performed by one organizational element
(Oil and Utility Analysis) which data messages (used here to mean
document types or messages) are input to each activity, which other
organizations receive output from those activities, and which types
of data are associated with both the organizations and the information systems. This sort of matrix assists in selecting areas of the
enterprise for computer support and determining system boundaries.

The total I.S. planning activity will typically include analysis of
business performance, resources, problems and other aspects of the
business which lead to a plan for I.S. support which provides value
to the business as a whole. This plan would normally be in terms of
providing computer support to specific processes and business entity
types, phased over time.

The prime, but not sole, output of the planning activity is the list
of committed application development projects and associated priorities. Other factors such as I.S. management organization, policies
and practices should also be revised in the light of the plan.

One of these policies might well be to build integrated data bases,
with one set of consistent data for each category of business data.
Another might be to build common systems across departmental boundaries, for example, for order processing, purchasing control, inventory control, cost control and so on.

These policies will represent top management's strategic thinking,
and the objectives behind them may include not only the achievement
of operational level benefits to both I.S. and the end user departments, but business planning and control benefits to executive
management over a strategic time frame.

In attempting to plan for the implementation of discrete application
projects within the context of integrated data base and common
systems policies, the planning phase may well attempt to produce

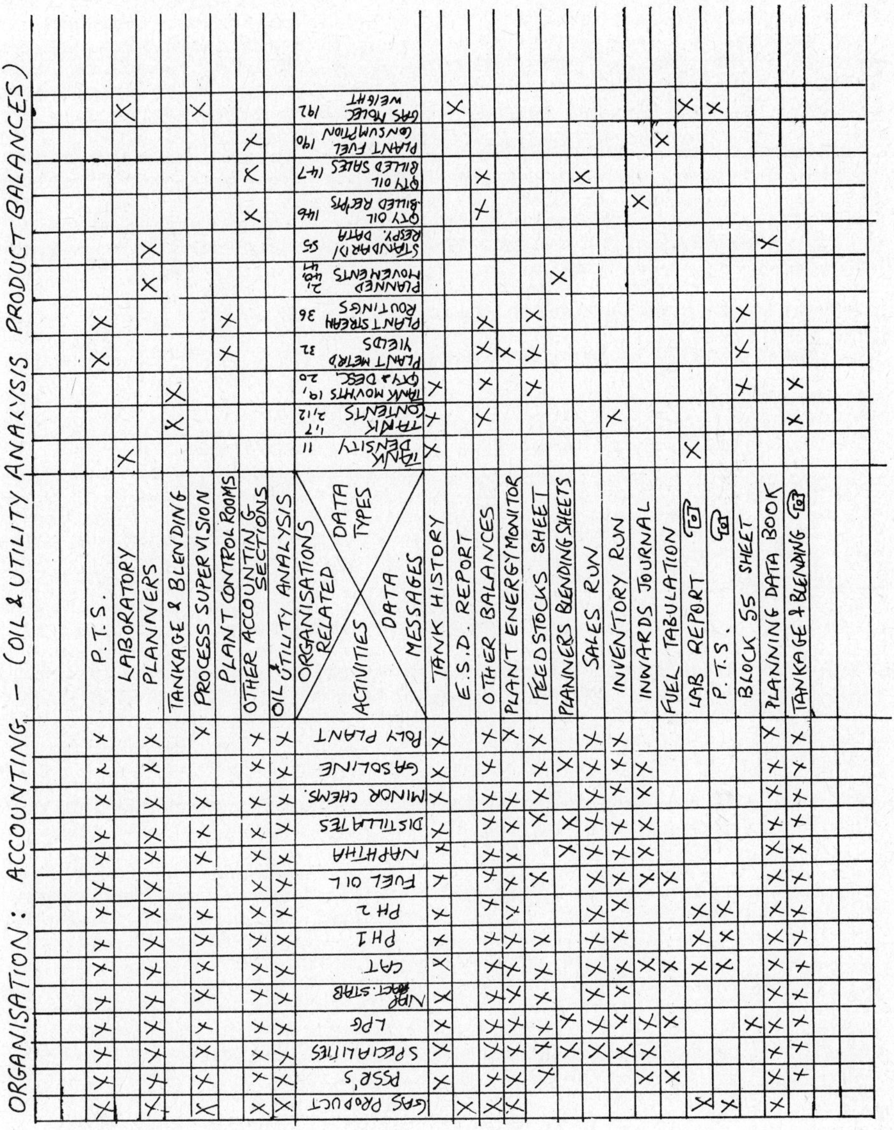

ORGANISATION: ACCOUNTING — (OIL & UTILITY ANALYSIS PRODUCT BALANCES)

Column headers (organisation / related activities):
- P.T.S.
- LABORATORY
- PLANNERS
- TANKAGE & BLENDING
- PROCESS SUPERVISION
- PLANT CONTROL ROOMS
- OTHER ACCOUNTING SECTIONS
- OIL UTILITY ANALYSIS

ORGANISATIONS RELATED ACTIVITIES / DATA TYPES / DATA MESSAGES

Data types (top, reading right):
- TANK DENSITY 11
- TANK CONTENTS 1.7, 2.12
- TANK MOVMTS 1.9, OXY.DESC. 20
- PLANT METRD YIELDS 32
- PLANT STREAM ROUTINGS 36
- PLANNED MOVEMENTS 21, 40
- STANDARD/RESP. DATA 55
- QTY OIL BILLED REPTS 146
- QTY OIL BILLED SALES 147
- PLANT FUEL CONSUMPTION 196
- GAS MOLEC WEIGHT 192

Data messages (right columns):
- TANK HISTORY
- E.S.D. REPORT
- OTHER BALANCES
- PLANT ENERGY MONITOR
- FEEDSTOCKS SHEET
- PLANNERS BENDING SHEETS
- SALES RUN
- INVENTORY RUN
- INWARDS JOURNAL
- FUEL TABULATION
- LAB REPORT (cot)
- P.T.S. (cot)
- BLOCK SS SHEET
- PLANNING DATA BOOK (cot)
- TANKAGE & BLENDING (cot)

Activities (rows):
- POLY PLANT
- GASOLINE
- MINOR CHEMS
- DISTILLATES
- NAPHTHA
- FUEL OIL
- PH 2
- PH 1
- CAT
- NBF RECT. STAB
- LPG
- SPECIALITIES
- PSSR'S
- GAS PRODUCT

Activities and Messages

Fig. 2

some sort of overall framework within which each project must fit.

There is considerable experience in how I.S. planning techniques can
help towards the development of a committed application plan. There
appear to be few, if any, techniques which help to ensure that
multiple, potentially concurrent, discrete application development
projects fit together to support an integrated data base.

A framework for development is required to ensure such coherence.
It should define all the project boundaries, the business functions
they are to support, the data categories that are involved, and the
information flows between projects. Thus, for example, it might
include the definition of what the enterprise considers to be the
meaning of the term "Customer".

"Customers are considered to include:

1. Those currently doing business,

2. Named prospective customers,

3. Those whose last transaction is less than 5 years old

and exclude:

1. Competitive enterprises with whom we exchange products(e.g. as
    amongst oil companies),

2. Internal locations, and subsidiary companies, between which
    product deliveries are made for internal use".

Such a constraint forces the subsequent system and data base design
to operate in a specific way consistent with an enterprise view, as
distinct from the view of an individual project.

Thus we have shown:

1. That I.S. planning has two purposes, one for planning individ-
    ual I.S. projects, and the other for developing and maintaining
    a framework for their development.

2. That I.S. planning produces specifications of various aspects
    of the business, such as its organization, business processes,
    information systems, and entity types. These specifications
    form, initially, the framework for development.

APPLICATION/DATA BASE DESIGN FOLLOWING AN I.S. PLAN

Typically the application/data base(A/DB) analyst will begin by
analyzing the detailed procedures, documents, data and information
flow within each prospective user's department. From there, he will
determine additional user information requirements made possible by
automation. Entity, or data, analysis will proceed either on parallel, or sequentially, to produce, for that project, some sort of
data base specification. Entity analysis is the process of analyzing the data types used in an enterprise for their meaning, structure, relationships with each other, and their usage in business

activities with the ultimate purpose of designing data bases and
providing disciplined data descriptions to users of all kinds. This
specification might be in terms of relations, Bachmann diagrams or
other sorts of tabular or diagrammatic representation. The outputs
of I.S. planning will contain, typically, some form of process or
activity model of the enterprise and a high level data model,
showing the major business entities and their relationships.

There thus appears considerable similarity between the two conceptual levels. The key points of difference, however, are:

1. The level of detail

2. The sources of information

For planning purposes the quantity of detail concerning a process or
data model must be small. That is, a relatively small number of
processes and data types will be named, sometimes to include or
subsume all lower conceptual levels. For example the high level
process "Marketing" will include the lowest level procedure "Receive
Order".

However certain architectural decisions are made at the high level.
For example, on the process side, it may be recognized that all
procedures concerned with product distribution are basically similar, and that during provision of computer support for that process
for one product group or market sector due consideration should be
given to providing extensibility to remaining product groups or
market sectors.

As far as data is concerned, for example, it may be decided that
instead of considering just existing employees as a resource to be
managed, that all individuals with whom the enterprise deals should
be considered within the class 'Employee'. This would include
candidates, both current and those previously rejected, past employees, contractors or suppliers' staff who require constant access to
enterprise locations and so on.

These and other architectural decisions materially influence the
individual A/DB project which will, in general, be concerned with
only a subset of enterprise processes and entity types. Thus, for
example, the project leader concerned with implementing a payroll
system for monthly-paid staff might be motivated towards considering
designing a system and data base extensible to all paid employees,
but might feel it reasonable to leave out extensibliity for candidate employees or registration of suppliers' staff when project
schedules start to slip.

However tendency this must be countered by firm management commitment, based upon benefits to be derived from adherence to the I.S.
plan. For example, the I.S. plan might have identified the need for
a project concerned with company costs, and another with reporting
revenues. At the planning stage the added value of providing
extensibility of these two systems to support profit analysis could
well be determined as considerable. Thus if either project short
cuts their design to meet their stated timescales, so as to remove
the required extensibility, then the added value from Profit Analysis must be assigned as a cost to the offending project. If adequate
financial controls exist in respect of system development projects
then this move could help to ensure development consistent within

the I.S. architecture.

The problem that management has is in appreciating the 'information technicalities' of candidates versus employees or of the difficulties of making costs and revenues systems consistent with each other. Too often these issues go unrecognized let alone resolved. Once the I.S. planning phase has ended -- and it is unlikely to be repeated frequently -- there is no one person or function who has the broad systems picture in sufficient detail to make judgements on the short versus the long term.

The sources of information to the A/DB analyst are, of course, the end user, and informed colleagues. The A/DB analyst has to know precisely how the system will work in every little detail as he is reponsible for its implementation. The sources of information to the I.S. planner are somewhat different. While probably including some operational end users the information sources will span all levels of management in the enterprise, and may be concentrated mainly at the upper levels.

What follows from this is that the architecture may be inaccurate as to detail and consequently require modification as detailed understanding develops. Also the A/DB design, if done independently of any framework, will be inaccurate in so far as it implements or reflects enterprise policies, and be subject to heavy revision as interfaces to future developments become necessary. Since modifications are easier to apply at the architecture stage than during implementation, the benefits of having the systems architecture actually directing systems development seem apparent.

So far the need for an architecture to be developed and maintained beyond any one I.S. planning exercise has been expressed. The requirement for a person to have the responsibility for building the architecture and ensuring its relevance to business needs and to see that applications are developed which conform to it is self-evident. He is the Information Sytems Architect. What methods does he have at his disposal?

METHODS FOR THE I.S. ARCHITECT

Methods to be employed by the I.S. architect must assist him in developing the architecture, communicating it to top management, communicating it to systems and data base developers, ensuring development proceeds so as to conform to the architecture, and updating the architecture as his understanding improves. The broad relationship between his function and A/DB analysts is depicted in Figure 3.

In one internal IBM I.S. department a recently-established "Systems Architecture" function has responsibility for producing the first two phases of each project's documentation. This means that the architects are responsible for the Feasibility Study and Outline Requirements phases. The individual project leader starts with a very clear and fairly detailed specification given to him by the Systems Architect. This procedure ensures that architectural constraints are reflected in project specifications, but probably

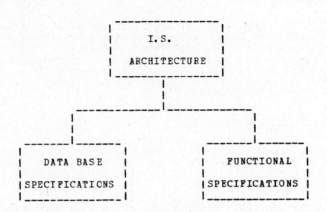

The Architect and Analyst Relationship

Figure 3

implies a sizeable architecture group.

So what actually might the architecture comprise? To answer this question requires looking in more detail at I.S. planning techniques.

Components of an Architecture

Architecture is one of these simple-sounding words with a very fuzzy meaning. With respect to information systems I intend it to include the following functions:

1. Describing, at a high level, the entire enterprise, or major part(s) thereof, and encompassing multiple individual projects.

2. Describing future enterprise information requirements, beyond current development projects.

3. Controlling inter-project interfaces ensuring that resultant systems work together satisfactorily.

4. Ensuring current projects make provision for extensibility to support known future information requirements.

Thus the components of an architecture must include some form of enterprise specification. This means disciplined descriptions of the way the enterprise operates, and what information is required to support such operations. The main parts of this specification are an enterprise process model and an enterprise data model.

Enterprise Process Model

There are different approaches to the creation of a process model
which have been used in practice. One approach involves covering all
of the lower level processes, which might number in the thousands.
Another approach may record only processes at the highest levels.
For example, 'Selling', 'Engineering', 'Purchasing'. This approach
allows for the gradual, step-wise, refinement of process specification into its component processes, as in Figure 4.

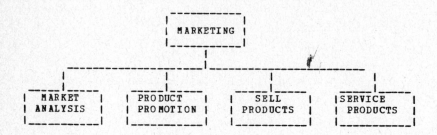

An Enterprise Process Model

Figure 4

Each of these functions can be further described by means of HIPO
(IBM Manual No. GC20-1851) charts which show the inputs and outputs
to each process in terms of messages of information. Additional
documentation includes lists of all processes and messages and
cross-references of processes and messages.

There is a third method which has been used in a number of organizations in the process industry. This method also produces both an
activity and a data model. However it has been considered useful to
allow the planning documents to cover multiple conceptual levels of
process without attempting to impose any conceptual hierarchy as
depicted in Figure 4. Thus one planning document might refer to
"Marketing", "Plan Daily Production", and "Record Overtime Worked".
This has the advantage of allowing the team involved in producing
the plan to concentrate on the various activities requiring computer
support to whatever level of detail is deemed necessary. While being
conceptually inelegant it has been considered economical in terms of
planning effort. An example of the matrices produced via this
technique is shown in Figure 5.

All of these variations in building an enterprise process model
derive from different experiences. All seem to work as planning
methods, to a greater or less degree. As part of an I.S. architecture, however, a complete picture is required, encompassing as much
of the enterprise and to as great a level of detail as possible. The
I.S. architect is not working in 'study' mode, as I.S. planning
tends to, and thus economy of specification effort is less important. However he must be able both to understand the "big picture"

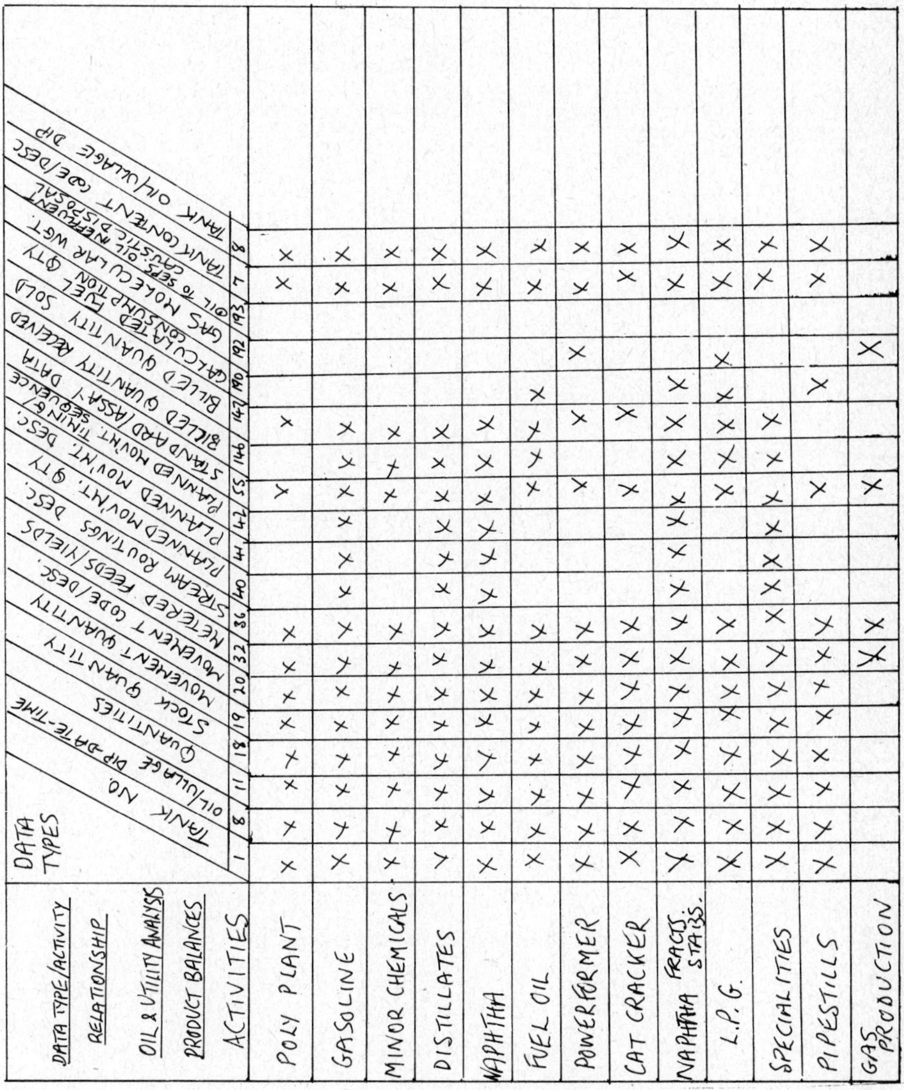

An Activity and Data Matrix

Fig. 5

and to control the overall strategy. The architect must be able to
dive to low levels of detail to ensure that individual developments
conform to architectural standards aimed at inter-system consistency
and future extensibility.

Indeed a Process Model covering multiple levels of abstraction, from
the most general to the most specific, is the means to enable the
architecture to be meaningful to an individual A/DB project team.
See (Moehrke & Dunham, 1975).

Enterprise Entity Model

Much has been written about data (or entity) models, (Bachmann &
Daya, 1977),   (Chen, 1976),   (Senko, 1975),   (Smith &   Smith, 1977),
(Codd, 1979), for example, without a great deal concerning the
process of establishing them. I.S. planning techniques involve
production of a model describing the types of information that the
enterprise requires for its operation. Models are normally generated via discussion among the study team and/or via interviews with
end users.

The BSP approach favours the construction of a Business Entity Model
(see Figure 6) at the highest conceptual level. This model identifies

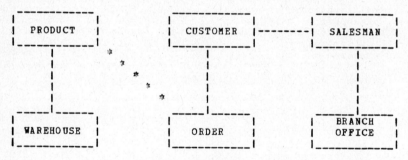

A Business Entity Model

Figure 6

as many entity types as possible at this level and their relationships, depicting them in Bachmann-like diagrams. At this level all
relationships are assumed to be many-to-many (e.g. many products per
warehouse and many warehouses per product) to allow for
extensibility.   Extensibility is needed should any current
one-to-many relationship change into a many-to-many as a result of a
change in the way of doing business. (e.g. building a second warehouse to stock the same products.)

Another approach has involved the use of multiple levels of data
types, without attempting to distinguish between the different
levels. For example "Product Information", "Inventory Data", and
"Product Standard Cost" are used without specifying that "Product"
is an entity type, "Inventory Data" represents a collection of
product attributes, and "Product Standard Cost" is an individual
product attribute. While this may appear confusing it reflects the
need for different levels of detail depending on the knowledge and
experience of the study team. It allows some things to be highlighted while leaving others deliberately vague.

As far as an I.S. architecture is concerned, as with the process
model, the breadth and depth of the model are both important. It is
the job of the I.S. architect to expand, rationalize, and refine the
models produced during the I.S. planning phase to produce a conceptually consistent architecture.

The point should be made that via an extended, perhaps multi-phase,
I.S. planning study the I.S. architecture should result. In most
cases however the architectural output of a planning study is
likely to be sketchy. The job of the architect is to flesh it out to
address all the types of specification required.

Other Types of Specification

The other types of information comprising a candidate I.S. architecture would normally include some description of the organization,
the current inventory of computer systems, and the current and
planned development projects. The planned costs and benefits are
also an important component as they will strongly influence the
architect in establishing and maintaining priorities. The key to
this information is its relationship to the process and entity
models. For example each development project should be defined, in
part at least, in terms of the subset of the process and entity
models that it addresses. For example Figure 7 shows a
project/entity type relationship. A similar matrix can be produced
for business processes and projects.

The I.S. architect has also to be aware of all the existing files
and data bases containing data about each entity type in order to
understand the implications of the new developments for existing
systems. See Figure 8.
Both of these matrices hide a great deal of further detail the
architect requires to perform his function. Quite where the precise
boundary where the architect's specifications stop and the project
analyst's start needs further investigation and may well vary from
enterprise to enterprise depending on the resources committed to the
architecture function.

Entity Type / Project	Customer	Product	Sales Order	Customer Account	Cost Centre	Vehicle	......
Sales Accounting	X			X			
Order Processing	X	X	X	X		X	
Inventory Control		X	X		X		
Product Costing		X			X		
...							

Project/Entity Relationships

Figure 7

Entity Type / Files	Customer	Product	Sales Order	Customer Account	Cost Centre	Vehicle	
Name & Address	X						
Sales Accounts	X		X	X			
Stock Master		X					
Pricing Master	X	X					
Sales Stats	X	X		X	X		
etc							

File/Entity Relationship

Figure 8

LINKING THE ARCHITECTURE WITH IMPLEMENTATION

Application development within an architectural framework does not represent a radical change. What is being imposed on each project is essentially the need to conform to externally imposed standards and constraints. The architecture should free the project leader from concerns as to the scope of his project and enable him to concentrate entirely on the achievement of clearly-defined objectives. Also the architecture should form an important input source of analysis and design documentation.

The key points to be noted in order for the I.S. architecture to be developed and followed in A/DB development are as follows:

1. An I.S. architecture must be developed consisting of models of the enterprise's processes, data, and a plan of implementation segmented into projects, each covering portions of the enterprise.

2. The I.S. architecture should be documented with a methodology consistent with techniques employed in A/DB development. For example HIPO (IBM Manual No. GC20-1851) can be used at the architectural and implementation levels for functional specification. Also Bachmann diagrams can be used at the architectural level and at the individual project level.

3. The division of responsibility between the architecture function and individual application projects should be clearly spelled out. The resolution of conflict between the strategic and the short term requirements must in the end be the prerogative of the I.S. manager.

4. I.S. architects should actually specify the initial phases of projects to ensure the above points are implemented and that architectural objectives are achieved.

5. I.S. architects should review, and have authority to reject, individual project specifications to ensure continued consistency with the architecture and to update the architecture either with greater detail or to correct previous errors.

CONCLUDING REMARKS

This paper has outlined the nature of some I.S. planning techniques and why current experience has indicated difficulties in actually constraining and guiding Application and Data Base development to operate within an overall architecture.

The concept of an Information Systems Architect is proposed as a role to maintain and develop the I.S. plan and to influence and guide individual A/DB projects.

Some methods are outlined for use by the I.S. architect in creating
the framework. However much further work is required to develop a
clear and comprehensive job specification.

Such work should address developing precise methods for building
entity and process models to cope with both current and future
requirements, and for defining projects in terms of the portions of
these models that they are to support. It should cover computer
support for the I.S. Architect, and developing consistency between
the sets of methods to be used at the I.S. planning, architecture
and data base design levels.

<u>REFERENCES</u>

1.   Business Systems Planning, Information Systems Planning Guide,
     IBM manual no. GE20-0527.

2.   IPT Overview, IBM manual no. GE19-5086.

3.   HIPO -Design and documentation technique, IBM manual no.
     GC20-1851.

4.   Moehrke & Dunham, Top-Down Design by Information Modelling,
     A.O. Smith Inc., Data Systems Division, Milwaukee, November
     1975.

5.   Bachmann C.W. & Daya M., The Role Concept in Data Models, in:
     Proceedings of the Third International Conference on Very Large
     Data Bases, Oct. 6-8, 1977, Tokyo, Japan

6.   Chen P., The Entity-Relationship Model: Toward a Unified View
     of Data, ACM Transactions on Database Systems 1 (1), March
     1976, pp. 9-36.

7.   Senko M.E., Information Systems: Records, Relations, Sets,
     Entities, and Things, Information Systems 1 (1), 1975, pp.
     1-13.

8.   Smith J.M. & Smith D.C.P.,Database Abstractions: Aggregation
     and Generalisation, ACM Transactions on Database Systems 2 (2),
     June 1977.

9.   Codd E.F., Extending the Data Base Relational Model to Capture
     More Meaning, IBM Research Report, Jan 1979.

The Information Systems Environment
Lucas, Land, Lincoln, Supper (Editors)
North-Holland Publishing Company
© *IFIP, 1980*

INFORMATION AND MANAGEMENT: THE CYBERNETICS
OF A SMALL COMPANY

Raul Espejo

Management Centre
University of Aston
Birmingham
U.K.

The design of Management Information Systems should take into
consideration problems of organizational effectiveness. For
this purpose, it is argued, we need to understand the conditions,
internal to the organization, that are limiting its learning
and adaptation; that is, we need to understand the cybernetics
of the organization. An application of this approach has been
undertaken in a small company. The results of the intervention
are reported in this paper. With the support of that experience
some general and particular propositions are made in relation
to information relevant to management.[1]

INTRODUCTION

The understanding of why a company behaves as it does seems to be a necessary
step before propositions are advanced to improve its effectiveness. Therefore
understanding of the "cybernetics" of the organization seems necessary when we
approach the design of corporate models or management information systems. A
system for the design of these managerial tools was developed by the author in a
previous paper (Espejo and Watt (1979)). In this paper the aim is to explore in
some detail the cybernetics of a small company to support a more precise
connection between management information needs and criteria for organizational
effectiveness.

Beer's model of the organizational structure of any viable system (Beer (1972)
(1979)) is used as a reference for effectiveness. The implications of this model,
in particular its account of the architecture of complexity and the processes of
learning and adaptation in viable systems, are extremely relevant when we think
of "designing" information systems. The regularities in the organization of
complexity, which become apparent once Beer's model is understood, can account for
substantial simplications in the design of computer applications for management
purposes.

In this paper I shall first give a few details of the company in which the study
was done; we shall call it "PM Manufacturers". Secondly, I shall discuss in
general, Beer's organizational model of any viable system. The application of
this model to PM Manufacturers is in the core of the report. A major conclusion
of this application is the need for measures of performance. Though it is clear
that measurement can be done in many ways, poor approaches make learning and
adaptation very difficult. While introducing a particular approach for measurement, planning and information processes become apparent in an organizational
context.

PM·MANUFACTURERS

PM Manufacturers is a small UK Company in the electrical engineering sector. At

present their main concern is the manufacturing of engine driven electrical
generating sets. However, some non-manufacturing activities like "technical and
procurement services" to customers are increasing in relevance.

The company has 40 employees and gross sales of £2 million per year. It is part
of a larger engineering group with two more operating companies, one related to
land development and the other to civil engineering. Altogether the group has
600 employees.

The company sells standard and non-standard generating sets to order and does not
stock products. Their market is mainly abroad, in particular Nigeria and the
Middle East. Company organization is shown in Figure 1.

There is a very limited use of computers in the company, certainly not for policy
purposes. Information procedures in the form of management reports have been
developed over the years. However, just as their computer counterparts in larger
organizations, they are not highly regarded or widely used by managers. The
company has been in operation for about ten years. However, only in the past five
years has it developed an identity and shown a will for growth.

CONCEPTUAL FRAMEWORK

The behavior of PM Manufacturers, in particular their problems for learning and
adaptation, cannot possibly be deduced from an organization chart. For these
purposes we need a model to study both the nature of the interactions of the
company with its relevant environment and the interactions between the several
organizational parts.

From a cybernetic point of view Beer's model of the organization structure of any
viable system is one representation (Beer (1972)(1979)). Hopefully, the model and
its application will answer the very question of what is relevant information for
management. Methodologically we study the company's mechanisms for learning as
implied by Beer's model, so that cybernetic questions can be asked in relation to
organizational effectiveness. The understanding of this model is central to an
understanding of the rest of the presentation. Unfortunately in the present
context we cannot aim at more than an introduction to the subject.

A very short summary of Beer's model is presented below. A system is viable if it
is capable of responding to environmental changes even if they were not foreseen
at the time the system was designed. If a system is to be viable it needs to
develop five basic functions:

(a)   policy,

(b)   intelligence,

(c)   control,

(d)   co-ordination,

(e)   implementation.

These functions are necessary and sufficient for system's viability. The policy
function implies a systemic capacity to choose few among the multiple possible
responses to environmental disturbances. For this purpose the system needs an
intelligence function scanning the environment, structuring problem situations,
identifying opportunities and threats. However, it is not enough for the policy
function to have a good filter of environmental situations; it also needs
information about the system as it is today. This information is provided by the
control function. The effective implementation of policies is the responsibility

Figure 1   Organizational Chart of PM Manufacturers

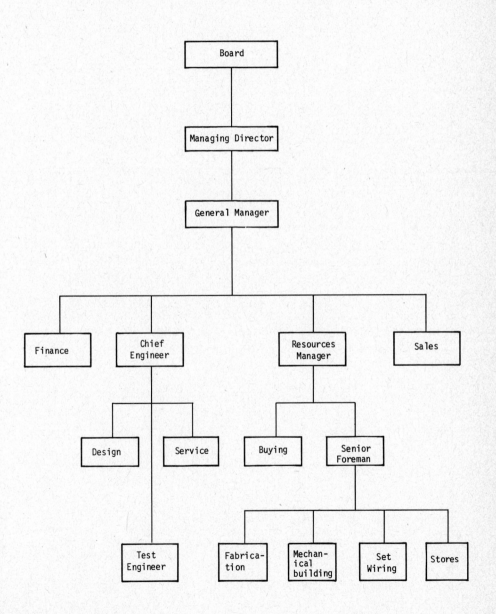

of this function. In this sense control should support policy decisions well
rooted in reality. The control of the implementation of policies implies the
responsibility for resource allocation, and, of course, the control and monitoring over time of implementation activities.

A major organizational strategy to make the policies of a system viable is to give
discretion to subsystems for carrying out particular areas of policy. These
subsystems, actually doing what the system is supposed to do, are the parts of the
implementation function. Central to this function is the degree of autonomy that
subsystems can exercise while implementing policies. The extremes of centralization and decentralization are clearly nonviable. The autonomy of subsystems
implies that they themselves have to develop viable organizations. The control
function cannot possibly consider in advance their response to all environmental
disturbances: the complexity of the environment is too large. Subsystems should
develop internal capacity to respond to unforeseen situations; that is, they
should develop a viable organization. Finally, subsystems, to a larger or lesser
degree, are operationally interconnected. Because of their autonomy they are
bound to make uncoordinated decisions. There is no mathematical algorithm or
computer capacity to predefine with complete precision the interfaces among subsystems. As an on-going process the system needs the coordination function which
is a damping mechanism.

Perhaps the most central aspect of thid model is the replication of the overall
organizational structure in each of the parts, that is, the subsystems. This
replication is the recursive property of the model and implies that the whole is
encapsulated in the parts.

The linkages between the five functions, and the interaction of the system with
its environment are schematically presented in Figure 2. These linkages and
interactions define the multiple regulatory loops that should be carefully
considered to understand the system's behavior.

Ashby's law of requisite variety (Ashby (1964)) is central in understanding these
regulatory loops. Ashby's law says that "only variety can absorb variety".
Variety is a measure of complexity and is defined as the number of possible states
of a situation. The more complex the task a system has to perform, the larger the
environmental variety it has to deal with. If the system fails to match or absorb
that variety, it will not achieve the task as stated. This possibility implies
that the task may be achieved at a lower level of performance. The law will
assert itself in any case.

It is not difficult to accept the concept that environmental variety is far larger
than organizational variety, yet one has to match the other if the organization is
to achieve its objectives. If this matching does not happen at a level consistent
with objectives, matching will happen anyway at a lower level of complexity,
reducing performance, and perhaps endangering viability.

Learning and adaptation is related to the ability of the organization to recognize
which environmental states are most likely to become actual, so that matching
capacity is developed only to cope with these most likely states.

The same law is relevant to understand the effectiveness of all internal linkages,
however, it is particularly difficult to understand the way it works between the
implementation and control functions. It is not difficult to perceive that the
variety of the implementation function is far larger than that of the control
function, yet if control is to be exercised, the actual complexity of the
implementation function has to be matched by the variety of the control function.
In Figure 2 we can see that control is linked to implementation by three
communication lines, the command, coordination and monitoring channels. This is a
complex control device necessary to achieve requisite variety. The more

Figure 2   Organization Structure of Viable Systems

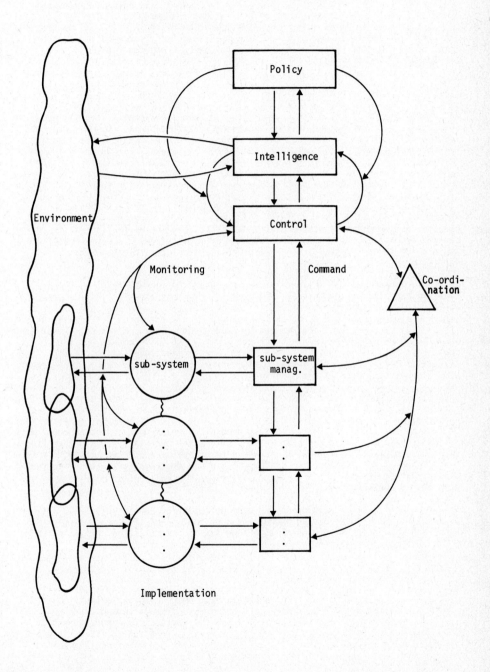

discretion allocated to the implementation function, potentially the more complex it can be; therefore, (because the law of requisite variety) the more complex ought to be the control function. However, this complexity cannot be achieved along the command channel. The more is commanded the lower is discretion. To sort out this apparent paradox the control function has to amplify its control capacity by inducing self-regulation, and this is done by coordination, and by structuring a monitoring capacity so that no more and no less discretion is used by implementation than that consistent with the system's viability.

CYBERNETIC STUDY OF PM MANUFACTURERS

With reference to Figure 2 we need to agree on some diagrammatic conventions. The autonomy of subsystems is exercised along the horizontal axis. Command or inter-ference with autonomy comes down the vertical axis. For instance, the three operating companies of the group are autonomous, however, their autonomy is limit-ed by the fact that they are parts of the same group. This condition is diagram-matically represented in Figure 3. The three operating companies are doing what the "Group" is supposed to do, thus they are the implementation function of that level of recursion.

The focus of our study is just in one of these operating companies - PM Manufact-urers. In Figure 4 we find the diagrammatic presentation of the cybernetic analy-sis of PM Manufacturers. It illustrates an in-depth study of one of the horizon-tal axes of Figure 3, namely the environment, operations and management of PM Manufacturers.

In what follows we shall discuss the way in which the company responds to the complexity of its environment and draw some conclusions about its effectiveness. Whether balance is achieved between the complexity of the environment and the response of the company depends on the objectives or references for behaviors that are implicit or explicitly recognized by management. More complex objectives imply the need to respond to more states in the environment. If this is not the case, that is if the company does not respond to this implied level of complexity, its objectives will be de facto achieved at a lower level of performance. The law of requisite variety will assert itself anyway.

The actual response of the company to the complexity of the environment is achieved through its implementation function; that is the subsystems which are doing what the organization is supposed to do. Thus the organization of these subsystems is of central relevance in studying effectiveness. However this is not enough; even if their organization is good, if the subsystems are not integrated to the company then the organization of the whole may not be effective. Moreover, even if this integration is achieved but the company as a whole does not have a capacity to assess whether it is 'doing' the right things it may well be the case that the company may not survive in the long run.

Following this logic our study of the cybernetics of PM Manufacturers will be done in three steps. First we shall study the organization of its implementation function, second the way in which this function is controlled by corporate manage-ment and finally corporate management itself.

Implementation Function

At Figure 4 we find two horizontal axes - these are the two activities defining the implementation function of PM Manufacturers: manufacturing activities and non-manufacturing activities (spares and services). Manufacturing is responsible for 90 per cent of the company's turnover and the rest is non-manufacturing. These two areas are the activities of the company in relation to its environment. In theory both are performing complex activities that need managerial autonomy. The recognition of these two subsystems is a cybernetic conclusion that is not

Figure 3   Group's Implementation Function

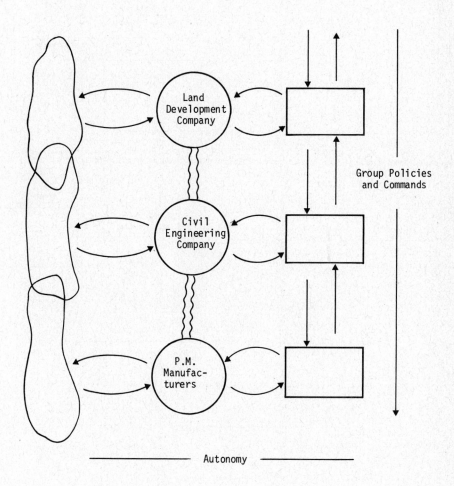

Group Policies
and Commands

———————— Autonomy ————————

Figure 4   PM Manufacturers: The Cybernetics of its Organization

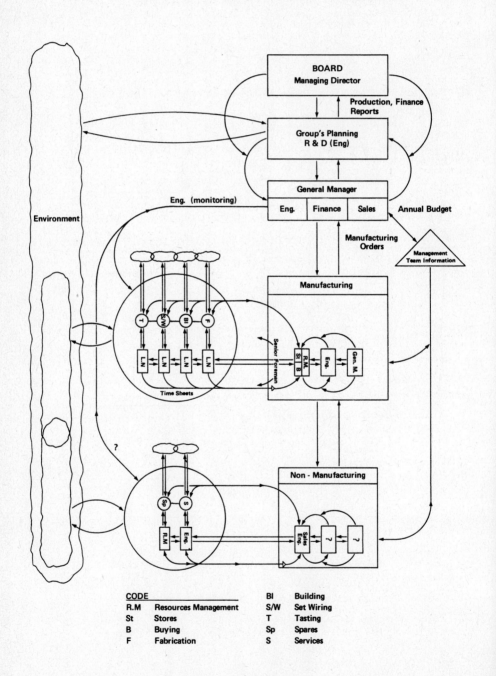

CODE
R.M	Resources Management	Bl	Building
St	Stores	S/W	Set Wiring
B	Buying	T	Tasting
F	Fabrication	Sp	Spares
		S	Services

apparent in the company's formal organization structure. While manufacturing activities are clearly the responsibility of the Resources Manager, the management of "non-manufacturing" is disseminated in several organizational parts. There is no recognition of the subsystemic nature of non-manufacturing activities, and certainly this is creating organizational problems. The subsystemic nature derives from the fact that the components are "doing" activities in direct connection with the company's environment.

This fact implies that these activities are facing a large variety, that in the long run cannot possibly be matched effectively unless their management has learning and adapting capabilities. This condition implies discretion and autonomy, both distinctive characteristics of a subsystem.

In what follows, we shall study the organization of both subsystems. This means, following the logic of structural recursion, that we shall study for this lower structural level essentially the same aspects that we are studying for the over-all organization. The study includes the way in which the implementation functions of the subsystems are controlled as well as the characteristics of the management of these subsystems. Because the level of resolution of our study is the overall company we do not get inside the organization of the sub-subsystems.

Manufacturing Subsystem

The manufacturing subsystem is responsible for the assembly of electrical generators. In Figure 5 we find a flowchart of the several related operations, doing what the manufacturing subsystem is supposed to do. Thus, they are the parts of the implementation function at this new level of recursion. At present only four of the five operations are active:

fabrication - manufacturers bed frames for generators;

building   - mechanical assembly of engines and alternators
              (the two major components of a generator);

set wiring - installing electrical system for the generator
              (this includes an electronic control panel);

testing   - generators are tested under several loading conditions.

Although the factory has capacity to produce control panels, their production is at present subcontracted. The four operating sub-subsystems are diagrammatically represented at Figure 4 along the manufacturing horizontal axis.

In the formal organization structure the "testing" sub-subsystem, manned by the testing engineer, is under the control of the Chief Engineer and not under the control of the Resources Manager who is responsible for manufacturing activities.

Each of the other sub-subsystems is under the control of a "leading hand"; the three leading hands formally report to a Senior Foreman, who in his turn reports to the Resources Manager.

The relevant environment for these operations is by and large "technological". The task of the operations is to perform as efficiently as possible within the technological constraints imposed by the available resources. Of course, these duties can be discharged in multiple ways, but whatever is the way chosen it has to be consistent with market standards. This fact presents the main source of complexity for them. (In Figure 4, the clouds representing the operations environment should be embedded in the environment of the manufacturing activity, however, this is not possible in this diagrammatic representation).

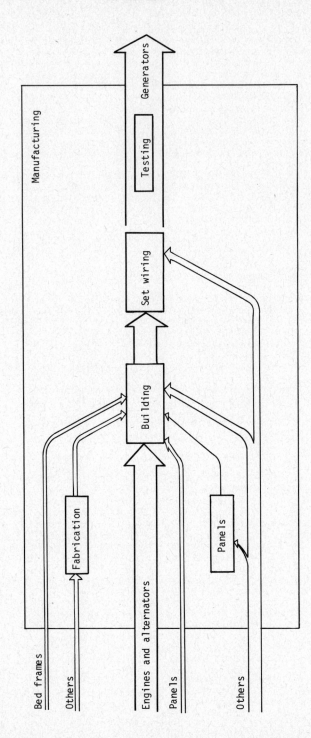

Figure 5   Quantified Flowchart

First our concern is the way in which these sub-subsystems are controlled by the subsystem's management. Production scheduling and control are formally tasks of the Resources Manager, apparently leaving to the Senior Foreman the role of co-ordinating the several operations. In fact, the Senior Foreman is commanding only in a very limited sense; perhaps only in the definition of very short term priorities. Most of his time is allocated to:

transferring information from one operation to the other, that is, co-ordination; and

monitoring production as a result of his permanent interaction with all people on the shopfloor.

Cybernetically we may say that the Senior Foreman is amplifying the control capacity of the Resources Manager by supporting the coordination and monitoring of production. This observation is clearly seen on the shopfloor.

Monitoring manufacturing production is fairly hazy at present. I have already mentioned that the Testing Engineer is under the control of the Chief Engineer. In fact, the Testing Engineer has two functions. The first is testing generators and the second is quality control by "auditing" production overtime. There is a perception that this auditing has to be done by someone outside manufacturing. However, in systemic terms, on the one hand the Testing Engineer is not outside manufacturing and on the other the auditing of manufacturing operations seems to be the role of the Senior Foreman. This condition obviously creates problems. It seems the problem is the confusion between two levels of recursion. While manufacturing has to monitor its own operations, the company has to monitor manufacturing. Therefore, at the higher level, the concern should be subsystems and not sub-subsystems; this extra monitoring seems to be an intrusion in their autonomy.

The task of the Resources Manager is to control the operations so that a given level of performance is achieved. In addition to production control the supply of materials is under the direction of this level of management. For the latter purpose the Resources Manager has the support of the "buying" and "stores" departments. (In the organization chart the Senior Foreman is responsible for Stores, a task for which he does not have requisite variety; Buying and Stores are close-ly interdependent - a point that is missed in the formal structure, and is a natural source of conflicts.)

Whether the Control Function achieves requisite variety in relation to manufact-uring operations depends on the desirable levels of performance. In practice these levels are loosely defined. Production capabilities are only known in general terms. Anyway they are larger than present volume of sales. Thus the Resources Manager can rely upon slack resources to achieve output as necessary. In this sense we may say that the control function does have requisite variety, however, the situation may change if demand grows beyond production capabilities. Requisite variety is now achieved because the levels of performance to achieve output are fairly low.

Second, with regard to the management of the subsystem itself, the intelligence function of manufacturing is mainly discharged by the Engineering Department. One of the concerns of this department is product development. For instance, a "welder" has recently been designed, aiming at diversifying present product lines. While this example illustrates very well the concerns of the intelligence function, it is insufficient to give a perception of whether "manufacturing" is coping properly with threats and opportunities in the market.

The competitive nature of PM's products is a measure of their level of response to the needs in the market. The company's limited success in the UK is an area of managerial concern and perhaps a measure of an imbalance of this activity in relation to its relevant environment. The perception of this imbalance seems to underlie present efforts to incorporate microprocessors into the control panels of the generators. This feature would give the company a distinctive product with which to approach the market.

The management of the interactions between the Resources Manager and the Chief Engineer is the role of the General Manager, who, therefore, is performing the policy function at this level of recursion.

The subsystem "manufacturing" does not have discretion in financial and sales matters. The complexity of its environment is related to production and supplies. By and large the problem is the efficient manufacturing of products demanded by the market and for this purpose "manufacturing" controls, more or less, a technology and procurement and manufacturing processes.

Non-manufacturing Subsystem

This subsystem is not formally recognized by the present structure. In other words, there is no unifying managerial capacity related to this task. As suggested before, this fact may imply the nonviability of the task in the long run.

Despite this situation we shall briefly refer to the way PM Manufacturers absorbs the complexity related to nonmanufacturing activities. In Figure 4 we can see two sub-subsystems doing what each subsystem is supposed to do. They are:

> services - maintenance of generators on request (two service
>   engineers, under the formal supervision of the
>   Chief Engineer, to do this task);
>
> spares   - the company sells its procurement capabilities
>   mainly to foreign customers (the operational
>   capabilities necessary to discharge these
>   activities are done by the "buying" and "stores"
>   departments, both under the control of the
>   Resources Manager).

The control and coordination of these activities occupies one of the sales engineers. He does all the administration and does not have direct link with customers. The fact that these functions are not performed effectively is reflected by the number of operational problems regularly occurring in stores, buying and engineering.

The intelligence and policy functions may be related to the hazy concern of the company's senior management to developing this line of activities. This lack of concern is limiting its viable expansion.

The way in which the complexity relevant to this subsystem is absorbed implies an overloading of corporate management with the details of an activity which represents no more than 10 per cent of the company's sales. The relevant environment of this subsystem is represented by the complexities in performing a high quality service. Financial and sales matters are clearly not dimensions of this environment.

Control of Operations; Control and Coordination Functions

The second step of our cybernetic study is related to the way corporate management controls the implementation function. We are concerned with the question whether effective control is achieved. This question implies focussing attention on

linkages between control, coordination and implementation functions. Does the
control function have requisite variety to control the implementation function?
The non-recognition of 'non-manufacturing' activities as a subsystem has far
reaching implications in the way control is exercised in the company.

While the non-manufacturing subsystem is responsible for a relatively small part
of the business it proportionally consumes a far larger amount of managerial
variety. But non-manufactruing is a highly profitable activity, and management is
quite prepared to allocate control variety in this direction. However, a subsystem would make it possible on the one hand to absorb a far larger variety of
non-manufacturing activities and on the other, it would make it possible to
allocate corporate variety more effectively elsewhere. The present 10 per cent of
company sales related to non-manufacturing is still marginal; however, this
market opportunity might be wasted if organizational viability is not given to the
activity. Operationally there is no reference level to assess the performance of
this subsystem, a fact which is limiting organizational learning.

The corporate control of the company's operations, that is the subsystems, is the
responsibility of the General Manager. To discharge these responsibilities he has
the support of the Engineering, Sales and Finance Departments.

The Engineering Department has, as one of its control activities, to attenuate the
variety of manufacturing. Historically the company has evolved from producing a
large variety of models in small quantities to larger quantities of few standard
sets. Today standard sets are responsible for 70 per cent of the company's sales.
This change has simplified not only manufacturing but also sales and financial
activities. For instance, the production of standard sets allows a "price list"
that simplifies the interactions with customers. Quotations are done only for
non-standard sets which represent 20 per cent of the company's sales.

Potentially non-standard sets can be standardized once the company feels it has
enough expertise on that product. Engineering is permanently updating the list of
standard sets.

Whether engineering is discharging this role effectively is a difficult question
to answer. For instance, there is evidence that delays in producing non-standard
sets are related to "design" problems. This may suggest the need for a larger
design capacity. However, this proposition makes sense only as long as we have
references to assess performance, and this information is not present available in
the company.

It was suggested before, that Engineering has the responsibility for auditing
"implementation" activities. This audit function would be a mechanism to amplify
the control capacity of the General Manager. In practice, as it was explained
above, there is a confusion of recursion levels and engineering seems to be doing
the auditing at the wrong level of recursion.

Monitoring the "right" level may imply, for instance, the assessment over time of
whether the level of manufacturing activities is well matched to the factory
capabilities, or whether the resources allocated to non-manufacturing operations
are reasonable for the magnitude of the task. However, we may argue whether these
are engineering activities at all.

In the Sales Department - marketing is a fundamental dimension of environmental
complexity at this level of recursion. While at lower levels problems are mainly
technology and supplies, at this level they imply the capacity to sell.

Operations - manufacturing and non-manufacturing - would be out of control if their
capabilities were not matched by a parallel capacity to put those products in the
market. Sales is interacting with the environment through the implementation
function. This function is necessary to make viable the "doing" of the company.

Sales is a mechanism to amplify the organizational capacity to interact with its environmental variety and a mechanism to filter this variety. For instance, the quality and "personality" of the company handouts may imply very different levels of amplification. In PM Manufacturers as yet very little attention has been paid to the filtering role of sales. For instance, only one of every ten quotations prepared by sales is successful. No analysis is made of the nine unsuccessful quotations.

The assessment of this function's performance is also difficult because of the lack of clear reference levels. The only reference is budgeted sales for a year, for example £2 million in 1978.

A proof of manufacturing slack resources is given by the procedure of accepting manufacturing orders. Orders are accepted by the Sales Manager after consultation with the General Manager and Managing Director. However, the Resources Manager is not consulted. He receives manufacturing orders in a way that practically implies that scheduling of production is done by the Sales Manager.

In the case of the Finance Department, it is easy to understand the support that this function gives to the Control Function. By and large, Finance is adding the dimension of financial viability to whatever is done by the implementation function. Most of the practical levels of reference to assess performance are expressed in financial terms. For instance, in this company we find sales, gross margin and profit references for manufacturing and non-manufacturing activities. Perhaps this information is the only tool available to control non-manufacturing performance.

Though cost analysis is done for each manufacturing order, the variety generated by this effort is not matched by managerial variety, thus by and large this potential information is not used. There is no cost analysis for product lines, a level of aggregation for which the requisite managerial attention is certainly lower and perhaps possible.

With regard to the coordination function, in Beer's model coordination is a systemic mechanism supporting self-regulation, limiting the need for managerial intervention in the details of the implementation function.

In the context of PM Manufacturers, there is a risk of confusing the need for co-ordination between the Engineering, Sales and Finance Departments, and the co-ordination between the managers of the two subsystemic operations, manufacturing and non-manufacturing. In systemic terms there is a difference between these two co-ordinations. While inter-departmental coordination is a mechanism to increase, to amplify the variety of the control function, the self-regulation of subsystems is a mechanism to decrease, to filter the variety reaching that function. Because the variety of the implementation function is far larger than that of the control function, the latter mechanism has a far more relevant systemic meaning.

PM Manufacturers fails to recognize non-manufacturing as a subsystem, so the company is not benefiting from this damping mechanism. Senior management is operating at a fairly detailed level, which is limiting its capacity to deal with more strategic issues, thus reducing PM's effectiveness.

Senior management is not controlling the company's operations very effectively. In addition to the chaotic management of non-manufacting activities which is directly affecting the possibilities for effective coordination and monitoring of subsystems, the lack in general of references for behavior or objectives in the non-financial dimensions of management is limiting severely the possibilities for organizational learning. There are no references to recognize errors and there-fore to support inquiries for organizational learning.

Despite all this control is achieved at least for the present level of activities,

that is, there are no evident signs that operations are out of control. This
situation seems to be possible because there is manufactruing slack and the
company enjoys a captive market abroad. In other words it appears that while it
may be argued that higher levels of demand will most likely overload management
seriously, the real problem of the company is that if present markets are lost
the company may not be competitive enough in other markets.

Corporate Management; Control, Intelligence and Policy Functions

Functional capacity "to create" the company's future involves the need for a
mechanism to make less painful the firm's learning and adapting processes.
Unfortunately it is not uncommon to wait for the pain before something is done.
Most of the time we sort out this problem by reducing our levels of performance
- in my view PM Manufacturers is not an exception to this behavior.

Planning is indeed a very limited activity in this company. PM's corporate plan
is the result of a limited exercise once a year with the participation of senior
management; the plan is finally structured by the Group's Planning Unit. In
this scenario the most important pay-off of planning, the process itself, is
happening outside the boundaries of the company. Planning to be effective has to
be done continuously by the whole organization and not only by a few of its
members, let alone by people outside its boundaries. Further development of the
meaning of planning as an activity of the whole organization is the concern of
our next section.

In the end, the balance between the intelligence and control functions necessary
for effective adaptation is strongly dominated by the latter function. Supporting
this view is the information normally prepared for Board meetings. By and large
this information concerns production and financial details. Thus the policy
function is plunged into operational details, far from the normative role that is
suggested by our cybernetic model.

The corporate identity of PM Manufacturers seems still to be fairly weak and so
also is its ability to respond to unexpected changes in the market. While we
could observe some efforts to make manufacturing activities viable, albeit with
very limited resources, we do not recognize a parallel effort at the corporate
level. The development of non-manufacturing activities - the result of a free
opportunity in the market - unfortunately has not been well structured. All this
accounts for the present fragility of the company which is extremely dependent on
the demand of only one customer. In cybernetic terms this situation could be
explained both by the lack of intelligence activity at the corporate level, and
the ineffective way in which control is exercised. The control problem is highlighted by the limited development of sales in the context of a perhaps too
detailed management.

MEASUREMENT

The cybernetic analysis of PM Manufacturers gives us criteria to define relevant
information for management. The problem of information is related to the measurement of the interactions between the company and its environment and between
several organizational functions. Viability and control are not related to
objective values but to relative measures concerning desirable and/or necessary
levels of performance.

In what follows I shall suggest a particular way of undertaking measurement which
is based on the cybernetics of the organization. Its power lies in the fact that
it integrates all organizational members in a joint effort for planning and
managing the whole organization. In this framework organizational learning and
adaptation is not a task delegated to few planning people, certainly lacking in

requisite variety, but a comprehensive effort of the whole.

In Figure 6, we have a diagrammatic definition of a system of indices. They can be applied to any organizational activity (a detailed analysis of these indices can be found in Beer (1972) and in Espejo and Watt (1979)). What is done today, the actuality, is compared with what could have been done. The comparison considers the present levels of resources and constraints as if everything had been optimally organized; that is, the capability. This comparison gives the so called index of productivity. If we remove constraints and allocate resources we ought to achieve a better value than capability; this is potentiality. The index of latency is a measure of possible organizational development considering resources that are present but not active. The index of performance integrates present behavior with future possibilities. It seems important to point out the relevance of capability as a "systemic" concept. While potentiality is essentially a normative value and actuality is a fluctuating value, capability is a measure of the present organizational resources.

Indices and Planning

In Figure 6, the concepts of actuality, capability and potentiality are related to tactical, strategic and normative planning. What does this mean?

Indices are designed for organizational activities at different levels of aggregation. Aggregation is a function of the recursion levels and the discretion allocated to that level of management. Both are outputs of our organizational analysis. Indices are designed for middle and senior management, as well as for people on the shopfloor.

Indices are just an instrument to structure in formal terms something that in one way or another is well known by the people concerned. However, lack of precision or haziness does have an important organizational impact: relationships and linkages are poorly structured. Peter knows his situation, John knows his, yet their interaction may be poorly structured as a result of the imprecision in expressing that knowledge. This is an important point if we remember that a vital aspect of our organizational analysis is that criteria to assess performance are solely linked to relationships.

Capability is the best we can do in a given activity considering existing resources and constraints. The point is to make explicit what the capability is and which are the resources and constraints related to that capability. The continuous process of updating capabilities all over the organization is the process of strategic planning. Thus we are not talking of one strategic plan for the company, but of the many plans that in continuous process are supporting the organizational awareness of the firm's capabilities. If resources and constraints are made explicit, people within the organization have references with which to interact and assess performance.

Capability gives a reference to assess present productivity. Annotations of productivity, part of the many strategic plans, explain why productivity differs from its optimal value.

As for tactical planning, it is essentially a reference projection of what we ought to be doing if we keep to present levels of productivity. Each manager knows capability and present productivity, therefore he knows what he can actually do.

A third planning concept related to each of the activities measured by indices is normative planning. This process, as the others, is a comprehensive effort of the whole organization and not only of a planning department removed from actual situations. For each activity a value of what we ought to be doing if we remove

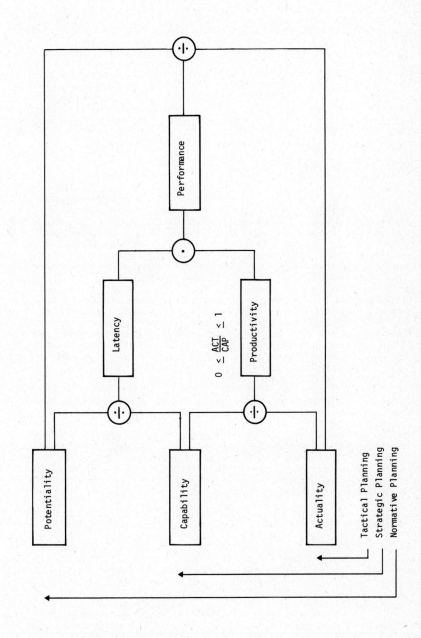

Figure 6   Indices and Planning

constraints and develop resources is defined. This is a role of the intelligence function at each level of recursion. Annotations of latency are defined for all activities. They spell out under which conditions potentiality can be achieved.

It should be apparent that this system of planning is in itself an information system. Two aspects, even at the risk of repetition, are worth mentioning:

there is no one plan but as many plans as indices are defined. Indices are matched to specific functional capacities - to people and functions that have the capacity to absorb the variety relevant to the activity being measured;

a data processing capacity has to be developed to control indices' behaviour in real time (an approach for this purpose can be found in Beer (1975) and Espejo (1979)).

Indices for PM Manufacturers

A tentative list of indices for PM Manufacturers is shown in Figure 7. They were derived from the organizational analysis discussed in a previous section. I expect that this list will change over the period of its implementation. For instance, I am assuming that non-manufacturing activities will be structured in a subsystem. Whatever is finally done, at this stage the problem is to appreciate the "variety engineering" implicit in Figure 7. The control of production is the discretion of subsystems. Decisions related to supplies, materials, technological standards and so forth are the discretion of managers at a subsystemic level. Yet these decisions are under the meta-systemic control of the General Manager supported by Sales and Finance. Indices for this latter level of management do consider production capabilities. For instance, one possible index for sales has production capacity for a given period as the capability for sales in that same period. This capability is adjusted by a factor which is derived from sales experience in the past, so that we can calculate over time whether the firm orders we have today will support an effective use of production capabilities in a given period.

Definition of indices is certainly different for different organizations. There is no simple rule or algorithm. For instance, data collection practices in a company will influence the selection and design of indices. A methodology to approach this design was discussed in an early paper (Espejo and Watt (1979)).

Definition of capabilities may be crude at the beginning. It is hoped that the organization will learn about them over time. For instance, if we want an index to control "fabrication" of bed frames for a product line, we may define capability as the best time ever achieved in that operation for each standard set. If the best time is challenged as a reasonable definition of capability, we are already in the learning process.

CONCLUSIONS

The purposes of this paper were twofold; first to illustrate the application of cybernetic concepts to a particular social system and second, the normative use of the results of this application to structuring relevant information for management.

The study was undertaken in a small company to reinforce the idea that managing complexity is as much a problem for large enterprises as it is for small businesses. It must be apparent at this stage that the organizational aspects discussed in this paper, that is the organization of the implementation function, the control of this function and the characteristics of general management are common to all enterprises. Moreover, from a cybernetic viewpoint, the same

Figure 7 Variety Engineering

Recursion (Indices)			Production			Sales							Finance					
						Manufacturing			Non-manufacturing			Total	Gross Margin				Profits	Cash flow
Sub-sub-system	Sub-system	System	SS	NS	T	SS	NS	T	Se	Sp	T		SS	NS	NM	T	T	
Fabrication	Manufacturing	PM Manufacturers	X	X	X													
Building			X	X	X													
Set wiring			X	X	X													
Testing			X	X	X													
Service				X	X													
Spares					X													
	Non Manufacturing					X	X	X	X	X	X	X	X	X	X	X	X	X

criteria of effectiveness is valid to all of them.

From an information perspective these criteria of effectiveness give the
references to structure relevant information for management. For instance, in
PM Manufacturers the lack of a 'non-manufacturing' subsystem implied that
corporate management had to deal with far more information than would have been
the case had they recognized the autonomy of that activity. It is in this sense
that the implications of the cybernetic study for management information are of a
normative nature.

In this paper, no attempt was made to design a MIS, yet the output was the
proposition of a set of dimensions (likely to be expressed in the form of indices)
relevant for effective regulation of the company's activities. These dimensions
were related to the specific managerial capabilities of all company members, not
only of senior management.

At PM Manufacturers there is a standard accounting system, yet we found very few
relevant measures to support the assessment of the company's performance over time.
In fact, in several instances it was suggested that the lack of information to
assess performances was limiting organizational learning. A cybernetic study
should help us to understand that the answers to these questions of effectiveness
are not a one-off problem; on the contrary, as the organization evolves, answers
may change and a conclusion valid today may not be so tomorrow. The lack of
information on references is in fact the lack of an information system for
management. It is in this sense that I think the study of the cybernetics of the
organization is a pre-requisite to the design of information systems.

In other words, while objectives or references for behavior are necessary to
attenuate situational complexity, they always fall below the overall problem of
viability. Objectives are always implicitly or explicitly changed in response to
a change in perceptions of viability. Thus our system implies an on-going effort
for the identification of organizational objectives. These are the necessary
references at all organizational levels to support learning and adaptation.

FOOTNOTES

1. The research reported in this paper is part of the project "Alternative
   Methods to Computer Applications" directed by Professor Robert Trappl of
   the University of Vienna and sponsored by the Jubilaeumsfonds der
   Oesterreichieschen Nationalbank, Project No. 1079.

REFERENCES

(1) Ashby, R., An Introduction to Cybernetics (Methuen, London, 1964).

(2) Beer, S., Brain of the Firm (Allen Lane, Penguin, 1972).

(3) Beer, S., Platform for Change (Wiley, London, 1975).

(4) Beer, S., Heart of the Enterprise (Wiley, London, 1979).

(5) Espejo, R., Cybernetic Filtering of Management Information, University of
    Aston Management Centre Working Paper Series No. 126. (1979)

(6) Espejo, R. and Watt, J.C., Management Information System: A System for
    Design, in: Journal of Cybernetics, 9 (1979) 3.

The Information Systems Environment
Lucas, Land, Lincoln, Supper (Editors)
North-Holland Publishing Company

LEGOL AS A TOOL FOR THE STUDY OF BUREAUCRACY

Sandra Cook and Ronald Stamper

The LEGOL Project
The London School of Economics
and Political Science
Houghton Street
London, England WC2A 2AE

The LEGOL Project deals with a fundamental problem in informatics, i.e. how to specify an information system with sufficient precision and detail necessary for building computer systems. In a more general sense, LEGOL analysis is appropriate to the study of organizational concepts.

The general nature of the research is introduced, the LEGOL semantic model is described and the analogy between legal systems and formal organisation is explained. This explanation provides the groundwork for showing how the theory enables one to elucidate certain organizational concepts (such as power, responsibility and authority), factors affecting the information systems environment. Finally, it is suggested that research is yielding techniques which may alleviate a certain type of bureaucratic dysfunction, and thus influence the interaction of information systems and the organization.

INTRODUCTION

The LEGOL Project is developing a language, a system and a technique of analysis to enable legislation to be expressed in a form which may be interpreted by computer. This practical application of LEGOL is illustrated by Jones & Mason (1980).

The major objective of the LEGOL Project is to find improved tools for systems specification. In order to study data-processing systems in general, the project has used legislation for its experiments. By studying legislation, we are studying the rules which specify all of the major government bureaucracy. A body of statues in effect defines a large and complex formal information system. By trying to devise a formal language which can express whatever is in the statutes, we are forced to explore the fundamental problems of systems definition at the highest level, i.e. saying what should be done without saying much about the procedures of how to do it. Therefore, in the LEGOL language, as in legislation, one can express rules which say what should happen in the world, rules which logically imply certain patterns of bureaucratic activity such as making observations, transmission and storage of messages and taking action.

LEGOL analysis is based upon the theory of signs: semiotics. It models the legal process by paying minute attention to the use of signs to represent both descriptions of the world and prescriptions for changing part of the world. As a technique for modelling organizations, LEGOL must express an unusual degree of detail because this is essential for the design of computer systems which might help administer legislation. For example, consider a computer system which would help administer the Family Allowances legislation, by keeping records, generating benefit collection documents, calculating benefits, etc. The LEGOL

system is intended to simulate the operation of the resulting information
systems.

One of the intended applications of the LEGOL model is to understand formal
organizations. LEGOL should interest organizational theorists insofar as it is
able to capture many important features of bureaucratic systems based on
legislation. Although only a subclass of organization, these governemntal systems
are of great practical importance.

Insofar as legislation is a means of making explicit general rules of conduct,
LEGOL should be capable of representing non-legislative rules which can be
perceived by an analyst while studying any organizational system. It is possible,
therefore, that LEGOL has relevance beyond the class of government bureaucracies.
In short, we are studying norms which have been made explicit in the law. If our
language can express those, it ought to be able to express other kinds of norms.
So if one views patterns of organization as being patterns of behavior governed
by norms (and it seems that an appropriate way to describe an organization is
to specify norms, which are not explicit, but which are expressed as stable
patterns of behavior), then we have a language equal to it.

As legislative rules can be modelled in LEGOL, so can organizational rules and norms.
And as the organization is the information systems environment, analagously, it
can be modelled in LEGOL. Finally, organizational concepts such as power,
responsibility, and authority can be elucidated using the LEGOL technique of
analysis. These environmental, organizational factors will certainly influence
information systems existing within the organization. Thus, understanding these
factors (i.e., where power is located) will be necessary to understanding and
predicting the interaction of the information system and its environment; which
is, in turn, essential to successful information systems design.

INTRODUCTION TO THE LEGOL MODEL

A person who reads legal text must understand a great deal about the world to
understand those rules. Similarly, the computer, to interpret rules in LEGOL,
must have the use of a semantic model[1] representing the relevant knowledge of
the world, and giving the meanings of all the data in the system. The analyst must
specify a particular semantic model for a legal problem area. The data on
relevant cases, together with this semantic model, comprise the semantic database. For the purposes of this paper it is only necessary to indicate the general
principles adopted in constructing a semantic model. The major components of
the model are indicated in Figure 1, and the underlying ideas are spelled out in
detail in Stamper (1978a), (1977), (1978b).

Surrogates

As illustrated by Jones and Mason (1980), the rules for the Family Allowances Act
1965 apply to operands that represent entities in the real world. The data about
the real world, suitably encoded, function as surrogates of the real world,
accessible to the formal model. Both particulars and universals are represented
here. Elsewhere, Stamper (1978a), (1978b), it has been shown that the meanings
of the surrogates are the actions which we perform in the world. For a given
problem these should be the same whatever language we are using.

Languages

Languages are handled as another part of the model. The data may be thought of
as represented in a lanugage-free internal code. The data dictionary functions
belong in this part of the model. Aliases, synonyms and various forms of a
name or descriptor belong here. These encodings are linked to the universals in
the surrogate division. The language division provides the link to the user,

who, generally speaking, is expected to know the meanings of words given the context.

Rules

As we have seen, the real world consists of things we may observe (such as persons and their various characteristics), together with legal fictions which owe their existence to legal rules (such as 'right to an allowance' or 'rate of allowance'). Many social constructs, such as 'childhood' and 'family', are treated as legal fictions and are given precise meanings in the context of the problem by the use of legal rules. These rules comprise the third major component of the model. Many legislative rules take effect quite formally once names and descriptors have been assigned.

Contexts

The fourth major component of the semantic model concerns contexts. The obvious one is the linguistic context. When words are used it is essential to know in which language they are to be interpreted. Explicit treatment of language context becomes potentially valuable if one is dealing with the variant specialist vocabularies which may be used by different groups within a single organization for historical reasons, and where these differences may be an important source of misunderstandings. In a legal context only gross differences of language are significant.

The relationship between entities and action has been shown to be dependent upon the problem or purpose being considered. This is true even when dealing with physical objects, Stamper (1977), and more obviously true when dealing with legal fictions. Thus, when dealing with the inheritance of property and family allowances, the meaning of 'family' is likely to be quite different. The semantic model must therefore contain a structure showing problem contexts and their inter-relationships.

Clearly, prescriptive rules are enforceable and therefore meaningful only within a limited jurisdiction. The jurisdiction is an essential part of the contexts definition for legal systems. More generally, if the rules are being used to represent norms, then the jurisdiction corresponds to the social community in which those norms are valid.

LEGAL SYSTEMS AND FORMAL ORGANIZATIONS

Using the above model we are studying the kinds of structures and rules which must be defined before information technology can be employed in an organization. Legal systems are our source of experimental material and it is our working hypothesis that these systems embody all the complexity that we need to consider. Perhaps we may consider legal systems to be like organizations in general operating in slow motion. If this analogy is correct then our research should eventually be of value to the organizational theorists. The extent to which the analogy fails is the extent to which there are organizational structures which have no counterpart in any law.

The law has the advantage of having made these structures explicit and therefore, more readily subject to analysis. Any particular law must leave a great deal unsaid but, generally, it is capable of being extended to make explicit further organizational structures whose definition is shown to be necessary as a result of the operation of the law.

Lying outside the formal, law-like systems are many complex patterns of human behavior, particularly those concerned with the transmission of attitudes and values. The sorts of behavioral norms which can be made explicit in legislation will be shaped by the surrounding value systems, particularly those of the law

makers. Once enacted, the use made of the body of law is also a function of the
values of those who have access to and govern the use of the law. A LEGOL
analysis makes more visible the points at which the value systems impinge upon
the machine-like formal structures. It does this by making explicit the points
where value-judgements are supplied and also the leverage which they exert
through the formal machinery.

Machine-like Systems

The structures we are concerned with analyzing are machine-like. But for
several reasons they are not entirely automatic in their application:
(a) human judgement will frequently be exercised; (b) the application of all
rules is not mandatory; and (c) when they are, their effect is a function of
the descriptors used to present the facts. These main areas of discretion are
like the discretion we have in using a lathe. We can choose the way we feed the
work piece into the lathe; we are not always obliged to use the tool;
and the lathe is equipped with handles and levers that give us considerable
control over its movement.

In the theory of organizations, it may be valuable to be able to make quite
distinct those components of an organization which are machine-like in the sense
suggested above. Organizational behavior is partly a response to these
machine-like components, but the machine-like systems are also a response to
the problems for which the organization exist. The rules which govern the
behavior of an organization in this sense may never have been made explicit as
prescribed norms. They may exist only as stable patterns of behavior which a
careful analyst may be able to describe. That is, just as the legal draftsman
has to make the social norms explicit in law, so the systems analyst expresses
what he finds (when he looks at the organization) in LEGOL rules. In this case
it seems to us that our method of analysis should be useful as a descriptive
tool, thus enlarging the potential field of relevance of our work in organization
theory.

Limitations

We do not wish to obscure the limitations of our method. The explanation of
organizational behavior is incomplete in terms of norms which are brought into
play by flows of information that can be made fully explicit. The kind of
analysis we are making exposes the points where judgment is exercised, but it
can say nothing about the forces that influence the attitudes of decision-makers.
The current techniques for the formal specification of computer-based information
systems do not even cope with the explicit part of the information system unless
it is quite machine-like. LEGOL is an advance from that point of view. An
analogy with electrical circuitry may be useful: in addition to the functions
performed by components upon the flows of signals conducted by the wires
connecting them, the components generate, and are affected by electromagnetic
fields. LEGOL deals with the circuits but shows where the field effects are
likely to be felt. Social fields are, in this analogy, the forces which
influence attitudes.

At the very least, we can claim that our methods are appropriate for the study
of the computer-assisted components of organizations. Therefore, those
organizational theorists who are concerned with the use of computers in
organizations may find our work of interest. Having placed upon record our
reservations about the possible relevance of LEGOL to organizational theory, we
shall take the liberty of using the expression 'formal organization' to refer
to the structures which LEGOL can describe, even abbreviating this to
'organization' when the context permits.

STRUCTURAL FEATURES OF FORMAL ORGANIZATIONS

LEGOL takes apart the formal organizations as one might dismantle a machine. This enables us to see some of the structures that may be of organizational significance. The earlier section of this paper dealing with the LEGOL semantic model reveals some of those structures. If one considers a formal organization as an expression of the norms in a task directed group, then those norms find their place in relation to the semantic model. The group itself is defined by the jurisdiction and language contexts while the problem context corresponds to the task. Roughly speaking, perceptual norms are given by the surrogate division, the behavioural norms by the language division, the cognitive norms by the descriptive rules and evaluative norms by prescriptive rules. While this equation is an approximate one, it would be fair to claim that the LEGOL semantic model gives a related classification of these norms. It helps to show what the parts of the LEGOL model refer to in the real world organization (as suggested in Figure 2).

Substantive vs. Procedural

Within the model, and considering only entities and rules, we may identify important subcategories which are related by their ability to refer to one another. A partial analysis of these is shown in Figure 3. We begin by distinguishing in reality those things which we are interested in for their own sake (physical and legal reality) from those other things which interest us because they refer to something else (signs or messages). For example, the passbook which enables a family to claim family allowance is real enough, but we are interested in it because it refers to people and such legal fictions as 'family' and 'entitlement to an allowance'.

Within the semantic model we distinguish between substantive entities (which are surrogates for physical and legal realities) and procedural entities (which are surrogates for messages and records or other signs). The rules we write have operands which may be interpreted as surrogates so we may distinguish between substantive rules (which refer to substantive entities) and procedural rules (which refer to procedural entities). We can also distinguish action rules, which in certain states of affairs generate commands, from sanction rules, which serve to make the other kinds of rules effective as prescriptions. There are also second-order rules which govern the structure of legislation, such as rule-making rules which govern the selection, extension and amendment of other rules.

The organizational significance of some of these groupings should be obvious. Perhaps the one obscure distinction is that between substantive and procedural entities or rules. This distinction becomes clear when one attempts, as in LEGOL, formal analysis of legislation. Legislation serves to "program" patterns of human activity. At the substantive level the subject matter of those rules will be people, their relationships, their activities and so on. At the procedural level the rules will refer to reports or messages about those persons and activities. In the example based upon the Family Allowances Act, Jones and Mason (1980), the rules analyzed are substantive ones. One can imagine giving effect to the substantive rules of the Family Allowances Act by a great variety of procedural systems. The kernel of the organization which the legislation defines is given by the substantive rules. These imply a logical minimum of observations and commands and record keeping. Any procedures used by the organization should be logically consistent with the substantive definition of the organization.

This distinction, though acknowledged, is not one which organizational theory draws very precisely. In systems analysis it is a distinction that has received little attention because of the prevailing conceptual notions of semantics which enable one to describe an organization in terms of message flows, (orders, invoices, back-orders and so on) assuming that a human user of the messages, through his "concepts", makes an adequate interpretation of their content. In the LEGOL model it will be seen that the procedural entities refer to

substantive entities. This relationship gives a precise interpretation of
the notion of the information content of a record or message in terms of the
part of the part of the substantive model represented.

POWER, RESPONSIBILITY AND AUTHORITY

Power

Power is a central notion of organization, Etzioni (1964). And some aspects of
power, at least in relation to formal organizations, may be explicated using
the LEGOL model. The analogy with the machine tool is useful here, but the lathe
is too simple a machine. While a lathe is operated by an individual and extends
his capabilities, a formal organization is a machine without a "key operator":
it simultaneously confers power upon and restricts the behavior of many people.
It demands certain predictability and uniformity of behavior so that it can weld
together the diverse and complicated activities of many individuals into a
result which would be unobtainable by any individual.   This does not
pre-judge the question of who benefits by the result. It may be a contract
that requires the performance by all parties of duties which will be beneficial
to each, or it may be an instrument of control serving some tyrannical
management. It may be a system of rewards that is so manipulated by the labor
force that it displaces the goals of the organization. The extent to which the
various levers on the machine are placed in the hands of different individuals
or groups determines the distribution of power which is effected by the machine.
This sort of power is the basis of control conferred by the formal system.
The way in which that power is exercised lies outside the field of study in
which we are engaged. So also does the formation of attitudes and the
transmission of value systems which are likely to predispose the protagonists'
uses of the power conferred by the formal organization. But let us see where
the power is accessible.

Power and the Data Model

Let us start with the naive view that the formal system is specified at the
substantive level and that it is supported by immediate and accurate flows of
information, while the participants are supposed to have a full and accurate
perception of the formal system and its workings.

The most obvious power conferred at this level is that of making judgements when
they are explicitly called for by certain rules. An example from the Family
Allowances Act 1965 is the allocation of a child to a particular family where
there is a choice that is in dispute. The individual who resolves this conflict
will exercise power.[3]

More or less power, depending upon the entity being specified, is conferred upon
the person or group given the responsibility for assigning descriptors, so that
a particular state of the real world can be operated upon symbolically by the
formal organization. The Family Allowances Act 1965 very carefully minimizes
the scope for assigning the descriptors 'child' or 'family' by relating these
to other descriptors more easily determined objectively, such as 'apprenticed'
or 'disabled'. Some entities, such as 'rate of allowance', do not correspond
to objective entities in the world. Rather, they serve as levers through which
influence may be exerted upon the machine-- in this case, by the minister
concerned.

An intermediate descriptor is 'disabled', which would probably have to be applied
by a qualified doctor of medicine before it confers the right to family allowance
on a person under nineteen. Many of the entities which determine the outcome of
a set of rules are themselves the outcomes of other formal organization; for
example, the upper limit of compulsory full-time education is a major parameter
in the family allowance systems, and is determined by the Education Act.

These preceding remarks should make clear the importance of the discussion about the semantic model. An exact semantic model should facilitate the analysis of power within an organization. Certain data elements could be altered a great deal without having any significant effect upon the outcome of any automatic decision-making process. Others might be adjusted only marginally before provoking an important change in the decision resulting from the rules. Those who select the data values which enter a formal system, who attach <u>labels</u> and who exhibit choice in <u>naming</u> things, hold its levers of symbolic power. For example, the fixing of the school leaving age has enormous consequences. Power is exercised by those who provide value judgements, and less obviously, by those who make observations. Even more subtly, power is exercised by those who determine who shall have the duty to make value judgements or observations. The points at which these assignments are made (names, labels, value judgements) is revealed by LEGOL in the semantic model. It reveals exactly where the power is and the extent to which it can be exercised.

An example comes form the Housing Finance (North Eastern Housing Association) Order 1972 subsection 6(3), "The Secretary of State may reduce, suspend or discontinue the payment of residual subsidy to the Association if it leases or otherwise disposes of any of its dwellings in respect of which it is entitled to such a payment." A Housing Association receives a subsidy in respect of its dwellings. Now the LEGOL analysis requires the specification of the <u>identifiers</u> of an entity. Thus the act of disposing of a dwelling is identified by the dwelling and the association, while the subsidy is identified by the giver (the law, e.g. the Housing Finance Order) and the receiver (the association) but not by the dwelling (subsidies are given as a whole, not for a particular dwelling). We can represent the situation by the diagram:

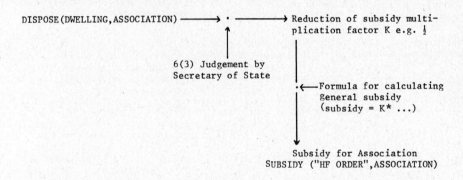

The lack of DWELLING as an identifier for SUBSIDY reveals the drastic nature of the intervening judgement; the disposal of a single dwelling could lead to, at worst, complete withdrawal of the general subsidy. This illustrates clearly how it is that the LEGOL data modelling technique can reveal a power location and especially, the extent to which that power can be exercised. Furthermore, the degree of power available in this judgement (i.e. the extent to which power can be exercised) is <u>not</u> apparent until this analysis is performed.

Another example can be found in the Family Allowances Act. In this case, the LEGOL analysis reveals a possible source of power which the Act may not have intended to allow. The LEGOL technique forces the analyst to define what is meant by the period of existence of an entity.[4] The Act, in Section 3, defines a family as a man and/or wife and any children, but does not specify if the family exists when there happen to be no children, perhaps when the first child becomes too old to be deemed a child according to the Act and the second child is not yet born. For the sake of exposition, Jones and Mason chose, in their

LEGOL version of the rules specifying 'family', to treat this as a gap in the existence of the family, but equally, one could take the view that the family "nucleus", i.e. the parents, still "exist" and, therefore, so should the family.[5] The analyst would be entitled to ask who should make this choice since it confers power on an anonymous part of the administrative machine set up to give effect to the Act. Other Acts, such as the National Insurance Act 1965, refer to this ambiguous definition of family and, thus, the choice may have wide ranging effects on peoples' rights.

In short, power lies where people manipulate values and judgements. The LEGOL analysis reveals precisely this, i.e. where the formal system may be controlled by the adjustment of data values, and the extent to which the power can be exercised. It is therefore a useful tool for locating power in an organization.

Power and rules

The naive view of formal organization specified at the substantive level and operating smoothly and openly has to be modified. Introducing the procedural system, we see that the opportunity exists to influence the making of observations and taking of actions, or at least the flow of information involved on both the input and output side. The procedural system also involves record keeping and, therefore, the choice of what information to retain and when to erase it. Procedural rules may be written to specify how these messages are to flow and how the records are to be maintained. This can certainly limit the power of the people who are gate-keepers on the information flow, but the favorite means of evading this sort of constraint is to leave the gate-keepers with discretion to time the flow of messages. Even when procedures are determined by rules, power is given by the allocation of tasks within the system, especially the information processing tasks.

Involvement in its procedures confers a certain useful familiarity with the machine and how it might be deployed. The extent to which the machinery is exposed to the people who are influenced by it is a major source of power. In Britain, great ingenuity is devoted to preventing potential recipients of supplementary social security or subjects of immigration legislation from knowing the detailed codes operated by the functionaries. This is an important aspect of power being conferred or denied by the degree of access to the formal organization. Similar aspects are the need for specialists' knowledge to be able to make use of such very complicated legislation, or the amount of public awareness of even quite simple provisions which may be controlled by the amount of publicity they are given. The "small print" in standard contracts illustrates the use of these devices.

Access to the power conferred by the formal organization depends upon recognizing its relevance to a given situation. Even when relevance is recognized, there may be conferred upon some persons or groups the discretion whether or not to invoke a system of rules. The public prosecutor or the judge in a legal system certainly has such power but in business organizations, this is an important kind of power given to managers and administrators.

The power to invoke rules is particularly important where the rules relate directly to sanctions. The power to apply sanctions is perhaps the most obvious way of conferring power through a formal organization, but as we have seen, this is by no means the only one.

The power to invoke or to set aside rules is an aspect of the power to adapt the system of rules itself. Rules which govern rule-making confer power of a very high order. A great deal of legislation is of this enabling character and in normal business organizations, this is an important way of establishing the area of authority of a manager.

The making of rules also has its procedural aspects. The power of the person who drafts legislation is increased if the rules have a complexity which is not matched by the power of scrutiny available to the person with substantive power to make rules. In the legislative system, we see this power at its strongest when complex secondary legislation or regulations are enacted without an opportunity for political scrutiny. Much of the power of the EEC commission is thought to be of this kind. In the typical business situation, the drafting of detailed rules often falls to the systems analyst, who is introducing a computer. In many detailed ways, he is the rule-maker. Although his power is procedural, it is real enough because the recondite nature of his work places it beyond the scrutiny of the substantive rule-maker.

The making of rules is an important source of power, but rules are relatively open to adjustment. More stable than the rules are the structures of entities used to depict the world. The person who fixes these has the power to determine what part of the world is seen and how it is structured by the formal organization in question. It is precisely this activity in which the information analyst is engaged. We suspect that any deep ideological differences between groups will appear in the different entity structures which they would devise for dealing with the problem. This entails, of course, determining what the problem shall be and this brings us in turn to one of the fundamental sources of power: the ability to determine what is upon the agenda.

Responsibility and Authority

Having indicated some of the source of power associated with formal organizations of the kind to which LEGOL is relevant, we can turn to the questions of responsibility and authority, also in the narrow context of LEGOL. Responsibility is conferred upon a person (legal or individual) when he is subject to sanctions as a result of actions in a certain field known as his area of responsibility. The notion could be made quite precise in the context of the LEGOL model, by examining whether or not sufficient power exists to enable a person to have responsibility.[6] Similarly, the notion of authority can be made precise in terms of the granting of the powers to make rules, to invoke them or set them aside, to invoke sanctions, to exert values and to assign meanings. And in fact this is consistent with notions commonly put forward in general organization theory, as in Arrow (1974), Simon (1957).

In this precisely determined context it would make sense to consider carefully the logic of relationships between responsibility and authority. This applies also to the sharing of responsibility and authority through patterns of formal organization achieved by negotiation when the parties are evenly balanced in the crude sanctions they can use to define their negotiating positions. We hope that if LEGOL can be adequately developed, it will become a valuable tool for studying negotiation.

THE MITIGATION OF BUREAUCRACY

In The Bureaucratic Phenomenon, Crozier (1963) mentions the dilemma of bureaucracy, pointed out by Michels, that "... democratic social action is possible only through bureaucratic organization and bureaucratic organization is destructive of democratic values." The undesirable features of bureaucracies stem partly from the way in which they treat their client population and partly from the way in which they use human components. Crozier asserts that "... a bureaucratic organization is an organization that cannot correct its behavior by learning from its errors."[7] He also underlines the poor quality of a working situation that demands rigid conformity to impersonal rules that tend to become more detailed and inflexible in order to reduce the tensions which they themselves generate.

If we look at bureaucratic systems as predominantly comprising the kind of formal organization we have been discussing here, we can perhaps see ways of mitigating the dysfunctions of bureaucracy. It helps to see the formal organization as a machine, useful and capable of being designed and, if well designed, capable of being changed. Bureaucracies which are built from human components could be built, and perhaps more appropriately built, from machine components. The displacement of clerical labor this way is not unimportant, but is a secondary problem from our point of view. Those who are interested in the intelligent use of informatics in our society might reasonably set the mechanization of bureaucracy as a worthy goal. This would certainly mitigate the effect of bureaucracy on the minds of those who now perform the mechanistic functions in such organizations.

Unfortunately, we do not know how to design computer systems which are easily adaptable. Manual bureaucracies which deal with very complicated sets of rules still have the advantage over computer systems because of their greater adaptability. Crozier's complaint that bureaucracies are unable to learn from their errors can be laid even more justifiably at the doors of many computer departments. However, one of the purposes of LEGOL is to discover techniques of analysis and design which will make it easy to adapt computer-based systems.

The LEGOL approach to data modelling is a positive step in this direction. In the LEGOL analysis this activity always precedes the writing of any rules or generation of any design. The LEGOL data analysis is performed in the initial phases of the organizational specification in order to identify the fundamental data resources of the organization. The LEGOL method requires that the inherent data structures be analyzed at the substantive level, independently from the details of the applications (the procedural level). This very high level activity permits the design of flexible file structures which can support a number of related activities and which are capable of sustaining changes in applications. Conversion of applications is subsequently easier due to the fundamental understanding of the data involved. The LEGOL method, therefore, promotes adaptability and flexibility in the resulting computer systems.

Also, by treating bureaucracy as machine-like, formal organization we can approach it more intelligently with an engineering outlook. Using LEGOL analysis we hope that the functioning of the component of an organization which comprises its formal rules can be better understood, criticized and tested. This is an essential part of the procedure required to make bureaucracy responsive to its errors. This responsiveness is a prerequisite to any drive to simplify bureaucracy. If it is difficult to change the rules then the architect of the system is beholden to make sure that the rules are as detailed and complete as possible. If the malfunctioning of a system of rules can be detected quickly and the rules, thereafter, quickly amended, then the rules can be kept simple.

This suggests that there should be a general design principle for formal organizations, that of finding the minimum rationality needed for the task. This is one of our aims and represents a large problem area in the field of information system design which has yet to be explored. It raises fascinating problems such as the possible need for retrospective rule making, obviously within a framework of constraints, but sufficient to remedy consequences of inadequacies in the design as they are encountered. This question of retrospective rule-making is a nettle indeed. We suggest that it should be grasped by the organizational theorist who is studying bureaucracy.

CONCLUSION

We have worked under the assumption that the systems analyst will be unable to seize the essentials of an organization until he has a language in which he can say what has to be done without being forced to say it in terms of how certain data are to be processed. Within this framework, we are developing a systems

specification language which permits legislation to be interpreted by computer.
We believe a theory which deals with the microstructure of an organization should
make possible new kinds of explanation and prediction of organizational behavior.

The LEGOL model then amounts to a theory of formal organization. Most
administrative theories are discursive on detail and able to make testable
statements only about aggregate behavior (such as the contingency theories of
organizational behavior, Woodward (1965)).   The LEGOL method supplements the
work being done in the main tradition of organizational theory because it is
concerned with field effects (attitudes), whereas the LEGOL method provides
techniques for looking in a precise way at the circuitry of the organization
(rule-following aspects). Managerial ideologies, general classifications of
organizations by size, industrial sector, type of technology and so on are
concepts at a level of aggregation far above the detail which is essential in
analyzing and designing an information system. Although such concepts are
relevant, the systems analyst also needs to perceive the machinery of the
organization in great detail.

Finally, LEGOL can be seen as a tool (1) for explication of organizational concepts
and (2) to assist change and thereby mitigate the bureaucratic dilemma.
Therefore, our kind of formal analysis reaches significantly into the area of
interest of organizational theorists. It helps to analyze and explain the
information systems environment, so that the interaction of the information
system and the organization within which it exists can be understood and
predicted. This explanation should result in more effective information systems
design, and a recognition that technical analysis can be relevant to those
interested in organizational theory.

Figure 1: LEGOL Semantic Model

SURROGATE DIVISION
    particulars (entities)
    universals (domains)
	CONTEXT DIVISION
	problem

LANGUAGE DIVISION
    encodings of natural language
    informal dictionary entities
	language

RULE DIVISION
    descriptive (natural constraints)
    prescriptive (legal constraints)
	jurisdiction

Figure 2: What the Semantic Model Refers to in an Organization

model
{
Context Division ──────────→ task
Surrogate Division ──────────→ perceptual norms
Language Division ──────────→ behavioral norms
Rule Division ──────────→ evaluative norms
──────────→ cognitive norms
}
group boundary
organ-
isation

(Note: only a rough set of equivalents)

Figure 3: Network of References among Entities and Rules

(Note: only a partial analysis)

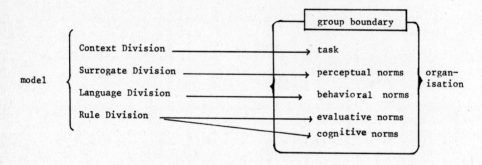

rule-making rules

action rules   sanction rules

messages and records ← procedural entities ← procedural rules

physical and legal reality
REALITY
substantive entities ← substantive rules

<u>FOOTNOTES</u>

1

The importance of the discussion of the semantic model will become
especially clear at the point in the paper where organizational concepts
are discussed. For example, an exact semantic model should facilitate the
analysis of power and influence within an organization.

2

A totally prescriptive characterization of formal organization, owing to the
Classical Theory of Administration (perhaps more appropriately called
"scientific management") is this: a blueprint according to which
organizations are to be constructed and to which they ought to adhere,
Etzioni (1964).

3

Using the LEGOL system, the points at which these judgments are called for
(i.e. locations of power) are illustrated dramatically. Where the rules
are entirely formal, the computer can proceed unaided. But in the cases
where human judgment is required, the LEGOL interpreter will intervene
and request values, i.e. ask for judgment to be exercised by an
appropriate administrator. Specific variables will be at the administrator's
disposal, and he must supply the values within constraints that the rule may
impose. This interruption makes these power points obvious in a way in
which merely reading the legislative prose may not.

4

A LEGOL entity representation is made up of the following: one characteristic
attribute, zero or more identifier attributes and two time attributes, in
that order. In LEGOL, <u>all</u> entities have these two time attributes, a start
and an end, distinguishing LEGOL entity representations from other relational
structures.

5

Space permits only a mention of how the entity 'family' is derived in LEGOL,
but the complete analysis with supporting arguments can be found in
Jones and Mason, (1980).

6

Power to invoke sanctions is necessary if real responsibility is to be
conferred. It is just illogical to confer responsibility on a person for
a particular area unless he has sufficient power to invoke sanctions.
As a postscript, the reader may be interested in a subsequent paper
(Stamper 1980) which presents more of the formal machinery for explicating
concepts such as power, authority, autonomy, right, privilege, duty,
liability, disability and immunity.

7

The inability to be self-correcting and adaptive runs exactly counter to the
basic features of organization (e.g. as expressed by Etzioni, (1964) p.1,
"An organization continually evaluates how well it is performing and tries to
adjust itself accordingly to achieve its goals,") and to the requirements
for organizational effectiveness (i.e. to maintain effectiveness through an
adaptive-coping cycle, which requires internal flexibility,
Edgar H. Schein, (1965), pp.15-17 & p.98.) This breakdown, then, represents
a real dysfunction of organization.

REFERENCES

(1)   Arrow, K.J., The Limits of Organization (W.W. Norton & Co., New York, 1974).

(2)   Crozier, M., The Bureaucratic Phenomenon (University of Chicago Press, Chicago,1963).

(3)   Date, C.J., Introduction to Database Systems, Second Edition (Addison-Wesley, London, 1977).

(4)   Davenport, R.A., Data Analysis for Database Design, The Australian Computer Journal, Vol.10, No.4. (November 1978).

(5)   Etzioni, A., Modern Organizations (Prentice Hall, Inc., Englewood Cliffs, N.J., 1964).

(6)   Jones, S., Mason, P., Programming the Law, in: Lucas, H.C. (ed.), The Information Systems Environment, Proceedings of the IFIP TC 8.2 Conference, Bonn, West Germany, 11-13 June 1979 (North-Holland, Amsterdam, 1980).

(7)   Schein, E.H., Organizational Psychology (Prentice Hall, Inc., Englewood Cliffs, N.J., 1965).

(8)   Simon, H., Authority, in: Arensberg, C.M. (ed.), Research in Industrial Human Relations (Harper and Bros., New York, 1957).

(9)   Stamper, R.K., Aspects of Data Semantics: Names, Species and Complex Physcial Objects, in: Bracchi, G., and Lochemann, P.C. (eds.), Information Systems Methodology (Springer Verlag, Berlin, 1978a).

(10)   _____, LEGOL: Modelling Legal Rules by Computer in: Niblett, B., Proceedings of CREST Course in Computer Science and Law (Cambridge University Press, Cambridge, 1980).

(11)   _____, Physical Objects, Human Discourse and Formal Systems, in: Nijssen, G.M. (ed.), Architecture and Models in Data Base Management Systems (North-Holland, Amsterdam, 1977).

(12)   _____ ,Towards a Semantic Model for the Analysis of Legislation, in: Martino, A.A., Maretti, E., and Ciampi, C. (eds.), Informatica e Diritto 2: Logica, Informatica, Diritto (Le Monnier, Firenze, 1978b).

(13)   _____, Towards a Semantic Normal Form, in: Bracchi, G., and Nijssen, G.M. (eds.), Data Base Architecture, Proceedings of the IFIP Working Conference on Data Base Architecture, Venice, Italy, 26-29 June, 1979 (North-Holland, Amsterdam, 1979).

The Information Systems Environment
Lucas, Land, Lincoln, Supper (Editors)
North-Holland Publishing Company

PROGRAMMING THE LAW

Peter Mason

London School of Economics, London WC2A 2AE

Susan Jones

The City University, London EC1

LEGOL[1] is a language for writing rules defining information
systems at a very general level so that they can be interpreted
automatically to discover whether they will have the desired
effect. Administrative legislation has the desirable properties
of a high-level system specification, providing precise
definition of what ought to be done, without saying how. The
objective in designing LEGOL is to provide an interpretable
formalism with similar characteristics, and the language has
been developed by considering what structures would be required
to express the provisions of various pieces of legislation.
LEGOL is seen as a tool for a systems analyst to simulate an
information system prior to detailed design of a computer
system.

INTRODUCTION

LEGOL is a language for writing rules defining information systems at a very
general level, so that they can be interpreted automatically and tested to
discover whether they will have the desired effect (Jones et al, 1979).

Administrative legislation has the desirable property of a high-level system
specification, providing a precise definition of what ought to be done, without
saying how. The objective in designing LEGOL has been to provide an
interpretable formalism with similar characteristics, and the language has been
developed by considering what structures would be required to express the
provisions of various pieces of legislation in an algorithmic form. The example
here shows how part of the Family Allowances Act, 1965 could be translated into
LEGOL. First, it is necessary to give a brief survey of the language, introducing
some necessary terminology and pointing out some unusual features.

ENTITY SETS

The language is intended to allow its users to refer directly to substantive
entities which have some observed existence (for instance persons and their family
relationships) or which can be derived by the application of a law (for instance
rights to, or obligations to pay, an allowance). Entity sets (e.g. persons,
marriages, allowances) are represented in the form of tables in which each entry
stands for one member of the set and each column contains a different "attribute"
of the entity. The tables are in third normal form, but some additional constraints
are imposed on the number and type of attributes, Stamper (1979).

325

Attribute Structure

Each entity representation will contain one "characteristic" attribute. It may
consist of a name, criterion, or a value, depending upon the nature of the thing
being represented.

Most entities also have "identifier attributes". For example, representations
of states of a person, or relationships between persons, include the person's
names as identifiers. All entities have two "time attributes". These delimit
the period during which the entity exists, for instance giving the dates of
birth and death of a person, or the start and end dates of some condition such
as "childhood", "marriage", etc.

Entity representations are referred to in the LEGOL language by the table name,
followed by a bracketed list of "identifier labels". For instance, the
expression "E(I,J)" refers to the table E having a characteristic attribute
also labelled E, and two identifier attributes labelled I and H respectively.
Time attributes may be referred to explicitly in such expression as
"start of E(I,J)".

THE LEGOL RULE

A LEGOL specification consists of a series of "rules" rather similar to
assingment statements in a programming language, e.g.

$$T(I) \Leftarrow R(J) \text{ while } S(I,J).$$

The right had side of the rule, known as the "source" consists of an expression
which, when evaluated, yields a table, the entries of which are added to those
of the table named on the left hand side, i.e. the "target". Assignment is
non-destructive; the new entries are added to any already in the target, so
the operation denoted by " =" is known as "update"; conceptually, it adds new
facts about the world without destroying the old. Source expressions consist of
entity references connected by operators. Particularly important are the
temporal operators such as "while", "during", "until", etc. which act upon and
generate time attributes.

ILLUSTRATIVE EXAMPLE

To illustrate these features of the language, the remainder of the paper will
discuss a LEGOL version of section 2 of the Family Allowances Act, 1965.

A number of LEGOL functions and operators will be seen in use, but for a precise
specification of their effect the reader is referred to Jones et al (1979).

The Act is concerned with specifying under what circumstances a family will be
entitled to an allowance, and how much it will be. Its first section enunciates
a very general principle, i.e.

> 1. Subject to the provisions of this Act, there shall be paid by the
> Minister for every family which includes two or more children, and for
> the benefit of the family as a whole, an allowance in respect of each
> child in the family other than the elder or eldest at the rate of eight
> shillings a week in respect of the first child other than the elder or
> eldest and ten shillings a week in respect of each other such child.

This section appeals to concepts such as "child" and "family" which, although
commonly understood in everyday use, require a precise definition here.
Section 2 begins to give us the required precision:-

2. (1) A person shall be treated for the purposes of this Act as a child -

(a) during any period while he is under the upper limit of the compulsory
     school age; and
(b) during any period before he attains the age of nineteen while he is
     undergoing full-time instruction in a school or is an apprentice;
     and
(c) during any period before he attains the age of sixteen while he is
     by reason of illness or disability of mind or body incapacitated,
     and likely to remain for a prolonged period incapacitated, for
     regular employment.

This paragraph refers to basic observable entities;- "persons" who may at
certain periods of their lives be undergoing "full-time education" or
"apprenticeship". We can represent such observed facts in the following way:-

PERSON

PERSON	PERSON	start (i.e. date of birth)	end (i.e. date of death)
	ARTHUR	1/4/20	1/10/55
	KATHLEEN	1/1/21	-
	JOHN	1/2/36	-
	SUSAN	1/4/42	-
	DAVID	1/3/47	-
	LINDA	1/3/57	-
	PHILIP	1/8/69	-
	THOMAS	1/2/74	-
	CATHERINE	1/11/77	-

FULL-TIME EDUCATION

FTE	(PERSON)	start of education	end
-	JOHN	1/9/41	1/7/51
-	SUSAN	1/9/47	1/7/63
-	DAVID	1/9/52	1/7/68
-	DAVID	1/9/69	1/7/71
-	LINDA	1/9/60	1/7/72
-	PHILIP	1/9/73	-

APPRENTICED

APP	(PERSON)	start	end
-	JOHN	1/7/51	1/7/54
-	DAVID	1/7/68	1/9/69

Note that in these tables there are some "unknown" end times, e.g. dates of
death of still living persons. Also, in the tables FTE and APP, the characteristic
attribute has no assigned value. Here all the relevant information for this Act
is given by the other attributes, i.e. that the persons named were in those
situations between the stated times. The characteristic attribute could be
conceived as holding the value "true". (e.g. "It is true that John was an
apprentice between July 1951 and July 1954".)

From tables like the above, we have to generate periods of "childhood".
According to the prose, there are three different criteria, and it will be
necessary to combine them to arrive at a total period. We require an
intermediate table:

CHILDHOOD (PERSON), periods of childhood (of a person), to hold details of
individual times during which the child satisfied any <u>particular</u> criterion.

The start of any person's childhood is the start of his or her life. This is
an implicit assumption which must be made explicit by a LEGOL rule[2] :-

      start of CHILDHOOD (PERSON) ← start of PERSON

Subsection 2-(1) (a) seems straightforward but is complicated by a further
subsection 2-(2) (b) which says that a person who reaches the school age limit
shall not be treated as under that limit at any time in the future even if the
limit is subsequently raised. For this brief explanation of LEGOL we shall
ignore this complication and consider the next two subsections.[3]

Subsection 2-(1) (b) extends the period of childhood by that time during which
the child was under 19 and either apprenticed or in full-time education. The
rule can be written:-

      CHILDHOOD,"2(1)(b)"(PERSON) ← FTE(PERSON) or while APP(PERSON)
                 until start of PERSON + 19

The "or while" operator in the source expression amalgamates any overlapping or
adjacent periods of full-time education and apprenticeship for the same person.
e.g. the data for John and David give:

CHILDHOOD	(PERSON)	start	end
-	JOHN	1/9/41	1/7/54
-	DAVID	1/9/52	1/7/71

"Until" sets a latest end time of P's 19th birthday to any period so obtained.
Note that in this rule, it is not a single start or end time which is transmitted
to the target, but a whole period, hence the slightly different form of the
update operator.[4] A literal subsection label "2(1)(b)" is assigned as
characteristic attribute value of the derived entries:

CHILDHOOD	(PERSON)	start	end
2(1)(b)	JOHN	1/9/41	1/7/54
2(1)(b)	DAVID	1/9/52	1/3/66

Although David was in full-time education until 1971, March 1966 becomes the
end of his childhood since he reached 19 then. The remainder of section 2 can
be treated similarly, i.e. with the rule:-

CHILDHOOD,"2(1)(c)"(PERSON) ← INCAPACITATED(PERSON) until start of PERSON + 16

We can now amalgamate, using the "whenever" function, all the separately defined
periods of childhood for each person into one:-

      TOTAL-CHILDHOOD,"SECTION 2"(PERSON) ← whenever of CHILDHOOD(PERSON)

The subsection labels in CHILDHOOD will not be transferred by this operation,
since several periods may be amalgamated into one, and can no longer be
separately named. For example, suppose John is a child between 1/2/36 and
1/2/51 according to 2(1)(a) and between 1/9/41 and 1/7/54 according to 2(1)(b);
according to Section 2 as a whole he is a child between February 1936 and
July 1954:

TOTAL-CHILDHOOD	(PERSON)	start	end
Section 2	JOHN	1/2/36	1/7/54
Section 2	DAVID	1/3/47	1/3/66

A Section 3 specifies when these "children" are deemed to belong to a "family".
For lack of space in this paper, let us now write the rules for Section 1
above, assuming we have generated the following table by applying the rules
representing Section 3.

NUM-CHILDREN	(FAMILY)	start	end
1	KING	1/4/42	1/3/47
2	KING	1/3/47	1/4/61
1	KING	1/4/61	1/3/66
1	SNOW	1/8/69	1/11/77
2	SNOW	1/11/77	1/8/85
1	SNOW	1/8/85	1/11/93
1	LANE	1/2/74	1/2/90

The allowance can be represented as a legal relation between the "Minister",
referred to in section 1, and any eligible family, derived by:-

ALLOWANCE("Minister",FAMILY) ←NUM-CHILDREN(FAMILY) > 1

i.e. the allowance is payable while the number of children in the family is
greater than 1. However, this immediately raises the point that, in fact, the
right to an allowance exists only after the Act has been passed. Moreover,
the conditions under which it is payable, and the amount payable, will in practice
change over time. So, although the text of the Act in 1965 contained the words
"eight shillings" etc., its provisions might be more generally translated by
representing the actual amount of the allowance as a time-varying prescriptive
entity, like the school-leaving age. We define:-

RATE (NUM-CHILDREN), rate of allowance (according to number of children),

into which appropriate values can be inserted:-

RATE	(NUM-CHILDREN)	start	end
£0.25	2	1/6/52	1/6/65
£0.60	3	1/6/52	1/6/65
£0.40	2	1/6/65	1/6/70
£0.90	3	1/6/65	1/6/70
£1.00	1	1/6/70	-
£2.50	2	1/6/70	-

The provisions of section 1 can now be expressed simply and in a time independent
manner by writing:-

ALLOWANCE("MINISTER",FAMILY) ⇐ RATE(NUM-CHILDREN) while NUM-CHILDREN(FAMILY)

Matching the number of children attribute associates the correct rate with each
family, and this is transferred to become the characteristic value of the
derived relation:-

ALLOWANCE	("MINISTER",	FAMILY)	start	end
£0.25	MINISTER	KING	1/6/52	1/4/61
£1.00	MINISTER	SNOW	1/6/70	1/11/77
£2.50	MINISTER	SNOW	1/11/77	1/8/85
£1.00	MINISTER	SNOW	1/8/85	1/11/93
£1.00	MINISTER	LANE	1/2/74	1/2/90

CONCLUSIONS

We have seen then how representations of legal relationships can be derived from representations of basic observed facts, using rules corresponding to units of the original legislation. Most important, every piece of data, whether observed or derived, is accompanied by a pair of times delimiting its period of existence.

We may link this expression of legislative rules in a concise, computer interpretable form to information systems design by imagining the following activity:

"An analyst is required to set up a computer-based organisation to pay family allowances; to collect facts, to calculate correct allowances, and to order and monitor appropriate payments by the government. He first specifies the procedures for calculating the eligibility for, and the amounts of, allowances. These are independent of the message flows he will subsequently design to collect and disseminate information. He knows these procedures are minutely specified by legislation but because of the latter's length, complexity, and form of expression:

- the raw legislation is not suitable as program specifications;
- there will be a long time-lag between the specification and the checking of program results;
- the running system will be comprehended by computer people in terms of its response to specified inputs rather than in terms of the original legislation. This will make changes to the system, caused by amendments to the legislation, difficult to specify.

He therefore specifies the logic as a LEGOL "program" which he runs (inefficiently) against sample data supplied by the government department. He checks his results with the user department before converting his LEGOL specification into flowcharts etc. for the programmers. He stores his LEGOL program as "active documentation" which can be altered and re-run quickly to test the correctness and impact of changes in the running system caused by changes in the legislation."

The analyst chooses an interpretation which he must check is correct. Even in our limited example we have the new idea of a time-varying rate of allowance based upon the number of children in a family, rather than constant amounts relating to each child. Such ideas aim to simplify the computer system (which would not need rules to specify who is the eldest, second eldest child etc. at any given time), and to allow flexibility (subsequently, rates may change or the legislation may be changed to pay an allowance for every child). They may, however, incorporate incorrect assumptions of the analyst and a LEGOL "simulation" should help to reveal these.

LEGOL has been applied to administrative legislation e.g. Jones (1978), Jones (1979), and to d.p. system specification, Jones, Mason (1980). A prototype interpreter has been written in POP-2 (Burstall et al, 1971), for a DEC-10. An interpreter for use by collaborators will be available on a microcomputer in October 1980.

REFERENCES

(1)   The LEGOL project is supported by the U.K. Scientific Research Council
      and Social Science Research Council.

(2)   The update " **<=** " transfers the person's name because the attribute label
      is the same in both source and target. The "double arrow" form of update
      also forces a transfer between attributes explicitly referred to;
      the start of a person becomes the start of childhood.

(3)   The LEGOL version of 2-(1) (a) and 2-(2) (b), discussed in Mason, Jones (1978)
      shows how concisely such a language can express the complicated time
      processing required by a prose rule:
          PROSE   2-(1) (a): as above, 2-(2) (b):"a person who at any time
      attains the upper limit of the compulsory school age shall not be treated
      as being under that limit at any time thereafter, notwithstanding any
      subsequent change in that limit":
          LEGOL   end of CHILDHOOD,"2(2) (b) & 2(1) (a)"(PERSON) **<=** first for
                  PERSON of (start of PERSON + SLA during SLA)

(4)   The update **<—**   automatically transfers the time period of an evaluated
      expression to the target. The previous rule overrode this default by
      specifying the transfer of a time instant using **<=** and explicit
      reference to an instant (start of PERSON).

Jones, S., Mason, P.J., Stamper, R.K., LEGOL-2.0: A Relational
Specification Language for Complex Rules, in: Information Systems,
Vol. 4, No. 4 (1979) 293-305.

Stamper, R.K., Towards a semantic normal form, IFIP TC2 Working Conference
on Database Architecture, Venice, Italy (June 1979).

Jones, S., A LEGOL Example: Intestate Succession, LSE Paper in
Informatics L19. (1978).

Jones S., Control Structures in Legislation, presented at CREST Course,
Computers and the Law, Swansea, (September 1979).

Jones, S., Mason, P.J., Proceduralism and Parallelism in Specification
Languages, Information Systems Vol. 5 No. 2. (1980).

Burstall, R.M., Collins, J.S., Popplestone, R.J., Programming in POP-2
(Ediburgh University Press, 1971).

Mason, P.J., Jones, S., Programming and the Law. This is a fuller version
of the paper presented here. LSE Paper in Informatics L30 (1978).

PERSONAL VIEWS AND SPECULATIONS

The Information Systems Environment
Lucas, Land, Lincoln, Supper (Editors)
North-Holland Publishing Company
© *IFIP, 1980*

TECHNOLOGICAL CHANGE AND BUSINESS ENVIRONMENT

S A DAY

The subject of this short paper is the changing environment in business and
trading activities brought about by technological developments in computing,
and the need for managements to be aware of, and to control, these changes.

For centuries the trader was a lone individual, or at most he formed a part
of a loose associations of individuals, and even when these associations
developed into powerful companies they retained much of their individualistic
character. The first industrial revolution concentrated and enlarged trading
units (and by trading I include production, manufacturing, transport and
marketing) but in the main throughout the 19th century they remained
localised; even within international companies the local branches had much
of the character of autonomous agencies. The 20th century, and in particular
the second half, has seen the rapid growth of large multi-national combines
and, despite the efforts of politicians to counter monopoly and
extraterritorial control, many of them are tightly controlled from the
centre. This development, although strictly speaking evolutionary, is of
such magnitude and rapidity that it has some of the turbulence of revolution.

As organisations grow and disperse problems of control increase. Where
management is vested in one man or even a small group, the lines of
communication may be simple; where control is vested in a series of
managerial units the problems of communication become difficult. Complex
organisational frameworks are designed to facilitate communication,
frequently they hinder it. Their purpose is to provide a channel of
information upwards from operating points, to enable management to
consolidate and assess the results of trading activities, and downward from
management to enable the operators to be aware of management policies and to
receive instructions. The need for horizontal communication is not always
realised, and when it is, the resulting organisational matrices are often
difficult to understand and operate.

Although the means of physical communication have increased rapidly over the
last hundred years, the techniques for handling information barely changed
until the second half of the 20th century, and are still fairly primitive.
The assembly of basic information about a company's activities is still
time-consuming and expensive, and the analyses applied to company results is
in many cases trivial and naive. Although in many companies problem-solving
techniques are used, these are predominantly aimed at technical activities;
the application of such techniques to the business functions is in most
companies slight if not non-existent. On the part of many commercial
managers there remains positive resistance to the idea that mathematical
tools can aid their decision processes. A large part of the information
which filters through the various layers of many companies consists of
pre-programmed tabulations which are designed as a compromise between
numerous requirements, and the criteria for which is an often misconceived

idea of what is called "cost-effectiveness". They are often little different from the returns which were the staple information diet of managers in pre-computer days.

The lack of sufficient information to support the requirements of the business has a number of undesirable side effects. It creates a sense of dissatisfaction and inadequacy in responsible management, whilst at the same time providing a permanent excuse for bad decisions. It restricts the capacity of managers to manage, and organisations are structured to try to overcome deficiencies in communication rather than as an aid to dynamic management. It is widely held that an individual manager can control directly relatively few people, otherwise he becomes a bottleneck. This is not because of difficulties in making decisions once the facts of a situation are known, but rather because of the time spent in extracting and absorbing the facts themselves. If information reporting and processing were improved, managers would have more time and could control more people. This would remove the need for much of the bureaucracy, which is designed to overcome difficulties of communication, but all too often stultifies decision making rather than encourages it.

As a result of limitations in the communication of information, when decisions are made they tend to be subjective and clear cut, instead of an unemotional assessment of risks and probabilities with options being preserved for as long as possible. A manager's competence is frequently judged on his willingness to make inspired and usually random decisions rather than the care with which he assembles and assesses the relevant date.

The Seventies have seen far less progress in applying computer technology to the communication of management information than was hoped and foretold in the Sixties. The term "management information" was coined at least twenty years ago and the need for improvements in business information has been widely perceived for far longer. Lack of suitable hardware and software is not sufficient to account for this; there were data processing outfits in the Sixties who operated effective database systems and many of them had the potential to offer considerable benefits in the processing of information for decision making. Some of these have continued and progressed and made some impact, but this is not so generally.

One reason for lack of progress is that managements have been reluctant to make substantial investments where benefits appear intangible and non-quantifiable. They have, though often reluctantly, invested in data processing equipment and people for the prospect of manpower savings, but the considerable act of faith required for the development of expensive information systems has been more than many of them have been prepared to make. To some extent data processing practitioners and computers companies have themselves to blame for this; their promises have too often not been fulfilled and their systems have too often not worked.

Whilst in general technical managers have embraced computers as tools of their trade and used them, often adventurously, for many years, most commercial managers have been reluctant to learn new methods of information assessment and decision making. Again, too many ideas have not worked, but the users themselves must accept a large part of the blame for this. They have been happy to leave information processing to technicians. The lack of user interest was an important reason for the many poor procedural systems which have been developed. Unless management are sufficiently interested to become closely involved, the attempt to develop effective information systems will be a waste of time and energy.

In the last ten years a number of portable data base systems have been made available, most of them in significant respects unsatisfactory, but many of them offering useful facilities. This development, by itself, has been so far disappointingly inadequate to stimulate the widespread growth of business information systems. But the availability of mini-computers capable of operating data base systems offers a new prospect. (In this context a mini-computer is one which does not require a specifically prepared environment or specially trained operators for its use).

The advent of the usable mini-computer may well prove to be the most significant advance since computers were first applied in commerce. Managements no longer have to commit themselves to great expense in order to achieve useful benefits from information processing, so that cost should become less of an obstacle to progress. Business managers tend to be conservative, necessarily so; adventurous accountants frequently spell disaster. But the continued use of traditional decision methods may also prove disastrous. In large organisations, and these are increasingly predominant, decision-making becomes less and less an entrepreneurial activity and more and more a corporate examination of facts and probabilities. With few exceptions today's successful business man is a careful career manager, trained in the process of corporate decision making and increasingly familiar with the use of decision techniques. Decision making becomes a cold blooded exercise, less like a game of poker, more like a game of chess. If decision making is to depend on the consolidation and analysis of information and if decisions are to be taken by committee rather than by individuals, the processes of decision making depend on analytical tecniques which, in general, will demand the use of some form of computer. These techniques include the collection and consolidation of data into an accessible data base, facilities for generating interactive retrievals and processing; facilities for answering hypothetical questions ("what-if" questions as they are sometimes called).

The technology to achieve many of the benefits is already available to a limited but usable degree. The techniques needed to process data for corporate information are slowly being developed. The attitudes and backgrounds of commercial managers are gradually changing as the computer generation succeeds to positions of management. But there is much not yet done which could be done with today's resources, and there are many companies poised for a step forward. There are several things which are ripe for action, and some of the most important are:

(a) Manufacturers and practitioners need to concentrate on ways to reduce the cost of data as a raw material. Much has been done to improve the economics of data entry at the computer, but the administrative cost of preparing data for entry is still very high in most cases.

(b) There is a research requirement for a systematic study to develop and improve techniques for the processing of business data to provide useful output for decision making. A great deal of work is being done in this area, but to the business data processor it seems fragmentary and unco-ordinated.

(c) Users must devote more time, as a matter of competitive necessity to considering the areas of their activities which can be made most susceptible to computer-aided mathematical analysis.

(d) Managements should seek and improve ways of bridging the gap which still exists between commercial managers and DP practitioners, by more careful training and career planning and by raising the status of information projects within their organisation.

(e) Managements should already be re-thinking their methods and
    organisation. Organisation is communication and changes in the mechanics
    of communication will have a profound effect on organisation and, through
    organisation, to basic methods of work.

The development of extensive corporate information systems is not in doubt;
the only question is how fast the process will be. Such systems are already
perceived by some enlightened managements as a means of competition, and when
this is more widely understood the present trickle of demand will become a
flood. The balance of supply and demand may soon change and the bottleneck
be, not reluctant managers, but insufficint practitioners. The decisions to
be taken will become harder, not only because the business activity becomes
more complex and more extensive, but also because more and more of the easy
decisions will be taken by computers. A substantial proportion of the time
of most senior managers has in the past been taken up with reactive decisions
which (with known technology and techniques) a computer can be programmed to
make. The decisions which are left will be those of such complexity that
they cannot easily be broken down into logical processes. It should
therefore become tougher at the top - it is already a lot more intellectual
than it used to be.

Organisations will become simpler as the middle layers disappear. The role
of middle management in the past has been to act as the implementing link
between the policy decision makers and the shop floor operatives. Their days
have been spent in interpreting management to workers and workers to
management, and in taking fairly simple reactive decisions. The reactive
decisions will be taken by computer systems, and as the shop floor becomes
more and more automated, the need for communication will disappear. A large
number of old fashioned managers will be replaced by a few supervisory
technicians.

With simpler organisation, accountability will become clearer. The
availability of more data and better analytical techniques will on the one
hand aid decision making and on the other remove the traditional excuses for
poor decisions, insufficient information and bad advice. (It remains to be
seen whether some remnant of middle management will be kept in being to share
the blame for the blunders).

With the introduction of the so-called "automatic office" the number of
administrators and clerical staff will also decline. With declining numbers
of staff and better communications, what need for an office? It is grossly
uneconomic and anti-social that millions of people should travel many miles
every day, all passing each other criss-cross en route, simply because of the
need to communicate with business colleagues. The day is coming when we
shall sit surrounded by our communications equipment making corporate
decisions in our own homes. And the dispossessed will be not only those
whose job is to administer to the needs of large organisations and their
staffs, but also those who transport them daily between home and office, and
the restaurants and cafes whose lifelihood depends on the working migrants.

These developments will take time to be released, but the trends are already
here,. It is significant that in the UK, for example, there are
one-and-a-half million unemployed, but an acute shortage of applicants for
well-paid and interesting technological jobs. Future society is taking
shape, based on an aristocracy of intellect. At the top, scientists,
technologists and managers who are capable of shaping and running a
computerised society; at the bottom, a few uncomputerised menial tasks
perhaps, but in the main the consumers who have to be fed and kept occupied.
In the middle a substantial number of providers - doctors, entertainers,

politicians and police, whose task is to keep the consumer in good order and happy.

I cannot see that democracy will cope with such a society - the class divisions will be too great. The danger is that the new aristocracy will fail to live up to its responsibilities. The old aristocracy. deriving largely from physical strength and political cunning had few scruples in running society to suit their ends. The new aristocracy, being by nature intelligent and sensitive, may be insufficiently ruthless. If this turns out to be so, the result could be anarchy and a new Dark Age. If we are to avoid this the architects of the new society must have the courage to build it, and the ruthlessness to operate it.

The Information Systems Environment
Lucas, Land, Lincoln, Supper (Editors)
North-Holland Publishing Company
© IFIP, 1980

SOME SOCIAL EFFECTS OF AUTOMATION

Charles N Read

INTER BANK RESEARCH ORGANISATION

Introduction

Information technology is advancing at an almost breathtaking pace and the social environment within which it is increasingly being employed has changed dramatically in recent decades. But people's basic attitude and habits do not change quickly and so the process of adaption to the new technology is complex. The young adapt more readily than the old, the rich more easily than the poor, and behavioural patterns can be seen to spread from higher to lower socio-economic groups almost like fashion trends.

Although the social effects of automation can be profound, more often than not they are not predicted or anticipated in any way but only realised with hindsight. Such effects are in fact very difficult to predict and meaningful experiments are almost impossible to contrive. There is therefore a paramount need for better observation of such effects and a faster feedback to the design and implementation process.

In anticipation of this improved feedback, the design of systems which may have widespread social effects need to be better formulated particularly with regard to their objectives, which in general need to more wideranging and inclusive of indirect as well as direct effects. Technical elegance and least cost to the implementor are too narrow and inevitably inadequate objectives.

If the narrow view is taken one is leaving it to others such as Consumerist bodies, Government regulatory agencies, one's own staff or even the public at large, to detect the deficiencies and irresponsibilities and to enforce subsequent modification of the automation. This is demonstrably unwise and also, more parochially, wasteful of resources.

This paper tries to illustrate these general propositions with the changes which are taking place with one basic social activity - the making of payments.

Making Payments

Payments are made and received by all sectors of society; by individuals; by all forms of corporate bodies and organisations, and by all departments of government. Rapid changes are taking place in the means by which many payments are made. In general terms these changes are concerned with the developing use of non-cash methods of making payments, both from credit accounts and from accounts in which real funds are held. It is the automation of payment systems which is making these changes possible and indeed many of these changes are technology led. It is the social effects of this use of automation with which this paper is concerned.

To make non-cash payments one needs to have an account at a bank or similar
financial institution. The ability of such institutions to handle
economically large quantities of accounting and payments information in
computerised systems and the increasing use of computers by private and
public sector organisations of all kinds, make possible the spread of the
banking habit to an ever wider proportion of the population.

Before examining these developments more closely it is important to put them
into a proper perspective. The extent of the spread of the banking habit
varies widely between countries and appears to depend primarily upon the
means by which individuals receive their income. In the UK 50% of the
working population still receive their income weekly in cash. By contrast,
in the USA and in some European countries, the figure is 5%, while in Italy
for example the figure is 95%. But in all countries it is still
predominantly a cash-based society. Thus in the UK, of all payments larger
than £0.5 made throughout society, still 94% are made in cash and only 6% are
made by non-cash methods through the banking system. The picture is much the
same in the USA and in all other Western countries.

The use of non-cash payments in time spreads down through society, like
fashion from the higher to the lower socio-economic groups. No longer is it
available only to the elite few who are known and trusted payers. Equally,
no longer can the payment systems depend upon the payers being known and
trusted. Means have had to be devised whereby unknown payers are vouched for
or guaranteed by a known and trusted bank. Hence, for example, the concept
of the guaranteed cheque.

And now a further stage of development is being entered. By on-line
telecommunication methods the fund-worthiness of the payer is checked for
each transaction he makes, and if he is not in funds with deposited monies,
or with a permitted line of credit, he will not be permitted to make the
payment. Developments of this type remove the need for a guarantee by a
financial institution and make it possible for non-cash payment methods to be
made available even to those with very low incomes such as the young, the old
and the under-privileged (assuming of course that the costs of so doing can
be satisfactorily met).

Changes in patterns of social activity

Accompanying the changes in the payment systems are the changing needs which
those systems must meet. People are more mobile nowadays and their payment
needs can no longer be met by a local branch bank. In effect the whole
banking system has to be made available to them

Rising living standards; rising numbers of women in employment; the motorcar;
the development of supermarkets and self-service shopping technology; all
contribute to changing the patterns of people's expenditure. For example,
less frequent shopping expeditions for larger quantities of goods made
possible by the motorcar, and often enforced by working hours, cause the size
of individual payments to retailers to rise and thus make non-cash methods
more viable as well as more convenient to payers.

Similar factors plus restricted bank opening hours make getting to a bank
branch increasingly more difficult, and thus stimulate the development and
use of banking terminals such as cash dispensers and auto-tellers, which are
operated by the banks' customers as a form of 'Do-it-Yourself' banking
service.

Television has led to the ever-increasing provision of entertainment in the
home rather than in public halls. Further development of that information

medium in association with the telephone system provides the Viewdata
facilities, which permit the selection and use at home of information from
many computer-based sources. These developments seem likely, among other
things, to extend both purchasing and bill-paying activities into the home
and thereby to diminish the need to leave the home to make purchases and
payments.

Major items of expenditure and regular payment commitments such as those for
house purchase, insurance, public utility services and so on, are
increasingly effected by various forms of pre-authorised payments in which
the relevant amounts are taken automatically from payers' accounts and
transferred to the beneficiary's account. Retaining full control of one's
financial affairs as procedures of this kind are increasingly employed
requires a level of sophistication in planning and management which is far
removed from putting cash into several money boxes in the privacy of one's
home; especially when the feed-back information about remote-controlled
payments is often far less than adequate.

The wide availability of credit through the medium of credit cards provides
similar difficult problems of financial control for many people, especially
for those who have a number of different and unrelated credit and banking
accounts. And the "Buy now, pay later" exhortation is a far cry from the
Protestant work ethic and the moral value of thrift which we were encouraged
to practice not that long ago.

Changes in individual behaviour People adapt to payment system changes just
as they do to other changes in society, and there is interesting evidence of
major shifts in behaviour given some of the facilities now available.

In the UK banking system there is now long and widespread experience of the
usage of cash dispensing terminals. It seems that many people much prefer
the machines to the bank counter staff. They queue at the machines while
counter staff are free and they have made a major change in their habits of
withdrawing cash from their accounts. Roughly speaking, they go to the
machine twice as often as they used to go to the teller and they take half
the amount of money at each visit. It seems that the impersonal machine
allows them to take small amounts of cash without feeling "small", as they
would do when face to face with the bank staff. And the machine makes no
comment whey they come again the following day for another small amount of
cash. They are free now of a constraint and they can behave as they prefer.
There are parallels to this in the use of VDU terminals for medical patient
examination where it has been found that there is a more honest and fruitful
response to the terminal than to a human doctor. Again a form of
embarrassment has been removed and a certain freedom given.

Credit cards in the UK can be used to obtain cash at a bank branch. This
facility is now quite widely used despite the high interest rate charge on
such cash advances. It seems this is preferable to asking the bank staff for
permission to overdraw one's chequing account. Embarrassment avoidance
again.

These behavioural shifts were not foreseen and they are clearly not
emphemeral changes. They illustrate our poor understanding of the real
desires and preferences of the people for whom automated systems of this kind
are being provided.

Gradually people are becoming more financially aware. They now show signs of
using facilities in ways which were not intended and the progressive decline
in the amount of money left in non-interest bearing accounts registers their

growing knowledge of cash-flow management - once a subject solely for
corporate treasurers.

The balance of power between organisations and individuals

The control of the timing of payments is an important factor in cash-flow
management. The choice of the method by which payments are to be made is
often critical, since the timing of the payments and the location of the
ability to control it has wide variations. Thus when paying by cash or by
cheque the payer can control the amount and the timing of payment of, for
example, an electricity bill. If he pays by Direct Debit the Electricity
Authority has control. If he pays by banker's Standing Order the bank has
control on his behalf. Cash-flow management advantages lead corporate
treasurers increasingly to take control wherever they can, often to the
unrecompensed disadvantage of private citizens. Government too can be
guilty. Pensions are paid late by means of technical lags, or beneficiaries
are provided with payment advices which require, for example, a trip to the
Post Office to convert them to usable cash. Many non-cash payment methods are
imprecise as to when the value of the payment is actually withdrawn from the
payer's account and when it is credited to the beneficiary's account.
Sometimes the lack of precision is unavoidable, but at other times it is
deliberately obscuring what amounts to a hidden tariff. Automated systems
often enhance that obscurity.

When knowledge is not equal and when relative bargaining power is not equal,
as it frequently is not between the two parties to a payment, fairness cannot
be ensured. Complex automated payment systems generate opportunities for
unfairness between organisations and individuals. This, of course, is not
inherent in information technology which equally could be used to make
fairness inevitable if that were a design objective of the system.

Confidentiality and Privacy

The increasing use of non-cash payment brings with it another social effect
of considerable importance. One of the great merits of cash is anonymity.
By contrast, non-cash payments inevitably are recorded in information systems
and one's pattern of payments can be highly disclosive of one's movements,
tastes and behaviour.

The traditional standards of confidentiality of professional bankers are, of
course, reassuring, but other organisations with no such ethic and no similar
commercial motivation are now in possession of automated data banks of
considerable sensitivity. Payment of subscriptions to Societies and Trade
Unions, or to particular publishers and so on, can be revealing. One's
employers, the Local Government Authority under whose jurisdiction one comes,
and of course such bodies as the Taxation Authorities, are but a few of those
involved.
It is not difficult to imagine a scenario in which one's earnings are first
provided and then largely disposed of against unavoidable commitments, such
as regular bills and taxation, with very little self-determination left to
the individual and in which the remaining self-determination is itself
recorded and kept under surveillance!

Payment systems provide an interesting microcosm of the wider need for Data
Protection in a society where ever-increasing use of information technology
is both inevitable and in many ways desirable.

It is clear that the individual in society has a number of legitimate
interests in regard to information about himself. Privacy, it has been said,

consists of the right to determine who shall know what about oneself. But at
the same time the organisations in our society which handle information about
individuals have definable legitimate interests in the posession and use of
such information. And society itself has a proper interest in seeing that
information about people is used in ways beneficial to society. These three
interests can and do conflict. In this paper examples have been given of
such conflicts of interest with non-cash payment systems exacerbated by
automation technology. Both in such a narrow sphere and in the broader
sphere of all personal information, ways have to be found of striking a
proper balance between these conflicting interests.

An independent regulatory authority - independent of government as well as of
all other interest groups - is clearly required to achieve all-round
protection of personal data. The determination of what may and may not be
done with personal data is perhaps the most important factor in shaping our
future social and commercial environment. Value judgements have to be made
and information system objectives have to be clarified if a fair and decent
society is to exist. Technology must not be allowed to lead us to where we
do not wish to go, and simplistic and parochial economic objectives deifying
least-cost solutions must not be allowed to either.

The quality of life must not be degraded by a failure to recognise values
other than technical excellence and lowest cost. I take comfort in the
changing climate of opinion which is leading to the enactment of Data
Protection legislation in many countries, and in the growing signs that
employees are increasingly unwilling to design and operate information
systems which are undesirable either for the general public or for the
employees themselves, and in the self-determination of the public in how it
will make use of some sorts of facilities to get what it wants rather than
what certain planners think it ought to want.